D1524922

Public Goo

Theories and Evide

Raymond G. Batina
Toshihiro Ihori

Public Goods

Theories and Evidence

With 13 Figures
and 10 Tables

Springer

Professor Raymond G. Batina
Department of Economics
Washington State University
Pullman, WA 99164-4741
USA
E-mail: rbatina@pullman.com

Professor Toshihiro Ihori
Department of Economics
University of Tokyo
7-3-1 Hongo, Bunkyo-ku
Tokyo, 113-0033
Japan
E-mail: ihori@e.u-tokyo.ac.jp

Cataloging-in-Publication Data
Library of Congress Control Number: 2005925028

ISBN 3-540-24174-4   Springer Berlin Heidelberg New York

Springer is a part of Springer Science+Business Media
springeronline.com

© Springer-Verlag Berlin Heidelberg 2005
Printed in Germany

Cover design: Erich Kirchner
Production: Helmut Petri
Printing: Strauss Offsetdruck

SPIN 11370956   Printed on acid-free paper – 43/3153 – 5 4 3 2 1 0

Preface

This book is a broad survey of the literature on public goods. There has been an explosion of research in the last ten years in a broad variety of areas in this literature and the time seems right for a survey of this work. This includes the recent work on dynamic theories of public goods, second-best financing methods, surveys and contingent valuation in determining the willingness-to-pay (WTP) for public goods, voting models, privately produced public goods, charity and national radio, experiments on public goods, public inputs, public capital and infrastructure, the Tiebout sorting mechanism, local public goods (LPGs), club goods, and fiscal competition and coordination. We survey developments in the theory and the empirical work in each area. We also present the classic results to place the new developments in context.

This book is appropriate for advanced undergraduates, graduate students who wish to learn the latest research in this area, and for practitioners who want to broaden their knowledge outside their own area of expertise. We present the background for each result and try to give the reader a feel for how a particular area of the literature developed. The technical results are provided and an intuitive explanation for them is also given. We also present some new results in many of the chapters as well. Each chapter is reasonably self-contained. A variety of models are studied in each chapter and are fully described so the reader can open the book to any chapter and begin reading without missing any of the notation or technique.

This book was almost three years in the making. We are indebted to a number of colleagues and students for helpful conversations along the way. In particular, we would like to thank Junichi Itaya, Hirofumi Shibata, Jim Feehan, Chris Annala, and especially Jeff Krautkraemer, who passed away just before we completed the manuscript. Jeff was a great friend and a terrific colleague who was always very generous with his time and always provided solid feedback. He will be greatly missed.

The camera-ready manuscript was handled by Atsusi Nakamoto. We are indebted for his skilled word-processor technique. We are also grateful to Martina Bihn and Yumi Onuki for their editorial assistance in preparing this book.

We would like to thank our families Lori and Julia, and Nami and Kumi, for their encouragement, love, and laughter. Without them this book would not have been as much fun to do. And finally we would also like to thank our parents for their support and encouragement along the way.

Raymond G. Batina
Washington State University

Toshihiro Ihori
University of Tokyo

Contents

1 Introduction

One of the most important ideas in all of economics is that self-interested behavior in the marketplace leads to the best products being produced and sold at the lowest possible prices and that this is socially optimal. This is one of the standard results in Welfare Economics. While this is certainly true in a variety of circumstances, problems do emerge and one of the biggest problems is that there is a class of goods that provides utility or improves the efficiency of production, but which the private sector has great difficulty providing, public goods.

The public sector has an important role to play in providing such goods and in generally supporting the activities of the private sector. Examples include defending the country through national defense, protecting property rights by providing police protection and a legal system to adjudicate conflict, building infrastructure that reduces transportation costs, supplying standards like a national currency, or driving on one side of the road rather than the other, providing for the general health of the population through clean air and water and sanitation and vaccination programs, and funding basic research. These activities provide a fundamental foundation that supports the private sector and that cannot be provided by the private sector itself, for the most part.

Two problems immediately arise, determining how much of each public good to provide and how to finance it. Unfortunately, information is asymmetric and this leads to the free rider problem. Individuals have more information about their own tastes and endowments than the government, and other private individuals for that matter, and this provides them with an incentive to reveal that information strategically in some situations. There is a large amount of research on the free rider problem. Indeed, coming up with a solution is perhaps the "holy grail" of public economics and a number of ideas on that score have been put forth. Subsidizing private alternatives, mechanisms that provide an incentive to reveal the truth, and the famous Tiebout hypothesis serve as examples.

In this book we will survey the literature on public goods and provide critical commentary as well as some extensions of the literature. We will take a broad view when defining "public" goods. Indeed, it is some of the special cases of goods that exhibit exclusion, congestion, or both that provide for some of the most fascinating research.

1.1 A Classification

The classic case is of a pure public good, where the marginal cost of providing another agent with the good is zero, and where no one can be excluded from enjoying its benefits. Examples include national defense, clean air and water, pristine natural habitats, the existence of an endangered species, the ozone layer, scientific research and knowledge in general, air travel safety, homeland security, peacekeeping operations, vaccinations that improve the general health of the population, and mosquito spraying to eradicate the West Nile Virus. The private sector has difficulty providing such goods since it is difficult to charge those who benefit from the good and to exclude non-payers from enjoying the good once it has been provided.

Clearly, changes in technology can alter the nature of a public good. For example, a television signal in the 1950s can be interpreted as a pure public good since a technology that could scramble the signal did not exist back then. The subsequent development of such a technology created the possibility of exclusion. Once exclusion can be practiced, the private sector can provide the good, charge a price for it, and earn a normal rate of return on its investment. Of course, there may be situations where exclusion is possible but inappropriate, e.g., local schools. However, it is possible for the private sector to provide a public good even in the absence of exclusion if another method of financing the good can be found. For example, advertising is used to pay for television programs in many countries and in other countries government provides the funding.

Some public goods are privately provided. Charity is a prime example, contributing to public radio is another example. There are numerous ways of modeling such behavior. For example, one could assume the individual cares about the total amount contributed. Or, one could assume the donor cares about her own contribution alone because she receives a 'warm glow' from the act of donating. The difference between the two models is substantial. For example, in the former model there is an externality across agents, whereas in the latter there is not if all donors only obtain a warm glow from donating. Public policy will have very different effects in the two models. There are other possible ways of modeling privately provided public goods and we will discuss several of them.

Some public goods specifically affect the efficiency of production. Public infrastructure such as roads, bridges, highway networks within a city and between cities, airports, ports and docking facilities, and water and sewer systems, can have a significant impact on the economy. Indeed, there is a large amount of empirical evidence that such investments can have a positive impact on the private sector. Building a highway network, for example, can reduce transport costs, allow for the expansion of markets and the exploitation of economies of scale. Some industries will be affected greatly by public capital like manufacturing and farming that must transport their goods, while others may not be affected at all, especially those providing services, e.g., hair styling and banking.

Many public goods are impure because they exhibit exclusion, congestion, or both. There are many examples of such goods at the local level, e.g., city streets, sidewalks, and traffic lights. These goods have been labeled local public goods (LPGs) primarily because they are typically provided locally and the benefits tend to be local as well. In addition, there are other goods provided by the private sector in some cases that have public good characteristics. Examples include so-called "club" goods like a tennis, golf, or swimming club. For many such goods the quality of the facility is a pure public good, but there is also congestion of the facility, and this raises the issue of the size and characteristics of the group sharing the facility. Indeed, the notion of a sharing group is more general than this. In a sense, when one shops at the same grocery store, for example, one is in effect joining a "club." Season ticket holders to the opera are joining a club, and are joining one that has very different characteristics than those who buy season tickets to watch the local football team. Other examples of a club in the abstract sense are a group of people who frequent the same tavern, those who buy the same luxury sports car, and those who park their car in the same parking lot every day. LPGs and clubs share many features in common. However, the main difference between them in our view is that exclusion can be practiced with regard to clubs but not with respect to LPGs. This allows private "club firms" to charge those who join and use the club a price. Another issue that arises is whether the good in question should be provided by the public sector or the private sector.

We will assume throughout that preferences and technologies are well behaved. Let the representative consumer's preferences be represented by a utility function of the form $u(x, G)$, where x is a vector of private goods and G is a public good, or possibly a vector of public goods. We will assume the utility function is typically quasi-concave, twice continuously differentiable, and monotone increasing in each argument. The technology of the representative firm producing a private good is $y = F(k, k^G)$, where k

is a vector of inputs and k^G is a vector of public capital goods that affect production. It is concave, twice continuously differentiable, and increasing in each argument. We will also assume that the cost of the public good is well behaved. It may, however, depend on the number of agents enjoying the benefits of the public good when there is congestion.

Unfortunately, the economy's resource constraint may not define a convex set even when the various technologies for production of the private and public goods are well behaved. It is well known that non-convexities may arise in the presence of public goods and other externalities and this may cause problems of existence, uniqueness, and stability. Regardless of this, we will also generally assume that agents that are observationally equivalent are treated in the same way by the policies of the government. Well known examples have appeared in the literature where it is optimal to treat identical agents differently because of a non-convexity in the economy's constraint set. We will assume there is a social constraint involving horizontal equity that prevents this.

There are other possibilities for modeling public goods, as mentioned above. For example, if the public good is privately provided and g^i is donor i's contribution to a public good, then $G = \Sigma\ g^i$ is the total amount donated. The individual may have utility for G, g^i, or both taken separately. If the government makes a contribution, the individual may have utility for that separately as well. The point is that it may matter to the individual who is contributing to the public good.

Public capital enters the technology and in that case the returns to scale of private production becomes an important issue. If there are constant returns in private inputs, pure economic profits will not exist. If there are constant returns in all inputs, including publicly provided inputs, then profits will exist. Public infrastructure can also affect utility. For example, a good highway system may reduce commuting time. In terms of LPGs and club goods, the individual may have utility for the number and type of people consuming the good. For example, u(x, g, n) might describe utility, where n is the number of people using the public good facility. The larger n is, the more congestion there is, and this may lower utility as a result.

1.2 Summary of the Book

In Part One we cover the classic case of a pure public good. Various aspects of the first-best case are studied in Chapter Two where we drive the famous Samuelson-Bowen- Lindahl rule for providing a pure public good. We also show that the rule must be adjusted for the method of financing, which includes a lack of person-specific taxes, pre-existing distortions, and the position of the economy relative to the golden rule expansion path. In Chapter Three we study the second-best case where taxes that distort decisions at the margin must be used to finance public spending. It is shown that there are a number of effects that need to be considered and that both the rule and the level of the public good will be affected. These include the excess burden of the distorting taxes, the provision of the public good on taxed commodities, the effect of the taxes on the willingness-to-pay (WTP) for the public good, and the position of the economy relative to the golden rule in the second-best case.

In Chapter Four we study the determination of the public good by voting and through a mechanism designed to elicit the individual's true WTP. As it turns out, there are difficulties with both methods. Two additional methods are discussed in Chapter Five, contingent valuation, which employs surveys, and indirect estimation techniques. The pros and cons of both methods are presented. All of the methods in Chapters Four and Five are attempts to handle the asymmetric information problem as it pertains to public goods. Agents may reveal information about their preferences for various public goods and policies strategically and cleverly designed voting procedures, mechanisms with tax incentives, carefully worded questionaires, and estimation techniques that use indirect information, all try to get at this information with some degree of success, although none are completely successful.

Another area that has received a large amount of attention recently is privately provided public goods, which comprises the subject of Part Two. In Chapter Six we present several models of privately produced public goods including the subscriptions model and the warm glow model, and various hybrid models. We also present a critique of each model. In Chapter Seven several extensions of the basic models are discussed. The famous neutrality theorem is studied in Chapter Eight. If the private sector is in equilibrium and is providing a public good such as charity or public radio and the government attempts to redistribute so as to provide more of the good, the private sector may alter its provision in a manner that offsets the government's policy. This is somewhat disconcerting since it is generally thought that the government can redistribute so as to allow the competitive economy to support a given optimal allocation. Indeed, this is the whole point of the Second Fundamental Theorem of Welfare Economics.

Charity is a good example of a privately provided public good and in Chapter Nine we present the empirical results on the estimation of charity functions. Tax policy can have an enormous impact on charitable donations. Many countries allow a write off of donations against taxable income, which provides agents with an incentive to donate. Income is also an important determinant of charity. Both variables have some empirical support for influencing charitable donations, in addition to a variety of other variables that have been included in empirical models. In Chapter Ten we study additional evidence on privately provided public goods. One of the main problems is ensuring that the comparison across donations made by different donors including the government is done on a fair basis. Typically, it has been assumed that charities are perfect substitutes for one another so that when two agents give to different charities they are both providing the same public good. This may or may not be true, but becomes especially problematic when including government programs and studying the neutrality result empirically. One of the best attempts to deal with this problem involved private and government donations to the same public radio stations. Suffice it to say, that there is virtually no empirical support for the neutrality theorem; researchers have uncovered only partial "crowding out." Finally, in Chapter Eleven we present some of the results on experiments involving public goods. Laboratory experiments allow the researcher to carefully control the environment in which the economic interaction takes place. Early work indicated that test subjects willingly donated a large amount to a pure public good from which all benefited when they clearly had an incentive to free ride. This result held up surprisingly well under various extensions, e.g., repeated games. It seems fair to say that some subjects will willingly contribute to a public good completely understanding the incentives they face. This could be due to a sense of altruism, cooperation, fairness, or an attempt to communicate to other players.

In Part Three we study the impact of public capital on the economy. The theory of public inputs is presented in Chapter Twelve, where we study the impact of public inputs on the firm and the economy. Public capital can improve productivity if public inputs are complementary to private inputs. For example, manufacturing firms need to ship their goods and quality roads, highways, and bridges lower cost and allow competitive firms to charge lower prices. The response of the economy will depend on the capital intensity of production across the different sectors of the economy. Dynamic models of public capital are studied in Chapter Thirteen. In particular the rules governing the optimal provision of public capital are derived and it is shown that a weighted average formula is appropriate if the government does not have complete control over prices. In addition, the long run growth rate of the economy may be positively related to the stock of public capital, although the taxes required to finance it can reduce the growth rate. Congestion may also blunt the effect of public capital on growth as well. In Chapter Fourteen we present results from the voluminous literature on empirical tests of the impact of public capital on the economy. Early results using time series data for the U.S. indicated a potentially large effect. However, more recent results suggested the effects were much smaller than originally thought, and there are some researchers who uncovered no effect at all.

In Part Four we study the important literature on clubs and local public goods. Tiebout responded to Samuelson's pessimistic claim, about the difficulty of overcoming the free rider problem, by arguing that individuals will reveal their preferences for LPGs in their choice of location thus solving the free rider problem. We present several models of this sort of behavior, including various versions of Buchanan's club model, and provide a critique of the hypothesis in Chapter Fifteen. In Chapter Sixteen we introduce the literature on tax competition and fiscal federalism. When one local government imposes a policy, some individuals may migrate, or may shift their mobile resources like capital to other locations, and this will have a spillover effect on other communities. This has become known as a fiscal externality. For example, a tax on mobile capital in one community will cause capital owners to shift some of their capital to other locations. If those other locations tax capital, this increases their tax base, and hence their tax revenue. Indeed, some have argued that this may constrain the rate of growth in local government spending. If local governments compete for a mobile tax base there may be downward pressure on tax rates to attract mobile resources and this can severely limit the sort of policy a local government can impose. However, there are also cases where taxes and spending may be greater than in the absence of competition. Finally, in Chapter Seventeen we present some of the empirical results on testing the Tiebout hypothesis and estimating the demand for local public goods. For example, if agents migrate in response to policy, then the price of locally traded goods like housing may capitalize the impact of local policy. If the schools in one community are better than in another, for example, families with children may move into that community and may bid up the price of housing in that community. The price will tend to fall in the other communities experiencing an out-migration. So one might expect a positive correlation between the price of housing and the quality of the local schools, as measured by standardized test scores, for example. There is some empirical support for this hypothesis, although there are critics.

1.3 New Areas

We cover a number of areas that have not been previously covered or emphasized in other books on related subjects. First, we extend a number of the static results to dynamic models. This is important since some results do not carry over from the static models. For example, the position of the economy relative to the modified golden rule is critically important for some results and it is unclear whether the government has enough policy tools at its disposal to keep the economy on the golden rule path.

We also discuss methods of determining the willingness-to-pay (WTP) for public goods. These include voting, mechanisms, surveys and contingent valuation, and indirect estimation. To our knowledge, contingent valuation has not been discussed in general books on this subject, but has received a great deal of attention, especially in the last few years.

Third, we contrast the various models of privately produced public goods at length. The subscriptions model and the so-called warm glow model have very different implications. We also describe the various hybrid models that have received considerable attention. We also provide a discussion of how the implications of the models may differ for empirical work.

We present specific results from the literature on the empirical work on charity, an example of a privately provided public good. Much of this work relies on the warm-glow model for its justification. We also fully discuss the empirical literature that tests the famous neutrality theorem. And the results from the experimental economics literature on public goods and the free rider problem are presented in detail.

Finally, we also discuss the work on public capital. We derive a number of important implications in both static and dynamic models, and we present the large empirical literature on the public capital hypothesis. This evidence comes from aggregate data, state data, industry studies, and international data from different countries and OECD sources.

1.4 A Last Word

Research on public goods is an exciting area of the current literature on public economics. The enormous bibliography we provide is a testament to this ongoing research. This book is an attempt to guide the reader through much of this stimulating work. We hope the reader finds this work as interesting as we do.

2 First-Best Public Provision of Pure Public Goods

In this chapter we will study Samuelson's (1954, 1955, 1958, 1969) famous rule involving the optimal provision of a pure public good, e.g., national defense, quality of a museum, or scientific knowledge. At the first-best social optimum the public good should be supplied so that the sum of the willingness-to-pay (WTP) for those who benefit from the good is equal to the marginal production cost.[1]

The key to understanding the rule involves the duality of a pure public good relative to a private good. For a private good everyone pays the same price, but is free to consume as much or as little as they want; consumers adjust the quantity they consume given the market price. For a pure public good everyone consumes the same amount of the "good" but is willing to pay a different price for it; consumers adjust their WTP for the public good given the quantity supplied.

There are two critical problems in implementing the rule in a competitive economy. First, the WTP for the public good must be determined. Unfortunately, consumers may not have an incentive to reveal their true WTP for the good. There is an incentive to understate the true preference for the public good if a consumer believes taxes will be tied to the WTP; consumers "free ride" in the hope that someone else will be truthful. On the other hand, there is an incentive to overstate the preference for the public good if the consumer believes the tax payment is not related to the WTP at all to ensure the good gets produced. In this chapter and the next we will assume the aggregate WTP is known in order to develop the intuition behind the rule and how the rule must be adjusted in a second-best environment.

Second, there is the problem of decentralizing the rule and this involves the method of financing the public good. Under Lindahl's financing mechanism each individual who benefits pays a share of the marginal production cost based on his or her WTP for the public good, where the sum of the shares is equal to one by design. Person-specific lump sum taxes can also be used to finance the first-best level of the public good. Since both methods of finance are tied to the individual, providing the public good does not affect the distribution of utility and, therefore, equity is not an issue.

Unfortunately, such financing methods are rarely available.[2] If they are unavailable, then we are in the realm of the second-best. In that case, the distribution of utility will be affected by provision of a public good. For example, if people with a large social marginal value of income are willing to pay more for the public good than people with a low social marginal value of income, the net social cost of the public good is lower than would otherwise have been the case. A second problem that emerges is that there may be pre-existing distortions in the economy and this will also affect the optimal second-best provision of a public good. For example, suppose there is a separate program financed by a distorting tax and that this acts as a constraint on the government's choice involving the public good. If the demand for the taxed good is affected by provision of the public good, then this will also influence the optimal choice of the public good even if person-specific taxes are available. Finally, the impact of the public good on the position of the economy relative to the optimal growth path will also affect its optimal provision. If provision of the public good moves the competitive economy closer to the optimal growth path, for example, this will reduce the net social cost of providing the public good. We provide an example where this also increases the level of the public good.

In the next section we derive Samuelson's rule. We also study the Lindahl financing mechanism and introduce the free rider incentive problem. Several examples are provided in section 2.2. We study the problem of decentralized financing of a public good when imperfect tax policies must be used in section 2.3; equity, pre-existing distortions, and the growth path of the economy are important considerations. And section 2.4 concludes the chapter.

2.1 Efficient Provision of a Pure Public Good

2.1.1 Samuelson's Classic Rule for Providing a Pure Public Good

Consider an economy where there are N consumers, n private goods, and one pure public good. Let $E = (E_1, ..., E_n)$ be the economy's endowment vector of the n private goods, let $Y = (Y_1, ..., Y_n)$ be the production vector of private goods, let $X = (X_1, ..., X_n)$ be the vector of demand for private goods, let $E^h = (E^h_1, ..., E^h_n)$ and $x^h = (x^h_1, ..., x^h_n)$ represent agent h's endowment and consumption vectors, and let G represent the public good. Consumer h's preferences are represented by a utility function according to

$U^h(x^h, G)$, which is twice continuously differentiable, quasi-concave, and monotone increasing in each argument. The aggregate technology is represented by $F(Y, G) = 0$. The resource constraints are

$$E_j + Y_j = X_j = \Sigma_h x^h_j, \text{ for } j = 1, ..., n.$$

The social planner's problem is to choose production and consumption to maximize the social welfare function $\Sigma_h \phi^h U^h(x^h, G)$, subject to the technology constraint, $F(Y, G) = 0$, and the resource constraints, where $\{\phi^1, ..., \phi^N\}$ is a set of social weights. The first order conditions imply the following,

$$\Sigma_h(U^h_G/U^h_1) = F_G/F_1, \tag{2.1a}$$

$$U^h_k/U^h_j = F_k/F_j, \text{ for } k, i = 1, ..., n \text{ and } h = 1, ..., N, \tag{2.1b}$$

$$\phi^h U^h_j = \phi^k U^k_j, \text{ for } j = 1, ..., n, \quad \text{and } h, k = 1,..., N, \tag{2.1c}$$

where $U^h_i = \partial U^h/\partial x^h_i$ is the marginal utility of good i and $F_i = \partial F/\partial Y_i$. A solution (Y^*, X^*, G^*) satisfies the first order conditions and the constraints. If $U^h(\ )$ and $F(\ )$ are strictly concave functions, there is a unique solution to the concave programming problem for a given set of social weights and the contract curve can be mapped out by adjusting the weights.

Equation (2.1a) is Samuelson's rule for providing a pure public good. The rule states that the level of the public good should be chosen so that the sum of the marginal rates of substitution between the public good and a private good, say x_1, $\Sigma_h(U^h_G/U^h_1)$, is equal to the marginal rate of transformation between the two goods, F_G/F_1, evaluated at the optimal allocation. Since $m^h = U^h_G/U^h_1$ is agent h's WTP for the public good in units of the first private good, and F_G/F_1 is equivalent to the marginal production cost of the public good in units of the first private good, the rule also states that the sum of the WTP is equal to the marginal production cost. Equation (2.1b) is the usual condition for two private goods, where the marginal rate of substitution between private goods k and j is equal to the respective marginal rate of transformation for each consumer. And equation (2.1c) equates the social value of the marginal utility of the jth private good across consumers for any given private good.

For example, suppose there are two people, a and b, two private goods, one public good, production is linear, and the economy is endowed with E units of a single resource which can be used to produce the private goods or the public good at constant marginal cost. The resource constraint is $E = X_1 + pX_2 + qG$, where the marginal production requirements for the three

outputs are $(1, p, q)$, respectively, and the utility function is $U = \alpha^h \ln(x^h_1) +$
$(1 - \alpha^h)\ln(x^h_2) + \beta\ln(G)$, where tastes differ by α. Let $\phi^a = \phi$ and $\phi^b = 1 - \phi$.
The Samuelson rule is $\beta(x^a_1/\alpha^aG + x^b_1/\alpha^bG) = q$, and the solution to the
social planner's problem is given by

$$(x^a_1, x^a_2, x^b_1, x^b_2, G) = (\phi\alpha^aD, \phi(1-\alpha^a)D/p, (1-\phi)\alpha^bD, (1-\phi)(1-\alpha^b)D/p, \beta D/q),$$

where $D = E/(1+\beta)$. The social weight parameter ϕ indexes the contract
curve. As ϕ increases from zero to one we trace out the contract curve for a
given level of the public good. If the individuals are identical, $\alpha^h = \alpha$, $\phi =$
$1 - \phi = 1/2$, and the solution is unique $(x^a_1, x^a_2, x^b_1, x^b_2, G) =$
$(\alpha D/2, (1-\alpha)D/2p, \alpha D/2, (1-\alpha)D/2p, \beta D/c)$.

   The duality of a pure public good can be exhibited geometrically. To
obtain the market demand curve for a private good we sum horizontally by
picking a price and adding up all the individual quantities at that price.
Continuing in this manner allows us to trace out the entire market demand
curve for a private good. For a pure public good we fix the level of the
public good and sum the marginal WTP across all consumers of the public
good undertaking a vertical summation instead. This is depicted in Figure
2.1, where c is the constant marginal cost of the public good.[3]

   Person a has a downward sloping demand for the public good while b's
demand is perfectly elastic. The aggregate demand for the public good is the
vertical sum of the individual demands. The optimum occurs where the aggregate demand for the public good is equal to the aggregate supply at G^*.

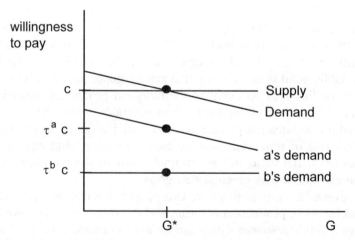

Fig. 2.1. Determining the Optimal Amount of a Pure Public Good

The question then becomes one of financing the optimal level of the public good in a competitive economy.

2.1.2 The Lindahl Financing Mechanism

Under the Lindahl financing mechanism each agent pays a share of the marginal production cost of the public good proportional to her marginal willingness-to-pay for the good.[4] Thus, in Figure 2.1, once $G*$ has been determined, type a agents would pay $\tau^a c$ at the margin under the Lindahl financing mechanism, while type b agents would pay $\tau^b c$ instead, where the total $\tau^a c + \tau^b c$ is capable of financing the public good. The rectangle with height $\tau^a c$ and base $G*$ is person a's total tax payment, and similarly for b.

It is certainly possible that this financing mechanism is feasible if the population can usefully be divided into a small number of groups and the demand for each individual group can be assessed in some reasonable way. For example, the public good might be the general health of the population and prescription drugs might be the good that produces "general health." The population can be segmented into two groups, the young and the old, and the two groups might be charged a different price for prescription drugs. As another example the public good might be a national park and the population of visitors might be separated into serious hikers and casual tourists. The former can be charged a higher price for entry into the park than the latter if their WTP is higher.

More formally, let τ^h be person h's tax share or Lindahl price. Agent h chooses demand $x^h = (x^h_1, ..., x^h_n)$ to maximize $U^h(x^h, G)$ subject to the budget constraint, $\Sigma_i p_i E^h_i - \tau^h c G = \Sigma_i p_i x^h_i$, where p_i is the market price of good i and $\Sigma_i p_i E^h_i$ is the market value of h's endowment, or income. We will assume that competitive forces drive profit to zero. The first order conditions imply $U^h_G / U^h_i = \tau^h c / p_i$. Summing across agents, $\Sigma_h (U^h_G / U^h_i) = (c/p_i) \Sigma_h \tau^h = c/p_i$ since the tax shares sum to one. Under competition, c/p_i is the MRT between the public good and private good i. A Lindahl equilibrium is a policy $(G, \tau^1, ..., \tau^H)$ and relative prices $(p_1, p_2, ..., p_n)$ such that agents optimize, markets clear, tax shares sum to one, $\Sigma_h \tau^h = 1$, and the Samuelson rule holds. The Lindahl financing policy can sustain an optimal allocation.[5]

However, there are several problems with this mechanism. First, it might be too costly to separate the population into different groups based on their WTP. It might be optimal to charge different drivers using a bridge a different toll. For example, commuters in a hurry to get to work would be willing to pay a high price, while tourists with plenty of time to

spare might only be willing to pay a low price. However, it may be difficult for a tollbooth attendant to differentiate among the different types of
drivers. Indeed, the Lindahl pricing rule requires that each individual
should be charged her marginal WTP. If each individual is literally unique,
each should be charged a different price. Clearly, this would be impracti-
cal.

Second, the mechanism becomes unworkable if individuals can easily
mask their type. For example, type a people in Figure 2.1 would try to
"look like" type b people to pay the lower tax share. This forces the pro-
vider of the public good to design a more complicated tax rule that provides agents with an incentive to provide the correct information. An example of this is the so-called Clark-Groves tax.[6] These "incentive tax"
rules can be very complicated and thus difficult to introduce in real world
settings. They can also be very costly to implement as well. And coalitions
may form to subvert the mechanism through strategic behavior.

Third, the Lindahl mechanism can be subverted if the good in question
can be resold. A group that is charged a low price will have a strong incentive to purchase the good and resell it to other groups paying a higher price. The profit from undertaking this sort of transaction is only limited by
the amount of the good available. While this is impossible for pure public
goods, it may be possible for other goods provided by the government,
e.g., rent vouchers, food stamps.

Fourth, there may be other social norms like horizontal equity or fairness that may be violated by differential treatment under this mechanism.
It might be considered unethical to charge the elderly more for the public
good "safety" than other individuals even though they may have a greater
WTP for it. An ambulance might have a greater WTP to use a toll bridge
than commuters or casual tourists, however, most would regard charging
the ambulance a higher toll as unseemly.[7]

In general, it follows that if fewer prices can be used than there are
groups in the population, some agents will be subsidizing others. For example, if everyone pays the same tax price, then people with a high WTP
for the public good will be subsidized by people with a low WTP. Some
may try to subvert the pricing rule and the resulting equilibrium may not
be socially optimal.[8]

2.1.3 The Free Rider Incentive Problem

The main problem with any simple pricing mechanism, as stressed by
Samuelson in his original paper on the subject, is that people may have a
strong incentive to misrepresent their preferences and thus "free ride" by

not contributing to the public good. This is easily seen in the following simple game. Suppose there are two families, a and b, that live at the end of a dead end street. The two heads of the households meet and agree that both would benefit from the provision of a streetlight and they agree to split the cost evenly. Assume that if the streetlight company receives a check from only one family, it sends that family a bill for the remaining cost. Let B be the benefit an individual family receives from the light, let C be the cost, and to make the problem interesting, suppose $C/2 < B < C$. Thus, neither family alone has an incentive to provide the streetlight itself; both have an incentive to free ride completely. The payoff matrix is depicted in Figure 2.2. The private individuals know the payoffs and everyone knows that everyone else knows this. The one-shot game has a unique Nash equilibrium where neither family contributes to the streetlight. This is because not contributing to the public good is a dominant strategy since $B > B - C/2$ and $0 > B - C$ for both players in the game, by assumption.

However, Johansen (1977) disputed the prevalence of the free rider problem. He argued that economics makes the homo oeconomicus assumption that people will only exhibit honest behavior if they have an economic incentive to, not if they simply have a moral incentive. Yet, he argued, there is little evidence to support this view. Indeed, it would be difficult for a society to survive without some honest behavior. Furthermore, he argued that people reveal their preferences through the political system and that it is difficult, especially for politicians, to systematically misrepresent their preferences in such a system. A liberal politician, for example,

	b Contribute	Don't Contribute
a Contribute	B - C/2, B - C/2	B - C, B
a Don't Contribute	B, B - C	0, 0

Fig. 2.2. The Streetlight Game

cannot consistently vote for conservative measures without changing the perception voters have of him.

There may be an economic incentive to cooperate if the interaction occurs more than once. To capture the notion that agents may undertake actions that support a public good for economic reasons, we can study a repeated game. Consider the streetlight game and suppose the two families interact once each period simultaneously for an infinite number of periods. Let β be the discount factor, where $0 < \beta < 1$, and assume $C > B > C/2$, as before. Suppose both families employ the strategy "never cooperate." This constitutes a Nash equilibrium in the infinitely repeated game. The payoff to such a strategy is zero and unilaterally deviating from this strategy by cooperating only lowers the payoff in the period the deviation takes place since $B < C$ and does not raise it in other periods if the other player is playing the strategy "never cooperate." Therefore, the strategy pair (never cooperate, never cooperate) for a and b is a Nash equilibrium.

Next, suppose both families play the strategy "always cooperate." The payoff is $(B - C/2) + \beta(B - C/2) + \beta^2(B - C/2) +.... = (B - C/2)/(1-\beta)$. Consider a unilateral deviation from this strategy. The payoff increases in the period a player unilaterally deviates by not cooperating since $B > B - C/2$ and does not fall in the other periods. The player thus benefits from unilaterally deviating. It follows that the strategy pair (always cooperate, always cooperate) is not an equilibrium.

This tends to suggest that cooperation may be unlikely to occur in this sort of "prisoner's dilemma" environment. However, there are more complicated strategies that can support the cooperative outcome in this set-up. Consider, for example, the so-called trigger strategy. A simple trigger strategy has two parts. First, the player begins by cooperating and continues to cooperate if the other player cooperated in the previous period. Second, if the opponent unilaterally deviated from cooperation in the previous period, the player punishes the opponent by playing non-cooperatively for a number of periods. We will consider the case where the player punishes the opponent forever for deviating.

If both families play the trigger strategy and cooperate each period the payoff is $(B - C/2)/(1 - \beta)$ for each family. Now suppose family b "cheats" in the first period of the game. Family b's payoff is B in that period instead of $B - C/2$ so it is better off in the period it deviates. However, in the second period family a finds out about b's "cheating" and "punishes" family b by choosing not to cooperate. Family b's payoff after the first period is 0. So in deciding whether to deviate or not, family b compares its payoff under cooperation, $(B - C/2)/(1-\beta)$, with that when it deviates and is punished, B. If the former is greater than the latter, $(B - C/2)/(1-\beta) > B$, or, after simplifying, if $\beta > C/2B$, then family b will cooperate and contribute to the streetlight each period. If this is also true of family a, they will also co-operate, and the trigger strategy can support cooperation.

The intuition is that the agent who "cheats" receives a larger benefit be-fore the other player finds out than he receives under cooperation. Once punishment begins, however, the "cheater's" payoff falls below the payoff he would have received under cooperation and this is the cost of cheating. Since the cost occurs in the future, it seems reasonable to discount it. The larger the discount factor β, the more weight the "cheater" places on the cost associated with cheating. If the discount factor is high enough, then these costs are large enough to induce cooperative behavior. For example, if the cheater doesn't care about the future at all, $\beta = 0$, and the cost of cheating has no effect on his behavior. In addition, the longer it takes for the other player in the game to discover that cheating has occurred, the greater the benefit to cheating and the less likely cooperation will be.

In the streetlight game we assumed that the private individuals knew the payoffs of the game. If this were literally true, the government could hire one of the agents to tell it everyone's payoff for the public good and then charge the appropriate Lindahl prices. In a more complex setting private agents might not know the exact payoffs B^h precisely but may know that $C/2 < B^h < C$ for each agent h. A more interesting case to consider is where the discount factor differs across agents. Suppose that the payoff and the discount factor differ across agents and there is equal cost sharing. Then under a trigger strategy, agent h will contribute if $\beta^h > C/NB^h$, when there are N agents, given that the other N - 1 agents are contributing. The lower the unit cost, the greater the number of agents, and the larger the individual payoff, the more likely it is that a trigger strategy will be successful. Indi-viduals with a low benefit, or a low discount factor may fail to contribute.

2.2 Examples

2.2.1 A Static Model with Labor

Suppose each agent is endowed with one unit of labor. There is one private good, x, one public good, G, and one input, labor, L, which is used to pro-duce the two outputs. There are N identical agents. Each is endowed with one unit of labor. The goods are produced according to the following tech-nology,

$$NL = \beta_1 Nx + \beta_2 G, \tag{2.2}$$

where $\beta_k > 0$ for $k = 1, 2$. Agents care about the private good, leisure, and the public good. The preferences of the representative agent are given by

$$U = \alpha_1 \ln(x) + \alpha_2 \ln(1-L) + \alpha_3 \ln(G), \qquad (2.3)$$

where $\alpha_k > 0$ for $k = 1, 2, 3$, and $\Sigma_k \alpha_k = 1$.

The social objective function for the planner is NU and the planner's problem is to choose (G, x, L) to maximize NU subject to (2.2) and (2.3). The solution is

$$(G, x, L) = (N\alpha_3/\beta_2, \alpha_1/\beta_1, \alpha_1 + \alpha_3) \qquad (2.4)$$

The public good is increasing in the taste parameter α_3 and population, and decreasing in the input requirement parameter β_2.

2.2.2 Heterogeneity

Next, consider an extension of the last model to include heterogeneity. The provision of a public good may affect the distribution of utility and hence equity may be an important consideration when determining the optimal amount of a public good to supply.

Suppose there are N private agents and that agents only differ in their labor productivity. Let w^h index productivity. To fix ideas, assume $w^1 > w^2 > \ldots > w^N$, so agent one is the most productive worker. Also assume $\beta_1 > \alpha_2 E(w)$, where $E(w) = \Sigma_h w^h / N$ is average productivity. The resource constraint is

$$\Sigma_h w^h L^h = \beta_1 \Sigma_h x^h + \beta_2 G. \qquad (2.5)$$

Suppose the planner's social objective function for simplicity is the unweighted sum $\Sigma_h U^h$. The planner chooses (L^h, x^h) for $h = 1, 2, \ldots, N$ and G to maximize the social objective function subject to (2.3) and (2.5). The solution is given by

$$G = N\alpha_3 E(w)/\beta_2, \qquad (2.6a)$$

$$x^h = \alpha_1 E(w)/\beta_1, \qquad (2.6b)$$

$$L^h = 1 - \alpha_2 E(w)/\beta_1. \qquad (2.6c)$$

The public good is affected by the parameters of the model in much the same way as in the first example. In addition, a technological innovation that increases the mean of the distribution of productivity reduces the amount of labor needed for production and hence increases the amount of both the public good and the private good. However, a change in technology that alters the distribution but does not affect the mean has no impact on the optimal allocation. For example, consider either $dw^1 = -1$ and $dw^N = 1$, or $dw^1 = 1$ and $dw^N = -1$. Both changes imply that $dE(w) = 0$ and hence $dG = 0$.

Also, notice that as long as tastes are the same across agents and utility is separable in the public good, N appears in the numerator in (2.6a) rather than the summation sign. If there is also heterogeneity in α_3, for example, the Samuelson rule becomes more complicated; N is replaced with a sum across agents indexed by α_3.

2.2.3 A Simple Dynamic Model

It is of some interest to consider the impact of introducing a public good into a dynamic environment. The position of the economy relative to an optimal growth path may have an important effect on providing a public good. Tastes for a public good may change as one ages and changing demographics may affect the provision of a particular public good. And many governments tax capital income to finance public spending.

Suppose the economy lasts two periods and there is one private agent. There is one private good and one public good available each period. The economy is initially endowed with K_1 units of capital in the first period that can be used to produce output. For simplicity, we will assume that output of the private good in period two is linear in capital and is given by $Y_2 = \psi K_2$ for $\psi > 0$. Output in the first period can be consumed, converted to private capital for use in the second period, or converted into the public good at a constant cost of p_1 per unit. Output in the second period can be consumed or converted into the public good at cost p_2 per unit. The resource constraints of the economy are

$$K_1 = K_2 + C_1 + p_1 G_1, \tag{2.7a}$$

$$Y_2 = C_2 + p_2 G_2. \tag{2.7b}$$

The planner's objective function is given by $U(C_1, G_1) + \beta U(C_2, G_2)$, where $\beta = 1/(1+\rho)$ is the discount factor, ρ is the rate of time preference, and where $U = \ln(C_k) + \alpha_k \ln(G_k)$. The planner's decision problem is to choose $(C_1, G_1, C_2, G_2, K_2)$ to maximize the objective function subject to (2.7), and the technology, taking K_1 as given. We can solve the first order conditions to obtain

$$(C_1, C_2, G_1, G_2) = (AK_1, A\beta\psi K_1, A(\alpha_1/p_1)K_1, A(\beta\psi\alpha_2/p_2)K_1), \tag{2.8}$$

where $A = 1/(1 + \alpha_1 + \beta(1+\alpha_2))$.

There are several new elements here. First, it is certainly possible for α_1 $\neq \alpha_2$. This captures the idea that an individual's preference for a public good may change over the course of his or her life cycle. Police protection, which creates the commodity "safety," may become more important as one gets older. On the other hand, a rugged wilderness area may become less desirable with age. Second, an individual may discount the future so a public good or service produced in the future will not be as valuable as the same service produced today. Also notice that each good depends on the initial capital stock. The greater the initial capital stock, the wealthier the economy and the greater the amount of each good society will provide in our example. However, demanding more of the public good in the future may require greater saving and investment today.

2.2.4 Public Goods in an Overlapping Generations Economy

Next, we will study provision of a public good in a version of Diamond's (1965) classic overlapping generations model due to Batina (1990a). At time t there are $N_t = N$ identical agents born. Each agent is endowed with one unit of labor when young and none when old, each lives for two periods, saving and supplying labor in the first period, and consuming in both periods. The representative consumer's preferences are given by a well behaved utility function, $U(c_{1t}, c_{2t}, G_t)$, where c_{kt} is the agent's consumption in period of life k when born at time t and G_t is the level of a public good available when the person is young. We could easily include G_{t+1} to capture the utility of the public good when old without changing the main results. There is one private good and one public good. The private good is produced via a neoclassical technology according to $Y_t = F(K_t, L_t)$, where Y is output, K is capital, and L is labor. We will assume the technology exhibits constant returns to scale so it can be written in intensive form, $y_t = f(k_t)$, where y is output per worker, k is capital per worker, and f(k) is concave. There is an initial old generation and each is endowed with K_1/N units of capital. The resource constraint at time t = 1, 2, ... is

$$f(k_t) + (1-\delta)k_t = k_{t+1} + c_{1t} + c_{2t-1} + C(G_t)/N,$$

where δ is the depreciation rate and C(G) is the cost of the public good. In a steady state this becomes,

$$f(k) = \delta k + c_1 + c_2 + C(G)/N.$$

The social planner chooses (k, c_1, c_2) to maximize steady state per capita welfare subject to the resource constraint. It is easy to show that the Samuelson rule holds, $N(U_G/U_1) = C_G(G) = dC/dG$. Second, intertemporal consumption is chosen by the planner so that $U_1/U_2 = 1$. Finally, at the optimum the economy evolves along the modified golden rule path characterized by $df/dk = f_k(k^{gr}) = \delta$, where k^{gr} is the capital labor ratio on the modified golden rule path. This steady state path is unique when $f(\;)$ is strictly concave.

If the economy evolves along a different path, it will necessarily be inefficient in a long run sense and output of the private good in a steady state will be suboptimal as a result. This will affect the amount of resources available for production of the public good in the future. So even though the Samuelson rule will still hold, the level of the public good will differ from the first-best case if the economy evolves along a different steady state path. This has not been fully appreciated in the literature.

To see this let $U = \alpha_1 \ln(c_1) + \alpha_2 \ln(c_2) + \mu \ln(G_t)$, $\alpha_1 + \alpha_2 = 1$, and $C(G) = G$, and suppose the economy evolves along an arbitrary path k^* in a steady state. It is straightforward to show that the first order conditions of the social planner's problem imply $G^{gr} = [N\mu/(1+\mu)][f(k^{gr}) - \delta k^{gr}]$, and similarly for G^*. It follows that

$$G^{gr} - G^* = [N\mu/(1+\mu)][f(k^{gr}) - f(k^*) + \delta(k^* - k^{gr})].$$

If we approximate the technology with the following Taylor's series expansion,

$$f(k^{gr}) = f(k^*) + (k^{gr} - k^*)f_k(k^*),$$

then,

$$G^{gr} - G^* = [N\mu/(1+\mu)](k^{gr} - k^*)[f_k(k^*) - f_k(k^{gr})],$$

where we have used $f_k(k^{gr}) = \delta$. This is unambiguously positive. If the economy is undercapitalized relative to the modified golden rule, then the level of the public good is lower than would have been the case had the economy been on the optimal path since $k^* < k^{gr}$ and $f_k(k^*) > f_k(k^{gr})$, and similarly, if the economy is overcapitalized relative to the optimal path since $k^* > k^{gr}$ and $f_k(k^*) < f_k(k^{gr})$.

2.3 Financing Public Goods

The next question is whether an optimal allocation can be supported in a decentralized way by government policy. We imagine a private economy where consumers choose demands and supplies to maximize utility subject to constraint. Firms choose inputs and which private goods to produce to maximize profit. Markets are competitive so no one has any market power and markets clear in equilibrium. The question is: what rule should the government use for providing a public good in such an environment? And, more to the point, how should the rule be adjusted if first-best taxes are not available?

2.3.1 First-Best Decentralization: Person-Specific Taxes

Suppose there are n private goods, one pure public good, one input, labor, N agents, the technology is linear, which serves to fix producer prices, and that the representative agent is only endowed with one unit of labor. Her tastes are represented by a well-behaved utility function, $U^h(E^h - L^h, x^h, G)$, where E^h is her endowment of labor, $E^h - L^h$ is leisure, L^h is labor supply, and x^h is an n-vector of private goods. The individual's budget constraint is given by $w^h L^h - T^h - p.x^h = 0$, where w^h is the wage, T^h is the person-specific tax, and $p.x^h$ is an inner product. The solution to the consumer's decision problem of maximizing utility subject to her budget constraint is the demand system, $x^h(p, w^h, I^h, G)$, where $I^h = w^h E^h - T^h$ is net full income.

The indirect utility function is given by $v^h(p, w^h, I^h, G)$ and it has the following important derivative properties, $\partial v^h / \partial p_k = v^h_k = - \lambda^h x^h_k$ for k = 1, 2, ..., n, and $\partial v^h / \partial T^h = v^h_T = - \lambda^h$, where $v^h_I = \lambda^h$ is the private marginal utility of income. We can define the expenditure function in the usual way,

$$e^h (w^h, p, G, u^h; E^h) = \min\{w^h(E^h - L^h) + p.x^h \mid U^h(x^h, G) \geq u^h\},$$

where $\partial e^h / \partial p_k = e^h_k = x^h_k(w^h, p, G, u^h; E^h)$ is the compensated demand for the kth private good and $\partial e^h / \partial w^h = E^h - L^h(w^h, p, G, u^h; E^h)$ is the compensated demand for leisure. Obviously, $e^h = w^h E^h - T^h$. It is also useful to recall the Slutsky equation for private goods, $x^h_{ik} = s^h_{ik} - x^h_k x^h_{iI}$, where $x^h_{ik} = \partial x^h_i / \partial p_k$ is the uncompensated cross price effect, s^h_{ik} is the compensated cross price effect, and $x^h_{iI} = (\partial x^h_i / \partial I^h)$ is the income effect.

Following Wildasin (1979, 1984), King(1986), and Batina(1990b), we can define the marginal WTP for the public good as the amount of expenditure the consumer is willing to give up for one more unit of the public good holding utility constant, $- \partial e^h / \partial G = m(w^h, p, G, u^h; E^h)$, where $\partial e^h / \partial G < 0$ so that $m^h > 0$. It is straightforward to show that $v^h_G = \lambda^h m^h$. We also have a Slutsky equation for the response to an increase in the public good, $x^h_{iG} = s_{iG} + m^h x^h_{iI}$, where $x^h_{iG} = \partial x^h_i / \partial G$. If private good i and the public good are uncompensated complements (substitutes), $x^h_{iG} > (<) 0$. If they are compensated complements (substitutes), $s^h_{iG} > (<) 0$. Finally, we also have the response of the WTP to the same parameters, $\partial m^h / \partial G = m^h_G = m^h_{Gu} + m^h m^h_I$ and $\partial m^h / \partial p_k = m^h_k = m^h_{ku} - x^h_k m^h_I$, where

m^h_{Gu} and m^h_{ku} are compensated effects, $m^h_{Gu} < 0$, and m^h_I is an income effect. Since $m^h_{ku} = - e^h_{Gk} = - e^h_{kG} = - s^h_{kG}$, the compensated responses m^h_{ku} and s^h_{kG} will be of opposite sign, i.e., if the kth private good is increasing (decreasing) in the public good, the WTP for the public good is decreasing (increasing) in the price of the kth private good.

The government's decision problem is to choose the person-specific taxes $(T^1, ..., T^N)$ and the level of the public good G to maximize social welfare subject to its budget constraint. The social welfare function is $\Sigma_h \phi^h V^h(p, w^h, w^h E^h - T^h, G)$, where the social weights are $(\phi^1, ..., \phi^N)$, and its budget constraint is $\Sigma_h T^h = C(G)$. The first order conditions of the government's decision problem are $- \phi^h \lambda^h + \gamma = 0$ and $\Sigma_h \phi^h \lambda^h m^h = \gamma C_G$, where we have used the properties of the indirect utility function. These conditions clearly imply the Samuelson rule, $\Sigma_h m^h = C_G(G)$, and it follows immediately that a first-best allocation can be supported by this tax system. And the person-specific taxes should be chosen so that the social marginal utility of income is constant, $\phi^h \lambda^h = \gamma$ for all h.

2.3.2 Non Person-Specific Taxes

Unfortunately, the rule must be modified since first-best taxes are usually not available. First, suppose person-specific taxes are not available. The government's budget constraint in this case is $NT = C(G)$, where everyone pays the same tax. We derive the following modified Samuelson rule in the Appendix,

$$\Sigma_h m^h = C_G(G) - cov(\phi^h \lambda^h, m^h)/E(\phi^h \lambda^h), \qquad (2.9)$$

where $E(z)$ denotes the simple mean of z.

The Samuelson rule must be modified to reflect the impact of the imperfect tax system on the distribution of income and thus equity becomes a concern. This is captured by the term in the covariance between the social marginal utility of income $(\phi^h \lambda^h)$ and the WTP (m^h) for the public good. If the covariance is positive, this lowers the net social cost of providing the public good, and raises it if it is negative. For example, if the WTP is increasing in income and the social marginal utility of income is decreasing in income, the covariance is negative and a concern for equity raises the social cost of the public good. The intuition is that the wealthy are more willing to pay for the public good at the margin than the poor are when the WTP is increasing in income. However, imposing the same tax on everyone to finance the public good adversely affects the income distribution and this raises the social cost of providing the public good.

2.3.3 Pre-Existing Distortions

Next, consider the case of a pre-existing distortion. Suppose there is a separate government program that depends on the economic behavior of the private sector and that person-specific taxes are available. To keep matters simple, assume there is a second public good H that is financed by a tax on x_n. The additional government budget constraint is $C(H) = \tau X_n$, where τ is the tax rate and $C(H)$ is the cost of H. One interpretation is that a separate government agency is mandated to provide H financed through a specific tax on x_n. The government chooses G and the person-specific taxes $(T^1, ..., T^N)$ to maximize social welfare subject to the two budget constraints, taking τ as given. The first order conditions imply the following version of the modified Samuelson rule for G,

$$\Sigma_h m^h = C_G(G) + (\eta\tau/\gamma)\Sigma_h s^h_{nG}, \qquad (2.10)$$

where γ is the multiplier for the budget constraint involving G, η is the multiplier for the separate program involving H, and where we have used the Slutsky equation to simplify.

The new effect, captured by the term $(\eta\tau/\gamma)\Sigma_h s^h_{nG}$, is an indirect compensated provision effect. Provision of the public good may affect the demand for the taxed good x_n and thus the amount of tax revenue collected under the pre-existing program. If the taxed good is a compensated complement (substitute) for G, tax revenue under the pre-existing distortion will increase (decrease) and this will lower (raise) the social cost of providing G. For example, suppose H is a highway, the taxed good x_n is gasoline, gasoline taxes are earmarked for highway repair, and G is a wilderness area. Provision of a wilderness area that causes people to drive more may increase gasoline tax revenue thus reducing the social cost of providing the wilderness area.

2.3.4 The Economy's Expansion Path

Government debt can be used to maintain the position of the economy relative to the optimal expansion path. However, many times debt policy is not available and cannot be chosen optimally. Suppose the government cannot perfectly control the manner in which the economy evolves over time. How does this affect the Samuelson rule?

To study this question, consider the overlapping generations model introduced earlier. Agents are identical and each is endowed with one unit of labor supplied inelastically to the labor market in exchange for a wage. The agent's budget constraints are given by

$$w_t - c_{1t} - s_t - T_t = 0,$$

$$(1 + r_{t+1})s_t - c_{2t} = 0,$$

where w is the wage, s is life cycle saving, r is the interest rate, and T is a lump sum tax paid when young. The agent chooses consumption and saving to maximize utility subject to the two budget constraints. The solution to the decision problem is a saving function $s = S(w_t - T_t, r_{t+1}, G_t)$. The agent's indirect utility function can be defined as

$$v(w_t - T_t, r_{t+1}, G_t) = u(w_t - S(\,.\,) - T_t, (1+r_{t+1})S(\,.\,)).$$

The new element here is that in general the public good will affect savings unless the utility function is separable in the public good.

Firms choose capital per worker to maximize profit. The real interest rate is thus given by $r_t = f_k - \delta$, where $df(k_t)/dk_t = f_k$ is the marginal product of capital per worker. This implicitly defines the demand for capital per worker. When the technology exhibits constant returns to scale, the wage will be given by $w_t = f(k_t) - k_t f_k(k_t)$. It is straightforward to show that an increase in the capital labor ratio increases the wage and reduces the real interest rate.

The government's budget constraint is $NT_t = cG_t$, where c is the constant marginal production cost. The equilibrium condition equates the supply of capital through life cycle saving to the capital stock next period, $K_{t+1} = N_t s_t$. Writing this in per capita terms and using the information about the wage, real interest rate, saving, and the government's budget constraint, we obtain

$$k_{t+1} = S[f(k_t) - k_t f_k(k_t) - cG_t/N, f_k(k_{t+1}) - \delta, G_t]. \qquad (2.11)$$

This is a difference equation in capital per worker. Following the literature, we will assume the equilibrium exists and is stable. However, in order to guarantee uniqueness additional restrictions would be required.[9] Locally, we require that $|dk_{t+1}/dk_t| < 1$ for stability. Since $dk_{t+1}/dk_t = kS_w/(S_r - (f_{kk})^{-1})$, where S_x is the derivative of the saving function with respect to x, if saving increases with the real interest rate, i.e., $S_r > 0$, then $S_r - (f_{kk})^{-1} - kS_w > 0$ implies the steady state equilibrium is locally stable.

The steady state equilibrium condition is given by,

$$k = S[f(k) - k f_k(k) - cG/N, f_k(k) - \delta, G].$$

Differentiate and solve to obtain the following result.

$$dk/dG = [S_G - (c/N)S_w]/(1 - S_r f_{kk} + k f_{kk} S_w), \qquad (2.12)$$

where the denominator is positive to ensure stability. There are two effects to consider. The first term S_G captures the effect of providing the public good on saving. For example, if the public good is 'public safety,' people may accumulate more assets if they feel those assets will be protected. The second term in (2.12), $- (c/N)S_w$, captures a tax effect associated with financing the public good. It will be negative if saving is a normal good.

To obtain the effect on welfare in the steady state, differentiate the indirect utility function and simplify using $dr/dG = f_{kk}(dk/dG)$ and $dw/dG = - kf_{kk}(dk/dG)$, to obtain

$$dv/\lambda dG = (Nm - c)/N + [kf_{kk}(\delta - f_k)/(1+r)](dk/dG)$$

where $\lambda = u_1$ is the marginal utility of first period consumption and $m = (u_G/u_1)$ is the WTP. Set this derivative to zero to obtain the modified version of Samuelson's rule in this case,

$$Nm = c + [Nkf_{kk}(f_k - \delta)/(1+r)](dk/dG) \qquad (2.13)$$

The second term captures the impact of the position of the economy relative to the modified golden rule and takes the sign of $(\delta - f_k)(dk/dG)$.

If the decentralized economy is undercapitalized relative to the modified golden rule, and provision of the public good increases the private capital stock, then this term is negative; provision of the public good moves the economy closer to the golden rule path and this lowers the social cost of providing the public good.[10] The opposite is true if the public good reduces private capital accumulation. If the government can choose its stock of debt optimally, it is well known that this tool can maintain the economy on the modified golden rule path. However, if its debt policy is restricted, then the impact of the public good on the position of the economy relative to the optimal path may be critically important.

2.4 Conclusion

We derived the classic formula governing the efficient provision of a pure public good, the Samuelson rule. In addition, we showed that the rule can be supported by a decentralized government policy if person-specific taxes are available. In that case, taxes should be optimally adjusted so that the social marginal utility of income is constant across agents. It is then appropriate to use the Samuelson rule in choosing the efficient level of spending on a pure public good.

However, there are several considerations that need to be taken into account in the realistic case where first-best policies are unavailable. Equity, pre-existing distortions, and the position of the economy relative to the optimal growth path will imply that the Samuelson rule needs to be modified and a first-best optimum will be unattainable. For example, if the government's debt policy cannot be chosen optimally, the economy will generally be off the modified golden rule path and the impact of the public good on the economy's expansion path will be an important consideration in modifying the Samuelson rule.

Appendix: Lump Sum Taxes

The government chooses its policy (T, G) to maximize social welfare subject to its new budget constraint. We obtain the following first order conditions to the government's optimization problem: $\Sigma_h \phi^h \lambda^h = N\gamma$ and $\Sigma_h \phi^h \lambda^h m^h = \gamma C_G(G)$, where γ is the multiplier, and $\phi^h \lambda^h$ is the social value of h's marginal utility of income. The former condition implies that $\gamma = \Sigma_h \phi^h \lambda^h / N = E(\phi^h \lambda^h)$. Add $\gamma \Sigma_h m^h$ to both sides of the second condition, subtract $\Sigma_h \phi^h \lambda^h m^h$ from both sides, divide both sides by γ, and simplify to obtain the modified Samuelson rule.

---

[1] Samuelson (1954, 1955) cited Lindahl (1919) and Bowen (1943) as deriving precursors to this rule. For citations to the early literature see Musgrave (1939, 1959), and the papers collected in Musgrave and Peacock (1958), which contains a translation of Lindahl's paper and the important paper by Wicksell. See also the comments on Samuelson's early work by Margolis (1955) and Strotz (1958), and Shibata's (1971) paper on bargaining.

[2] Kaplow (1996, 1998) has argued that the emphasis on adjusting the Samuelson rule for second-best financing is misplaced since there is always a way of financing the public good that is not distortionary. If each agent's income tax liability is adjusted so that the additional tax burden is balanced by the extra benefit of the public good, then the first-best rule should be used. Unfortunately, his method requires person-specific information on each individual's marginal willingness-to-pay and this information is subject to the typical free rider incentive problem. Since it is unlikely that the government will have this information, his financing method cannot be relied upon as a practical matter. See the exchange between Kaplow (1998) and Browning and Liu (1998).

[3] A version of this diagram appears in Samuelson (1955), who first noted the duality between private and public goods in terms of horizontal versus vertical summation. See Chart 5 on page 354. See also Figure 1 in Bowen's (1943) seminal paper, page 31, for a clear description of vertical summation.

[4] See Lindahl (1919) for the original statement of this idea and Johansen (1963) for a clear explanation of the basic idea. See Foley (1967, 1970), Muench

(1972), Roberts (1974), and Kaneko (1977) for the seminal theoretical work on the Lindahl model. For some of the more recent extensions, see Mas-Colell and Silvestre (1989), Diamantaras and Wilkie (1994), and Tian (2000).

[5] Since only relative prices matter, one equilibrium condition is redundant.

[6] See Clarke (1971) and Groves and Ledyard (1977a, b, 1980, 1987).

[7] Another problem arises with the Lindahl financing mechanism if agents are mobile. Suppose there are people with a high demand for the public good and others with a low demand living in the same locality. One would expect that an intermediate level of the public good will be produced in such a setting. Under Lindahl financing, high demand people pay more, and low demand people pay less, as in Figure 2.1, but no one consumes their preferred amount of the public good. With perfect mobility it may be optimal for the two groups to form their own separate communities so that each can consume its preferred level of the public good. Sorting and mobility are at the heart of the Tiebout (1956) hypothesis studied later in part 4.

[8] Other alternative tax schemes can be used to distribute the net benefit of the public good. For example, Hines (2000) proposed a linear tax whereby everyone pays the same tax price τ^* for the public good, rather than a personalized price, and receives a transfer. Transfers are designed to compensate agents for not being able to buy as much of the public good as they would like at the fixed tax price. For example, agents who would like to buy more of the public good at τ^*, but cannot since only one level of the good can be chosen, would receive a positive transfer. The main problem with this tax scheme is that if the public good is a normal good, wealthy individuals will pay a low tax price and receive a large transfer to compensate them for not being able to buy more of the public good at the low price. It follows that this tax scheme is regressive and is more regressive the higher the income elasticity of demand for the public good.

[9] See the discussion in Azariadis (1993).

[10] Abel, et. al. (1989) presented evidence that the U.S. economy is undercapitalized.

3 Second-Best Public Provision of Pure Public Goods

Pigou (1928, 1947) provided the key insight when distorting taxes must be used to finance spending. He argued that the social marginal cost of a public good is greater if distorting taxes are used because of the "indirect damage," or deadweight loss, caused by such taxes. Furthermore, if the deadweight loss did raise the social cost of providing the public good, he argued it is optimal to produce less of the public good as a result.[1]

This is of some importance because governments usually impose taxes that distort economic behavior and a large enough distortion can conceivably affect decisions on public projects. A gasoline tax may reduce sales of SUVs, lower miles driven, and increase carpooling and public transportation use enough to reduce the optimal size of a new bridge, or highway for commuters. An entry fee for a national park may reduce visits to the park and affect decisions on how much of the park to maintain. And higher college tuition may lower enrollments enough to affect library acquisitions, or construction of new buildings on campus.

Recent research in this area has made Pigou's argument mathematically precise, clarified the argument, and uncovered additional effects that need to be considered. Diamond and Mirrlees (1971) showed that provision of the public good might affect taxed commodities and thus indirectly affect the social cost of the public good. Stiglitz and Dasgupta (1971) derived the rules governing the second-best provision of a public good under various assumptions involving the tax instruments available. Atkinson and Stern (1974) pointed out that Pigou actually raised two separate issues, the "rule" issue and the "level" issue. They decomposed the social marginal cost of funds (MCF) in the second-best equilibrium into two effects, which may work in opposite directions on the MCF.[2] Wildasin (1984) provided further clarification on the rule issue and showed how fragile empirical estimates of the MCF are to the assumptions made. King (1986) and Batina (1990b) showed how a concern for equity might affect the rule. And Batina (1990a) argued that the Samuelson rule must be modified to take account of the position of the economy relative to the optimal expansion path.

On the "level" issue, Atkinson and Stern presented a Cobb-Douglas example where the level of the public good was greater in the first-best than in the second-best. Wilson (1991a) provided a CES example that supported this contention, although Wilson (1991b) presented an example where the reverse was true. More recently, de Bartolome (1998), Gaube (2000), and Chang (2000) argued that taxes may affect the marginal benefit of the public good and presented examples where the second-best level of the public good was greater than the first-best level as a result.

We study the classic results on the Samuelson rule when it must be modified to account for distorting taxation in section 3.1. In section 3.2 we present several extensions of the classic result. In section 3.3 we study the level comparison across equilibria. In section 3.4 we study the second-best provision of a public good in a dynamic model. We discuss the marginal cost of funds literature in section 3.5 and section 3.6 concludes the chapter.

It should be kept in mind that the purpose of the literature on optimal policy design is not necessarily to derive specific recommendations such as, "Tax gasoline at 9% and food at 2%," or to make statements such as, "The net social cost of a new highway is 3.7% to 9.1% higher because of the use of distorting gasoline taxes." The purpose of this literature is to make arguments logically correct through careful modeling, and to point empirical researchers toward estimating the parameters of interest. For example, statements like, "The social cost of a new bridge is higher because distorting taxes are used in its financing," can be supported by a logical argument. And a statement such as, "A higher tax on gasoline than food can be justified if its demand is more inelastic," will hopefully point empirical economists toward estimating the relevant elasticities and narrowing the range of estimates. So this literature is really about justifying an argument and refining empirical estimates, rather than giving specific policy advice.

3.1 Second-Best Provision: Distorting Commodity Taxation

Suppose there are N identical private agents, one pure public good, n private goods, and the government imposes a distorting commodity tax system on private goods $(x_1, ..., x_n)$ at rates $(\tau_1, ..., \tau_n)$. Let leisure be the numeraire good, let $q = p + \tau$ be the consumer price vector, and let w be the wage. The technology is linear, which fixes producer prices.[3] The cost of producing the public good is C(G), where $dC/dG = C_G > 0$ and $C_{GG} > 0$ for $G > 0$.

Each consumer is endowed with E units of labor and L units are supplied to the labor market. The preferences of the consumer are represented
by a well-behaved utility function, $U(x, E - L, G)$. The consumer's budget
constraint is $wL = q.x$, where $z.y$ denotes an inner product between the
vectors z and y. The representative consumer chooses (x, L) to maximize
utility subject to her budget constraint. The solution is a demand and supply system, $x(q, w, I, G)$ and $L(q, w, I, G)$. The indirect utility function is
$v(q, w, I, G)$, where $I = wE$ is 'full' income. It has the usual derivative
properties, $v_I = \lambda$, $v_G = \lambda m$, and $v_k = - \lambda x_k$, where λ is the private marginal
utility of income, and m is the willingness-to-pay (WTP) for the public
good.

The government's budget constraint is $N\Sigma_i\tau_ix_i = c(G)$ and its decision
problem is to choose its tax and spending policy (τ, G) to maximize $Nv(q,$
$w, I, G)$ subject to its budget constraint, taking into account the behavioral
response of the private sector. The first order conditions are

$$Nv_G + \gamma N\Sigma_i\tau_ix_{iG} - \gamma C_G(G) = 0 \qquad (3.1a)$$

$$v_k + \gamma(x_k + \Sigma_i\tau_ix_{ik}) = 0 \text{ for } k = 1, ..., n \qquad (3.1b)$$

where γ is the Lagrange multiplier for the government's budget constraint,
x_{ik} is the response of good x_i to the price of good k, and x_{iG} is the response
of good x_i to the public good. Equation (3.1a) governs the optimal choice
of the public good, while (3.1b) governs the optimal choice of the kth distorting tax rate. Equations (3.1) and the government's budget constraint are
n+2 equations that determine the second-best equilibrium policy and the
multiplier.

Following Atkinson and Stern, we can write equation (3.1a) as

$$(\lambda/\gamma)Nm + N\Sigma_i\tau_ix_{iG} = C_G(G). \qquad (3.2)$$

Alternatively, we could rewrite this equation as,

$$Nm = (\gamma/\lambda)(C_G - N\Sigma_i\tau_ix_{iG}). \qquad (3.2')$$

The difference between (3.2) and (3.2') is minor. In (3.2) the term
$N\Sigma_i\tau_ix_{iG}$ is interpreted as an indirect benefit, while it is used to adjust the
marginal production cost in (3.2') instead.

The first critical point to notice is that the term $N\Sigma_i\tau_ix_{iG}$ captures the indirect effect of providing the public good on taxed commodities. If taxed
commodities are generally complementary to the public good, provision of
the public good, e.g., lighthouse, raises demand for the private good, e.g.,
boats, and increases tax revenue if the private good is taxed. This raises the
net benefit calculation in (3.2), or lowers the net social cost of providing

the public good in (3.2'). This effect was first noted by Diamond and Mirrlees (1971) and we can label it the 'uncompensated provision effect.' Bradford and Hildebrandt (1977) later argued that a complementary relationship exists between many private and public goods. Examples include air travel and air safety, automobiles and a traffic light, private boating and a lighthouse, tennis rackets and tennis courts, picnicking and mosquito control, and even the ownership of private property and national defense. Of course, the opposite is true if they are substitutes instead, e.g., private security guards versus police.

The coefficient (γ/λ) in (3.2') is sometimes referred to as the marginal cost of funds (MCF), e.g., Ballard and Fullerton (1992). It is equal to one when a non-distorting tax is employed since $\lambda = \gamma$ in that case. However, it will generally differ from one when distorting taxes are used to finance public spending. If it is greater than one in magnitude, then the net social cost of providing the public good, $(C_G - N\Sigma_i\tau_ix_{iG})$, is magnified relative to the first-best level. If it is less than one, then the net social cost is constricted.

To derive Atkinson and Stern's first main result, use the Slutsky equation in (3.1b), multiply by τ_k, sum over k, use the government's budget constraint, and rearrange to obtain

$$\gamma/\lambda = 1/[1 + S/C(G) - \Sigma_i\tau_ix_{iI}], \qquad (3.3)$$

where $S = \Sigma_k\Sigma_i\tau_is_{ki}\tau_k \leq 0$ is a measure of the substitution effects caused by the tax system and is non-positive by the properties of the Slutsky matrix, as pointed out by Diamond and Mirrlees. The term S/C captures the static efficiency effect of using second-best distortionary taxes mentioned by Pigou. It seems to confirm his conjecture since it tends to make the MCF at least as great as one in magnitude. However, there is a second term in formula (3.3) that depends on the income effects associated with the tax system, Atkinson and Stern's so-called revenue effect, $\Sigma_i\tau_ix_{iI}$. If most taxed goods are normal goods so that the sum $\Sigma_i\tau_ix_{iI}$ is positive, this effect reinforces the Pigou effect to make the MCF greater than one. However, Atkinson and Stern pointed out that the revenue effect depends on which goods are taxed. If public spending is financed solely by a tax on labor income and leisure is a normal good, then the revenue effect works in the opposite direction of the Pigou effect. If the revenue effect dominates the Pigou effect, the MCF is less than one in magnitude. This provides a second possible reason why the social cost of the public good might be lower than in the first-best case.

Alternatively, we can rewrite the first order conditions using Diamond's (1975) concept of the social marginal utility of income,

$$\mu = \lambda + \gamma \Sigma_i \tau_i x_{iI},$$

where γ is the multiplier for the government's budget constraint and hence the social value of a dollar of tax revenue. The social marginal utility of income is the value society places on giving an extra unit of income to an agent. λ captures the private value of the extra income, while $\gamma \Sigma_i \tau_i x_{iI}$ captures the social value when the extra income is spent on taxed commodities. With diminishing marginal utility and non-satiation, the private marginal value of income is decreasing in income. However, if taxed commodities are a normal good, demand will increase with income and this will in turn raise additional revenue. It is possible for the social marginal utility of income to be increasing in income even though the private marginal utility is not because of the second term in the definition.

To derive an alternative exposition of the main effects, first use Diamond's definition of the social marginal utility of income and the Slutsky equation in (3.1a) to obtain a compensated version of the public goods rule,

$$Nm = (\gamma/\mu)(C_G - \Sigma_i \tau_i s_{iG}). \tag{3.4a}$$

Next, use the Slutsky equation in (3.1b), multiply through by τ_k, sum over k, and use the government's budget constraint to obtain,

$$\gamma/\mu = 1/(1 + S/C(G)). \tag{3.4b}$$

The 'compensated provision effect' is captured by the term $\Sigma_i \tau_i s_{iG}$ in (3.4a). This effect reinforces (reverses) the Pigou effect if taxed commodities are compensated substitutes (complements) for the public good. Second, the 'compensated', or utility constant, marginal cost of funds, γ/μ in (3.4b), is unambiguously greater than one since S is non-positive. This captures the 'compensated Pigou effect.' We can combine (3.4) to obtain a modified Samuelson rule, which captures the two new effects concisely,

$$Nm = (C_G - \Sigma_i \tau_i s_{iG})/[1 + S/C(G)], \tag{3.5}$$

where the MCF is $1/(1+S/C) > 1$.

Finally, consider the following development initially due to Wildasin (1984). Add the term γNm to both sides of (3.1a), use the Slutsky equation and Diamond's definition of the social marginal utility of income in (3.1a,b), multiple (3.1b) by τ_k, sum over k, substitute into (3.1a), and rearrange to obtain,

$$Nm = C_G - SNm/C(G) - N\Sigma_i \tau_i s_{iG}. \tag{3.6}$$

The second term on the right hand side in (3.6) captures the compensated Pigou effect and is unambiguously positive, which serves to increase the net social cost of the public good. The third term captures the compensated provision effect. This last formula is written in the spirit of the first-best Samuelson rule where the new effects are captured by additive terms.

3.2 Extensions

3.2.1 Heterogeneity in the Second-Best: Commodity Taxation

Following King (1986) and Batina (1990b), suppose agents only differ in their marginal productivity and this is reflected in the wage rate. Assume that $w_1 > w_2 ... > w_N$ and that the technology is linear. In addition to the commodity taxes, suppose there is a common lump sum tax, T, that can be used to finance provision of the public good. Person h's optimal demands are given by $x^h(q, w^h, I^h, G)$ and the indirect utility function is $v^h(q, w^h, I^h, G)$, where net full income is $I^h = w^h E - T$. The government's budget constraint is $NT + \Sigma_h \Sigma_i \tau_i x^h_i = C(G)$. We will take the simple sum of indirect utility across agents, $\Sigma_h v^h$, to be the social welfare function without loss of generality.

The government chooses a policy $(\tau_1, ..., \tau_n, T, G)$ to maximize $\Sigma_h v^h(q, w^h, I^h, G)$ subject to its budget constraint. In the Appendix we derive the following results governing the tax system

$$\gamma = E(\mu^h), \tag{3.7}$$

$$cov(\mu^h, r^h) = \gamma S, \tag{3.8}$$

where $r^h = \Sigma_k \tau_k x^h_k$ is the commodity tax revenue collected from person h and S is now defined as $S = \Sigma_k \Sigma_h \Sigma_i \tau_i s^h_{ik} \tau_k$, which captures the substitution effects of the tax system. Since $S \le 0$ by the properties of the Slutsky matrix and $\gamma = E(\mu^h) > 0$, it follows that taxes should be imposed so that the social marginal utility of income and tax revenue are inversely related, $cov(\mu^h, r^h) < 0$ by (3.8). This is a critically important implication. At the optimum agents with a high social marginal value of income should pay less in tax than agents with a low social marginal value of income. If, for example, the social marginal utility of income is decreasing in income, then commodity taxes should be imposed in such a way as to raise more tax revenue from those with higher incomes. This can be used to justify taxing luxury items such as tennis rackets, golf clubs, and Rolex watches at a higher rate than goods like food.

We also derive the following modified Samuelson rule in the Appendix,

$$\Sigma_h m^h = C_G - \text{cov}(\mu^h, m^h)S/\text{cov}(\mu^h, r^h) - \Sigma_h \Sigma_i \tau_i S^h_{iG}. \tag{3.9}$$

This formula extends (3.6) to include a concern for equity captured in the second term, where $\text{cov}(\mu^h, r^h)$ captures an equity effect associated with the tax system and $\text{cov}(\mu^h, m^h)$ captures the impact of the public good on equity. The second term in the covariances combines the Pigou effect and the equity effects. It takes the opposite sign of the covariance between the social marginal utility of income and the WTP, $\text{cov}(\mu^h, m^h)$, when the optimal tax system is imposed since $\text{cov}(\mu^h, r^h) < 0$ and S is non-positive. If, for example, wealthy people have a low social marginal value of income but are willing to pay more for the public good, e.g., uncongested tennis courts, at the margin than the poor, then provision of the public good has an adverse effect on equity. Formula (3.9) can then be used to justify the argument that this raises the social cost of such a public good at the margin.

3.2.2 A Reform Analysis

It is instructive to consider a policy reform analysis since many policies are proposed as reforms of the current system. Recall that the agent's indirect utility function is $v^h(p+\tau, w^h, w^h E - T, G)$ and the social welfare function is $W = \Sigma_h v^h$. In the Appendix we use this function and the government's budget constraint to find a direction dG that improves social welfare,

$$dW/\alpha = (\Sigma_h m^h - C_G)dG + \Sigma_h \Sigma_j \Sigma_k \tau_k s^h_{kj} d\tau_k + \Sigma_h \Sigma_k \tau_k s^h_{kG} dG \tag{3.10}$$

$$+ \text{cov}(\mu^h, dv^h/\lambda^h)/E(\mu^h).$$

The first term in (3.10) captures the Samuelson first-best case for introducing a small project dG. The second term, $\Sigma_h \Sigma_j \Sigma_k \tau_k s^h_{kj} d\tau_k$, captures the compensated Pigou effect and is non-positive. The third term, $\Sigma_h \Sigma_k \tau_k s^h_{kG} dG$, captures the compensated Diamond - Mirrlees provision effect and is positive (negative) if taxed goods are complementary to (substitutable for) the public project. And the last term captures the effect of the reform on equity and is positive (negative) if those who benefit from the project have a high (low) social marginal utility of income.

It is of interest to consider the special case where the reform is financed by an equiproportionate increase in tax rates, $d\tau_k = z\tau_k$ and the size of the project is chosen optimally, where $dW = 0$. In that case, (3.10) becomes

$$(\Sigma_h m^h - C_G)dG = - z\Sigma_h \Sigma_j \Sigma_k \tau_k s^h_{kj} \tau_k - \Sigma_h \Sigma_k \tau_k s^h_{kG} dG$$ (3.11)
$$- cov(\mu^h, dv^h/\lambda^h)/E(\mu^h).$$

This formula provides a very straightforward depiction of the various effects and is very intuitive. The Pigou effect is captured by the first term on the right and is non-negative, which raises the social cost of the project above $C_G dG$. The provision effect is once again ambiguous. However, if Bradford and Hildebrandt's argument is correct, it will work in the opposite direction of the Pigou effect. Finally, if people with a high social marginal utility of income are made better off by the reform than people with a low value, then the equity term serves to reduce the net social marginal cost of the project.

Next, the equity term can be decomposed into two separate effects to obtain

$$(\Sigma_h m^h - C_G)dG = - z\Sigma_h \Sigma_j \Sigma_k \tau_k s^h_{kj} \tau_k - \Sigma_h \Sigma_k \tau_k s^h_{kG} dG$$ (3.12)

$$+ cov(\mu^h, r^h)/E(\mu^h) - cov(\mu^h, m^h dG)/E(\mu^h).$$

The term $cov(\mu^h, r^h)/E(\mu^h)$ captures the equity effect associated with the tax reform while the term $cov(\mu^h, m^h dG)/E(\mu^h)$ picks up the effect of the project on equity. If people with a low social marginal utility of income finance a greater share of the reform than people with a high social marginal utility of income, then the financing of the reform improves equity and lowers the social cost of the public good project. Similarly, if people with a high social marginal utility of income are more willing to pay for the project than people with a low social marginal utility of income, then the project itself improves equity and also lowers the net social cost of the reform at the margin.

3.2.3 Labor Income Taxes

We can also consider the case where the public good is financed by a tax imposed on labor income instead of a commodity tax. This is of interest since many governments impose such a tax. Let τ be the tax imposed on labor earnings and let T be a lump sum element associated with the tax. Indirect utility is now given by $v^h(p, w^h E - T, w^h(1 - \tau), G)$, and the government's budget constraint is $NT + \tau\Sigma_h w^h L^h = C(G)$. The government chooses its policy (τ, T, G) to maximize social welfare subject to its constraint.

The first order conditions are presented in the Appendix. They can be combined in a manner similar to the commodity tax to obtain the following implications, $\gamma = E(\mu^h)$, $\gamma\tau S = - \text{cov}(\mu^h, r^h)$, and

$$\Sigma_h m^h = C_G + \text{cov}(\mu^h, m^h)S/\text{cov}(\mu^h, r^h) - \tau\Sigma_h s^h_{wG}, \qquad (3.13)$$

where S is now defined as $S = \tau\Sigma_h(w^h)^2 s^h_{ww} > 0$ and once again captures the aggregate substitution effects, s_{wG} is the compensated response of labor to the public good, and $r^h = \tau w^h L^h$ is now the labor income tax revenue collected from person h.

Once again, the optimal labor income tax rate is imposed so that more revenue is collected from those with a low social marginal value of income than with a high social value, $\text{cov}(\mu^h, r^h) < 0$. The last term in (3.13) captures the compensated provision effect. If labor and the public good are complements (substitutes), the last term serves to reduce (increase) the net social cost of the public good. For example, if the public good is a new highway, people might increase their labor supply if it is easier to get to work. Or, if the public good is a new docking facility, labor supply might decrease as the demand for leisure boating increases. Finally, if people with a greater WTP have a high (low) social marginal value of income, the second term is negative (positive) and this serves to reduce (increase) the social marginal cost of providing the public good.

We can also undertake a reform analysis similar to the last section. Following the same procedure we obtain

$$(\Sigma_h m^h - C_G)dG = z\Sigma_h(\tau w^h)^2 s^h_{ww} - \Sigma_h \tau w^h s^h_{wG}dG$$
$$+ \text{cov}(\mu^h, zr^h)/E(\mu^h) - \text{cov}(\mu^h, m^h dG)/E(\mu^h),$$

where $dW/\alpha = 0$, $\alpha = E(\mu^h)$, and $d\tau = z\tau$, $z > 1$. The same considerations come to bear as in the discussion of (3.12). The first term on the right captures the Pigou effect and is unambiguously positive. The second term captures the provision effect. And the last two terms capture the equity effects associated with the change in policy. If the social marginal utility of income is decreasing in the wage, and the WTP for the project is increasing in the wage, then $\text{cov}(\mu^h, m^h dG) < 0$ and this increases the social marginal cost of the public good due to a concern for equity.

3.3 Level Comparisons

3.3.1 Identical Agents

We will present a method for studying the level issue that is new to the literature. First, consider the model of section 3.1 where taxpayers are identical. The agent's uncompensated WTP in the first-best case is $m^f = m(p, w, wE - T^f, G^f)$ and her WTP in the second-best case is given by $m^s = m(p+\tau^s, w, wE, G^s)$, when commodity taxes are used to finance the project, where an 'f' superscript denotes the first-best and an 's' superscript denotes the second-best.

To facilitate making level comparisons across equilibria we will approximate the latter function with the former according to a Taylor's series expansion,

$$m^s \cong m^f + T^f m_I + (G^s - G^f) m_G + \Sigma_i \tau_i m_i, \qquad (3.14)$$

where m_I is an income effect, $m_G < 0$ if the substitution effect dominates, and m_i is an uncompensated cross price effect. We can also approximate the cost function as well,

$$C_G(G^s) \cong C_G(G^f) + (G^s - G^f) C_{GG}(G^f). \qquad (3.15)$$

Subtract the first-best rule, $Nm = C_G$, from the second-best rule (3.6), use (3.14) and (3.15), and rearrange to obtain the following result.

$$(G^f - G^s)(Nm^f_G - C^f_{GG}) = Nm^s S/C(G^s) + N\Sigma_i \tau_i s^s_{iG}$$
$$+ N\Sigma_i \tau_i m^f_i + NT^f m^f_I, \qquad (3.16)$$

where $S = \Sigma_k \Sigma_i \tau_i s^s_{ki} \tau_k$. If the substitution effect dominates, the WTP for the public good is decreasing in the public good, and $m_G - C_{GG} < 0$. It follows that the sign of $G^f - G^s$ is the opposite of the sign of the terms on the right hand side.

The first term on the right hand side of (3.16) captures the compensated Pigou effect and is negative thus contributing to $G^f > G^s$. This captures Pigou's second conjecture that the higher social cost due to distortionary taxation implies that the optimal level of the public good should be lower.

However, there are several other effects to consider. The second term in (3.16) captures the compensated provision effect and is ambiguous. If taxed goods are substitutes for (complementary to) the public good, this effect reinforces (reverses) the Pigou effect. The third term captures the effect of the commodity tax rates on the WTP function and is also ambiguous. This is the WTP financing effect. Commodity taxes raise prices and this may cause the WTP function to shift. If the agent's WTP is decreasing (increasing) in prices and tax rates raise prices, the WTP financing effect reinforces (reverses) the Pigou effect. Finally, the last term captures the income effect of financing the first-best level of the public good. If the representative consumer's WTP is increasing in income, this works in the opposite direction of the Pigou effect.

Notice that if indirect utility is represented by the popular Gorman form extended for a public good, $v = a(q) + (I + G^\beta)b(q)$, then $m = v_G/v_I = \beta G^{\beta-1}$ and the WTP is independent of income and prices so $m_i = m_I = 0$. In addition, the expenditure function is $e = [u - a(q)]/b(q) - G^\beta$ so the compensated demands are independent of the public good hence $s_{iG} = 0$. Only the Pigou effect remains and it follows from (3.16) that the first-best level of the public good is greater than the second-best level.

3.3.2 Alternative Formulation

We can also expand the compensated WTP function, $m(q, w, G^s, u^s)$,

$$m^s \cong m^f + \Sigma_i \tau_i m^f_{iu} + (G^s - G^f)m^f_{Gu} + (u^s - u^f)m^f_u \qquad (3.17)$$

where m_{iu} is a compensated cross price effect of q_i on m, $m_{Gu} < 0$ is the compensated effect of the public good on the WTP function, and m_u captures the income effect. Recall that $m_u = -e_{Gu}$, $m_I = -e_{Gu}\lambda$, and $m_{iu} = -e_{Gi} = -e_{iG} = -s_{iG}$. We can combine this information, (3.17), and the first and second-best rules to obtain

$$(G^f - G^s)(m^f_{Gu} - C_{GG}) = N(u^s - u^f)m_I/\lambda + NmS \qquad (3.18)$$

$$+ N\Sigma_i \tau_i s^s_{iG} - N\Sigma_i \tau_i s^f_{iG}.$$

The first term on the right hand side of (3.18) captures the income effects associated with the two policies. It is unambiguously negative if the agent's WTP is increasing in income. This works in the direction of making the first-best level of the public good greater than the second-best level. The second term captures the Pigou effect and works in the same direction as the first effect. The third and fourth terms capture the compensated provision effect and the compensated WTP financing effect, respectively, and are both ambiguous. In general, these two effects will not necessarily cancel one another since the derivatives s^s_{iG} and s^f_{iG} are evaluated at different points. It is immediate that if the compensated effect of the public good on private demands is zero ($s^s_{iG} = s^f_{iG} = 0$), or constant ($s^s_{iG} = s^f_{iG}$), then the first-best level is larger than the second-best level when the WTP is increasing in income.[4] In addition, (3.18) also shows definitively that $\Sigma_i \tau_i(s^s_{iG} - s^f_{iG}) > 0$ is a necessary condition for the second-best level to be greater than the first-best level when the WTP is increasing in income.

de Bartolome (1998) and Gaube (2000) presented examples where the WTP shifts out when taxes are imposed. If this effect is strong enough, it is possible for the second-best level of the public good to be greater than the first-best level.

If preferences are given by $v = a(q) + Ib(q) + G^\beta$, then private demands are $x_i = - (a_i + b_iI)/b$ and the WTP is $m = \beta G^{\beta-1}/b(q)$. If $b_i < 0$, then the private good x_i is normal and $dm/dq_i = m_i = - \beta G^{\beta-1}b_i/b^2 > 0$. In that case, the WTP financing effect works in the direction of making the second-best level of the public good greater than the first-best level. This generalizes Gaube's CES example.

These results generalize to the case of heterogeneous agents. Following the same procedure under commodity taxation, we obtain

$$(G^f - G^s)(\Sigma_h m^h_{Gu} - C_{GG}) = \Sigma_h[u^h(s) - u^h(f)]m^h_I/\lambda^h$$

$$+ \; cov(\mu^h, m^h)S/cov(\mu^h, r^h) + \Sigma_h\tau_i s^h_{iG}(s) - \Sigma_h\tau_i s^h_{iG}(f),$$

where $u^h(z)$ is utility in equilibrium $z = f, s$, and $s^h_{iG}(z)$ is the compensated response in equilibrium z. The new element is the concern for equity embodied in the second term on the right in covariances. If the tax system is imposed optimally, $cov(\mu^h, r^h) < 0$, and the sign of the second term depends on the sign of $cov(\mu^h, m^h)$. Thus, $cov(\mu^h, m^h) > (<) 0$ works in the direction of making $G^f < (>) G^s$. If people who have a high social marginal utility of income also have a large WTP for the public good, then providing the public good in the second-best environment improves equity and this works in the direction of making the level of the public good in the second-best equilibrium greater than in the first-best case.

3.4 Public Goods in the Overlapping Generations Model

Many governments also impose taxes on labor and capital income and it is of some interest to see what impact this may have on the supply of public goods in a dynamic environment. We will extend the overlapping generations model of the last chapter to include endogenous labor supply.

3.4.1 The Optimal Second-Best Rule

Agents choose consumption, saving, and labor supply when young to maximize lifetime utility subject to their lifetime wealth constraint. The government imposes taxes on labor and savings income. The representative consumer's utility is $U(c_{1t}, c_{2t}, E - L_t, G_t)$ and the budget constraint is

$w_{nt}L_t - c_{1t} - R_{nt+1}c_{2t} = 0$, where $w_n = w(1 - \tau_w)$ is the after tax wage, $R_n = 1/(1+r(1-\tau_r))$ is the after tax "price" of second period consumption, and the tax rates on labor and saving income are τ_w and τ_r, respectively. The solution to the consumer's decision problem is $C^1(w_{nt}, R_{nt+1}, G_t)$, $C^2(w_{nt}, R_{nt+1}, G_t)$, and $L(w_{nt}, R_{nt+1}, G_t)$, and the indirect utility function is $V(w_{nt}, R_{nt+1}, G_t)$.

The government chooses an infinite sequence $\{\tau_{wt}, \tau_{rt+1}, G_t\}_{t=1,\infty}$ to maximize society's welfare subject to the economic behavior of the private sector, the government's own budget constraint, and the equilibrium conditions of the economy. We will take the social welfare function to be $\Sigma_t N\beta^t V(w_{nt}, R_{nt+1}, G_t)$, where β is the discount factor. The economy's resource constraint is

$$F(K_t, NL_t) + K_t - Nc_{1t} - Nc_{2t-1} - C(G_t) - K_{t+1} = 0, \qquad (3.19)$$

and the equilibrium condition in the capital market is given by

$$K_{t+1} = Ns_t = N(w_{nt}L - c_{1t}), \qquad (3.20)$$

where s is the representative agent's first period saving. It can be shown that the optimal steady state growth path is now given by $f_k = \rho$.

Following Atkinson and Sandmo (1980), King(1980), and Batina (1990a), we will find it convenient to rewrite the government's decision problem to have it choose the sequence $\{w_{nt}, R_{nt+1}, G_t\}_{t=1,\infty}$ instead.[5] To facilitate this, use the capital market equilibrium condition (3.20) in (3.19) to obtain

$$F(K_t, NL_t) - Nw_{nt}L_t + K_t - Nc_{2t-1} - C(G_t) = 0. \qquad (3.21)$$

Next, use the agent's wealth constraint in (3.19) and simplify to obtain

$$F(K_t, NL_t) - Nw_{nt}L_t + K_t - Nc_{2t-1} - C(G_t) + NR_{nt+1}c_{2t} - K_{t+1} = 0. \qquad (3.22)$$

where $L_t = L(w_{nt}, R_{nt+1}, G_t)$ is labor supply at time t, $c_{2t-1} = C^2(w_{nt-1}, R_{nt}, G_{t-1})$ is second period consumption of the current old, and $c_{2t} = C^2(w_{nt}, R_{nt+1}, G_t)$ is second period consumption of the young next period when old. Equations (3.21) and (3.22) form the constraints to the government's decision problem.

In the Appendix we derive the following modified Samuelson rule,

$$Nm = C_G - NmS/C(G) + \beta Nmr\tau_r s(\rho - r)/C(G) - N\Gamma, \qquad (3.23)$$

where $S < 0$ captures the substitution effects of the tax system, Γ captures the compensated provision effect, and the second term captures the static Pigou effect.

The third term in ρ - r captures a dynamic efficiency effect and it takes the sign of (ρ - r). If the government can use its debt policy to maintain the economy on the optimal expansion path, it is well known that r = ρ in this model, and this term drops out. However, if the government cannot perfectly control the evolution of the economy, as seems most likely, then the position of the economy relative to the optimal expansion path will affect the choice of the public good. For example, if the economy is undercapitalized relative to the optimal path, r > ρ. In that case, the tax system can be chosen partly to improve the position of the economy relative to the optimal growth path and this lowers the social cost of the public good.

3.4.2 Level Comparisons

In order to make level comparisons between equilibria, we can denote the compensated WTP for the public good in the OG Model as $m(w^f, R^f, G^f, u^f)$ in the first-best and $m(w_n, R_n, G^s, u^s)$ in the second-best. We can then approximate the compensated WTP for the public good in the second-best in the following way,

$$m^s \cong m^f + \Psi + (G^s - G^f)m^f_{Gu} + (u^s - u^f)m^f_u. \qquad (3.24)$$

where

$$\Psi = (w^s_n - w^f)m^f_{wu} + (r^f - r^s(1-\tau^s_r))R^s_n R^f m^f_{Ru},$$

captures the WTP financing effect.[6] Using the approximation (3.24), the approximation of the cost function for the public good, the first-best rule $Nm = C_G$, and (3.23), we obtain,

$$(G^s - G^f)(Nm_G - C_{GG}) = (u^f - u^s)m^f_u - NmS/C(G) - N\Gamma \qquad - \qquad (3.25)$$
$$N\Psi + Nm\beta r\tau_r s(\rho - r)/C(G).$$

The first term on the right captures the income effects associated with the different policies and contributes toward making the first-best level of the public good greater than the second-best level if the WTP is increasing in income. The second term captures the static Pigou effect and reinforces the first term. The third term $N\Gamma$ captures the compensated provision effect and is ambiguous. The fourth term $N\Psi$ captures the WTP financing effect and is also ambiguous. It includes the effect of tax policy as well as the effect of a change in gross factor prices. Finally, the last term captures the dynamic Pigou effect and takes the sign of ρ - r. If the economy is under-capitalized (overcapitalized) relative to the modified golden rule, the dynamic Pigou effect works in the direction of making the second-best level greater (less) than the first-best level.

We can formulate various propositions regarding the comparison of the first and second-best levels of the public good using (3.25). For example, suppose the indirect utility function is of the form $v = [I + D(w) + A(G)]B(R)$. In that case, $m = v_G/v_I = A_G(G) = dA/dG$ is independent of prices and income, and the compensated private demands are independent of the public good. All that remains are the static and dynamic efficiency effects. If $\beta r \tau_r s(r - \rho) > - S$, then the second-best level of the public good is greater than the first-best level.

3.4.3 Self-Selection and Heterogeneity

Pirttila and Tuomala (2001) combined a version of Mirrlees's (1971) model of optimal taxation with that of Atkinson and Sandmo's overlapping generations model by incorporating a second type of labor into the model and allowed the public good to affect production. Agents are assumed to differ in their ability and ability is unobservable. This imposes a severe constraint on the government's ability to redistribute income and is captured by a self-selection constraint; agents are provided with an incentive to correctly reveal their type under the optimal second-best policy. Unfortunately, the self-selection constraint also hinders the government's ability to use its policy to redistribute income.

They showed that the Samuelson rule must be modified to take the impact of this self-selection constraint into account. For example, if the more productive agents are more willing to pay for the public good than the less productive agents, then the government can ease the self-selection constraint by providing more of the public good. This allows it to redistribute income from the more productive agents to the less productive agents more easily than would otherwise have been the case.

3.5 The Marginal Cost of Funds (MCF)

The marginal cost of funds plays an important role in assessing the optimality of a particular spending policy. Wildasin (1984) developed a formula for the MCF in a partial equilibrium framework similar to the static model studied earlier in this chapter. Stuart (1984) undertook a simulation study of the marginal cost of funds in a general equilibrium setting. Browning (1976, 1987) attempted to calculate the marginal cost of funds empirically for the U. S. tax on labor earnings and generally found MCF's in excess of one. Mayshar (1990, 1991) generalized the analytical results to allow for a difference in average and marginal tax rates. Snow and Warren (1996) reconciled the disparate formulae presented in the literature as being determined by different policy experiments and different assumptions about labor supply elasticities. Finally, Sandmo (1998) considered the effects of introducing heterogeneity in the population explicitly.

3.5.1 Labor Income Taxation and the MCF

The literature has tended to focus on labor income taxes. Suppose agents are identical and the government imposes a labor earnings tax to finance provision of a public good. Then following our general procedure we obtain the following equations for G and τ,

$$Nm = (\gamma/\lambda)(C_G - N\tau wL_G),$$

$$\gamma/\lambda = 1/(1 - \theta\varepsilon),$$

where $\varepsilon = (w(1-\tau)/L)L_w$ is the uncompensated wage elasticity of labor and $\theta = \tau/(1-\tau)$. The MCF is γ/λ.

Clearly, whether or not the MCF is greater than one in magnitude depends critically on the uncompensated labor supply elasticity in this simple case.[7] If $\theta\varepsilon < 1$, then MCF > 1. If the labor supply curve is 'backward bending,' then $\varepsilon < 0$ is possible and MCF < 1 as a result. Much attention has focused on this case. However, while a backward bending supply curve may characterize some workers in the population, it is unlikely that it characterizes the average worker in a large economy.

Most of the literature on the MCF assumes agents are identical for tractability. More generally, the case where there is heterogeneity may be of interest. Following Sandmo (1998), assume agents only differ in their marginal productivity as measured by their wage rate. The first order conditions in section 3.2.3 govern the optimal choice of policy in the presence of heterogeneity and a linear tax. In particular, the equation governing the optimal choice of the public good is

$$\Sigma_h \lambda^h m^h = \gamma(C_G - \Sigma_h \tau w^h L^h_G).$$

Let $E(\lambda^h) = \Sigma\lambda^h/N$, add $E(\lambda^h)\Sigma m^h$ and subtract it from the last equation, divide through by $E(\lambda^h)$, and simplify to obtain

$$\Sigma_h m^h + cov(\lambda^h/E(\lambda^h), m^h) = [\gamma/E(\lambda^h)](C_G - \Sigma_h \tau w^h L^h_G) \qquad (3.26)$$

where $\text{cov}(\lambda^h/E(\lambda^h), m^h)$ is a normalized covariance. The term $(\gamma/E(\lambda^h))$ can be interpreted as the MCF in this case.

We can take the equation governing the optimal choice of the wage tax rate and develop it to get,

$$\gamma/E(\lambda^h) = [1 + \text{cov}(\lambda^h/(E(\lambda^h), w^h L^h)/WL](1 - \theta\Omega)^{-1} \qquad (3.27)$$

where $WL = \Sigma_h w^h L^h$ is aggregate labor earnings, $\Omega = \Sigma_h w^h L^h \varepsilon^h / \Sigma_h w^h L^h$, and ε^h is person h's uncompensated wage elasticity of labor supply. The term Ω simplifies to $\Omega = \varepsilon$ if $\varepsilon^h = \varepsilon$ for all h. The new element in (3.27) is the term in the covariance. If the covariance between the normalized marginal utility of income and labor income is negative, this lowers the MCF and works in the opposite direction of the term involving the elasticity of labor supply. However, one cannot conclude from this that the sum of the marginal benefits is less in the second-best than in the first-best since there are two additional terms in (3.26), the covariance term in λ and m and the provision effect.

If the lump sum tax T is chosen optimally, then

$$- \Sigma_h \lambda^h + \gamma N - \gamma\tau\Sigma_h w^h L^h_I = 0.$$

This can be rewritten as

$$\gamma/E(\lambda^h) = 1/(1 - \tau\Sigma_h w^h L^h_I/N).$$

If leisure is a normal good for all workers, it follows that $\gamma/E(\lambda^h) < 1$. If both the tax rate and the lump sum tax can be chosen optimally, then the right hand side of the last equation and (3.27) must coincide and the government will be indifferent between the two taxes in collecting the marginal tax dollar. This implies that there is a presumption that $\gamma/E(\lambda^h) < 1$ when both tax instruments of the linear labor income tax are chosen optimally. To reconcile this result with the empirical estimates which indicate that the MCF > 1, Sandmo noted that the empirical research did not take into account the influence of distributional concerns, nor did it include a public good in the estimation. It follows that the empirical estimates may be biased as a result.

3.5.2 Capital Income Taxation and the Marginal Cost of Funds

We can also extend the literature on the MCF to the context of a dynamic setting. In the overlapping generations model considered earlier, the equation governing the modified Samuelson rule in a steady state can be written as

$$Nm = (\gamma/\lambda)[C_G - (w\tau_w L_G + \beta r\tau_r C^2{}_G)],$$

where $MCF = \gamma/\lambda$. The equations governing the optimal choice of the tax rates in a steady state are given by

$$\lambda L = \gamma[L - (w\tau_w L_w + \beta r\tau_r C^2{}_w)],$$

$$\lambda c_2 + \alpha c_2 = \gamma[c_2 - (w\tau_w L_R + \beta r\tau_r C^2{}_R)].$$

Noting that $c_2 = (1+r_n)s$, multiply the first tax equation by $w\tau_-$, the second tax equation by $r\tau_r$, add the subsequent equations, and rearrange to obtain,

$$\gamma/\lambda = (1 + A)/(1 - N\Omega/C(G))$$

where $C(G) = w\tau_w L + \beta\rho\tau_R S$ is the total discounted tax revenue collected in a steady state, $A = \beta R^s(\rho - r)\pi/\lambda C(G)$, and $\Omega = (w\tau_w)^2 L_w + w\tau_w r\tau_R(L_R + \beta C^2{}_w) + (r\tau_R)^2 C^2{}_R$ is the behavioral response to the tax rates, where π is a multiplier.

There are two new elements in this calculation of the MCF, the position of the economy relative to the modified golden rule path becomes important and the behavioral response to taxation is more complicated. If the economy is on the modified golden rule expansion path, $r = \rho$ and $A = 0$ as a result. It follows that the MCF is greater (less) than one if the behavioral response is positive (negative), i.e., $\Omega > (<) 0$. However, if the economy is not on the modified golden rule path, then it is possible for the MCF to be less than one in magnitude even when the behavioral response is positive. This may occur if the economy is undercapitalized relative to the modified golden rule path since this implies that $A < 0$. A sufficient condition for the MCF to be greater than one is that $A + N\Omega/C(G)$ and $1 - N\Omega/C(G)$ be of the same sign.

3.5.3 Empirical Calculations of the MCF

Browning (1987) studied the MCF of labor taxation using aggregate U.S. data and attempted to reconcile the various estimates of the MCF at the time. He argued that the difference in earlier results was due mainly to different assumptions about some of the key parameters. His main result was that the estimate of the MCF for labor income taxes in the U.S. ranged from 10% of the revenue collected to 300%, based on realistic ranges for the key parameters. To see why a large range of estimates can lead to a problem, consider the simplest case of a static model of labor supply with identical agents. The MCF of a tax on labor income is given by $1/(1 - \theta\varepsilon)$, where $\theta = \tau/(1-\tau)$ and ε is the uncompensated wage elasticity of labor supply. Suppose $\tau = 0.3$ and that the range for the labor supply elasticity is (0.1, 0.5). Then the MCF ranges from 1.045 to 1.27. One might accept the project at the lower estimate but reject it at the higher end.

Feldstein (1997) estimated the marginal excess burden of a 10% increase in all income tax rates of 1.65 per dollar raised using a tax file of U.S. data. This was on the high side of the current estimates. He argued that the marginal welfare cost of income taxation was likely to be higher than previous estimates for several reasons. First, the appropriate area to calculate for a change in existing tax rates is the excess burden trapezoid, which is much larger in size than the so-called Harberger deadweight loss triangle. Second, labor supply is a very complicated process that includes occupational choice, human capital accumulation, and the effort decision, and these activities are bound to be highly responsive to taxation but are left out of the usual analysis. Third, employers may alter the form in which compensation takes place in response to the tax system. For example, if fringe benefits are not taxable, we should expect more compensation to be paid in fringe benefits, and this is also distortionary. Fourth, there are a number of items that are tax deductible like mortgage interest that is also inefficient and serves to raise the marginal excess burden.

3.6 Conclusion

We have studied the public provision of a pure public good in second-best environments where the first-best taxes are not available. We derived the so-called modified Samuelson rule in various second-best settings and showed how the first-best rule must be altered to take into account the second-best features of the economy.

In particular, we showed how the rule must be modified to take into account the use of distorting taxes, the impact of the public good on the demand for taxed commodities, the effect of the tax system on the WTP for the public good, the equity of both the tax system and the provision of the public good, and the position of the economy relative to the golden rule expansion path. We also compared the levels of the public good across equilibria and derived several general results.

We also studied the so-called marginal cost of funds (MCF) issue. When person-specific taxes are available the MCF is equal to one and the Samuelson rule holds. When such taxes are not available, the MCF will generally differ from one and various considerations need to be taken into account. The distortions associated with an imperfect tax system, equity concerns, and dynamic efficiency, will all play a role in determining the magnitude of the MCF in general. Unfortunately, current empirical estimates provide a range for the MCF that is too large to base policy advice on and do not take into account a number of these additional second-best effects.

Appendix A: Samuelson's Rule in the Static Model with Heterogeneity

It is straightforward to show that the following equation governs the optimal lump sum tax,

$$- \Sigma_h \lambda^h + N\gamma - \gamma \Sigma_h \Sigma_i \tau_i x^h_{iI} = 0, \tag{A1}$$

where γ is the Lagrange multiplier and x^h_{iI} is an income effect. The condition governing the optimal choice of the public good is

$$\Sigma_h \lambda^h m^h - \gamma C_G + \gamma \Sigma_h \Sigma_i \tau_i x^h_{iG} = 0. \tag{A2}$$

And the condition governing the kth commodity tax rate is

$$- \Sigma_h \lambda^h x^h_k + \gamma \Sigma_h x^h_k + \gamma \Sigma_h \Sigma_i \tau_i x^h_{ik} = 0, \tag{A3}$$

Use Diamond's definition of the social marginal utility of income in (A1) to obtain (3.7).

Use the Slutsky equation, $x^h_{ik} = s^h_{ik} + x^h_k x^h_{iI}$, in (A3), Diamond's definition of the social marginal utility of income, multiply the result by τ_k and sum over k to obtain

$$\Sigma_h (\mu^h - \gamma) \Sigma_k \tau_k x^h_k = \gamma \Sigma_k \Sigma_h \Sigma_i \tau_i s^h_{ik} \tau_k.$$

Since $\gamma = E(\mu^h)$, the left hand side of the last equation is a covariance. This is (3.8).

Next, use the Slutsky equation, $x^h_{iG} = s^h_{iG} + m^h x^h_{iI}$, in (A2), Diamond's definition of the social marginal utility of income, add and subtract $\gamma \Sigma_i m_i$ to (A2), use (A3) to eliminate γ, to derive the main result of this section.

Appendix B: A Reform Analysis

Differentiate the social welfare function to obtain,

$$dW = \Sigma_h(v^h_G dG - v^h_I dT + \Sigma_k v^h_k d\tau_k),$$

or,

$$dW = \Sigma_h(\lambda^h dG - \lambda^h dT - \Sigma_k \lambda^h x^h_k d\tau_k), \qquad (B1)$$

after using the properties of the indirect utility function. Differentiate the government's budget constraint,

$$\Sigma_h(dT + \Sigma_k x^h_k d\tau_k + \Sigma_k \tau_k dx^h_k) = C_G dG. \qquad (B2)$$

Also note that $dx^h_k = x^h_G dG - x^h_I dT - \Sigma_j x^h_{kj} d\tau_j$. Using this and the Slutsky equation $x^h_{kj} = (s^h_{kj} - x^h_j x^h_{kI})$, add and subtract $\alpha(\Sigma_h m^h + dT + \Sigma_k x^h_k d\tau_k)$ to (B1) for some $\alpha > 0$, substitute from (B2), use Diamond's definition of the social marginal utility of income, and simplify to obtain

$$dW/\alpha = (\Sigma_h m^h - C_G)dG + \Sigma_h \Sigma_j \Sigma_k \tau_k s^h_{kj} d\tau_k + \Sigma_h \Sigma_k \tau_k s^h_{kG} dG \qquad (B3)$$

$$+ \Sigma_h(\mu^h - \alpha)(m^h dG - dT - \Sigma_k x^h_k d\tau_k)/\alpha.$$

Note that $dv^h = \lambda^h(m^h dG - dT - \Sigma_k x^h_k d\tau_k)$. If $\alpha = E(\mu^h)$, then we can use this to rewrite equation (B3) as (3.11). Next consider the term $\Sigma_h(\mu^h - \alpha)(m^h dG - dT - \Sigma_k x^h_k d\tau_k)/\alpha$ in (B3). If $\alpha = E(\mu^h)$, the term in dT drops out. The remaining terms are then given by $cov(\mu^h, m^h dG)/\alpha$ and $- cov(\mu^h, r^h)/\alpha$. This gives (3.12).

Appendix C: Labor Income Taxation

The first order conditions governing the wage tax rate, the lump sum tax, and the public good are, respectively,

$$- \Sigma_h \lambda^h w^h L^h + \gamma \Sigma_h w^h L^h - \gamma \tau \Sigma_h (w^h)^2 L^h_w = 0,$$

$$- \Sigma_h \lambda^h w^h L^h + \gamma N - \gamma \tau \Sigma_h w^h L^h_I = 0,$$

$$\Sigma_h \lambda^h m^h + \gamma \Sigma_h \tau w^h L^h_G = \gamma C_G,$$

where L_G is the uncompensated response of labor to the public good.

Appendix D: Samuelson's Rule in the OG Model

In a steady state, the first order conditions for G, w_n, and R_n, respectively, can be written in the following form,

$$\lambda Nm = \gamma[C_G - (w\tau_w L_G + \beta r\tau_r C^2{}_G)], \tag{D1}$$

$$\lambda L = \gamma[L - (w\tau_w L_w + \beta r\tau_r C^2{}_w)], \tag{D2}$$

$$\lambda c_2 + \alpha c_2 = \gamma[c_2 - (w\tau_w L_R + \beta r\tau_r C^2{}_R)], \tag{D3}$$

where λ is the private marginal utility of income, $\gamma = \pi + \alpha$, and π and α are the Lagrange multipliers for the two constraints. The condition governing the evolution of the capital stock is

$$\beta(\alpha_{t+1} + \pi_{t+1})(1 + r) - \alpha_t = 0. \tag{D4}$$

It is well known in this model that if debt policy can be chosen optimally, $\pi = 0$ for all t. See Atkinson and Sandmo (1980), or Batina and Ihori (2000), for example. It follows from (D4) that $r = \rho$ in a steady state. If debt policy is unavailable, this will no longer be true.

Using Diamond's definition of the social marginal utility of income, $\mu = \lambda + \gamma(w\tau_w L_I + \beta r\tau_r R_n C^2{}_I)$, where X_I is an income effect for $X = L, C^2$, we can collapse (D1) - (D4) to obtain the following conditions in a steady state,

$$Nm = C_G - (\mu/\gamma - 1)Nm - N[w\tau_w L_{Gu} + \beta r\tau_r R_n C^2{}_{Gu}], \tag{D5}$$

$$(\mu/\gamma - 1)C(G) = S + \beta R^s(r - \rho), \tag{D6}$$

where $L_{Gu}, C^2{}_{Gu}, L_{wu}, C^2{}_{Ru}$, are compensated effects, $R^s = r\tau_r s$ is revenue collected from the tax on saving income from the representative consumer, and

$$S = [\beta r\tau_r R_n w\tau_w L_{Ru} - (w\tau_w)^2 L_{wu} + \beta(r\tau_r R_n)^2 C^2{}_{Ru} - \beta r\tau_r R_n w\tau_w C^2{}_{wu}] < 0$$

by the properties of the Slutsky matrix. Equations (D5) and (D6) can be combined to give the result in the text.

---

[1] To quote Pigou (1928), "When there is indirect damage, it ought to be added to the direct loss of satisfaction involved in the withdrawal of the marginal unit of resources by taxation, before this is balanced against the satisfaction yielded by the marginal expenditure. It follows that, in general, expenditure ought not to be carried so far as to make the real yield of the last unit of resources expended by the government equal to the real yield of the last unit in the hands of the representative citizen." (Pigou (1928), page 53. We are indebted to Charles de Bartolome for this quote.) Later, Pigou (1947) reiterated this point, "The raising of an additional pound of revenue ... inflicts indirect damage on the taxpayers as a body over and above the loss they suffer in actual money payment. Where there is indirect damage, it ought to be added to the direct

loss in satisfaction involved in the withdrawal of the marginal unit of resources by taxation, before this is balanced against the satisfaction yielded by the marginal expenditure. It follows that, in general, expenditure ought not to be carried so far as to make the real yield of the last unit of resources expended by the government equal to the real yield of the last unit left in the hands of the representative citizen." (Pigou (1947), pages 33 - 34.)

[2]   On the marginal cost of funds see Browning (1976, 1987), Stuart (1984), Wildasin (1984), Mayshar (1991), Ballard and Fullerton (1992), Kaplow (1996, 1998), Slemrod and Yitzhaki (1996, 2001), Feldstein (1997), Browning and Liu (1998), Sandmo (1998), Ng (2000), and Gronberg and Liu (2001).

[3]   We could assume a CRS technology without affecting the results.

[4]   This confirms Chang's main result. See Proposition 3 in Chang (2000). Our result generalizes his result.

[5]   Following the literature, we will also ignore the time consistency problem. For a recent discussion of this problem see Batina and Ihori (2000).

[6]   The sign of Ψ is ambiguous. If $k^s < k^f$, then $w^s < w^f$ and $r^s > r^f$. It follows that the first term takes the sign of m^f_{wu}. The second term takes the sign of $(r^f - r^s(1 - \tau^s_r))\, m_{Ru}$. Unfortunately, we know of no empirical evidence on this issue.

[7]   We should note that most of the literature on the MCF has focused on calculating the appropriate rule for the public good and not on the level issue. If the aggregate demand for the public good is strictly downward sloping, the marginal production cost is strictly upward sloping, and labor supply does not bend backwards, an MCF > 1 may still not imply that the second-best level of the public good is less than the first-best level due to the provision effect, equity effects, and the dynamic efficiency effect.

4 Determining Demand for Public Goods: Voting and Mechanisms

Voting is one method that has been used to assess the demand for public projects. Indeed, some have even suggested that votes can be taken on every issue of public interest in referendum style voting since the technology for collecting the votes exists. Simple electronic voting machines, e.g., palm pilots, laptops, could transmit one's vote wirelessly. Indeed, votes could even be structured so as to provide information on gradations of projects, e.g., two lane bridge, four lane bridge, four lane bridge with toll booths, and so on. Bowen (1943), Black (1948, 1958), and Downs (1957) contain some of the classic results on voting especially the median voter hypothesis.[1]

A second possibility for directly determining the demand for a public good is to confront the individual with a tax system that provides an incentive to correctly reveal privately held information about the agent's willingness-to-pay (WTP). These tax mechanisms, pioneered by Clarke (1971), Groves (1973), and Groves and Loeb (1975), based on Vickrey (1961), typically contain two parts, one to finance the project and a second part that provides agents with an incentive to reveal their true WTP for the project. The incentive part of the tax is based on everyone else's WTP, for example, or on the WTP of a subset of agents, and cannot be manipulated by the individual himself.[2]

Unfortunately, neither of these methods is infallible. A voting equilibrium may not exist due to a cycle, which is known as Condorcet's paradox. Arrow's well-known Impossibility Theorem generalizes this to social welfare functions; a non-dictatorial social welfare function that fulfills certain criteria does not exist. And Gibbard (1973) and Satterthwaite (1975) have shown there does not exist a non-dictatorial social choice mechanism that cannot be manipulated. Hurwicz (1972) pointed out that individuals have an incentive to misrepresent their tastes for private goods in order to manipulate market prices to their advantage, although the ability of an agent to manipulate the market outcome dissipates with the size of the economy. However, Roberts (1976) showed that the incentive for manipulative behavior remains as the size of the economy increases in the presence of public goods. These negative results provide the context in which one can impose additional restrictions and attempt to derive positive results, although one should not be sanguine about the prospects of either of these methods.

In what follows we will survey both areas, pointing out the strengths and weaknesses along the way. In the next section we discuss some of the well know results on voting and some of the more recent work. In section 4.2 we study the literature on mechanisms. And section 4.3 concludes the chapter.

4.1 Voting Models

Under his new principle of taxation, Wicksell (1896) proposed that a new tax be used to finance each new public project and that each policy receive unanimous consent. One can imagine various iterative procedures for determining such a policy. For example, a disinterested third party might state a set of tax shares, one for each agent of N agents, $T(1) = \{T^1(1), ..., T^N(1)\}$, and a level of the public good, $G(1)$, in the first round. If everyone is at least as well off as before, each will vote for it and this proposal then becomes the status quo. A new set of tax shares and level for the public good is then proposed, $(T(2), G(2))$, in the second round. If everyone is again no worse off and votes for it, this becomes the new status quo. The procedure iterates until an equilibrium on the contract curve is found.[3]

Such procedures might be difficult to implement for several reasons. First, the cost of collecting, analyzing, and disseminating the information is not included in the analysis but might be substantial. Second, voters might become exceptionally weary of going through the process for every decision. Third, voters might not vote honestly, but strategically, especially if coalitions form. Fourth, the process may not converge under unanimity. Finally, the generation of the proposals as the process evolves is a deus ex machina that needs to be taken into account as a practical matter. For these reasons interest has centered on the majority rule voting mechanism.

4.1.1 The Median Voter Hypothesis

Suppose there is a single political issue: to decide the level of a public good, G. There are N private agents, where N is an odd number, and two political parties. There is one private good X and one pure public good. The technology for the private good is linear and C(G) is the cost of transforming the private good into the public good. Private agents have well-behaved preferences for both the private good and the public good, $u^h(x^h, G)$, where x^h is individual h's consumption of the private good. Voter h's income constraint is $w^h = x^h + T^h$, where w^h is income and T^h is his tax. What level of spending on the public good would person h prefer? Clearly, it is the level that maximizes $u^h(w^h - T^h, G)$. Suppose the agent believes that his tax payment is an equal share of the cost of the public good, $T^h = C(G)/N$, so his utility is $u^h(w^h - C(G)/N, G)$. The voter's preferred level of the public good G^* is given by $u^h_G - C_G u^h_x/N = 0$, or $m^h = C_G/N$. Summing, we obtain $\Sigma m^h = C_G$, the first-best Samuelson rule. Thus, $G^* = G^f$, the first-best level. This is depicted in Figure 4.1 as point A, where $C(G) = cG$ and c is constant.[4]

If the agent's preferences are strictly convex as depicted, then there will be a unique level of spending that maximizes utility. The agent's preferences will be "single-peaked" as depicted in the right-hand diagram.[5] Point A can be interpreted as a "bliss," or "ideal," point since the individual achieves the highest level of utility possible given her budget constraint and the sharing rule for financing the public good.

It is certainly possible that the voter's preferences may not be single-peaked. For example, suppose the issue is spending on the military and the country is involved in a conflict. A voter might be indifferent to spending a small amount to maintain the status quo, or spending a huge amount to end the war, but might prefer both to an intermediate level of spending so the indifference curve might be 'U-shaped' instead, as depicted on the left in Figure 4.2. As a second example, Stiglitz (1974) suggested that preferences might not be single-peaked for public school expenditures. If G is less than G_0 on the right diagram in Figure 4.2, the agent prefers private

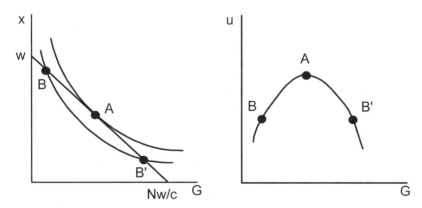

Fig. 4.1. Voting for a Public Good

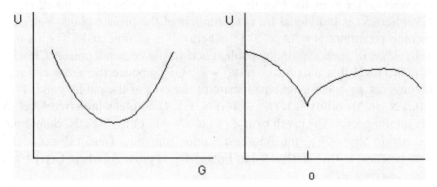

Fig. 4.2. Irregular Preferences

school to public school, but still has to pay taxes to finance the public school and her utility is decreasing with G until G_0. When G is greater than G_0, she switches to the public school. Thus, so long as the marginal benefit of the public school is greater than the marginal cost of the agent's tax burden, utility increases. For $G > G_0$, her indifference curve is U-shaped.

Under the median voter hypothesis the middle of the distribution of voters determines the outcome of the election and so political parties attempt to "capture the middle" of the distribution in order to win. To make this more precise, assume that voter preferences are single-peaked, that voters vote for the alternative closest to their ideal point, and that utility is transferable, $u^h = x^h + U^h(G)$, for simplicity, following the literature. Let G^* represent point A in Figure 4.1. Preferences are single peaked if $U^h(G_1) > U^h(G_2)$ when $|G^* - G_1| < |G^* - G_2|$, for any two points, G_1 and G_2, to one side of G^*, i.e., the point that is closer to G^* yields a higher level of utility, where $|x - y|$ is the distance between x and y. An "ideal" point for person h is a G^* such that $U^h(G^*) > U^h(G)$ for any G different from G^*. Finally, rank voters according to their ideal points and label them accordingly, $G^{*1} < G^{*2} < ..... < G^{*med} < ..... < G^{*N}$, where G^{*med} is the level preferred by the median voter. By definition there are N/2 voters to the left of the median and N/2 voters to the right of the median. The median voter result follows from this.[6] As a corollary to the proposition, the median voter outcome will satisfy the first-best rule and thus lead to an efficient provision of the public good if preferences are symmetric about the median and voters believe they pay a tax that is an equal share of the cost of the good.[7] Thus, the simple majority voting rule can support the first-best Samuelson rule, as described by Bowen (1943).

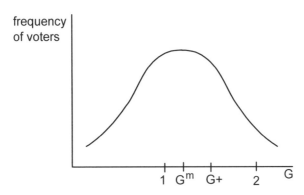

Fig. 4.3. A Continuous Distribution of Voters

This easily generalizes to a continuous distribution of voters, as might be the case in a large election if the distribution is symmetric. In Figure 4.3 we have depicted a symmetric distribution of voters. G^m is the median position and will win the election described above. Consider two parties that offer positions 1 and 2, respectively. G+ is the midpoint between the two positions. Voters to the left of G+ will vote for party 1 while voters to the right of G+ will vote for 2. Since G+ is to the right of the median, party 1 will win a majority of the votes. In Downs' classic model of political competition, party 2 will move to the left of position 2 in order to try to win the election, and policy convergence will ultimately be the result. When the distribution of voter ideal points is asymmetric, the two parties will still converge to a point of central tendency in order to win the election.

One can easily imagine a process where voting is used to determine the preferences of the population for a public good, or any policy for that matter. Under the median voter hypothesis and its corollary, the optimal amount of the public good will be provided. If true, this might be a cost effective way for determining policy.

4.1.2 Problems With the Median Voter Hypothesis

A variety of problems with the hypothesis have been mentioned in the literature. As the two parties converge, voters have little incentive to vote for one party over the other and may become indifferent as a result. Voters in the extreme tails of the distribution may become alienated and drop out as parties converge. In fact, a voter who observes a party alter its position away from her ideal point may also become alienated, even if the voter is not in one of the tails of the distribution. And many issues have a strong ideological following, yet voting on a yes-no basis hardly suffices to register the intensity of many voters' preferences. Some voters may drop out of the process as a result of indifference, alienation, the inability to register the intensity of their preferences, or some other reason. If enough voters drop out, the distribution may change, and this will be reflected in the final outcome.

There are also costs associated with voting and yet there appear to be few direct benefits. Why would anyone vote in a large election? Surely, a single vote does not matter in determining the outcome when thousands, if not millions, are casting a vote.[8] Of course, one could appeal to patriotic duty, or a desire to express one's ideology. However, including such a motive introduces an additional element into the model that may alter its predictions. For example, if voters vote to express their ideological beliefs, they may not vote for a party that opportunistically alters its policy simply to win.[9]

There may be some uncertainty that affects the outcome. A politician will sometimes state an ambiguous position on an issue to appeal to the largest number of voters. This can make it difficult for a voter to tell exactly what the candidate's true position is. The median position on an issue may change over time as new voters enter the process and older voters leave. Thus, there might be some difficulty ascertaining where the median position lies. This also seems realistic and may affect the model in a substantive way.

The country-specific nature of the institutional structure of elections might affect the outcome of the process. For example, in American politics, presidential candidates must first survive a grueling series of primary elections to become the nominee of a party. If the candidate must choose a set of positions to appeal to the median voter in the party, it might be difficult for the candidate to alter his position in order to win the vote of the median voter in the general election. Thus, the positions of the two parties might not converge because of the institutional restrictions.

We also tend to observe political parties that want to win an election in order to impose a particular policy, or ideology, rather than simply compete to win the election. The parties may thus stake out positions for ideological reasons and be less willing to sacrifice principle for a favorable outcome in the election. In that case, the parties may not converge to the median position.

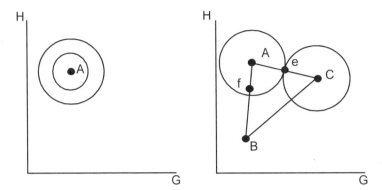

Fig. 4.4. Multi-Dimensional Voting

Finally, an equilibrium may not exist due to the famous problem of cycles. If some voters do not have single-peaked preferences, or there is more than one political dimension being voted upon, cycles may occur and an equilibrium may fail to exist. Suppose there are three voters A, B, and C, and let G_1, G_2, and G_3 be three levels of a public good, where $G_1 < G_2 < G_3$. Consider the following ordinal preference orderings for A, B, and C, respectively, A: $G_1 \gg G_2 \gg G_3$, B: $G_2 \gg G_3 \gg G_1$, and C: $G_3 \gg G_1 \gg G_2$, where $G_k \gg G_j$ means that level k is preferred to level j. Notice that if each voter's preferences are transitive, A prefers G_1 to G_3, B prefers G_2 to G_1, and so on. In a series of pairwise votes under simple majority rule G_1 beats G_2 and G_2 beats G_3. However, G_3 would also win over G_1 and an equilibrium will not exist. The problem is that person C's preferences are not single-peaked.[10]

The existence problem is exacerbated if there is more than one issue in the election. In Figure 4.4 we have depicted voter A's preferences for two issues G and H in the left-hand panel and ideal points for voters A, B, and C in the right-hand panel. Each agent has single-peaked preferences. Segment AB is the set of common tangency points for voters A and B, segment BC is the set of common tangencies for voters B and C, and so on.

There is no point that intersects all three segments AB, BC, and AC, and therefore, there is no majority rule equilibrium even though each voter has single-peaked preferences. Consider a point on segment AC, say e, and suppose it is an equilibrium. Voter B can propose point f to voter A and voter A will support it over point e since it is closer to his bliss point. However, voter C can respond by offering voter B a point that she prefers to point f, and so on.

However, Plott (1967) showed that a "median voter" hypothesis may be salvaged if there is an ideal point for at least one voter and all of the other voters come in pairs that are diametrically opposed to one another. In Figure 4.5 we have depicted the ideal points for a number of voters. First, consider the left-hand panel. The set of points on the line segment AB is a set of common tangency points between voters A and B, the set AC is a set of tangency points between voters A and C, and so on. Notice that point C, voter C's ideal point, is a majority voting equilibrium for these three voters. A point strictly in between points A and C makes voter A better off but makes B and C worse off and would be voted against by B and C, and similarly for points strictly between B and C. Point C is the only point in the intersection of the sets AB, AC, and CB.

Now suppose we add a pair of voters D and E whose preferences are diametrically opposed to one another relative to voter C. Point C is still a majority voting equilibrium. Consider a point on the segment CE. Voter E is better off, however, A, B, C, and D would be worse off and would vote against it, and similarly, for any other move away from point C. Voter C is a 'median voter in all directions.' This assumption is quite restrictive and Plott concluded that it was unlikely to occur.[11] Other analysts also provided necessary and sufficient conditions for existence. However, the required conditions tend to be highly restrictive.[12]

The question then becomes how prevalent is the problem of cycles.[13] Williamson and Sargent (1967), Niemi (1969), and Tullock and Campbell (1970) presented models where cycles are not likely to occur. Later, Tullock (1981) even posed the question as to why there was so much apparent stability in American politics. On the other hand, Plott (1967), Niemi and Weisberg (1968), Kramer (1973), Schofield (1978), McKelvey (1979), and Rubinstein (1979), argued that the conditions supporting existence of a majority rule equilibrium are very restrictive and probably do not hold in the real world. In so far as we seek information about voter preferences, the existence of a cycle is a serious problem.

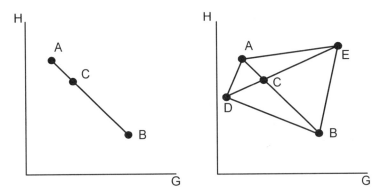

Fig. 4.5. Generalizing the Median Voter Hypothesis

4.1.3 Extensions of the Median Voter Model

In Hotelling's famous model of a spatial market there are two firms selling the same product to buyers who are uniformly distributed on a line. Firms choose price and location, and there is a linear transport cost depending on the distance of the buyer from the seller. Hotelling argued that an equilibrium occurs where the two sellers locate in the middle of the market and charge the same price. Applying this idea, Black and Downs argued that two political parties will move to the center of a distribution of voters on a one-dimensional issue if they only care about winning an election. However, d'Aspremont, Gabszcwicz, Thisse (1979) provided a counterexample to Hotelling's result. They assumed there is a quadratic transport cost and showed that firms locate as far apart as possible. Prescott and Visscher (1977) examined a sequential version of the Hotelling model where firms first choose location in the first stage and then choose price later, given location. They showed that locating as far apart as possible in the first stage is optimal. If the quadratic transport cost is interpreted as a cost of campaigning, or if political parties must choose an ideology first and then choose a position on an issue, then political parties may not converge to the median of the distribution.

Recently, a number of researchers have begun exploring models where political parties are ideologically motivated. It has been shown, for example, that partisan politics may keep policies from converging completely.[14] Political parties may wish to win an election in order to impose their own preferred policy based on their ideological preferences, the opposite of

Downs' view. Suppose there is one issue and that there are two political parties L and R with ideal points G_L and G_R, respectively, where $0 < G_L < G^{med} < G_R < G_{max}$, where G^{med} is the median voter's ideal level for G and G_{max} is the largest feasible level for G. Each party's preferences are single-peaked at their ideal point, and all voters also have single-peaked preferences. Also assume a party's utility falls the further away it is from its ideal point, and that each party also gains utility from winning the election. This creates an interesting tradeoff for the party. Each party would like to win the election and must move closer to the median to do so. However, each party would also like to impose its own ideal policy.

Alesina and Rosenthal (1995) showed that if both political parties know the distribution of voters, policy convergence occurs so that ideology doesn't matter. This follows since if one party chooses a policy proposal identical to its ideal point, the other party can win the election with perfect certainty by making a proposal slightly closer to the median position. Thus, both parties will be driven to the median position and policy convergence will occur. However, if there is enough uncertainty about the distribution of voters, then they showed that convergence is incomplete, $G_L < g_L < g_R < G_R$ is the equilibrium, where g_k is the k-party's policy proposal in the election.

Once a party has won the election, it has a strong incentive to impose its most preferred policy G_k instead of its promised policy g_k. This is an example of the time consistency problem.[15] The party should promise to pursue g_k but once elected impose G_k. As Alesina and Rosenthal point out, there may be mechanisms that impose a constraint on this sort of behavior. For example, a government where there are other political agents to deal with in passing policy, e.g., legislature, and the possibility of running for re-election, impose constraints on a politician. However, one cannot overlook the examples where a politician has very publicly reneged on a promise.[16] We would conclude that voting is a very imperfect method for determining the demand for a public good.

4.2 Mechanism Design with Public Goods

4.2.1 The Clarke Mechanism

The literature on mechanism design studies the institutional arrangements in an economy and seeks ways to improve on the existing institutions. It is imagined that agents transmit messages which when aggregated lead to an equilibrium outcome that can be evaluated using some sort of criterion like

Pareto optimality. The classic pure exchange Walrasian model with a complete set of markets in private goods can be formulated as a mechanism. The Center transmits a message involving prices and private agents respond by transmitting their excess demands for the private goods. As another example, the Center in the Lindahl model of a public good sends a message involving the prices of the private goods and the amount of a public good it will provide, while private agents report their excess demands for the private goods and their WTP for the public good.

Vickrey (1961) proposed a mechanism that provides agents with an incentive to reveal information truthfully, and Clarke (1971) and Groves (1973) independently rediscovered the basic idea.[17] In a first-price sealed bid auction the highest bidder wins the auction and must pay the winning bid. However, the winner will typically pay too much; the winner could have won the auction by submitting a bid equal to the second highest bid plus a small amount. It follows that there is an incentive to reveal a lower bid than the true value. Under Vickrey's second-price auction the highest bidder wins the auction but only pays a price equal to the second highest bid. Each agent has an incentive to reveal his true bid since there is no gain to be had from revealing false information. Revealing the truth is a dominant strategy regardless of the strategies chosen by the other bidders. In a sense, the winner of the auction imposes an externality cost on the other bidders, especially the second highest bidder, and by paying the second price internalizes that cost.

Following Clarke (1971) and Tideman and Tullock (1976), we can apply this idea to economies with public goods. Suppose there is one private good and one public good. Consider a project of fixed size where the public decision is whether to do the project or not. Let v^h be h's true value of the project net of her cost share and let d^h be her declared value that is revealed to the Center. If the agent reveals the truth, $d^h = v^h$. Since v^h includes the cost share, $v^h < 0$ is possible. Further assume utility is quasi-linear in the private good, $U^h = x^h + v^h G$, where x^h is h's consumption of the private good. Private feasibility requires $w^h - T^h \geq x^h$, where w^h is h's endowment of the private good, and T^h is the incentive tax. If $\Sigma_h d^h \geq 0$, then $G = 1$ and the project is undertaken, and if $\Sigma_h d^h < 0$, then $G = 0$ and the project is rejected. Agent h's incentive tax is given by the following formula,

$$T^h = |\Sigma_{j \neq h} d^j| \quad \text{if } (\Sigma_{j \neq h} d^j)(\Sigma_j d^j) < 0,$$

$$= 0 \qquad \text{if } (\Sigma_{j \neq h} d^j)(\Sigma_j d^j) \geq 0.$$

The agent only pays an incentive tax if she is pivotal and thus changes the social choice decision, in which case $\Sigma_{j\neq h}d^j$ and $\Sigma_j d^j$ are of opposite sign. The Clarke mechanism is a special case of the so-called Groves mechanism, where the tax can be defined as,

$$T^h = \Sigma_{j\neq h}d^j + R^h(d_{-h}) \text{ if } (\Sigma_j d^j) > 0,$$

$$= R^h(d_{-h}) \text{ if } (\Sigma_j d^j) \leq 0,$$

for some arbitrary real-valued function $R^h(\ )$, where $d_{-h} = (d^1, ..., d^{h-1}, d^{h+1}, ..., d^N)$.

First, suppose $\Sigma_{j\neq h}d^j > 0$, i.e., the group would choose to undertake the project in the absence of person h. There are a number of cases to consider. If $v^h > 0$ and agent h tells the truth, or understates her preference but not by enough to alter the decision, then she is not pivotal and pays no incentive tax. In that case, she experiences the same utility as if she had told the truth, namely, $U^h = w^h + v^h$. If she understates her true preference and $\Sigma_j d^j < 0$ as a result, $G = 0$ and she alters the outcome, and her incentive tax is $T^h = \Sigma_{j\neq h}d^j > 0$. Her utility in this case is $w^h - \Sigma_{j\neq h}d^j$, which is clearly lower than if she had told the truth. Next, suppose $v^h < 0$ but that $\Sigma_{j\neq h}d^j + v^h > 0$. If she overstates her preference she has no impact on the decision and her utility is $U^h = w^h + v^h$. If she understates her preference enough to alter the outcome, then $\Sigma_j d^j < 0$, her incentive tax is $\Sigma_{j\neq h}d^j$, and her utility is $U^h = w^h - \Sigma_{j\neq h}d^j$. Since the difference in her utility when she tells the truth and when she lies in this case is $v^h + \Sigma_{j\neq h}d^j > 0$, telling the truth is her best choice. Finally, suppose $v^h < 0$ and $\Sigma_{j\neq h}d^j + v^h < 0$. If she lies and the project is undertaken, her utility is $U^h = w^h + v^h$. If she tells the truth, she will alter the outcome since $\Sigma_{j\neq h}d^j > 0$ by assumption, pay an incentive tax of $\Sigma_{j\neq h}d^j$, and experience utility of $U^h = w^h - \Sigma_{j\neq h}d^j$. Since the difference in utility when she tells the truth relative to when she lies is $-v^h - \Sigma_{j\neq h}d^j = -(\Sigma_{j\neq h}d^j + v^h) > 0$, truth telling is optimal. The logic is the same for the various cases when $\Sigma_{j\neq h}d^j < 0$.

It follows that 'telling the truth' is a dominant strategy under the Clarke mechanism; the agent can maximize her payoff by correctly revealing her preference for the project regardless of what the other agents do. This is an important property since the agent does not have to figure out the strategy the other agents will choose. All that is required is that each agent understand how the incentive tax will be applied. In that case it seems reasonable to expect that agents will actually play the game as prescribed if they were to actually be confronted with this mechanism in a real situation.

More generally, suppose agent h is characterized by a parameter $\alpha^h \in A^h$ for a finite set A^h, which is private information. This can be interpreted as the agent's "type." Let $A = \Pi_j A^j$ be the space of types for the N agents, where $\alpha = (\alpha^1, ..., \alpha^N) \in A$. The agent's strategy is to announce a type a^h according to a decision rule, $a^h : A^h \longrightarrow A^h$. If the agent reveals the truth about his type, $a^h(\alpha^h) = \alpha^h$, the identity function. A mechanism that provides agents with an incentive to tell the truth is one where $a^h(\alpha^h) = \alpha^h$ is chosen for all h. An outcome function maps from A to the set of outcomes for the public good according to $\Gamma(a)$ for $a \in A$. Let h's payoff be given by

$$U^h = w^h - T^h + u^h(G; \alpha^h),$$

where w^h is the endowment of the private good, G is the public good, and T^h is h's tax. The social decision might be to do the project or not, in which case $\{0, 1\}$ is the set of admissible values for G. A strategy a^{*h} is dominant if

$$u^h(\Gamma(a^{*h}, a^{-h}); \alpha^h) - T^h(a^{*h}, a^{-h}) \geq u^h(\Gamma(a^h, a^{-h}); \alpha^h) - T^h(a^h, a^{-h}),$$

for any $a^{-h} = (a^1, ..., a^{h-1}, a^{h+1}, ..., a^N) \in A^{-h} = \Pi_{j \neq h} A^j$, and any other $a^h \in A^h$, where $T^h(x, z)$ is h's tax function. Under the Clarke mechanism, $a^{*h} = \alpha^h$ for all h. Another nice feature of a dominant strategy when information is private is that one doesn't have to formulate expectations about the types of the other agents when choosing one's own optimal strategy.

Unfortunately, the Clarke mechanism is not generally Pareto optimal since the budget does not balance identically ($\Sigma T^h = 0$) for all possible strategies.[18] For some messages a surplus of revenue is collected under the mechanism due to the incentive tax. The additional tax revenue cannot be spent without disrupting the incentives of the mechanism in a finite population. If the revenue is used in a systematic way that agents can predict, they will respond to the use of the revenue at the margin in a strategic manner and this may severely limit the ability of the mechanism to provide agents with the correct incentive. Tideman and Tullock (1976) argued that the wasted revenue is negligibly small in a large economy and can be ignored for all practical purposes. This may be true for some strategies. However, it is not true for all strategies. Alternatively, one can imagine a lump sum rebate of the excess revenue that would only cause a small distortion to incentives, which would go to zero asymptotically with the size of the economy.[19] However, even if the tax revenue falls as the economy increases in size, another problem emerges, as pointed out by Green and Laffont (1979); the agent has less of an incentive to tell the truth if the individual agent's incentive tax falls with the size of the economy. In that case the mechanism may fail to provide the appropriate incentive in large economies. Therefore, truth telling as a dominant strategy, budget balance and Pareto optimality appear to be incompatible.

4.2.2 The Groves - Ledyard Mechanism

An alternative to dominant strategy mechanisms is to use a different equilibrium concept. Groves and Ledyard (1977a, 1977b, 1980) devised a mechanism in the context of the classic Arrow-Debreu general equilibrium model and relied on the Nash equilibrium concept instead of one based on dominant strategies. Consumers maximize utility subject to their budget constraint, firms maximize profit subject to their technology, and markets clear. Consumers transmit a message involving their excess demands and their WTP for the public goods and they face a Groves tax rule that provides them with an incentive to truthfully reveal their WTP for the public goods. The government chooses how much of each public good to produce according to the stated WTP and its budget balances. In equilibrium the Samuelson rule is satisfied for each public good since agents reveal their true demand for the public goods. In a Nash equilibrium revealing one's true preferences for the public goods is the best one can do, given that everyone else is also revealing the truth.

Under the Groves - Ledyard 'quadratic government' mechanism each agent pays a share of the cost of the public good, $t^h cG$, and also pays an "incentive" tax according to

$$T^h = (\gamma/2)\{[(N-1)/N][m^h - \mu^{-h}]^2 - (\sigma^{-h})^2\},$$

where $\mu^{-h} = \Sigma_{k \neq h} m^k/(N-1)$ is the average of everyone's reported WTP except agent h and $(\sigma^{-h})^2 = \Sigma_{k \neq h}[m^k - \mu^{-h}]/(N-2)$ is the squared standard error of everyone's deviation except agent h. The incentive tax is increasing in the agent's deviation from the average WTP and decreasing in the squared standard error of everyone else's deviation. The consumer's total tax is $t^h cG + T^h$.

Groves and Ledyard showed that a competitive equilibrium exists. Furthermore, the equilibrium is Pareto optimal and a Pareto optimal allocation can be supported by a competitive equilibrium with the proposed tax rule of the quadratic government. Finally, they also showed that the government's budget balances. However, Groves and Ledyard (1977b) also pointed out some of the problems that may arise and advised caution be taken in applying the mechanism.[20]

The game can also be modeled as one of incomplete information using the Bayesian equilibrium concept, following Arrow (1979), d'Aspremont and Gerard-Varet (1979, 1983), Rob (1989), d'Aspremont, Cremer, and

Gerard-Varet (1990), Mailath and Postlewaite (1990), and Ledyard and Palfrey (1994, 1999), among others. In such a model information is private and each agent has beliefs about the preferences of the other agents and chooses a strategy to maximize his expected payoff. Bayesian incentive compatibility is imposed to ensure the mechanism will elicit the appropriate behavior ex ante. Suppose α^h is h's true type and he announces a^h as his type. Let $u(G; \alpha^h) + x^h$ be h's utility, where x^h is the private good and his constraint is $w^h = x^h + T^h$, where w^h is his endowment and T^h is a tax. Each agent has a probability distribution on the other agents' types. Let $p(a^{-h}| \alpha^h)$ be h's probability that the other agents are type a^{-h}. Let $G = \Gamma(a)$ be the outcome for the public good when a is the vector of announced types and let $T^h(a)$ be h's tax. Agent h's expected utility when he announces a^h is

$$\Sigma p(a^{-h}| \alpha^h)[u^h(\Gamma(a^h, a^{-h}); \alpha^h) + w^h - T^h(a^h, a^{-h})],$$

where the sum is over a^{-h}. The agent chooses an announcement about his type to maximize expected utility. The tax function is chosen by the government to finance the public good and provide agents with an incentive to reveal their true preferences. A mechanism is Bayesian incentive compatible if truth telling is a Bayesian equilibrium, i.e., if truth telling is optimal for each individual given that everyone else is telling the truth. The main result is that a Bayesian incentive compatible mechanism that is Pareto optimal (with a balanced budget) and implements the first-best allocation exists under certain conditions.[21]

Another interesting approach, due to Green, Kohlberg, and Laffont (1976), Green and Laffont (1979), and, more recently, Gary-Bobo and Jaaidane (2000), is to examine the mechanism within the context of statistical sampling. In particular, Gary-Bobo and Jaaidane study a polling mechanism where the planner chooses a sample from a large number of agents, elicits information about the WTP from the subset of agents in the sample while imposing a Clarke - Groves tax within the sample, and then implements a decision for the entire group. The surplus stemming from the incentive tax within the group is transferred to agents outside the sample. They rely on individual rationality in the interim, by which they mean that agents decide whether to participate in the mechanism ex ante before they know whether they will be part of the sample, or not. Mistakes made by the mechanism are small when the sample is large and the variance of tastes in the population is small by the law of large numbers since a statistical version of the Samuelson rule holds under their mechanism. If the public good is excludable, they further show that an optimal allocation can be obtained under their polling mechanism when there is free mobility.[22]

4.2.3 Multi-Stage Games

Crawford (1979) and Moulin (1979) first suggested that the subgame perfection refinement of the Nash equilibrium concept in multi-stage games could implement certain mechanisms that could not be implemented in one-shot games, or as simple Nash equilibria. Moore and Repullo (1988) pointed out that a mechanism could be devised as a solution to the free rider problem as a subgame perfect equilibrium.

It is imagined that agents move sequentially and Nash equilibria that incorporate incredible threats, i.e., threats that would be ignored were they ever to arise, are ruled out by the use of the subgame perfection equilibrium concept. This reduces the number of equilibria in the game and increases the likelihood of finding a mechanism that can solve the free rider incentive problem.

Following Moore and Repullo, suppose preferences for the public good are private information, and that agents know their own type and everyone else's, but the government does not. There are two agents and utility is transferable. Agent h's utility is given by $u^h(g, \alpha^h) - t^h$ and agent k's utility is $u^k(g, \alpha^k) + t^k$, where g is a decision on the public good, α^j denotes j's true 'type,' and t^h is a transfer from h to k, which may be negative. The public good decision is given by $g = G(a^h, a^k)$ when h and k have announced a^h and a^k. Suppose the government uses the following mechanism. In stage 1.1 agent h announces a^h. If agent k agrees with h's announcement in stage 1.2 the game moves to stage 1.3. If agent k disagrees in stage 1.2, she can announce another type for h, say $d^h \neq a^h$, and the game moves to stage 1.3. In stage 1.3 agent h has to choose an outcome for the public good and his tax, which also determines a transfer made from agent h to agent k. Stage 2 is the same as stage 1 with the roles reversed so the government can elicit k's preferences. If at stage 2.2 h agrees with k's announcement, the government then implements the decision. Since each agent has an opportunity to expose the other agent, truth-telling is optimal and $g = G(\alpha^h, \alpha^k)$. With more agents there would be more stages to the game. For example, agents h and i might interact in stage 1, agents i and j might interact in stage 2, agents j and k might interact in stage 3, and so on. What is necessary is that one individual be rewarded for penalizing another.

The key to this mechanism is that an agent may lie about his preferences in order to free ride. However, such a 'threat' is incredible because he knows that another agent can expose him in a later stage of the game. So the strategy of lying is not a subgame perfect equilibrium strategy. In addition, the budget is balanced in equilibrium. For some decisions the budget may yield a surplus out of equilibrium. However, if there are more than two agents, the transfer affecting h and k can be made to a third agent and hence the budget can always be made to balance by construction, even out of equilibrium. And the result does not depend on the assumption of transferable utility, i.e., quasi-linear preferences. All that is required is that there be one individual for each agent who knows the agent's type and is willing to truthfully reveal it.

Varian (1994b) has studied a version of such a mechanism and proposed it as a general solution to the externalities problem. There are two stages to the game, an announcement stage and a choice stage. In the context of the public goods problem, individuals announce subsidy rates under which other agents will be subsidized and are taxed to cover the cost of the subsidy in the announcement stage of the game. In the choice stage agents choose how much to contribute to a privately provided public good taking the subsidy rates as given. The resulting outcome is a Lindahl equilibrium where the government's budget balances.

One drawback to these mechanisms is that they require that some or all of the private agents know the preferences of other individuals and are willing to reveal their assessment of those preferences to the government truthfully, and that everyone understands this. An agent has to believe that someone else will expose him later if he lies. This raises several questions. First, how does the government know that agent k truly knows h's preferences? If k is mistaken about h, the resulting outcome will not be optimal since k may make the wrong decision in a later stage of the game. Furthermore, suppose k doesn't like h and exposes him to receive a transfer. If h never gets a chance to respond and other agents are unaware of the enmity between h and k, k can take advantage of h. In addition, it is possible that agents may exploit this to their advantage by forming coalitions. For example, what is to stop h and k from forming a coalition to exploit the mechanism and foist the cost of the public good onto agent m? What is to stop k from coming forward and stating that she knows h's preferences but lying about it to help agent h exploit the mechanism? In a sense, there is a stage 0, which has not been modeled, where the government has to ascertain which agents know the preferences of the other agents to be used in later stages of the game. So in stage 0, the government has to provide agents with an incentive to truthfully come forward and reveal which individuals they know. Clearly, this is problematic.

4.2.4 Problems with Mechanism Design

There are a number of drawbacks to mechanism design that may limit its usefulness in eliciting preferences for public goods and implementing social decisions. Groves and Ledyard (1977b) themselves expressed skepticism of the ability of mechanisms to solve the free rider problem completely. They listed five general limitations: the budget does not balance in many mechanisms which leads to allocations that are not Pareto optimal; some agents may be bankrupted under some mechanisms and choose not to participate; some mechanisms have equilibria that are unstable and may be unattainable as a result; some mechanisms can be manipulated by individuals; and, finally, coalitions of agents may form to manipulate a mechanism.

Some mechanisms will have a budget that is not identically balanced. Under some outcomes of the mechanism positive revenue will be generated that must be wasted. The Clarke and Tideman and Tullock mechanisms based on dominant strategies are examples. One way around this is to use a different equilibrium concept that incorporates a budget that is always balanced. Various alternatives have been used including the Nash and Bayesian equilibrium concepts, and subgame perfection. However, these equilibrium concepts are not without their own problems. For example, multiple equilibria may exist under the Nash and Bayesian concepts. And, under the Bayesian concept, the outcome of the mechanism can differ from the ex post optimum leading to possible inefficiency.[23]

Another major problem with many mechanisms is that they do not satisfy "individual rationality." If each individual is at least as well off with the outcome of the mechanism as not, then the mechanism satisfies individual rationality. A mechanism may bankrupt some agents, or make some agents worse off by participating in the mechanism than not participating. This possibility cannot be ruled out for many mechanisms including the Clarke mechanism, the Groves - Ledyard mechanism, and Bayesian mechanisms.[24] The reason for the success of the Groves - Ledyard mechanism, for example, is that there is no strategy whereby someone can escape paying a share of the cost of the public good while still benefiting from it even if the benefit is small. Unfortunately, some people with a low demand for the public good may find themselves paying such a high tax that their utility is lower than if they didn't participate at all.

Both Greenberg, Mackay, and Tideman (1977) and Muench and Walker (1983a, 1983b) have questioned the stability of the Groves - Ledyard mechanism based on the Nash concept and whether it would converge to a Nash equilibrium, or not. The mechanism has difficulties when the size of the economy increases. In particular, the mechanism either becomes very unstable, or the incentive to optimize diminishes as the economy increases in size so that an equilibrium under the mechanism may be unattainable in the limit. This raises a serious question as to how a Nash equilibrium could ever be attained. This may be especially problematic if there are multiple Nash or Bayesian equilibria, which is a possibility that also cannot be ruled out. In addition, the equilibrium may fail to exist in large economies, as discussed by Muench and Walker (1983b).

Another problem is that some mechanisms may be subject to manipulation when there is a finite number of agents. This is especially problematic if the mechanism involves an adjustment process. For example, an agent selling a private good can manipulate his message about his demand for the good in a small economy to raise its price artificially thus increasing his own income at the expense of other agents.[25] "Competitive" behavior is not generally rational for the individual once he realizes he can manipulate the outcome, and this is especially true in the context of a public good. Groves and Ledyard, for example, get around this problem by simply assuming competitive "price taking" behavior, which they acknowledge as a handicap. (1980, See page 807.) If agents come to understand that they have an impact on the mechanism, they will possibly manipulate the process to their advantage. This is also a problem with other mechanisms and many voting rules in general.[26]

Bennett and Conn (1977) and Green and Laffont (1979), and more recently, Laffont and Martimort (2000) studied the effects of coalitions on mechanisms. This can be a potentially serious problem. We would expect coalitions to form once agents come to understand clearly how the government will use the information provided to it. There is no guarantee that the outcome of a manipulated mechanism will be socially efficient.[27] So we would expect that unionized labor, non-unionized labor, and management groups will vie for power and influence in determining an array of public policy issues that affect labor. Pro-choice and pro-life coalitions will form on the abortion issue, pro-war and pro-peace coalitions will form whenever war is threatened, pro-environment and pro-development groups will compete on environmental issues, and so on. Much casual evidence supports this notion.

Finally, mechanisms have focused attention on the efficiency problem of providing a public good, and with good reason. Solving the free rider problem is one of the most important intellectual challenges in public economics. The tradeoff between efficiency and incentive compatibility is by now well understood. However, mechanisms may have harmful implications for the income distribution. For example, a mechanism may imply that those who place a high value on a public good pay more for it at the margin. If those agents are primarily at the low end of the income distribution, applying the mechanism without taking this into account may be socially inappropriate.[28] It is to that question we now turn.

4.2.5 Mechanisms and Social Weighting

Jackson and Moulin (1993) proposed a multi-stage mechanism that can implement the first-best allocation for a wide range of cost sharing arrangements. In the first stage each individual reveals an estimate of the joint benefits of the project, V^1, ..., V^N. If the largest value, say V^*, is less than the cost of the public good, C, the mechanism stops and the project is not undertaken. If $V^* > C$, the mechanism proceeds to the second stage where each agent states his own individual benefit from the project, b^1, ..., b^N. If $\Sigma b^h > V^*$ the project is undertaken, otherwise it is not. If the project is undertaken, a cost sharing rule is implemented. Cost shares are chosen to balance the budget and satisfy individual rationality. Jackson and Moulin proved that their mechanism implements the unique first-best Nash equilibrium where agents truthfully reveal their correct preferences, and allows a wide range of cost sharing rules that may include transfers among the agents. And an extension of the mechanism delivers an equilibrium that is also subgame perfect. The only downside is that some of the agents have to know the total valuation of the project, although this is less stringent than other mechanisms that require some agents to know some of the individual valuations.

Ledyard and Palfrey (1994, 1999) studied Bayesian mechanisms where social weights are included in the planning problem. They characterize the interim efficient incentive compatible mechanisms. When there are only two types of agent, high value and low value, and λ is the social weight attached to the high value agents, they showed that the public good is produced if the number of high value agents is greater than a threshold that depends on the social weight and the distribution of types. The larger λ is, the lower the threshold. If λ is higher, so more weight is associated with high value types, then the probability of the public good being produced increases and more of the cost is shifted to the low value agents, and vice versa if λ is lower. It follows that more (less) of the public good is produced relative to the first-best efficient case when λ is high (low) in an ex ante sense. And when interim individual rationality is imposed, they showed that the probability of producing the public good goes to zero with the size of the economy, as in Mailath and Postlewaite (1990).

When there are N agents and a continuum of types for each agent, a social weight $\lambda(v^h)$ can be associated with each type v^h, where v^h is h's value for the public project. The benchmark case is where $\lambda = 1$ for all h and all v^h. The public good is produced (G = 1) if $\Sigma v^h \geq C$, or not (G = 0) if otherwise. The distribution of the cost does not affect welfare in this case and so incentive compatibility does not cause a distortion relative to the first-best solution. More generally, however, with a different set of social weights it does. In general, when the public good is produced, the incentive tax includes an informational rent. This is rebated back to the agents by adjusting a constant term in the incentive tax. Ledyard and Palfrey showed that if $\lambda(v^h)$ is increasing (decreasing) in type, there is over (under) production of the public good relative to the Samuelson case in the interim efficient equilibrium. In general, there will be some distortion because when the welfare weights are not neutral, social welfare depends on the incidence of taxation in addition to the efficiency of providing the public good. The best way to lower taxes imposed on low (high) value types is to reduce (increase) the level of the public good because of incentive compatibility. Unfortunately, since Ledyard and Palfrey do not impose interim individual rationality, it is not immediately obvious that bankruptcy is avoided under this mechanism. And it does require some knowledge of the distribution of types, which may be problematic.

4.3 Conclusion

Voting may be a very blunt tool for determining society's preferences for a particular policy. Many voters may not vote for a variety of reasons, e.g., alienation. A voting equilibrium may not exist. It may be impossible to ascertain the intensity of preference for one policy over another. Some voters may vote strategically in order to alter the outcome of the vote and coalitions may form for this express purpose. And in a dynamic context, the promised policy may not actually be implemented after the election; the policy may be time inconsistent.

Mechanisms hold out promise that preferences may be elicited by providing individuals an incentive to truthfully reveal their preferences. The results in the literature are technically impressive, to say the least. Mechanisms exist which can implement the correct social decision in a variety of circumstances, but problems remain, especially involving individual rationality or the willingness of someone to participate in the mechanism. And ex post outcomes may cause some to drop out of the mechanism. Still, there is some experimental evidence, e.g., Chen and Plott (1996), that supports the notion that a successful mechanism can be designed in a carefully controlled environment.

[1] For a broad summary of the voting literature see Mueller (1989), the papers in Mueller (1997), and the books by Alesina, and Rosenthal (1995), and Alesina and Roubini, with Cohen (1997).

[2] For surveys on mechanism design see Hurwicz (1973), Green and Laffont (1979), and Campbell (1987), and the papers in the symposia in Public Choice (1977) and the Review of Economic Studies (1979). For the early literature on public goods mechanisms see Clarke (1971), Groves (1973), Groves and Loeb (1975), Tideman and Tullock (1976), Groves and Ledyard (1977a, 1977b, 1980, 1987), Green and Laffont (1977, 1979), Hurwicz (1979a, 1979b), Walker (1980, 1981, 1984), and Conn (1983), among others.

[3] There is no guarantee that such a sequential process will converge to the Lindahl equilibrium.

[4] Of course, with a different cost sharing rule a different outcome may occur.

[5] See Arrow (1951) and Black (1948) on single-peaked preferences.

[6] To prove this proposition, without loss of generality, consider a vote between G^{*j} and G^{*med}, where $G^{*j} < G^{*med}$. Then voters with an ideal point equal to or greater than the median will prefer the median. Voters with an ideal point equal to or less than G^{*j} will prefer it to the median. However, by the definition of the median, there will be at least $N/2 + 1$ voters who prefer the median level. Thus, G^{*med} will be chosen. For example, if $G^{*j} < G^{*j+1} < G^{*med}$ and G^{*med} is preferred by the $j+1$ voter to G^{*j}, then $N/2 + 2$ agents will vote for the median level. Since this simple argument also holds to the right of the median level, the median level will dominate under simple majority rule.

[7] Of course, if preferences are not symmetric, this will not necessarily be true. To see this, let $h = med$ denote the median voter. Then his optimal choice is given by $m^{med} = C_G(G^{*med})/N$. However, the first-best level of the public good must satisfy $\Sigma_h m^h = C_G(G^f)$. Subtracting, we obtain $(\Sigma_h m^h/N - m^{med})N = C_G(G^f) - C_G(G^{*med})$. Thus, $G^{*med} = G^f$ if and only if $m^{med} = \Sigma_h m^h/N$, the arithmetic average, which will be true if the distribution is symmetric.

[8] In the presidential election of 1960, one of the closest in US history, John F. Kennedy beat Richard M. Nixon by 49.72% to 49.55% of the popular vote, but well over 100,000 votes. Even in such a close election, a single vote would not determine the outcome of the election. In the election of 2000, another close election, Al Gore defeated George W. Bush in the popular vote by over 500,000 votes but lost in the Electoral College. Gore received 50,999,897 votes or 48.38% of the popular vote while Bush received 50,456,002 votes or 47.87%. Once again, an individual voter could not possibly believe that her vote would be decisive prior to the election. See http://www.fec.gov/pubrec/2000presgeresults.htm for the official data on the 2000 election.

[9] See Fiorina (1997) and Aldrich (1997) on voter motivation.

[10] On a more technical level, the set of preference lists in the above example of a cycle is said to form a "Latin square;" each possible alternative appears in each of the possible ordered positions. One can easily see this by placing the three sets one on top of the other and looking at the three resulting columns. In col-

umn one, the first choice for each voter, we have G_1, G_2, G_3. In column two, the second choice for each voter, we have G_2, G_3, G_1. And column three is composed of G_3, G_1, and G_2. If preferences were such that this did not occur, then a cycle would not occur. For example, if voter C's preferences are $G_3 >>$ $G_2 >> G_1$ instead, then G_2 would beat both G_1 and G_3 in pairwise votes and be the equilibrium choice. One can also see that columns two and three do not include all of the alternatives when C's preferences are $G_3 >> G_2 >> G_1$ and so the structure of preferences does not form a Latin Square.

[11] To quote Plott, "Samuelson has demonstrated that the equilibrium attained by the market mechanism for a public good will, in general, fail to be an optimum. The analysis here implies that a majority rule political process will fail to reach an equilibrium at all. Thus, in the case of public goods, society can count on neither the market, nor a majority rule political process to be a desirable allocative device." Plott (1967), pages 794 - 795.

[12] For other work on existence see, for example, Kramer (1973), Davis, DeGroot, and Hinich (1972) and Slutsky (1977, 1979).

[13] Enelow (1997) contains a useful survey of the literature on cycles.

[14] There is a large and growing literature in this area. See the references in Alesina and Rosenthal (1995), Alesina and Roubini with Cohen (1997), and Drazen (2000).

[15] See Kydland and Prescott (1977) for the original statement of the time consistency problem. See also Persson and Tabellini (1990) and Batina and Ihori (2000) for a discussion of the problem. Briefly, the future policy that was optimal at the beginning of the planning horizon is no longer optimal later when the future actually arrives and the policy must actually be imposed.

[16] A famous example of this occurred when President George Bush broke his "read my lips" promise not to raise taxes, which was made during his acceptance speech at the Republican National Convention in 1988. Many believe the budget deal he made with congressional Democrats in 1990 to balance the budget by raising taxes was the main reason for his losing the 1992 election.

[17] Groves and Ledyard (1977b, note 6) cite Vernon Smith as stating that Jacob Marschak had the essential idea in the early 1950s.

[18] A dominant strategy mechanism that is truth telling and Pareto optimal does not exist in the context of transferable utility models of pure public goods. They also do not exist in more general settings. See the discussion in Green and Laffont (1979) and especially in Walker (1980).

[19] See Green and Laffont (1979) and Rob (1982).

[20] Chen and Plott (1996) implemented the Groves-Ledyard mechanism in a laboratory experiment and discovered that the mechanism performed surprisingly well. The 'punishment' parameter γ had a strong influence on the outcome increasing the efficiency of the mechanism from 91% to 98% when it increased.

[21] A Pareto optimal Bayesian incentive compatible equilibrium exists regardless of the form of the utility functions for a large set of beliefs when there are two

types and more than two agents. If beliefs are independent, the budget is balanced. See d'Aspremont, Cremer, and Gerard-Varet (1990).

[22] Hurwicz (1979b) and Walker (1981) also put forth alternative mechanisms. In particular, Walker provided a simpler version of the mechanism that implements Lindahl allocations. Suppose h's utility is $U^h(x^h, G)$ and $x^h = w^h - T^h$. His tax is $T^h = cG/N + m^{h+1} - m^{h+2}$, for h = 1, 2, ..., N-2, and for agent N-1, $T^{N-1} = cG/N + m^N - m^1$, and $T^N = cG/N + m^1 - m^2$, where m^k is k's message, i.e., WTP. Each agent's tax is equal to the average cost of the public good plus a term that depends on the difference of the stated WTP of the next two agents. Agent h solves max $U^h(w^h - cG/N + m^{h+1} - m^{h+2}, G)$. Thus, $U^h_G/U^h_x = c/N$ since agent h takes the messages of the other agent's as given. Summing yields the Samuelson rule. The mechanism works because the individual's tax is not influenced by his own actions and is constructed in a clever way to achieve a balanced budget. Both Fundamental Welfare Theorems hold under Walker's mechanism. And, Walker showed how his mechanism could be defined in a model with a continuum of agents where the tax of a single agent is based on more than two agents. The model thus easily generalizes to the case where agents cannot manipulate the equilibrium in private goods and thus cannot manipulate the equilibrium in public goods.

[23] See Rob (1989, page 317) for an example of this.

[24] Mailath and Postlewaite (1990) showed that a public goods mechanism does not exist that is individually rational, Pareto optimal, incentive compatible, i.e., truth telling is a Bayesian equilibrium, and has a balanced budget. Rob (1989) derived a related result in a slightly different game involving an externality. Essentially, the assumption of individual rationality gives veto power to the individual and this favors the status quo. And the problem is exacerbated in large economies. Both Rob and Mailath and Postlewaite provided conditions under which the probability that the project is undertaken goes to zero with the size of the economy when interim individual rationality is imposed in a Bayesian framework, where 'interim' means that the individual knows his own type but not anyone else's when the mechanism is implemented. Imposing ex post individual rationality is an even greater restriction on the mechanism. Also, see the comments by Ledyard and Palfrey (1994), who pointed out that the ex post individual rationality problem can be severe and can lead to significant inefficiency when imposed in a large economy.

[25] See Hurwicz (1972, 1973).

[26] A well known example of this is rank order voting, where agents are asked to rank alternatives and the set of rankings is used to choose the best alternative. For example, an agent can falsify her ranking by placing her second choice last to manipulate the outcome toward her best choice.

[27] Although, see the skeptical comment by Tullock (1977) about coalitions.

[28] Mirrlees (1986, page 1217) has espoused this view.

5 Determining the Demand for Public Goods: Surveys and Indirect Estimation

In order to determine the WTP for a public project, one could simply ask people how much value they place on the project, as first suggested by Ciriacy-Wantrup (1947) for environmental goods. Indeed, Johansen (1977) optimistically suggested that people would correctly reveal their true preferences for a public good since they are generally honest. Thus, surveys and questionnaires could be used to gather information about the WTP for a public project.[1]

There is also the clever idea put forth by Maler (1971), Hori (1975), and Bradford and Hildebrandt (1977), among others, that public goods and private goods may be related and that market demand information on private goods may provide indirect evidence on the WTP for a particular public good. For example, the demand for automobiles may depend on the local street and highway network. Estimating the marginal impact of public infrastructure on the demand for automobiles by regressing local auto sales on local spending on the roads, among other variables, and then integrating back to the indirect utility function may reveal information about the demand for roads.

In the next section we discuss Bohm's survey in detail and the work on contingent valuation (CV) in 5.2. In section 5.3 we discuss problems with the CV approach. In 5.4 we study indirect estimation techniques and section 5.5 concludes the chapter.

5.1 Bohm's Survey

Under the interval method a group is split into at least two subgroups, one is given an incentive to overstate their WTP while another is given an incentive to free ride, and everyone is asked their WTP for the public good. If the subjects behave according to the incentives they face, this yields an interval where the lower bound is determined by the free riding group and the upper bound is determined by people who overstate their WTP. The project is accepted if the cost is less than the lower bound and rejected if it is greater than the upper bound. Of course, the lower bound should be zero under the free rider hypothesis.

Bohm (1972) designed an experimental test of the free rider hypothesis using a survey instrument carried out by the Swedish Radio TV Broadcasting Company. Six hundred and five people were drawn at random from the population of Stockholm and were asked to participate in the study for 50 KR. Participants were put into six groups. Each group was asked to watch a brand new television program and provide an estimate of their WTP for the program. They were told that if the sum of the stated valuations was at least as great as the cost of the program, 500 KR, the program would be provided. Each group was confronted with a different price for the program. Group one was told they would have to pay the amount they stated. Group two was told they would have to pay a percentage of the amount stated. Group three was told they would pay the amount stated, a percentage of that amount, 5 KR, or nothing, as determined by a random lottery. Group four was told they would pay a fixed price, 5 KR. And group five was told they would pay nothing; taxpayers would pay the cost. A sixth group (labeled VI:1) was asked hypothetically to state how much they thought the program was worth. In a later trial this group (labeled VI:2) was also asked to bid for a seat to see the program, were told only ten people out of one-hundred would be allowed to see the program, and that they would have to pay the amount they had bid. Finally, each group was given the impression that it was part of a much larger study.

Members of group one clearly had an incentive to understate their preferences and free ride, while group five had an incentive to overstate their preference since they would pay nothing. Group four also may have had an incentive to overstate their preference since their cost was fixed and not related to their stated WTP for the program. Bohm's main result was that there was no significant difference in the stated WTP among the different groups at the 5% level of confidence. For example, the mean response for group one was 7.6 Kr and the mean response for group five was 8.8 Kr, although the standard deviations were very large for both (over 6 Kr). He also concluded in passing that individuals may not reveal their true WTP in hypothetical situations since the mean response of the only group confronting a hypothetical question, group VI:1, was significantly larger than the first five groups.[2] This evidence perhaps suggests that the subjects in the study did not follow the economic incentives they faced.

Several remarks are in order. The large stand errors make hypothesis testing problematic and so Bohm's conclusions is unwarranted. After all, the WTP of the free rider group was lower than that of the group whose incentive was to overstate their preference. Second, arguments were employed to counter strategic behavior for each group, i.e., the subjects were instructed on the free rider problem before filling out the survey, and this may have tainted the results. Bohm also used open-ended questions like, "How much would you be willing to pay for the program?," rather than closed-ended questions like, "Would you be willing to pay $x for the program?" Using open-ended questions may increase the variance of the responses. An open-ended survey may also generate answers that don't make sense, e.g., offering to pay 50% of family income for a project with only minimal benefits to the family. Finally, no one actually had to pay for the program and this may have skewed the responses upward. These issues have all been raised in the more recent literature on contingent valuation.[3]

5.2 Contingent Valuation (CV)

The main use of CV is to elicit the WTP of non-marketed goods, mostly involving environment such as a natural habitat. The method has been used in a variety of situations including the environmental damage caused by the Exxon-Valdez oil spill.[4]

5.2.1 The Basic Method

In a popular form of CV analysis a randomly selected group of subjects is provided with a scenario regarding some issue X and asked a question or sequence of questions about X. In an open-ended survey subjects are simply asked, "What is your WTP for X?" In a closed-ended survey subjects are asked, "Would you favor spending $y for X, yes or no?" Sometimes it is phrased as a vote for or against $y. Depending on the answer, the subject might then be asked, "Would you favor spending $y plus or minus $z, yes or no?" A follow up question may be included to elicit the subject's WTP more precisely in a narrow interval. For example, if a subject states "yes" to $y, yes to $y plus $10, yes to $y plus $20, but "no" to $y plus $30, the subject might then be asked to state her maximal WTP in the interval [$y + 20, $y + 30].

Several other important features of a CV study are the implementation of the proposal, the relationship of the subject's tax payment to her stated WTP, and follow up questions. The researcher may wish to convince subjects that if enough of the subjects support the proposal it will actually be implemented. Subjects may be more willing to reveal their true WTP if they believe the program will actually be undertaken if it passes, than not.

Second, if the subject's tax is tied to her stated WTP, it is said to be coupled. If not, it is uncoupled. Under Bohm's interval technique, for example, the sample is split between those whose tax is coupled, who thus have an incentive to understate their WTP, and those whose tax is uncoupled, who have an incentive to overstate their WTP. Finally, there may be follow up questions to ensure that subjects understood the survey.

An open-ended study proceeds to estimate the relationship between the WTP obtained in the survey and various conditioning variables that may include the general attitude about the environment, for example, and personal socio-economic information. A closed-ended study proceeds by posing different dollar amounts to different individuals and collects information on the frequency of yes and no answers across those amounts, as well as other information such as general attitudes about the good in question and socioeconomic information. The resulting information allows the researcher to map out the cumulative distribution function of the WTP for the particular good in question across the dollar amounts chosen for the study.

Single, closed-ended, referendum CV studies have become popular of late. In fact, the single question format was endorsed by the blue-ribbon panel charged by the NOAA (National Oceanic and Atmospheric Administration). One reason for the single question format is that answers to follow-up questions can be heavily influenced by the first question posed, as noted by McFadden (1994). However, many CV analyses retain the sequential referenda format.

Hanemann (1994) described the foundation of a well-designed contingent valuation study particularly well in his defense of the general approach. First, subjects should be interviewed in-person in an environment where they have time to give serious thought to the questions posed, rather than being stopped and hurriedly asked a few questions in a shopping mall. The issue should be framed in a specific way, e.g., protecting the spotted owl's habitat, rather than in a general fashion, e.g., protecting a hypothetical wilderness area, and a full description of the scenario should be presented to the subject. The more specific the questions are, the more accurate the information will be. Subjects should be asked closed-ended questions, rather than open-ended questions. Phrasing the question as a vote is sometimes helpful. For example, the question, "Would you vote to spend $x to preserve the spotted owl's natural environment?", might be a useful way to get at the WTP. Finally, a "debriefing" session should be held to ensure the subject understood the questions and issues posed.

5.2.2 Common Problems

A number of problems with this methodology have been discussed in the literature. Subjects may not fully understand the questions posed, or become bored and give quick responses rather than honest ones. They may also give answers they believe the researcher is looking for rather than honest answers. The order of the questions may also affect the responses as well.[5] There may be so-called framing effects. For example, the respondent may not understand that "higher prices " corresponds to "higher taxes." In addition, there may be "interviewer effects," where subtle cues by the interviewer may affect the responses. Another problem is that of answering with what may be focal points rather than true responses. For example, a subject may give $10 as an answer, rather than his true valuation of $9.59 if $10 is a focal point. A clear description of the scenario and careful follow up can mitigate some of these problems.[6]

Finally, there is also the well-known problem that the willingness-to-accept (WTA) is typically much greater than the WTP for a given project. For example, subjects generally place a higher value on preserving a particular wilderness area if they are told the public owns the land and are asked, "Would you be willing to accept $z to allow a developer to develop the land?", as opposed to being told the developer owns the land and being asked, "Would you be willing to pay (WTP) $y for the right to maintain the land as a wilderness area?"[7] In general, the ratio WTA/WTP is typically much greater than one in the case of environmental goods. Thus, owners of a right seem to place a greater value on it than non-owners. This has been labeled the 'endowment effect.' A difference between the WTA and the WTP for a particular project can alter the decision on whether or not the project should be undertaken. For many environmental questions like drilling for oil in a wildlife refuge the WTA would appear to be the appropriate measure of non-market value since the public owns the right to the land prior to development. Since the ratio WTA/WTP is as great as seven in some studies, the land in the refuge may be seven times more valuable if the WTA is used instead of the WTP. This sort of difference in estimates can easily have a dramatic impact on public policy decisions, but also makes it harder to defend the general approach.

5.2.3 An Example of Contingent Valuation: Valuing Commuting Time

Calfee and Winston (1998) used a method similar to CV to place a value on commuters' time in order to assess various policy alternatives involving travel time and public infrastructure. They estimated the WTP of automobile commuters to reduce their travel time under various scenarios involving travel conditions and the potential uses of the toll revenue. Surprisingly, they found that the average value of time was lower than expected. This was also true for high-income individuals. In addition, the value of travel time was surprisingly insensitive to travel mode and the uses of the toll revenue.

1170 subjects were contacted and about 67% responded. Each respondent was contacted by mail and was sent a deck of 13 cards. Each card described a scenario involving the commuting time on congested and uncongested roads, the travel cost in the form of a toll, and whether trucks were allowed on the road or not. Each respondent shuffled the deck of cards and then rated each card on a scale of 1 to 10, where 1 was considered very unacceptable and 10 was very acceptable. They then ranked the cards from most acceptable to least acceptable. Separate samples were drawn for each of thirteen scenarios. For example, scenario 3 was "toll road with an unspecified use of toll revenues," scenario 4 was "toll road where tolls are used for maintenance and construction," and so on. Rank order logit was used to estimate a utility function with the arguments of travel time, price, and whether trucks were allowed on the road or not.

The average WTP ranged from 14 to 26 percent of the gross hourly wage and tended to rise with income. There was no evidence that WTP was affected by the use of the toll revenue. Indeed, the estimated value did not differ much across the thirteen different scenarios. Calfee and Winston speculated that people and businesses may have responded to previous congestion by relocating prior to the study, and that this reduced the stated value of their time spent commuting.[8]

Calfee and Winston seem to have avoided many of the common pitfalls of CV studies. Their method differed in that they were asking about something people were very familiar with, commuting, the question sequence was not a factor, subjects were not given an opportunity to give a response they thought socially appropriate, and interviewer bias was also not a factor. Of course, since people in the study did not actually have to pay for the good in question, one can always wonder if they really provided information on their true WTP for the good, or not.

5.2.4 A Unified Approach to Contingent Valuation

Cameron, Poe, Ethier, and Schultze (2002) developed a unified approach and compared seven elicitation procedures. One telephone survey and six mail surveys were done under the aegis of the Niagara and Mohawk Power

Company in New York. Subjects in the service area were chosen randomly and were asked to consider paying an additional amount per month on their power bill for various options under the Green Choice™ program, which had two parts. First, some homes would be supplied with power from renewable resources like solar energy. Second, thousands of trees would be planted to improve the environment. There were several options to choose from. For example, option A was "do nothing and pay nothing," option B was "plant 50,000 trees," option C was "provide renewable energy to 1200 homes and plant 50,000 trees," and so on.

Seven elicitation methods were used to gather the information, one actual choice and six hypothetical choices. Some subjects were asked if they wanted to join the program (option C) and pay an extra $6, where everyone paid the same price, against the option of doing nothing.[9] The second method was the same as the first but made hypothetical. Third, subjects were given a randomly chosen price that differed across agents and were asked if they would choose option C against the option of doing nothing at this price. Fourth, subjects were asked to state their WTP for option C in an open ended way. Fifth, a payment card was used, which typically requests a choice among a series of intervals. Sixth, subjects were confronted with thirteen different prices for option C and were asked how likely they were to choose that option under each price, e.g., definitely yes, probably yes, and so on. Finally, subjects were confronted with several options in addition to option C and were asked to make dichotomous choices among two options, A versus B, A versus C, and so on.

Cameron, et. al., assumed that a person's utility depends on the number of homes provided with renewable energy, the number of trees planted, and the price of the program. A dummy variable approach was used to identify individuals who chose one option over another. If the indirect utility function is linear, then under option A we have,

$$v^{hA} = \beta_0 + \beta_5 I^h + u^{hA},$$

where I^h is person h's income and u^{hA} is a random variable under option A. For option C,

$$v^{hC} = \beta_0 + \beta_2 C^h + \beta_5 (I^h - \text{price}) + u^{hC},$$

where C^h is a dummy variable equal to one if the person chose option C and zero otherwise. Thus,

$$v^{hC} - v^{hA} = \beta_2 - \beta_5 \text{price} + u^{hC} - u^{hA}.$$

The WTP is defined as the price that makes the individual indifferent between a particular option and doing nothing. Solving, WTP = β_2/β_5 +

$(u^{hC} - u^{hA})/\beta_5$. The parameters β_2 and β_5 are modeled as functions of socio-economic variables in order to identify the parameters. Their main finding was that there is a common underlying preference structure for four of the samples when the data is pooled.

5.3 A Critique of the Contingent Valuation Approach

Diamond and Hausman (1994) and Green, Jacowitz, Kahneman, and McFadden (1998) have been particularly critical of the methodology used in CV studies. Diamond and Hausman argued that there are several credible hypotheses alternative to the hypothesis that individuals are correctly stating a WTP for a public good. First, the subjects may be expressing a view in dollars because they were asked to, not because they really have one. Second, people may obtain a "warm glow" for their support of a good cause such as maintaining a wildlife refuge. Third, they may be expressing a general opinion about what they think is best for the country. And, finally, they may be expressing a view about certain actions taken rather than undertaking a careful assessment of a particular public good's value to them. Distinguishing among the various alternatives may be difficult if not impossible. Diamond and Hausman forcefully argued that much of the available evidence strongly suggests that people have a "warm glow" for various environmental issues and that stated valuations are not really measuring their true preferences.

In particular, they focused attention on several problems including the "embedding" problem and proposed an "adding up" test. Consider a "single question" survey, so the order of questions is irrelevant. Suppose one group is asked to value x, a second group is asked to value y, and a third group is asked to value x and y. Diamond and Hausman posed the question: how should we interpret the results if the value of x and y together is less than the sum of the separate valuations of x and y taken separately? The evidence they cited suggests that people value one, two, and three wilderness areas about the same and that the amount for several wilderness areas taken together is less than the sum of the areas taken separately. Furthermore, they argued that this is consistent with the warm glow idea if people generally support the environment since small changes in the environment apparently did not alter their WTP by much.

Nunes and Schokkaert (2003) provide evidence on this. They included a series of 26 questions on their CV questionnaire designed to elicit information about the subject's attitude toward the environment. The questions were designed to capture existence value, use value, and a warm glow value. There were three different versions of the questionnaire focusing on wilderness areas, WA, recreation areas, RA, and a joint program involving the sum of both, WA + RA. They found that both the mean and the median WTP's for the three alternatives were about the same across alternatives and thus WTP(WA+RA) < WTP(WA) + WTP(RA), suggesting a warm glow motive is operating. They then econometrically estimated the warm glow effect using the attitudinal measures and various other socioeconomic variables and calculated the WTP for each alternative after taking out the warm glow motive.[10] Their main result was that they could not reject the hypothesis that WTP(WA+RA) = WTP(WA) + WTP(RA) when the warm glow motive was eliminated. This suggests that the existence of a warm glow motive may be what is causing the embedding problem. It would be of some interest to continue this work to determine whether it is a warm glow per se or some other motive, e.g., sense of fairness or altruism, that is driving the result.

Green, Jacowitz, Kahneman, and McFadden noted that open-ended questions occasionally elicit outlandish responses that stretch one's belief that CV is getting at the true economic value of the non-marketed good in question. Closed-ended referenda get around this problem by simply avoiding those response intervals. This lends more confidence to the method than is perhaps warranted. Unfortunately, we don't know if any of the subjects in such a referenda study would have chosen such outlandishly high valuations had they the opportunity to do so. For example, suppose someone is willing-to-pay $2000 to save the spotted owl's habitat but that a closed-ended procedure stops at a maximum of $500. In that case, we will never know if respondents would have gone higher than $500 since they were not given the opportunity to do so.

They also noted that making transactions through the market is a learned behavior that the subjects have a great deal of experience with. However, their experience in valuing non-marketed goods is very limited. The costs and benefits of the non-marketed good may be hazy, or ill defined for the person and thus uncertain and difficult to place a value on. The link between the instructions given to the subjects and their subsequent beliefs may be weak. If the subject only believes part of the instructions, a serious bias may exist leading to misrepresentation. For example, if a subject believes that there is no link between his stated WTP and his payment and that he might be decisive, despite instructions to the contrary, then he may overstate his preference for the good to ensure it gets provided. Unfortunately, there is virtually no way to know precisely what the subject's beliefs are.

Another serious problem noted by Green, et. al., is that of anchoring. Imagine asking a group of subjects if Mt. Everest is taller than 5000 feet or less, and then asking them to estimate the height of Mt. Everest. The answers to the second question may very well cluster about 5000, even though this is ridiculously low. The number 5000 serves as an anchor pulling the subjects' answers toward it. There is significant evidence cited by Green, et. al., that anchors exist and can bias results. So the use of bid levels, e.g., $y, $y + $z, $y + $z + $x, when eliciting information in a sequence of questions, might create an anchor ($y) that is not closely related to the subject's true valuation.

Further evidence on this issue was provided by Dubourg, Jones-Lee, and Loomes (1997). On the basis of their CV analysis of road safety, they argued that preferences for non-marketed goods may be very imprecise and that imprecision may cause numerous problems when undertaking a CV study. Indeed, they argued that the recommendation of the NOAA Panel on CV studies, which proposed a dichotomous choice referendum scenario be used, actually prevents subjects from revealing the imprecision of their preferences. Indeed, their work calls into question the viability of the entire CV methodology for eliciting information on preference for non-marketed goods. Dubourg, et. al. chose a non-marketed good that was close to being a private good, a road safety device that could be attached to one's car that would reduce the risk associated with being in an accident. They used an iterative bidding procedure and a payment card to elicit pricing information. Respondents were asked to rank five possible states involving injury in a car accident, e.g., 1 - 4 weeks in hospital with severe burns and moderate pain, and then quantify the rankings numerically. Then they were asked questions on the WTP for a slight reduction in the risk of each of the five different injuries. Respondents were first given a price and asked if they would pay it for the given reduction in risk. The interviewer continued asking questions until an interval was determined giving the lowest and highest values the respondent would pay. Then respondents were asked to provide an estimate of their WTP in the interval.

They found strong anchoring effects. Starting with £75 led to point estimates typically more than twice the size of the estimate obtained when starting with £25. In addition, the brackets were also affected by anchoring. Therefore, the hope that there is a stable interval or bracket within which the WTP lies may be a false one. Indeed, the fact that there are anchoring effects with regard to the intervals themselves diminishes the confidence one has in the dichotomous choice scenario. In fact, it is highly likely that use of the dichotomous choice referenda may mask the impact anchoring can have on the intervals.[11]

Another problem with CV analysis is that the stated WTP under a hypothetical situation may differ from the WTP when payment must actually be made.[12] We would expect agents to reveal a larger WTP when payment is hypothetical than when an actual payment must be made. This is known as "hypothetical bias."[13] Cummings and Taylor (1999) set up an experiment with four public goods,[14] which varied in different ways, and elicited the WTP from the subjects when payment had to be made, the WTP under hypothetical payment, and the WTP under hypothetical payment including "cheap talk" instructions, where the subjects were informed about the general problem of "hypothetical bias" and were asked to give their true WTP. Cummings and Taylor found that hypothetical bias existed for three of the four public goods and that in each such case the cheap talk instructions eliminated the bias. It is not clear how general this result is and whether it carries over to other environmental goods and other public goods.

An alternative is to use another piece of information that is tied to actual behavior to confirm or reject the results of a CV analysis. Vossler and Kerkvliet (2003) and Vossler, Kerkvliet, Polasky, and Gainutdinova (2003) use actual voting behavior on a referendum to compare with the CV results. In the first study a project to improve the riverfront was proposed to the voters of Corvallis, Oregon financed by increased property taxes. A CV survey was conducted prior to the vote and the results were compared to the results of the vote using precinct data. They found that the results of the CV survey matched those of the actual vote quite well. In the second study, however, they found that the results only matched up if the "undecided" respondents were treated as choosing "no." The average WTP to fund an open space near Corvallis, Oregon from the election results was estimated at $48.89, while the estimated average WTP From the CV analysis was $75.43 without the "undecided" respondents and $49.67 when the "undecided" respondents were treated as a "no" response. The ambiguity about how to treat "undecided" people suggests that even this method is not foolproof.

5.4 Indirect Estimation: Weak Complementarity (WC)

5.4.1 The Basic Method

Consider a consumer who has a well defined preference ordering R over bundles of private and public goods (x^h, G), which is represented by a strictly quasi-concave monotone increasing utility function $u^h(x^h, G)$, where x^h is a vector of private goods and G is a vector of public goods.

Suppose the consumer chooses (x^h, G) to maximize utility subject to a budget constraint, $w^h = q.x^h + p.G$, where a.b is an inner product, w^h is income, and q and p are the price vectors for private and public goods, respectively.[15] The solution is given by the demands $x^h(q, p, w^h)$ and $G(q, p, w^h)$, and $v^h(q, p, w^h)$ is the indirect utility function. If the associated Slutsky matrix is symmetric and negative semi-definite, one can start with the demand system for (x^h, G) and integrate back to the ordinal preference ordering using Roy's identity, $x^h_k = -v_k/v_w$ and $G_j = -v_j/v_w$ for private goods k and public goods j. Of course, the public demands $G(q, p, w^h)$ are typically not observable.

Suppose instead that the consumer only chooses private demands optimally and takes G as given. The solution is the conditional demand system for private goods, $x(q, w^h, G)$. The issue is then one of recovering the preference ordering including preferences over public goods from information on the private demand system alone. Unfortunately, the complete preference ordering cannot be fully recovered in this case. Roy's identity can still be used to obtain the conditional WTP function, $m^h_j(q, w^h, G) = v_j(q, w^h, G)/v_w(q, w^h, G)$ for public good j. However, this function is not invariant to monotone transforms of the utility function. More information is needed.

Maler (1971, 1974), Hori (1975), Bradford and Hildebrandt (1977), Willig (1978), Freeman (1981), Bockstael and Kling (1988), and Neill (1988), among others, noted that many private goods are complementary to public goods. Examples include highways and cars, air safety and air travel, local public goods and choice of residence, mosquito control and picnics, public television and television sets, visits to a lake and the quality of the lake, and national defense and the ownership of private property. This connection may provide information that can determine the WTP for a public good indirectly.

Following Bradford and Hildebrandt, assume preferences are quasilinear for person h, $u^h = x^h_1 + U(x^h_2, G)$, and private good x_1 is numeraire. The WTP for the marginal unit of the public good is $m^h \equiv dU^h/dG = U^h_G(x^h_2, G)$. This is also the inverse demand function for the public good. The inverse demand for the second private good is given by $p = U^h_x(x^h_2, G)$, where p is its market price. By the rules of calculus,

$$m^h = U^h_G = \int_0^{x^h_2} (\partial U^h_G(s,G)/\partial x^h_2)ds + U(0,G).$$

Since $\partial U^h_G/\partial x^h_2 = \partial U^h_{x^h_2}/\partial G$, we can write the last equation as,

$$m^h = \int_0^{x_2^h} (\partial U_{x_2^h}^h(s,G)/\partial G)ds + U(0,G),$$

where U(0, G) is a constant of integration. The first term on the right hand side is the area under the inverse demand curve for the private good when it shifts due to the provision of the public good. The second term is the inverse demand for the public good when the consumer does not consume any of the second private good. Under the assumption of weak complementarity (WC), the public good only generates utility if the private good associated with it is also consumed. In that case the constant term is zero and we have,

$$m^h = \int_0^{x_2^h} (\partial U_{x_2^h}^h(s,G)/\partial G)ds.$$

Consider the following example. Suppose utility is given by $u = x_1 + x_2 G + (x_2)^\alpha (G)^\beta$. The inverse demand functions for x_2 and G, respectively, are $p = G + \alpha(x_2)^{\alpha-1}(G)^\beta$ and $m = x_2 + \beta(x_2)^\alpha(G)^{\beta-1}$. The cross partial derivative is $1 + \alpha\beta(x_2)^{\alpha-1}G^{\beta-1}$. And U(0, G) = 0.

The quasi-linear functional form allows for aggregation across agents and can be generalized to allow for the possibility of income effects. These results also hold for the aggregate inverse demand function as well. This follows because aggregation holds for certain forms of the utility function including the form chosen by Bradford and Hildebrandt.

More generally, let $u^h(x^h, G)$ be the utility function. It follows that the conditional expenditure function is $e^h(q, G, u^h)$. Suppose demand for the kth private good x^h_k is related to the public good, where $e^h_k = x^h_k(q, G, u^h)$ is the conditional compensated demand for good k. Since $m^h = -e^h_G$ by definition, and $e^h_{Gk} = e^h_{kG}$, we also have

$$m^h = \int_{q_k^*}^{q_k^{**}} (\partial e_k^h(s,q_{-k},G,u^h)/\partial G)ds + e_k^h(q_k^*,q_{-k},G,u^h),$$

where q_{-k} is a vector of private good prices other than k. Suppose there is a price q^*_k such that for all prices q^+_k at least as great as q^*_k demand for x^h_k is zero, $e^h_k(q^*_k, q_{-k}, G, u^h) = 0$. This is known as a 'choke' price. It ensures that the demand for x^h_k touches the price axis and makes the calculation of an integral under the private demand curve finite. In that case, we have,

$$m^h = \int_{q_k^*}^{q_k^{**}} (\partial e_k^h(s,q_{-k},G,u^h)/\partial G)ds.$$

Intuitively, when the private and public goods are complements, the compensated conditional demand for the private good will shift out when the public good is provided. The area under the private demand curve above the price that is added by the shift in demand due to the public good is an indirect measure of the individual's WTP for the public good. This is illustrated in Figure 5.1. The emphasized area between the two demand curves for the private good serves as a measure of the agent's WTP for the incremental amount of the public good for G" > G'. This area can be calculated as the difference between two consumer's surplus triangles using compensated demand, before and after the change in the public good. It is the compensating variation if the initial level of utility is used in the integrals and the equivalent variation if the new level of utility is used instead.

One can imagine a local government that wants to build a bridge, for example, and thus needs to know the WTP for different sized bridges. It can collect data on bridges in other locations, market data on complementary private goods in those locations, additional socioeconomic data, and empirically estimate the WTP for a new bridge using this indirect method. Then, if it is willing to make the inference that local demand is similar to demand at other locations, it can extrapolate those results to the local situation. Or, it can use local data from earlier bridges and public infrastructure projects built locally combined with market data on complementary goods and socioeconomic variables to make inferences about the current local demand for a new bridge if it is willing to assume local demand for such projects is relatively stable over time and similar to demand for the new bridge.

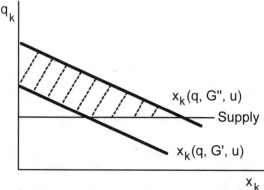

Fig. 5.1. Indirect Estimation

5.4.2 Problems

The main difficulty is that the assumption of WC is a cardinalization of preferences that cannot be tested. Herriges, Kling, and Phaneuf (2004) provide an example of this problem. Suppose we have estimated the Marshallian demand system and want to integrate back to preferences in order to make welfare comparisons across different public projects. Consider the following two utility functions,

$$U = \ln(x_1) + \Sigma\phi_i(G_i)\ln(x_i + \theta),$$

$$U = \ln(x_1) + \Sigma\phi_i(G_i)\ln(x_i/\theta + 1),$$

where x_1 is numeraire, ϕ_i is increasing in public good i, and θ is a parameter, and where goods i = 2, 3, ..., n are each related to a public good captured by the sum. The problem is that both of these functions yield the *same* first order conditions, and hence the same observable demands, but have different implications for complementarity. When the complementary private goods are not consumed, the utility of the public goods is $\Sigma\phi_i(G_i)\ln(\theta)$ and $\Sigma\phi_i(G_i)\ln(1)$ for the two functions, respectively. Weak complementarity holds for the first function only when $\theta = 1$, but holds for any value of θ for the second function. Since the two functions are observationally equivalent, it is impossible to design a test to determine if the first utility function explains the data better than the second. Furthermore, the same estimated demand equation may have different implications for welfare since the underlying utility functions differ.

Herriges, et. al., use the Kuhn-Tucker framework to estimate a travel demand model under the two different utility functions in order to determine the WTP for visiting a public good.[16] The 1997 Wetlands Survey in Iowa collected information on the use of wetlands and attitudes toward preservation. These areas provide outdoor recreation possibilities for activities like "hunting, hiking, and wildlife viewing." Prices can be calculated by determining travel distance to the wetland and time spent traveling and then imputing value to that information. They also used information on the pheasant count as a measure of quality and hence the public good aspect of the wetland. They found that the estimates of the WTP for a 20% increase in their measure of wetland quality differed significantly, $88 and $103, respectively for the two utility functions.[17] This is somewhat disconcerting because the WTP calculated in this manner might serve as a lower bound for valuing non-marketed goods since such goods might be valued for other reasons, e.g., existence value, in addition to their value when consumed in conjunction with private goods. The possibility that this lower bound might vary substantially is problematic.

Ebert (1998) showed that the conditional demands and WTP function, $x^h(q, w, G)$ and $m^h(q, w, G)$, are informationally equivalent to the unconditional demands, $x^h(q, p, w)$ and $G(q, p, w)$, in recovering the preference ordering. This makes it clear that the difficulty in recovering the preference ordering stems from the lack of information on the WTP. He also suggested that CV data could be used to supplement other sources of data in recovering preferences. For example, if CV data can be used to determine the conditional WTP function $m^k_j(q, w, G)$ for some public good j, this can be used to recover part of the ordinal preference ordering. However, this is subject to all of the aforementioned difficulties associated with CV analysis.

This method also requires a considerable amount of micro data in order to estimate the required equations, or choose functional forms that allow aggregation and use aggregate data. Such data is difficult to come by, however. And, since the public good data would have to be included as a regressor on the right hand side of the estimated equation, there would have to be some previous experience with the public good. Clearly, this will not work for new public goods where there is no previous experience like the space program, homeland security, or spraying for mosquitoes to kill the West Nile virus. In addition, there are the usual problems associated with multicollinearity, omitted variable bias, and simultaneity. It is entirely possible that one may not be able to obtain clean estimates of the relevant parameters even if the data exists.

5.4.3 Indirect Estimation as a Mechanism

Bradford and Hildebrandt also argued that their procedure for estimating the WTP for the public good from private demands can be thought of as a social choice mechanism, and furthermore, one that is not subject to manipulation. The presumption is that individuals take market aggregates as given, which would include the level of a public good as well. This should make sense. Would private agents try to manipulate their perceived WTP for a public good by altering their observed demands for private goods? For example, would someone buy a light pick-up truck, rather than a preferred SUV, just to signal a low WTP for new roads to avoid paying a higher tax? Since this sort of strategic behavior seems unlikely because it imposes a real cost on the individual, the indirect procedure would seem to fit the bill as a way of determining the WTP for a pure public good.

Suppose the mechanism operates in the following way. An auctioneer announces a vector of prices for the private goods, the level of the public good, and a vector of tax shares, (p, G, τ), and suppose the agent's tax share is unaffected by his announced private demands. Private agents respond with their market demands for private goods. If markets do not clear another vector is announced, demands are revealed, and so on. The process continues until markets for the private goods clear and Samuelson's rule for the public good is satisfied. The indirect estimation method would allow the auctioneer to determine the demand for the public good as the process evolves if some of the private goods are complementary to the public good. If the process converges, then in equilibrium the auctioneer will be able to determine the appropriate demand for the public good via indirect estimation. Bradford and Hildebrandt conjectured that private individuals would not manipulate the mechanism by altering their private demands.

O'Reilly (1995) has shown, however, that the incentive to manipulate the mechanism still exists in the case of an equal sharing cost rule where the tax is not specifically tied to the agent's demand but is uncoupled. O'Reilly cleverly constructed an example where agents truthfully reveal their WTP in their demand for the complementary private goods in equilibrium, but not out of equilibrium. This allows the individual agent to manipulate the mechanism as it gropes for the equilibrium. And since there is no cost to sending false signals to the auctioneer out of equilibrium, the incentive to misreport demand for private goods that are complementary to the public good in order to manipulate one's signal for the public good does not diminish as the size of the economy grows. Thus, revealing the truth out of equilibrium is not incentive compatible because the individual can manipulate the outcome so as to achieve an allocation he prefers. But, as O'Reilly admits, in practice such manipulation would be difficult to undertake.

5.5 Conclusion

We studied the use of surveys and indirect estimation for determining the WTP for a public project in this chapter. In a pioneering effort, Bohm undertook a survey where some subjects were provided with an incentive to undervalue the public good, while others were provided with an incentive to overvalue it. This allows one to calculate an interval that can be used to make a decision on a particular project. However, it has been suggested that the interval so calculated may not be stable and may not provide objective guidance.

The CV survey method was also described in detail. In addition to the problems of interviewer bias, the ordering of questions, the complexity of the issues involved, and the lack of experience in valuing non-marketed goods, anchoring may be a serious problem. And people sometimes give ludicrous answers to survey questions like valuing a small increase in the probability of protecting a natural habitat at two or three times their salary. We would conclude that great care must be taken when doing a CV study. Unfortunately, this may be the only way to get at the WTP for a public project never undertaken before.

Finally, we also described the indirect estimation method. This method exploits the complementarity of some private goods for a public good and may provide some information on the demand for public goods indirectly. Unfortunately, it requires a great deal of data, cannot be used when a new public good is under consideration, and requires a cardinalization of preferences that must be taken as given.

---

[1]   Carson (2000) lists a number of areas where CV has been used including "increasing air and water quality; reduced risk from drinking water and groundwater contaminants; outdoor recreation; protecting wetlands, wilderness areas, endangered species, and cultural heritage sites; improvements in public education and public utility reliability; reduction of food and health transportation risks and health care queues; and provision of basic environmental services such as drinking water and garbage pickup in developing countries." (p1413.) For a recent CV study on the WTP to save the Asian elephant in Sri Lanka see Bandara and Tisdell (2004), for example. They sampled a group of 300 residents of Columbo, educated them on the basic problem of preserving the elephant and compensating farmers whose crops are damaged, and asked a dichotomous choice question with bid values of Rs 500, 250, 100, 50, and 25. Actual payment was not required and alternative methods of financing were not surveyed. Extrapolating the results to the population of Columbo, they found that the aggregate WTP is Rs. 1996 million annually.

[2]   Cummings and Harrison (1994) used a non-parametric test of Bohm's (1972) data and concluded there was no difference among the mean responses of the first five groups. Second, the two stated mean values for group VI:1 and group VI:2 were the same. Finally, they also argued that it is difficult to say whether a hypothetical CV response is biased upward or downward from this data. The response of group I was significantly lower than group VI:1 and group I had an incentive to understate. This suggests that it is possible that the hypothetical response is an accurate reflection of the true WTP. But, they also could not reject the hypothesis that group V's response was different from group VI:1.

Since group V had an incentive to overstate, the hypothetical response may be biased upward. See Bohm's (1994) reply.

[3] Bohm (1984) also set up a similar experiment involving 279 local governments in Sweden choosing an actual public good, a large data set on housing. The governments were randomly assigned to two groups. Each government in the first group was told they could have access to the data if they paid a user fee and a percentage of its stated WTP. Each government in the second group was told they would pay the same user fee but would pay a small fee ($100) to cover the fixed costs where the fee was constant across governments. Group one had an incentive to understate their WTP, while group two had an incentive to overstate. The average WTP for group one was SEK 827 and for group two was SEK 889. However, the aggregate WTP was less than the fixed cost and so the project did not pass.

[4] Ciriacy-Wantrup (1947) first suggested asking people to state the value they placed on non-marketed goods. Other early work on contingent valuation methods includes Bradford (1970), who suggested a sequential bidding process be used, and Randall, Ives, and Eastman (1974), who used a sequential referenda process that elicited payment brackets. For a general introduction into the contingent valuation methodology see Hanemann (1984), Mitchell and Carson (1989), McConnell (1990), Freeman (1993). See Cameron and James (1987) and Howe, Lee, and Bennett (1994) on the econometrics of analyzing contingent valuation data. See the papers in Hausman (1993) for a critique of contingent valuation. And, for recent surveys see Smith (2000) and Carson, Flores, and Meade (2001).

[5] Samples and Holyer (1990) used a survey instrument to uncover the value of preserving whales and seals. They found that whales were valued at $125 when asked about first but $142 when asked second, and seals were valued at $103 when asked about first but only $62 when asked second. When asked about both together in two separate surveys they obtained $131 and $146. This is clearly not consistent with measuring preferences for preserving the different species. We are indebted to Jeff Krautkraemer for this example.

[6] Hanemann (1994) makes the point that all economic data may suffer from some of these same problems. For example, the data in the Current Population Survey and the Family Expenditure Survey has been criticized on similar grounds as data collected under the CV method. For references see footnote 16 page 27 in Hanemann's paper. However, the fact that other survey data may be contaminated in the same manner as contingent CV data does not make data used in CV studies any less tainted.

[7] See Horowitz and McConnell (2002) for a survey of the literature on the willingness-to-accept versus the willingness-to-pay for a project.

[8] To check on whether the study truly reflects low value of travel time, or that subjects did not believe tolls would reduce travel time, two scenarios did not include tolls. In scenario 2 the commuter can pay for a "smart" technology that

can guide the car to the least congested road or around construction sites and save time, rather than pay a toll. The estimate for this scenario was essentially the same as the other scenarios.

[9] By law the power company could only charge subjects one price.

[10] In their regression equations they included the attitudinal measures to capture the use, warm glow, and existence values, location (rural versus urban), several socioeconomic variables, e.g., age, occupation, and education, and several other variables. The warm glow coefficient was always highly significant.

[11] Dubourg, et. al., also found other anomalies. Respondents ranked one choice X (1 - 4 weeks in hospital with slight to moderate pain with a return to normal health in 1 - 3 years) over W (2 - 7 days in hospital with slight to moderate pain with a return to normal health in 3 - 4 months), but were willing-to-pay more for a reduction in the risk of W than X. Dubourg, et. al., suggest this is due to a lack of sensitivity to small changes in risk despite the ability of the subjects to initially rank the alternatives. This poses a serious problem for CV analysis since it is predicated on individuals being able to place a value on small differences in outcomes. Finally, they also found evidence of embedding. About 30% of the subjects were willing-to-pay the same amount for different reductions in risk.

[12] Bohm (1994) provided the following anecdote. A newspaper in Sweden sampled the population in 1966 and asked if the Swedish government should increase its foreign aid to LDCs from 0.0025 of GNP to 0.01 of GNP and 40% responded 'yes.' Those who stated 'yes' were then asked if they would accept the proposal if their taxes had to be raised to finance it. Only half of those who answered 'yes' to the first question also said 'yes' to the second question.

[13] See Cummings, Elliot, Harrison, and Murphy (1997), for example. Hypothetical bias does not always occur. See the discussion in Cummings and Taylor (1999) for examples.

[14] The four public goods were contributing to the local chapter of the Nature Conservancy that protects natural habitats, a non-profit group in Albuquerque NM that disseminates information to low income Hispanic households on testing the local water quality, the Nature Conservancy's "Adopt an Acre" program which buys land in the rain forests of Costa Rica to protect from development, and the Path Foundation which constructs bike and pedestrian paths locally in Georgia. The subjects were students at Georgia State University and were paid $10 to participate in the study. Information was elicited from referenda questionnaires and no one participated in more than one experiment.

[15] Ebert (1998) labels this a pseudo choice problem. Although, this type of decision problem might represent a consumer's choices if the consumer chooses location on the basis of the package of local public goods available.

[16] See Freeman (1993) for a survey of travel cost models. For a meta analysis of travel cost recreation studies see Smith and Kaoru (1990). And see Parsons, Jakus, and Tomasi (1999) who compared four different methods of linking site choice random utility models to a seasonal trip model. The latter makes predic-

tions aout the number of trips to the site whereas the former does not. All of the methods integrate a demand function to make welfare calculations.

[17] Following Herriges, et. al., let C^R be defined as the "revealable" compensating surplus according to $v(p, w, G^0) = v(p, w - C^R, G^1)$, where $G^1 > G^0$. The "revealable" compensating surplus can be decomposed into the "direct use value" and the "indirect use value." Direct use value is the area under the compensated private demand as discussed above. Indirect use value covers cases like deriving utility from the quality of a wetland site without visiting the site if that site reduced congestion at sites that one did visit, for example. It could also cover cases of altruism, where one cared about the number of sites rather than one's enjoyment of a particular site. C^R is the direct use value if there is no indirect use value and is the area under the compensated private demand.

6 Privately Provided Public Goods

There are many situations where private individuals make contributions to a public good. A charity is a prime example. People donate to charities that provide general relief such as the International Red Cross and Oxfam, organizations that support medical research like the American Heart Association, local charities like a soup kitchen, or a food bank, and many give to their alma mater. People also donate their time. They work in soup kitchens, volunteer at their children's school, coach a youth soccer team, take pledges over the telephone at a phonathon, or work at a crisis center. They volunteer to fight fires, fill sandbags during a flood, shovel snow for an elderly neighbor, donate blood, and walk to raise money for a worthy cause. Even mowing one's lawn and maintaining one's property contributes to the general beauty of a neighborhood, a pure public good to be sure. Countries may also make contributions to international public goods such as peacekeeping efforts and disaster relief.

In a recent study of the United States, for example, over 70% of all households reported giving to charities in 1998 and the average annual contribution was $1075, or about 2.1% of the household income of contributing households. 60% of all cash contributions went to religious organizations, 9% went to human services, 6.5% were given for health research, 6.4% went to education, and the rest went to youth development, the arts and culture, the environment, and various other local community programs. 55% of American adults also volunteered 19.9 billion hours with an estimated value of approximately $225 billion in 1998, mostly in providing direct services, fundraising, and counseling.[1]

As a specific case, Dawes, Orbell, Simmons, and van de Kragt (1986) describe a setting where the Association of Oregon Faculties wanted to hire a lobbyist in 1979 to lobby the state legislature for a pay raise and asked faculty as individuals to donate toward the lobbyist's salary of $30,000. The donations would be returned if less than the $30,000 was raised. The pay raise was considered a public good since it would apply to all faculty regardless of whether they had contributed to the salary of the lobbyist, or not. The goal was met and the lobbyist was hired.

There are several competing models of privately provided public goods.[2] Malinvaud's (1972) subscriptions model has received the most attention in the theoretical literature and generated quite a bit of controversy due to its stark predictions. In this model donors care about the total amount of a public good, which is taken to be the sum of the individual donations to the good. One prediction of the model is that the equilibrium is not affected by certain redistributions among donors. This in turn implies several interesting neutrality theorems. Warr (1983, 1984) and Bergstrom, Blume, and Varian (1986) first provided sufficient conditions where government programs "crowd out" private donations one-for-one, for example.[3] And Roberts (1984) referred to time series data for the U. S. that supported this contention; a shift in private donations from charities that alleviated poverty toward other charitable ventures, such as medical research and public television, occurred during the post World War Two era that also saw the rise of large government programs designed to alleviate poverty.

The second model we study is the warm glow model where donors gain satisfaction from the act of donating itself, where the donor's money donation enters the utility function as a separate argument. Most of the empirical literature on charity, e.g., Feldstein (1975a, 1975b), is based on this model. The donor's optimal supply of donations depends on the donor's income, wealth, the price of donating, and various personal characteristics like age, education, and family status. It follows that other variables such as the donations of others and the economic circumstances of the recipients do not influence donations at all in this model. In addition, if individuals really care only about their own donation and not those of others, an externality does not exist, and the resulting Nash equilibrium when it exists is optimal in this model.

We will also present several models of impure public goods and several hybrid models. The implications of these models are not quite as narrow as the subscriptions model or the warm glow model and can support a variety of empirical predictions. For example, as suggested by Cornes and Sandler (1984a, 1985a), it is possible that a model of an impure public good may predict "crowding in" rather than crowding out. An increase in government contributions to a public good may then lead individuals in the private sector to donate more, rather than less.

We will derive the implications of these models in this chapter and compare them. In the next section we will study the implications of the subscriptions model. The warm glow model will be presented in section 6.2. Criticisms of the two models will be presented in 6.3. We will present several models of imperfect public goods in section 6.4. In section 6.5 we study hybrid models that combine motives. In section 6.6 we briefly describe a model of fundraising activity where the marginal cost of making a donation depends on the amount of the contribution. And section 6.7 concludes the chapter.

6.1 The Subscriptions Model

There are N private agents, each agent obtains utility from a private good and a pure public good, and a subset of agents make a contribution to the public good, which is the sum total of all contributions. Agent h's utility function is given by $u^h(x^h, G)$, where x^h is the agent's consumption of the private good, $G = \Sigma_j g^j$ is the public good, and g^h is h's contribution to the public good. The technology is linear, which fixes producer prices, and it costs c units of the private good to produce one unit of the public good. Let w^h be h's income or endowment of the private good. Agents are not endowed with the public good.

The social planner chooses an allocation $\{x^1, \ldots, x^N, g^1, \ldots, g^N\}$ to maximize social welfare represented by a utilitarian sum of utilities, $\Sigma \phi^i u^i(x^i, \Sigma_j g^j)$, where ϕ^i are social weights, subject to the resource constraint, $\Sigma_i(w^i - g^i - x^i) = 0$. The necessary condition governing the optimum is the first-best Samuelson rule, $\Sigma(u^i_G/u^i_x) = c$. By altering the social weights the entire contract curve can be mapped out.

Can this allocation be attained under laissez faire? Agent h's budget constraint is $w^h = x^h + cg^h$, where c is the marginal cost of contributing, and h's decision problem is to choose (x^h, g^h) to maximize utility subject to her budget constraint, taking the contributions of the other agents as given.[4] The first order condition is $u^h_G/u^h_x = c$. By summing we obtain $[\Sigma(u^i_G/u^i_x)]/N = c$ and the resulting competitive Nash equilibrium is suboptimal. Each agent essentially ignores the positive impact she has on the other agents through her contribution to the public good. Cornes and Sandler (1984a, 1985a) referred to this sort of behavior as "easy riding," rather than "free riding," since agents may make a positive contribution to the public good but under-contribute relative to the Pareto optimal level. For example, suppose $u^h = \ln(x^h) + \beta \ln(G)$. Under equal weighting $\phi^h = \phi$, then at the social optimum, $G = (\beta/(1+\beta))W$, where $W = \Sigma_i w^i$ is aggregate income, while at an interior Nash equilibrium where everyone contributes, $G = (\beta/(N+\beta))W$.

We can solve the first-order condition stemming from the individual's decision problem and the budget constraint to obtain the agent's supply function for contributing to the public good, $g^h = \gamma^h(w^h, G^{-h}, c)$, where G^{-h}

$= \Sigma_{j \neq h} g^j$ is the sum of everyone else's contribution but h's. It is straight-forward to derive the implications of the model at the individual level. If utility is quasi-concave and $u^h_{xG} \geq 0$, then $\gamma^h_w = dg^h/dw^h > 0$ and $\gamma^h_G = dg^h/dG^{-h} < 0$. Second, it can be shown that $\gamma^h_G = c\gamma^h_w - 1$, or in elasticity form, $\gamma^h_G = \delta^h_g \eta^h_g - 1$, where $\eta_g = (w^h/g^h)(dg^h/dw^h)$ is the income elasticity of h's contribution and $\delta^h_g = cg^h/w^h$ is the contribution's share in h's income. Thus, a change in everyone else's contribution induces an income effect for person h in this model. If $\eta^h_g < 1/\delta^h_g$, then $dg^h/dG^{-h} < 0$. For example, if $\delta^h_g = 0.02$, a reasonable estimate for many countries, and $\eta^h_g < 1$, it follows that $dg^h/dG^{-h} < 0$ by a large margin. Obviously, it is even possible for the income elasticity to be greater than one and still have the inequality hold. This is a fairly strong prediction. Finally, a change in the cost of contributing induces the usual income and substitution effects. If the latter dominates, then $\gamma^h_c = dg^h/dc < 0$.

A Nash equilibrium in the subscriptions model (NESM) without government intervention is a vector of contributions $g^S = (g^{1S}, ..., g^{NS})$ and an allocation of the private good $x^S = (x^{1S}, ..., x^{NS})$ such that (x^{hS}, g^{hS}) solves h's decision problem, for all h, the following system holds,

$$g^{hS} = \gamma^h(w^h, \Sigma_{j \neq h} g^{jS}, c), \text{ for } h = 1, ..., N, \tag{6.1}$$

and such that (g^S, x^S) satisfies the resource constraint with equality,

$$\Sigma_h w^h = \Sigma_h x^{hS} + cG^S. \tag{6.2}$$

where $G^S = \Sigma_h g^{hS}$ is the level of the public good provided in equilibrium.

The reaction functions may be non-linear, as depicted in Figure 6.1. In the left-hand diagram we have depicted several indifference curves for each agent and their reaction functions, γ^1 and γ^2. Utility for agent 1, $u^1(w^1 - cg^1, g^1 + g^2)$, increases vertically upward in the diagram while utility for agent 2, $u^2(w^2 - cg^2, g^1 + g^2)$, increases to the right horizontally. The Nash equilibrium for the subscriptions model occurs at the intersection of the reaction curves, $\gamma^1 = \gamma^2$. In general, there may be multiple equilibria where the reaction curves intersect more than once. However, this can easily be ruled out if we assume the income response of donors is positive and less than one in magnitude. The PP curve in the right-hand diagram in Figure 6.1 is the set of Pareto optimal points where there is a common tangency between the two agents' indifference curves. At such a point the slopes of the indifference curves are equal, $cu^1_x/u^1_G - 1 = 1/(cu^2_x/u^2_G - 1)$. Rearranging yields the Samuelson condition for the first-best provision of the public good. Clearly, the Nash equilibrium is not Pareto optimal due to the externality.

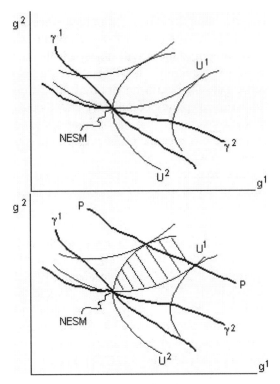

Fig. 6.1. Equilibrium with Non-Linear Reaction Curves

We can easily derive some of the predictions of the model from (6.1) and (6.2). To this end, totally differentiate (6.1), add $\gamma^h_G dg^h$ to both sides of the resulting equation, note that $\gamma^h_G = c\gamma^h_w - 1$, divide both sides by γ^h_w, sum across agents, and simplify to obtain,

$$\{c + \Sigma_h(1/\gamma^h_w - c)\}dG = \Sigma_h dw^h + \Sigma_h(\gamma^h_c/\gamma^h_w)dc. \tag{6.3}$$

If $\gamma^h_w < 1/c$, the term in braces is positive. In that case, a general increase in income will induce an increase in the public good. Thus, ceteris paribus, we should expect charitable donations to fall in a recession, for example, and increase during a period of economic growth. If true, this suggests that donations to charitable causes, such as shelters for the homeless, fall when they are most needed and rise when the need is less. Second, an increase in the cost of contributing will induce a decrease in the public good if the substitution effect dominates.

The equilibrium is invariant to small changes in the income distribution when the set of contributors remains unchanged since dG depends on the sum $\Sigma_h dw^h$ and not higher moments of the distribution. It follows that a small redistribution among donors will not affect the equilibrium as long as the donors continue donating. This means that the government cannot use person-specific taxes to attain an optimal allocation on the contract curve. Only if government policy completely crowds out private contributions can it use such taxes to reach an optimal allocation in this model. This is a striking notion but begs the broader question as to why the private sector evolved in such a way.

Young (1982) and Bergstrom, et. al. (1986, 1992) suggested the following alternative way of developing the model. We can rewrite the agent's budget constraint as $w^h + cG^{-h} = x^h + cG$, where $w^h + cG^{-h}$ represent the agent's "full" income. We can model h's contribution as a decision to increase the level of total contributions G above the level G^{-h} such that $G > G^{-h}$ if agent h decides to make a contribution to the public good, and $G = G^{-h}$ if not. Thus, agent h chooses G to maximize utility subject to the alternative budget constraint $w^h + cG^{-h} - T^h = x^h + cG$ and the inequality constraint, $G \geq G^{-h}$. For an interior solution, we have $G^* = \text{argmax}\{u^h(w^h + cG^{-h} - T^h - cG, G)\}$. The general form of the first order condition is the same as in the first version of the model and can be solved to obtain the following function, $G = \Gamma^h(w^h + cG^{-h} - T^h, c)$ when $G > G^{-h}$. More generally, the level of the public good is given by $G = \max\{\Gamma^h(w^h + cG^{-h} - T^h, c), G^{-h}\}$.[5]

6.2 The Warm Glow Model

In the pure version of the warm glow model the representative agent obtains utility from the private good and from her own contribution to the public good according to $u^h(x^h, g^h)$. Everything else about the basic model is the same as in the subscriptions model. The social planner chooses an allocation to maximize a utilitarian sum of utilities subject to the resource constraint as in the subscriptions model. The first order condition is $(u^h_g/u^h_x) = (u^k_g/u^k_x) = c$ for all h and k. The first-best Samuelson rule does not characterize the optimum since agents do not recognize the public good characteristics of good G in this model.

Under competition, the individual donor chooses consumption of the private good and a contribution to the "public" good to maximize her own utility subject to her budget constraint. The first order condition is $(u^h_g/u^h_x) = c$. Since the cost is the same across agents, $(u^h_g/u^h_x) = (u^k_g/u^k_x)$. It follows that the competitive equilibrium where agents donate to the "public" good satisfies the optimum in this model since the model is isomorphic to a model of two private goods without an externality. This is in stark contrast to the subscriptions model.

We can solve the individual's decision problem to obtain a contribution function of the following form, $g^h = \delta^h(w^h, c)$. This function will have all of the usual properties of a supply function if the utility function is well behaved, e.g. twice differentiable, quasi-concave, and monotonic. By differentiating the first order condition and the budget equation in the usual way, we can derive the agent's response to a change in a parameter such as income. For example, if the cross partial derivative of the utility function is non-negative, donating to charity is a normal good. One major difference between this model and the subscriptions model is that the donor in the warm glow model will not respond to a change in the donations of the other agents, $dg^h/dG^{-h} = 0$, including the government. If the government taxes donors and they respond by reducing their donation less than one-for-one, then the government can increase the amount of the public good through its own contribution.

A Nash equilibrium in the warm glow model (NEWGM) is a contribution vector $g^W = (g^{1W}, ..., g^{NW})$ and an allocation $x^W = (x^{1W}, ..., x^{NW})$ such that agents optimize and such that the resource constraint holds, where $G^W = \Sigma_h\delta^h(w^h, c)$ is the level of the public good provided. In general, g^S will differ from g^W. One implication is immediate. In general, the distribution of income will matter in the warm glow model in terms of determining the equilibrium level of the public good. Only in the special case where the supply of donations is linear in income and the Engle curve has the same slope across agents will the distribution not matter. To see this suppose $\delta^h = \alpha^h w^h + A^h(c)$ is the contribution function. The Engel curve is a straight line with positive slope α^h. Then $G^W = \Sigma\alpha^h w^h + \Sigma A^h(c) = \alpha\Sigma w^h + \Sigma A^h(c)$, and only national income Σw^h matters in determining G, not the distribution of income, when $\alpha^h = \alpha$.

The general equilibrium comparative statics of the model are easily derived. For example, a general increase in income will lead each donor to make a larger donation under the weak condition mentioned above and thus the total amount of donations will increase. An increase in the cost of donating will have the opposite effect if the substitution effect dominates the income effect for most agents. A transfer from one donor to another will generally affect the equilibrium unless their responses are perfectly offsetting. Perfectly offsetting responses are not guaranteed in this model so that a transfer across donors will generally affect the total amount of the public good provided.

The nice feature of the warm glow model is that it generates demand and supply equations that can easily be estimated. Indeed, we will discuss some of the work along these lines later. However, the tension in this model is that it does not explicitly include the essential properties of a public good, non-exclusion and non-depletion. If the public good in the model is truly a "public" good, the resulting warm glow equilibrium will not be Pareto optimal for the same reason as in the subscriptions model.

6.3 Criticism of the Models

Several analysts have been very critical of the subscriptions model. In particular, Young (1982) raised two issues. First, he argued that the social benefit of an extra dollar donated is potentially huge and hence not believable. To see this suppose agents are identical, donations are tax deductible, and consider a donor in tax bracket τ so the tax "price" of donating is $1 - \tau$ and let $\tau = 30\%$. Summing the first order conditions for donors in a Nash equilibrium yields $\Sigma MRS^h = 0.7N$, when there are N donors. The marginal benefit of a dollar donated, $0.7N$, can be quite large for even a small charity.

Second, the model makes odd predictions when income differs across agents. Suppose tastes are the same but income differs. Then for two donors the model implies $MRS^i(x^i, G) = MRS^j(x^j, G)$ when the price of donating is the same across donors. It follows that $x^i = x^j$ since G is the same and hence $w^i - w^j = c(g^i - g^j)$ from the budget constraint. But if $w^i > w^j$, then the entire increment in income across agents is spent entirely on the public good, an usual prediction to say the least. If tastes differ, then the wealthier donor may consume more of the private good if it is normal. However, in that case, a wealthy donor must have less of a taste for the public good than a poor donor, and this also seems somewhat implausible.

Sugden (1982, 1984, 1985) has been very critical of the model. Indeed, he argued that the model is seriously flawed and should be rejected as a general model of charitable donations. First, Sugden argued that the result $\gamma^h_G = c\gamma^h_w - 1 = \delta^h_g \eta^h_g - 1$ is a critical implication of the theory; it must hold for all donors. It seems most plausible that the income elasticity and the share of donations in income are both small in magnitude, e.g., $\delta^h_g = 0.02$ and $\eta^h_g = 0.5$ or less. So the right-hand side should be closer to minus one than zero in magnitude. However, it also seems plausible that the individual donor will only alter his donation by a small amount, or not all, if there is a change in everyone else's contribution. A donor giving \$100 to a large charity like the Red Cross will most likely not dramatically increase his contribution if the sum of everyone else's contribution falls by $100. Indeed, it seems intuitively reasonable to argue that a donor will not respond at all to small fluctuations in the income of a large charity. Thus, γ^h_G is probably closer to zero than to minus one. It follows that either $\gamma^h_G = \delta^h_g \eta^h_g - 1$ is inconsistent, or the theory cannot be used to study large charities, a major flaw.

Second, if a donor receives an extra dollar of income the public good will barely increase, according to the theory. To see this suppose $dw^k = 1$, $dw^j = 0$ for everyone else, and let $c = 1$. Then from equation (6.3)

$$dG = [1 + \Sigma_h(1/\gamma^h_1 - 1)]^{-1} = [1 + (E(1/\delta^h_g \eta^h_g) - 1)N]^{-1},$$

where $E(1/\delta^h_g \eta^h_g) = \Sigma_h(1/\delta^h_g \eta^h_g)/N$. Since $\delta^h_g \eta^h_g$ is close to zero, it's inverse will be much larger than one in magnitude and so will the mean, $E(1/\delta^h_g \eta^h_g)$. Thus the denominator is likely to be much greater than one in magnitude and thus dG will be much smaller than one. If $N = 100$, agents are identical, but only k receives extra income, $\delta^h_g = 0.02$, and $\eta^h_g = 1.0$, then $dG = \$0.000204$. This is so because every agent other than k responds to the increase in k's donation by reducing theirs and there are 99 other donors doing this. This sort of behavior also seems implausible.

Sugden also noted that the three key assumptions in the model are that there is an externality present, agents maximize utility, and agents behave in a Nash-like fashion ignoring any effect they might have on one another. Relaxing any of these assumptions may radically alter the implications of the model. First, Sugden argued that people might donate simply because they enjoy the act of donating, i.e., they receive a warm glow from giving. If so, the resulting equilibrium may be Pareto optimal if the agents do not recognize there is an externality. Second, if people do not maximize utility but use a simple rule of thumb in choosing their donation, e.g., donating 2% of every paycheck, they may actually donate more than the socially optimal amount. And, they may not respond to government policies in the same manner as predicted by the model. Finally, altering the Nash conjecture can also have serious consequences. For example, if an agent believes others will match his contribution if it is above a certain level but contribute nothing if it is below, then the agent may be inspired to meet the minimum level. If everyone behaves similarly then total contributions could be above the socially optimal level.

Other critics include Andreoni (1988a) and Bernheim (1986), among others. Both Andreoni and Bernheim show that the model predicts that all government policies can be perfectly offset or neutralized by changes in private behavior if private agents take the government's budget constraint into account when solving their individual decision problems. Since this implication is difficult to accept, they concluded there must be a flaw with the model. In addition, Andreoni showed that the model makes several predictions as the size of the economy grows that are counterfactual. The model predicts that as the economy grows in size the proportion of the donating population diminishes to zero, only the richest private agents contribute in the limit, total contributions increase to a finite amount, and the average donation diminishes to zero in the limit. The intuition behind these results is that agents feel more anonymous in large groups rather than small groups and are thus more likely to free ride in large groups. However, these results are counterfactual for large economies, and therefore, a problem for the pure form of the subscriptions model.[6]

The problems with the warm glow model are not quite as significant. The main problem is that it predicts individual donors will not respond to a change in a charity's circumstances. For example, the Kroc family of McDonald's fame recently made the largest single private donation ever of $1.5 billion to the Salvation Army. It is difficult to believe that this won't affect donations from other sources. Indeed, the Salvation Army immediately began running ads asking people to continue giving. Thus, assuming there is no externality effect seems problematic; if one is donating to a charity it is probably because one cares about the work being done by that charity. If such a donor discovers that the charity has suffered a drop in contributions from the government, for example, it seems unreasonable to argue that a donor will ignore this. One can include the donations of others as separate arguments in the utility function to capture this and this leads to a variety of impure public good models.

6.4 Imperfect Altruism Models

There are several ways to model impure public goods. One charity may be more efficient at producing the public good than another so contributions may not be perfect substitutes in production. Agents may not perceive contributions to be perfect substitutes in consumption. They may feel differently if they know one charity is providing the good rather than another. Finally, the "price" of contributing may differ across agents.

Bruce (1990) and Ihori (1992, 1994) considered a set-up where the individual contributions are imperfect substitutes for one another in producing the public good. Suppose the public good is produced according to, $G = \Sigma_j \psi^j g^j$, where the weights ψ^j differ across agents and the utility function is the same as in the subscriptions model. The subscriptions model is the special case where $\psi^h = 1$ for all k. Alternatively, suppose $G = \Sigma_j g^j$ and utility is given by $u^h(x^h, g^1, ..., g^N)$. This model captures effects like envy and peer pressure. For example, if h is envious of j's contribution, then h's utility may decrease in response to an increase in j's contribution.

These two models yield similar results in many cases. For example, in the first model a donor chooses g^h to maximize $u^h(w^h - cg^h, \Sigma_j \psi^j g^j)$. The first order condition is $u^h_G / u^h_x = c/\psi^h$, which is a slight generalization of the subscriptions model. We can solve this condition to obtain $g^h = \gamma^h(w^h, \Sigma_{j \neq h} \psi^j g^j, c, \psi^h)$. In this case, the agent may not respond to a change in k's contribution in the same manner as he does to a change in j's contribution unless $\psi^j = \psi^k$. A similar result for the charity function can be obtained with the alternative model. The donor's decision problem is virtually the same as in the previous model. Let $g^h = \kappa^h(w^h, g^{-h}, c)$ be the solution, where g^{-h} is a vector of everyone else's donation but h's, $(g^1, ..., g^{h-1}, g^{h+1}, ..., g^N)$. Donor h will only respond to a change in k's donation in the same way as she responds to changes in j's donation if k and j's donations enter her utility function in the same way.

A third possibility occurs when different agents confront a different price for making a contribution. Suppose the donor chooses g^h to maximize $u^h(w^h - p^h g^h, \Sigma_j g^j)$. The first order condition for a donor is $u^h_G / u^h_x = p^h$. Clearly, this may differ across agents depending on the context. For example, if G is a private charity, contributions are tax deductible, and the tax is progressive, the tax price of donating p^h will differ across agents. Different countries contributing to an international public good may have a different marginal cost of production and thus experience a different cost of contributing to the good, as another example.

It is straightforward to define an equilibrium in these models in a manner similar to the subscriptions model. Since the contributions of the other agents enter the individual agent's utility function in some way, there will be an externality and the resulting competitive Nash equilibrium will not be Pareto optimal. For example, if the price of contributing differs across agents, and price is exogenous, it may be optimal to only have the "low price" donor provide the good. Thus, if we observe price differentials and various agents donating, then the resulting equilibrium may be suboptimal for that reason as well as the usual reason associated with the externality.

Like the warm glow model, the equilibrium level of contributions to the public good will not be neutral with respect to the income distribution. In general, a change in the distribution of income will alter the total amount of the public good provided in these models. To illustrate the possibility that the government can have an impact on the equilibrium consider the following example. Suppose $u^h = \ln(x^h) + \alpha^h \ln(G)$ and $G = \Sigma_j \psi^j g^j$. It is easy to show that $g^h = A^h w^h/c - B^h G^{-h}$, where $A^h = \alpha^h \psi^h/(1+\alpha^h \psi^h)$ and $B^h = 1/(1+\alpha^h \psi^h)$. Differentiate to obtain

$$dg^h = (A^h/c)dw^h - B^h dG^{-h} - (A^h w^h/c^2)dc.$$

Subtract $B^h dg^h$ from both sides, multiply both sides by ψ^h, sum, and rearrange to obtain

$$dG = (\Sigma_h \psi^h dw^h)/(1+\Sigma_h \alpha^h) - [\Sigma_h(\psi^h w^h dc/c^2)]/(1+\Sigma_h \alpha^h). \qquad (6.4)$$

This differs from (6.3) in the term $\Sigma_h \psi^h dw^h$.

A general increase in income will lead to an increase in the public good while an increase in the cost of providing the public good will lead to a decrease. And a redistribution of income across donors will generally alter the level of the public good. Suppose $dw^1 = 1$, $dw^2 = -1$, and $dw^j = 0$ for all $j > 2$. Then $dG = (\psi^1 - \psi^2)/(1+\Sigma_h \alpha^h)$. The public good will increase (decrease) if income is transferred to a more (less) productive producer of the public good. By imposing differential taxes on agents the government can shift production of the public good to the more efficient donors, according to this model.

6.5 Hybrid Models

Given the foregoing analysis, one can construct models with various types of agent in them. First, there may be different kinds of agent in the model, each of whom has a different motive for making a contribution to the public good. Alternatively, each agent may have more than one motive for making a donation to the public good.

Cornes and Sandler (1984a, 1994) studied a joint products model of impure altruism where a contribution to the public good by an individual produces some of the public good and produces a private good as well. They assumed a contribution helps produce the public good according to $G = \Sigma_h g^h$, as before, and also produces a private good for the individual, say, y^h, where $y^h = \mu g^h = \mu(G - G^{-h})$ and $\mu > 0$ is fixed. Utility is given by $u^h(x^h, G, y^h)$, where x^h is a private numeraire good, and the budget constraint is given as before, $w^h + G^{-h} = x^h + G$, under the Young - Bergstrom, et. al. development of the model. Thus, the individual agent chooses (x^h, G) to maximize utility subject to the budget constraint and the same inequality constraint as before, $G \geq G^{-h}$, taking G^{-h} as given. Cornes and Sandler showed that the response of the agent's decisions become more complicated in this more general framework and this in turn broadens the implications of the model for policy. For example, the Nash equilibrium is sensitive to the income distribution. It follows that the neutrality propositions may fail. And it is possible that 'crowding in' may occur where government provision increases private donations.

Vicary (1997) studied a related model where private individuals donate to the public good and purchase a private good which also adds to the public good, e.g., buying cookies from the Girl Scouts. Suppose utility is given by $u^h(x^h, y^h, G)$, where x and y are private goods, G is the sum of explicit donations, and y is a private good sold by the charity to obtain further revenue. The individual's budget constraint is $w^h = x^h + qy^h + g^h$, where q is the price of a unit of y and the public good is given by $G = \Sigma g^j + \alpha \Sigma y^j$, where $\alpha > 0$. If $G = g^h + \alpha y^h + G^{-h}$, where G^{-h} is the sum of everyone else's contributions including their purchase of y, the individual agents's budget constraint is $w^h + G^{-h} = x^h + (q - \alpha)y^h + G$. Thus, the agent's "virtual" or full income is $w^h + G^{-h}$ and the "virtual" price of y is $q - \alpha$. Thus, α cannot be too large or the price would be negative and constitute additional income. Vicary showed that some of the properties of the subscriptions model hold such as the neutrality results under certain conditions. However, the results are more general. For example, y^h may increase with an increase in G^{-h}. Thus, 'crowding in' also becomes a possibility in this version of the model.

A special case of the preceding model is where a warm glow motive is included in the subscriptions model. In that case the individual gains utility from the total donation and his separate donation is like a private good in that it generates utility as well. Steinberg (1987), McClelland (1989), Andreoni (1989, 1990), and Ribar and Wilhelm (2002) have studied versions of this model extensively. In particular, Andreoni assumed the donor cares about the private good, the public good, and his own contribution to the public good, $u^h(x^h, G, g^h)$, where the third argument captures the warm glow motive for donating to the public good. The budget constraint is the same as before. The agent chooses (x^h, g^h) to maximize utility subject to her budget constraint.

Alternatively, we can use the definition $g^h = G - G^{-h}$, and set up the decision problem as Max $u^h(w^h + cG^{-h} - cG, G, G - G^{-h})$, following Bergstrom, et. al.'s discussion of the subscriptions model. The first order condition can be rearranged to obtain, $(u^h_G + u^h_g)/u^h_x = c$. We can solve this to obtain the supply of donations for this model, given by $G = \Omega^h(w^h + cG^{-h}, G^{-h}, c)$, where the agent's full income is $w^h + cG^{-h}$ once again. The second argument of the function G^{-h} captures the warm glow effect.

We can define the equilibrium in these hybrid models in the same manner as the subscriptions model. The equilibrium will generally not be Pareto optimal since the externality is perceived by the agents but not taken into account by them when choosing their own action. Other combinations are certainly possible. One can easily construct a model where some agents care about the level of the public good, some care about their own contribution, some have both motives, and some agents may view the contributions of others as imperfect substitutes for their own.

As an empirical matter, it may be very difficult, if not impossible, to distinguish between the various hybrid models. One immediate possibility is fairly straightforward, however. If the strictest version of the warm glow model is correct, then a donor only cares about his own contribution and thus entering the sum of everyone else's contributions, or entering government expenditures on a competing public good, in a donation function as a right hand side regressor, should yield a coefficient of zero when data is used to estimate the model. So if such a variable is entered into the regression equation and the coefficient is statistically different from zero, this is evidence against the strictest version of the warm glow model and the NEWGM concept.

6.6 Fundraising Costs

Another issue that has been raised is the fact that most charities actively seek donors and attempt to affect how much is donated at the margin through their fundraising efforts. In particular, Andreoni and Payne (2003) argued that fundraising is costly and that government policy could affect the marginal cost of raising funds by altering the charity's fundraising efforts. For example, if a charity receives a government grant, it has less of an incentive to raise funds itself. However, if the charity reduces its fundraising efforts, this may make it more difficult to raise funds at the margin.

One simple way to capture this is to assume the cost of making a donation is a function of the amount donated, $c(g^h)$. In that case, the first order condition in the subscriptions model becomes $u_G/u_x = c_g(g^h) = dc/dg^h$, and similarly in the warm glow model, $u_g/u_x = c_g(g^h)$. More generally, there will be a set of parameters confronting the charity, say φ, and these will also enter the marginal cost of donating. Some of the parameters may be endogenous. A change in a parameter may alter the marginal cost of raising charitable funds. One such parameter might be the receipt of a government grant.

It is also straightforward to define an equilibrium in a model that includes fundraising costs and to show that the equilibrium will not be Pareto optimal if an externality is included in the model. Furthermore, the equilibrium will be sensitive to the income distribution if the marginal cost of fundraising differs across agents.

6.7 Conclusion

We have reviewed some of the basic theory on privately produced public goods in this chapter. The workhorse model in this literature is the subscriptions model where each donor cares about the total amount contributed to a pure public good by all of the donors. The model has a number of interesting implications most of which stem from the prediction that the public good provided is independent of the income distribution. On the normative side, it is clear that the competitive equilibrium will not be Pareto optimal since each agent ignores the externality her donation causes for every other agent.

We also examined a warm glow model where agents receive a warm glow from contributing to the public good. This model is very similar to a model of a private good and hence the resulting equilibrium is Pareto optimal. One stark prediction of the model is that donors completely ignore other sources of donations. Thus, the donor in the warm glow model will ignore any change in the economic circumstances of the charity.

In addition, other analysts have studied models of impure public goods. It has been assumed that donations are imperfect substitutes in production and utility and that the marginal cost of contributing differs across agents. And the motives of the subscriptions and warm glow models have been combined. Not surprisingly, in each of these models the equilibrium will generally be affected by changes in the income distribution and hence by various government policies. And the equilibrium will generally not be Pareto optimal. Unfortunately, it can be difficult to design policies that improve upon the competitive Nash equilibrium because of the interaction among the private agents and the amount of information required. And it may be difficult to empirically test the differences in the models given the paucity of data.

---

[1]   See the National Survey of Giving and Volunteering, 1999, which is online at independentsector.org/GandV. In 1987, 71.1% of American households gave an average of $1134 (constant 1998 dollars) and donated about 19.6 billion hours. More people volunteered as a percentage of the population in 1998, but donated less time per person when compared to 1987.

[2]   For an interesting discussion of various "altruistic" motives see Arrow (1975, 1981).

3   This neutrality result is more general; private agents may alter their behavior in order to return to the initial pre-policy equilibrium thus offsetting some or all of the intended effects of a variety of policies. Becker (1974) noted that investment in private post secondary education has fallen as government support for post secondary education has increased and Peltzman (1973) provided some evidence in support of this conjecture. Parents might offset the intended effect of a subsidized school lunch program by feeding their children less at home. Barro (1974) put forth the idea that private individuals could alter their transfers within the family so as to offset changes in government debt and social security. See the debate between Barro (1976) and Feldstein (1976), Carmichael's (1982) correction of the basic argument, the papers by Bernheim and Bagwell (1988) and Bernheim, Shleifer, and Summers (1986), and Bernheim's (1989) survey.

4   On non-Nash conjectures see Cornes and Sandler (1984b, 1985b), Sugden (1985), and Scafuri (1988).

5   Bergstrom, et. al. (1986, 1992) proved existence of an equilibrium and uniqueness in this version of the model. See also Fraser (1992) on uniqueness and the elegant proofs in Andreoni and Bergstrom (1996). Nett and Peters (1993) proved uniqueness when the model is extended to include endogenous labor supply. Existence follows because the set $\Omega = \{g = (g^1, ..., g^N) \in R^N: g^h \in [0, w^h]$ for $h = 1, .., N\}$ is compact and the function $g^h = \max\{\Gamma^h(w^h + G^{-h}, c) - G^{-h}, G^{-h}\}$ is a continuous function from Ω into itself, and, therefore, a fixed point exists, which constitutes the Nash equilibrium. Uniqueness follows if $0 < d\Gamma^h/dI^h < 1$ for all contributors, where I^h is full income. See Nett and Peters for the more general case.

6   Fries, Golding, and Romano (1991) studied a version of the subscriptions model where there are T types of agent, each type has N agents, and agents differ in their preferences and income. They considered the altruism motive as the number N increases and showed that only one type will contribute to the public good if N is large enough and there is enough heterogeneity in the economy. This supports Andreoni's result for large but finite economies.

7 Extensions

In this chapter we will discuss several extensions of the models considered in the last chapter. First, we will study models of the charity firm, the other side of the donations market. Rose-Ackerman (1982, 1987), Bilodeau (1992), Bilodeau and Slivinski (1996), Glazer and Konrad (1996), Andreoni (1998), and Harbaugh (1998a, 1998b), aomg others, have made important contributions to this area of research. Charities compete amongst themselves for donations and this may lead to excessive fundraising since a single charity will ignore the impact it has on other charities. Charities may also undertake certain actions to increase the donations they receive such as announcing large contributions. Charities may exhibit a certain ideology and attempt to attract donors who share that ideology. And obtaining "seed" money for a new fundraising campaign may be important in getting over a critical hurdle. There may also be strong status effects when donating that need to be considered. Explaining this observed behavior is important in understanding this market.

Next, we consider Varian's sequential contributions game. Under certain circumstances a donor may choose to move first and attempt to play the role of a Stackelberg leader. Varian's main result is that the level of the public good will be lower in the Stackelberg equilibrium than in the Nash equilibrium where agents move simultaneously because of the manner in which the donors interact. Although, Romano and Yildirim (2001) showed that if there is a warm glow motive to donating, the reaction curves may slope upward causing donations to be greater in the game where donors move simultaneously. We also discuss several mechanisms involving private contributions to a public good due to Guttman (1978), Danziger and Schnytzer (1991), Varian (1994a), and Falkinger (1996). Each attempts to provide individuals with the appropriate incentive to make the socially optimal donation and are critical in understanding how policy might be designed to achieve a better outcome. Falkinger's mechanism is particularly straightforward to implement and has some experimental support for it, e.g., Falkinger, Fehr, Gachter, and Winter-Ebmer (2000).

We also study contributions in a dynamic model by extending the overlapping generations model to include a privately provided public good. A donor's contribution to a public good today may respond to a perceived change in everyone else's contribution in the future. This sort of anticipatory response has not been fully appreciated in this literature. We also show that saving will increase with an increase in everyone else's contribution today but decrease with an increase in everyone else's contribution in the future due to income effects and that the interest rate may affect the timing of donations. We also point out that to support the optimum a Pigouvian tax/subsidy for donations must be combined with a policy that maintains the economy on the modified golden rule path.

In the next section we study the behavior of charity firms. In section 7.2 we discuss sequential donation games and compare the results with the one-shot game and also describe several mechanisms that can be used to achieve the first-best outcome. In section 7.3 we present the OG model extended to include a public good and section 7.4 concludes the chapter.

7.1 Charities

So far we have studied the behavior of donors in several simple but important settings. However, charities, on the other side of the market undertake a number of activities like advertising, mass mailings, telemarketing, publishing names of donors, and so on, that are designed to generate more donations. Including this behavior leads to richer models and may be useful in developing testable implications.

7.1.1 Fundraising Under Competition

Rose-Ackerman (1982) presented a model where donors care about the cost of raising donations, e.g., advertising expenditures, the ideology of the charity, and obtain a warm glow from donating, and where entry into the charity market is endogenous. She assumed the charity solicits donations with information about the work of the charity, its ideology, and its fundraising costs and charity managers maximize donations net of these costs. If there is free entry and donors do not care about fundraising costs per se, the equilibrium is characterized by a large number of small charity-firms, donation revenue is equal to the cost of sending brochures to solicit more donations and is thus entirely wasted, and none of the charity-good is actually produced. The intuition is that no individual charity has any reason to take into account the impact its entry has on the amount of donations available to the other charities. This result is tempered if donors care about excessive fundraising costs. In that case, donation revenue will exceed the cost of soliciting donations in equilibrium so that some of the charity good is produced. However, fundraising will still be excessive. Furthermore, Rose-Ackerman (1987) argued that lump sum government grants to charities may have unintended effects. For example, charity managers may use grants to reduce solicitation of private donations and thus public grants may simply replace private donations. And such grants may also lessen the charity manager's accountability to private donors.

Rose-Ackerman also discussed several regulatory policies that might be pursued, forcing charities to provide information about their fundraising costs, limiting fundraising costs, and imposing entry barriers. Forcing charities to reveal fundraising costs does not eliminate the problem of excessive fundraising. Similarly, limiting fundraising expenses may be difficult to implement and enforce since a charity's total fundraising cost is dependent on variables that are difficult for the charity to control such as how many mailings are required to raise a donation. Thus, limiting entry into the industry may be the only way to avoid excessive fundraising. This may, however, also limit the range of ideology expressed in the charity market and so a tradeoff between the range of ideology and excessive fundraising may exist.

Bilodeau (1992) presented a model of a united fund that collects donations and then distributes them among a number of different charities. The united fund may reallocate donations across charities more efficiently than atomistic donors can.[1] Suppose there are two public goods G_1 and G_2 produced by two separate charities, the donor's utility is $u^h(x^h, G_1, G_2)$, and her budget constraint is $w^h = x^h + g^h_1 + g^h_2 + g^h$, where g^h_k is donor h's contribution to charity k, and g^h is her contribution to the united fund. Total donations to charity k and hence public good k are given by $G_k = \Sigma_i g^i_k + d_k$, where d_k is the united fund's contribution to charity k. The united fund's objective function is $u^0(x^0, G_1, G_2)$, and its constraint is $\Sigma_i g^i = x^0 + d_1 + d_2$. We can interpret x^0 as the cost of operating the united fund, although Bilodeau did not include this in his model.

Bilodeau described a two-stage game where private agents choose their contributions in the first stage and the united fund chooses its contribution in the second stage. The united fund can offset any reallocation across charities by an individual donor. To see this suppose $\Delta g^h_1 = - \Delta g^h_2$ for some h. If $\Delta d_1 = - \Delta d_2$ and $\Delta d_1 = - \Delta g^h_1$, then it follows that $\Delta G_1 = \Delta G_2 = 0$. Thus, the united fund can frustrate attempts by private donors to earmark funds to individual charities. Furthermore, if the united fund manager chooses the united fund's donations to maximize a Paretian social welfare function, the united fund may reallocate so as to improve efficiency. Thus, a united fund need not have a cost advantage in reallocating donations to improve efficiency; moving last may be the only advantage it needs to seek a reallocation. However, it is also possible that individual donors may donate less in the aggregate if they are unable to earmark their donations without having their earmarking undone by the united fund. This could offset the enhanced efficiency due to a more appropriate allocation of donations across charities.

Another question arises if the two-stage game is followed by another two-stage game, or if private donors can take an action after the united fund has acted. Consider a game with an infinite horizon and suppose each period is comprised of a two-stage game as assumed by Bilodeau. Private donors now have a chance to respond to the action taken by the united fund in the previous period. It is not clear that Bilodeau's results hold up under this extension. If the united fund in a two-stage game can undo the equilibrium achieved by private donors in the first-stage, it seems to follow that the private agents can undo what the united fund tries to achieve if the private donors can take an action after the united fund has acted. It is not immediately obvious that the united fund can still improve efficiency in that case.

Bilodeau and Slivinski (1996) also studied the role of competition among charities and showed that charities would have an incentive to specialize in a particular area of the non-profit sector rather than produce a broad range of "charity" goods. They modeled a three-stage game where agents decide whether to enter into the non-profit sector and pay a fixed cost in the first stage, donors make their donations in the second stage, and in the last stage charities decide how to allocate their donations between two public goods. The main implication of their model is that non-profit firms would tend to specialize, rather than diversify. This would explain why we observe charities funding medical research into one disease rather than many, for example. Furthermore, they also showed that the total amount of each public good available is greater under specialization than if there had been diversification since this allows donors to earmark their donations to a cause they are specifically interested in.

7.1.2 Status Effects and Charities

There are a number of interesting facts about charitable giving that are either difficult to explain using conventional models, or where the models do not make a prediction about the fact at all. For example, charities will publish the names of donors and the amount they give. Many charities use category reporting where they list donors in broad categories, e.g., an interval like $500 - $999, and publish the results. Donations tend to cluster near the lower end of the bracket rather than the upper end, i.e., the lower limit may serve as a focal point.

Glazer and Konrad (1996) presented a signaling model where donors make donations in order to signal their income status to other donors. Consider a prestigious university that accepts donations from alumni. An alumnus can signal her classmates about her income status by the amount she donates to the university if the information is made public. Thus, the university has an incentive to publish information on donations. Assume there is a continuum of agents who only differ in their income and let f(w) be the density function of income. Agents are atomistic and so no individual can influence the total amount of donations. This serves to highlight the signaling motive for donating. Assume the individual cares about her consumption of a private good and status, where status is determined by her belief in the expectation others have about her net income level, $E(w^h)$ - g^h, where $E(w^h)$ is that expectation. Utility is given by $u^h(x^h, E(w^h) - g^h)$ and the agent's budget constraint is $w^h - x^h - g^h = 0$, where g^h is the donation, x^h is consumption of the private good, and w^h is her income. Only the donation is observable. The agent uses the donation g^h to signal her relative income status.

Glazer and Konrad proved that a 'perfectly revealing' equilibrium exists so that the agent's donation reveals her income. They also showed that aggregate donations increase proportionately as the population increases, crowding out is only partial when the government taxes everyone to make its own contribution to the public good, and that a redistribution of income among private agents is generally not neutral. To see this suppose $g^*(w^h)$ solves the agent's decision problem of constrained utility maximization. If this function is concave, they showed that a redistribution of income that reduces the dispersion of income will induce agents to increase their donations. Intuitively, if the income distribution exhibits less inequality it is harder for the agent to signal her income status and so she must increase her donation accordingly. Furthermore, if the government uses a matching grant to reimburse donors at rate $\alpha/(1+\alpha)$, donors will increase their donation by $(1+\alpha)$ multiplied by their original donation, i.e., if $g^*(w^h)$ solves the agent's decision problem before the matching grant, and $g^{**}(w^h)$ does after, then $g^{**}(w^h) = (1+\alpha)g^*(w^h)$. These predictions are at variance with the subscriptions model, but do seem to fit the facts. For example, significant donations are observed in large economies. The subscriptions model predicts that they become trivially small relative to the size of the economy as the economy increases in size, while the Glazer - Konrad model predicts they increase proportionately.

Harbaugh (1998a, 1998b) studied a model that included both a warm glow motive for donating and a status effect and argued that many charities use reporting to increase donations and that different charities use different methods of reporting depending on the type of charity. Many charities use category (interval) reporting and many donors give just enough to make it into a particular interval, e.g., [$50, $99]. This might produce a status effect for the donor. However, there are other donors who give slightly more than the minimum amount to be included in a certain category, e.g., g^h = $70, and these donors might exhibit a warm glow in addition to the status effect, where the warm glow explains the excess donation, e.g., $20. Furthermore, Harbaugh presented evidence on alumni contributions to an unnamed "prestigious law school" that switched to category reporting. Donations increased dramatically at the minimum level of each category and decreased at every other level of donating but one. The model also explains why some charities provide donors with a free gift; publicly displaying a gift may produce status.

Harbaugh argued that charities come in three general types and that they choose different methods of reporting donations depending on their type in order to maximize donations. First, there are educational and cultural institutions that invariably use categories and almost always publicize donations. A university, for example, has a certain amount of monopoly power since there are no close substitutes for an alumnus to signal classmates of his status. Second, there are national charities that solicit a large number of small donations. Such charities generally will list several small categories in their mailings for the donor to choose from and almost never report donations. There are typically many close substitutes and this limits the ability of such a charity to generate status effects. Environmental groups are a good example of this. Finally, there are "umbrella" charities, or so-called united funds, like the United Way in the United States, that receive donations and then distribute them to a number of smaller charities. Harbaugh argued such charities are really a form of cartel designed to optimize the donations made to the member charities. For example, the United Way restricts solicitation efforts by its affiliated charities and uses categories for local charities in reporting donations which may generate local prestige effects.

Harbaugh (1998b) used data on donations and income from an anonymous law school to estimate the utility of the status effect under different econometric assumptions. He then simulated the model under two methods of reporting donations publicly, exact reporting and no reporting. The difference between the two being the amount of utility obtained from the prestige of having one's donation fully reported. The utility function in his model includes both the status effect and a warm glow effect, and is of the Stone-Geary form. The former effect would induce the donor to contribute just enough to make it into the bracket or category he wants revealed publicly. Donations above this amount in the same bracket are hypothesized to be due to a warm glow effect. Under the more conservative empirical model, he found that a switch from no reporting to full reporting would increase donations from 25% to 33%, quite a significant amount, which Harbaugh attributed to the status effect.

7.1.3 "Seed" Money

Andreoni (1998) noted that in the United States fundraisers are hired by over 115,000 organizations spending over $2 billion for their services. In addition, the top twenty-five charities spent about 14% of donations on fundraising, which came to about $25 million on average. A major focus of many charities is a capital campaign whereby the charity hopes to raise a great deal of money typically for a new purpose such as a new wing of a hospital, a building campaign at a university, or for a major acquisition by a museum.

Andreoni introduced a threshold into the pure subscriptions model that serves to create a potential barrier for the charity to overcome. This give fundraisers and "seed" money an important role to play in getting over the hurdle caused by the threshold. Let G^+ be the aggregate threshold. The technology for the public good in the presence of the threshold is assumed to be

$$G = \Sigma g^i \text{ if } \Sigma g^i \geq G^+, \text{ or } G = 0 \text{ if } \Sigma g^i < G^+.$$

Following Young (1982) and Bergstrom, et. al. (1986), suppose the donor solves the following decision problem in the absence of the threshold, $\max u^h(w^h + G^{-h} - G, G)$ subject to $G \geq G^{-h}$, where G^{-h} is the sum of everyone else's contribution other than person h. Let $G = f^h(w^h + G^{-h})$ be the solution. Thus, the charity function is described by,

$$g^{h*} = \max\{f^h(w^h + G^{-h}) - G^{-h}, 0\}$$

in the absence of the threshold. Let $g^{max} = \max\{g^1, ..., g^N\}$ be the largest single contribution.

If the threshold is below a donor's optimal contribution, it will have no effect on the equilibrium since that one individual will be able to overcome the threshold by providing "seed" money himself. If the threshold is greater than the donor's contribution, then the donor may choose not to contribute. Andreoni showed that the unique Nash equilibrium is where the public good does not get produced if the largest individual donation of the group of donors is less than the threshold, $g^{max} < G^+$. The intuition is that if donors behave atomistically and take the behavior of all other donors as beyond their control, and no single donor is willing to give enough to get over the threshold, then the charity won't survive, $G = 0$. On the other hand, if at least one donor can meet the threshold, then a Nash equilibrium with positive donations will exist.

Furthermore, Andreoni showed how a grant from the government can get over the threshold and thus ensure the public good gets produced. This provides a theoretical justification for government grants in the form of seed money. In fact, the result is more general than this. The government may give a grant that is below the threshold but just large enough to induce the most generous person to contribute enough to meet the threshold constraint. Andreoni also described a three-stage game of fundraising. The charity chooses a small group of donors to act as leaders in the first stage. In the second stage the charity solicits binding contributions from the leaders. In the third stage the charity announces the donations of the leaders to a larger group of donors who then make contributions themselves. The charity does this in order to ensure that $G = 0$ does not occur. This explains fundraising activities and the role played by large donors.

7.2 Sequential Contributions and Strategic Behavior

7.2.1 A Two Period Model

Varian (1994a) considered a case where agents choose a single contribution to the public good sequentially in a setting reminiscent of a Stackelberg duopoly game of leader - follower. We will illustrate the analysis with a simple example. Suppose there are N agents, one private good and one public good, tastes are the same and given by the log utility function, $u^h = \ln(x^h) + \alpha\ln(G)$, and the budget constraint is $w^h - x^h - g^h = 0$. In the Nash equilibrium when the agents choose contributions simultaneously, the individual agent's reaction function is given by

$$g^h = (\alpha w^h - G^{-h})/(1+\alpha) \qquad (7.1)$$

and the equilibrium level of the public good is $G^N = \alpha\Sigma w^i/(\alpha+N)$. This is illustrated in Figure 7.1 as point N, when there are two agents.

In the sequential move Stackelberg game the leader moves first taking the reaction of the followers into account when he makes his choice. In the second stage the followers choose simultaneously and each follower makes his choice taking the behavior of the leader and the rest of the N-2 follow-ers as given. The representative follower's reaction function is the same as in the simultaneous move game, (7.1). Summing across all followers and simplifying, the total contribution to the public good of the group of fol-lowers is

$$G^f = [\alpha\Sigma_f w^f - (N-1)g^1]/(\alpha+N-1) \qquad (7.2)$$

where h = 1 is the leader and $\Sigma_f w^f$ is the aggregate income of the followers. The leader's decision problem in the Stackelberg game is

$$\max \{\ln(w^1 - g^1) + \alpha\ln(g^1 + [\alpha\Sigma_f w^f - (N-1)g^1]/(\alpha+N-1))\}.$$

Differentiate with respect to g^1 and simplify to obtain the leader's opti-mal decision rule,

$$g^1 = (\alpha w^1 - \Sigma_f w^f)/(1+\alpha). \qquad (7.3)$$

To obtain the level of the public good in the sequential Stackelberg game substitute (7.2) and (7.3) into the definition of G and simplify,

$$G^S = [\alpha^2/(\alpha+N-1)(1+\alpha)]\Sigma_i w^i.$$

The sequential equilibrium is depicted in Figure 7.1 as point S, where agent h is the leader and k is the follower, and R^h and R^k are their respec-tive reaction functions. Clearly, the level of the public good is lower in the simultaneous move game than in the sequential game, $G^N > G^S$. Intuitively, the leader picks a point on the reaction curve of the follower that is to the leader's best advantage. It is in the interest of the leader to 'easy ride' on the follower knowing the follower will respond with a greater contribution than would have been the case in the simultaneous move game.

Varian proved a number of interesting propositions about the sequential equilibrium. For example, the neutrality theorem for small redistributions still holds; the sequential equilibrium allocation $(x^{1S}, ..., x^{NS}, G^S)$ is unaf-fected by a small redistribution among agents. He also shows in a more general setting that the level of the public good will be greater in the Nash equilibrium than in the Stackelberg equilibrium for an interior solution. Thus, the free rider problem is exacerbated if the agents move sequentially than if they move simultaneously. In that case, a charity would prefer that donors move simultaneously rather than sequentially.

It is straightforward to show in our example that the leader's utility is higher than a follower's utility. Thus, there is an advantage to be the first mover. Intuitively, the first mover gains by easy riding on the followers. But each individual has the same incentive to move first. If everyone faces the same incentive, this would lead to everyone trying to move first and we

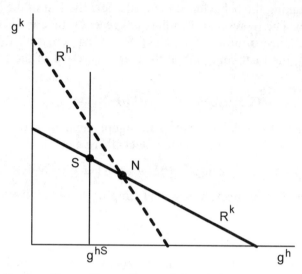

Fig. 7.1. Simultaneous Games Versus Sequential Games

are back in the simultaneous move game. If there are costs to moving first, then the agent with the lowest cost relative to the gain will be the first mover.

In a slightly different context, Konrad (1994) argued that if agents anticipate having to contribute to a public good in the future and wish to free ride, they will take actions now which make it easier for them to justify contributing only a small amount to the public good later. For example, an agent may choose to consume more leisure now by working less so that her future income will be lower. This might be used to justify making only a small contribution to a public good in the future. This result is contingent on everyone knowing how much is donated. If individual donations are not generally known, as would be the case for a large charity, for example, then this result might not go through.

7.2.2 Warm Glow Giving

Romano and Yildirim (2001) generalized the subscriptions model by including a warm glow effect and showed that this may lead to 'upward sloping' reaction functions. It is possible that donations may be higher in the sequential game when the reaction functions slope upward. In that case, the charity might try to get donors to play a sequential move game rather

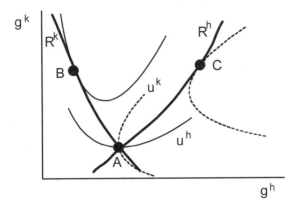

Fig. 7.2. Dynamic Games with Warm Glow Effects

than a simultaneous move game by revealing information about donations. To see this, consider a two agent game and suppose utility is given by $u^h(x^h, G, F(g^h, g^k))$, where $G = \Sigma g^i$. The function $F(\ )$ can take various forms depending on the agent's specific motive for giving. For example, if the individual has a warm glow motive, then $F = g^h$. If relative status is important instead, then $F = g^h/g^k$. The agent's budget is as before, $w^h = x^h + g^h$. The first order condition of the agent's problem now becomes,

$$u^h_G/u^h_x = 1 - F_1 u^h_F/u^h_x,$$

where the second term is new and the derivative F_1 depends on the additional motive for donating. The agent's reaction function may slope upward under certain conditions on the $F(\ )$ function and an increase in k's donation may lead to an increase in h's in this model.

This possibility can fundamentally alter the nature of the equilibrium. Suppose h's reaction function R^h is upward sloping as depicted in Figure 7.2 and k's reaction function R^k is downward sloping. The unique Nash equilibrium in the simultaneous-move game is at point A. However, if h can move first and announce his donation, he can become a Stackelberg leader and choose a donation that leads to a Stackelberg equilibrium at point B. Similarly, for k. The level of the public good will definitely be higher if k is the leader than if h is, which is easy to see by comparing point C with point B. If the charity knows this, it can try to rig matters so k donates first, the charity announces the donation, and then agent h donates. This will raise the greatest amount of donations possible in this setting.

If there are N agents and all agents have upward sloping reaction functions, then the charity can increase total donations by simply announcing the first donation. Furthermore, Romano and Yildirim also considered the case where the timing of donations is endogenous and showed there are three equilibria, a unique equilibrium in the simultaneous-move game, and two Stackelberg equilibria as in Figure 7.2, one where h moves first and one where k moves first.

7.2.3 Mechanisms

Since the Nash equilibrium is suboptimal when each agent ignores the effect his contribution has on the other agents, it is of some interest to consider possible mechanisms that may improve on matters. Guttman (1978, 1987) argued that private agents would have an incentive to set up an institutional arrangement whereby the resulting equilibrium is optimal. One such institution would entail private matching contributions. More specifically, Guttman studied a two-person two-stage game where each agent makes a lump sum contribution to the public good and matches the contribution of the other agent privately. In the first stage of the game each agent chooses a subsidy rate for the other agent's contribution. This is tantamount to choosing the price the other agent faces for contributing to the public good. In the second stage agents choose their lump sum contribution taking the subsidy rates as given. Guttman heuristically described an iterative process whereby the agents eventually choose the Lindahl subsidy rates and thus exhaust any gains from trade without the need for any government intervention. Thus, the resulting equilibrium with private subsidies is Pareto optimal under certain conditions. The key to this process is that each agent chooses a matching rate for the other agent and thus cannot affect his own matching contribution.

There may be several problems with this particular mechanism. It may be difficult to identify agents who free ride since the decision to make a contribution may be private and not readily known in many situations. And, even if everyone contributed, person h would have to choose N subsidy rates. If N is large, the process quickly becomes unmanageable and costly, and thus unlikely to work. We tend not to observe such processes, perhaps, because they are costly, or because they are inherently unworkable. For example, there are cases where a large company will match the contributions of its employees for a cause they deem worthy, e.g., public television, but they tend to be the exception rather than the rule.[2]

Danziger and Schnytzer (1991) generalized Guttman's formulation to the case where agents differ in income, income effects are present, and considered asymmetric equilibria. In the first stage of their two-stage mechanism, agents simultaneously announce a single price that they will use to subsidize every other agent's contribution. In the second stage agents announce their contributions. Let c be the constant unit cost of the public good and p^h be h's announced price in the first stage. Her budget constraint becomes

$$w^h - x^h - (c - \Sigma_{j \neq h}p^j)g^h - p^h\Sigma_{j \neq h}g^j = 0,$$

where $\Sigma_{j \neq h}p^jg^h$ is a transfer received from other agents and $p^h\Sigma_{j \neq h}g^j$ is a transfer paid to the other agents by h. Agent h's personalized price is $(c - \Sigma_{j \neq h}p^j)$ and her total contribution is

$$T^h = (c - \Sigma_{j \neq h}p^j)g^h - p^h\Sigma_{j \neq h}g^j.$$

The first order condition at equality is

$$u^h_G/u^h_x = c - \Sigma_{j \neq h}p^j.$$

Summing,

$$\Sigma_i u^i_G/u^i_x = cN - (N-1)\Sigma_i p^i.$$

If $\Sigma_i p^i = c$, then we have $\Sigma_i u^i_G/u^i_x = c$, the Samuelson condition.

Danziger and Schnytzer proved that if

$$\Sigma_i u^i_G(w^i, 0)/u^i_x(w^i, 0) > c,$$

then a Lindahl equilibrium exists under this mechanism and G, x = (x^1, ..., x^N), and the Lindahl prices are unique. However, the vector of individual contributions g = (g^1, ..., g^N) is not. The reason for this is that in a Lindahl equilibrium agent h is indifferent between whether he contributes to the public good or some other agent does so at the margin. Finally, summing the budget constraint yields $\Sigma w^i = \Sigma x^i + cG$ so the mechanism balances. Although, the indeterminacy of the vector g is somewhat problematic.

Varian (1994a) also considered a setting where agents subsidize one another in a two-stage game in a manner similar to Danziger and Schnytzer's mechanism. There are two agents and each agent chooses a subsidy rate for the other agent in the first stage. Agents receive their subsidy from the other agent and choose contributions in the second stage, taking subsidies as given. He shows that each agent would like the other agent to be subsidized. The intuition is that if agent h contributes to the public good he does so on a dollar-for-dollar basis. However, if he subsidizes someone else at rate $s^k < 1$ and that individual contributes a dollar, agent h's expense is only s^k. Furthermore, Varian showed that the agent will continue to increase his subsidy rate of the other agent until it is equal to the direct dollar cost to himself at the margin. This yields the Lindahl allocation. Thus, the unique Nash equilibrium with subsidies in the two-agent game is the Lindahl equilibrium.

More generally, if there are more than two agents, each agent would like someone else to subsidize agent k. Varian's mechanism then has agent 1 choose the rate that agent 2 will use to subsidize agent 3, agent 2 choose the rate that agent 3 will use to subsidize agent 4, and so on, so that agent N-1 chooses the rate that agent N uses to subsidize agent 1, and agent N chooses the rate that agent 1 uses to subsidize agent 2. The price confronting agent h is completely out of her control since it is chosen by someone else. Varian proves that the subgame perfect equilibria are Lindahl allocations. Of course, as N increases, the mechanism becomes more difficult, if not impossible, to implement.[3]

Falkinger (1996) introduced a mechanism where the individual's tax/transfer is based on the average contribution to the public good. The problem in the Subscriptions model is that if agents care about the total contribution but not it composition, it is difficult for the government to impose a policy that improves on the Nash equilibrium since agents will offset the policy is possible. Andreoni and Bergstrom (1996) give an example of a subsidy policy that can increase contributions even though agents anticipate the policy.

Consider the static subscriptions model where utility is $u^h(x^h, G)$ and $G = g^h + G^{-h}$. The agent's budget constraint is $w^h + \tau^h = x^h + g^h$, where τ is a transfer from the government, and is given by

$$\tau^h = \beta[g^h - G^{-h}/(N-1)],$$

and β is a subsidy rate. Agents who donate more than the average of everyone else's contribution, given by $G^{-h}/(N-1)$, receive a transfer, while agents who donate less pay a tax. Summing,

$$\Sigma\tau^h = \beta G - \beta(N-1)G/(N-1) = 0,$$

so the government's budget always balances. Assuming the agent takes the government's budget into account, the first order condition is

$$m^h(w^h + \beta[g^h - G^{-h}/(N-1)] - g^h, g^h + G^{-h}) = 1 - \beta,$$

where $m^h = u^h_G/u^h_x$ is the MRS.

If $0 < \beta < 1 - 1/N$, Falkinger showed that the Nash equilibrium including the subsidy is unique and that the level of the public good is increasing in the subsidy rate if the private and public goods are normal goods. If $\beta = 1 - 1/N$, the equilibrium is indeterminate. However, this problem can be surmounted if the population can be segmented into groups. Suppose the population is split into groups by income level and suppose $N = \Sigma N_k$, where N_k is the number of people in group k. Let the transfer to person h in group k be

$$\tau^{hk} = \beta[g^{hk} - G^{-hk}/(N_k-1)],$$

where G^{-hk} is the sum of everyone else's contribution in group k but person h's. If $\beta = 1 - 1/N \neq 1 - 1/N_k$, the Nash equilibrium is unique and Samuelson's rule holds.

Falkinger, Fehr, Gachter, and Winter-Ebmer (2000) set up a repeated linear public goods experiment with a control group, who played the game in the classic manner, and a second group that confronted Falkinger's mechanism.[4] In some series the solution was on the boundary so the Nash equilibrium entailed complete free riding, while the optimum entailed complete contribution. In other series the solution was in the interior. Falkinger, et.al. found that the control group mimicked the behavior in other experiments; contributions started at a high level when they should have been zero, there was significant decay, and contributions were still positive in the last trial. However, under the mechanism provision was close to the optimum, regardless of whether the optimum was on the boundary or in the interior. And several groups played the game in the classic way for ten trials but then were confronted with the mechanism for ten trials. Contributions were high and decayed in the first ten trials but as soon as the subjects were confronted with the mechanism, contributions jumped and were very close to the optimum by the end of the second set of ten trials.

7.3 A Simple Dynamic Model of a Privately Provided Public Good

7.3.1 Privately Provided Public Goods in the OG Model

We will consider including private donations to a public good in the two-period overlapping generations framework. Time is discrete and each period N agents are born who differ only in their fixed first period endowment of labor and their utility. In addition to the intertemporal consumption and saving decisions, agents can make donations to a public good in both periods of life. Utility is given by $u^h(c^h_{1t}, G_t, g^h_{1t}) + \beta u^h(c^h_{2t}, G_{t+1}, g^h_{2t})$, where c^h_{kt} is agent h's consumption of the private good in period of life k when born at time t, G_j is the public good available at time j, $G_t = \Sigma(g^h_{1t} + g^h_{2t-1})$ and similarly for G_{t+1}, and where we have included a warm-glow motive for donating as well. Not only is there an externality within each generation, there is also an externality across generations as well.

The agent's wealth constraint is

$$w_t L^h - c^h_{1t} - g^h_{1t} - R_{t+1}(c^h_{2t} + g^h_{2t}) = 0,$$

where w is the wage per unit of labor, L^h is the fixed endowment of labor, $R = 1/(1+r)$, r is the real interest rate, and g^h_{kt} is the cash donation made in period of life k. This can be written as

$$W^h_t - c^h_{1t} - G_t - R_{t+1}(c^h_{2t} + G_{2t}) = 0,$$

where $W^h_t = w_t L^h + G^{-h}_t + RG^{-h}_{t+1}$ is "full" wealth. The agent makes her choices so as to maximize utility subject to her wealth constraint. The solution can be written as consumption and donation functions for each period, $c^h_{kt} = C^{hk}(W^h_t, r_{t+1})$ for k = 1, 2, $G_t = \Gamma^1(W^h_t, r_{t+1})$, and $G_{t+1} = \Gamma^2(W^h_t, r_{t+1})$. Life cycle saving can be defined as

$$s^h_t = w_t L^h - c^h_{1t} - g^h_{1t} = w_t L^h - C^{h1}(W^h_t, r_{t+1}) + G^{-h}_t - \Gamma^1(W^h_t, r_{t+1}).$$

The individual's own donation functions are given by

$$g^h_{1t} = \Gamma^1(W^h_t, r_{t+1}) - G^{-h}_t,$$

$$g^h_{2t} = \Gamma^2(W^h_t, r_{t+1}) - G^{-h}_{t+1}.$$

For example, if preferences are given by $u = \alpha_1 \ln(c_1) + \alpha_2 \ln(c_2) + \alpha_3 \ln(G_t) + \alpha_4 \ln(G_{t+1})$, where $\Sigma \alpha_k = 1$, then $c_1 = \alpha_1 W$, $c_2 = \alpha_2 W/R$, $G_t = \alpha_3 W$, and $G_{t+1} = \alpha_4 W/R$, and saving is given by $s = wL - \alpha_1 W + G^{-h}_t - \alpha_3 W$, where $W = wL + G^{-h}_t + RG^{-h}_{t+1}$. The individual's donations are $g_1 = \alpha_3 W - G^{-h}_t$ and $g_2 = \alpha_4 W/R - G^{-h}_{t+1}$. Thus, for example, $dg_1/dG^{-h}_t = \alpha_3 - 1 < 0$ and $dg_1/dG^{-h}_{t+1} = \alpha_3 > 0$.

There are several new results of importance. First, saving depends on the donations to the public good by everyone else in both periods including future donations. Second, future donations by everyone else enter the donation function today. And, third, the interest rate generally affects donations in both periods. This strongly suggests that the estimated charity functions that we will study in later may be mis-specified since they generally do not include the interest rate, nor do they include the sum of the future contributions of everyone else. This means that the variables that are included, such as labor earnings and the tax price, may be picking up the influence of these omitted variables.

One can easily derive the donor's responses by differentiating the first order conditions of her decision problem. Unfortunately, general statements are difficult to make without imposing more structure on the model. We can obtain the following results if the utility function is additively separable in all its arguments. Consumption and donations in both periods are normal goods. Consumption in both periods is increasing in the sum of everyone else's current and future donations. The donation in period of life k decreases in the sum of everyone else's donation in period k if the income elasticity of donations is less than one. Donations in the first (second) period increase with the sum of everyone else's donation in the second (first) period. Consumption and donations shift from the future to the present with the interest rate if the substitution effect dominates. The intuition for the response of saving to the wage and the interest rate is the same as in the simpler model without donations. In addition, saving is increasing in the sum of everyone else's current donation if the income elasticity of current consumption and current donations sum to less than one, but decreasing in the sum of everyone else's future donation. The latter response occurs because G^{-h}_{t+1} represents income "received" in the future; an increase in future income means the agent can save less now and still maintain consumption in the future.

To close the model, we can assume the private good is produced via a neoclassical technology $y = f(k)$, where y is output per worker and k is private capital per worker. Profit maximization under constant returns to scale implies that the interest rate is determined by $r = df/dk = f_k(k)$. Solving, $K(r)$ is the demand for capital per worker, where $dK/dr = K_r < 0$. The wage is given by $w = f(k) - kf_k(k)$. Using $K(r)$ in the wage equation we obtain $w(r) = f(K(r)) - K(r)f_k(K(r))$, where $dw/dr = -k$. Each member of the initial old generation is endowed with K_0/N units of capital that they rent to firms who produce the private good.

An equilibrium is an infinite sequence of price pairs $\{(w_t, r_{t+1})\}$, savings $\{s^h_t\}$ for each h, and donation pairs $\{(g^h_{1t}, g^h_{2t})\}$ for each h, such that

$$\Sigma S^h(W^h_t, r_{t+1}) = K(r_{t+1}),$$

$$g^h_{1t} = \Gamma^1(W^h_t, r_{t+1}) - G^{-h}_t,$$

and

$$g^h_{2t} = \Gamma^2(W^h_t, r_{t+1}) - G^{-h}_{t+1}.$$

A steady state equilibrium is a price pair (w, r) and saving and donations such that $\Sigma S^h(W^h, r) = K(r)$, $g^h_1 = \Gamma^1(W^h, r) - G^{-h}$, and $g^h_2 = \Gamma^2(W^h, r) - G^{-h}$. It is assumed the equilibrium is stable. We should also point out that the income distribution is affected by significant changes in the economic environment in this model as long as there is a warm glow motive for some of the donors.

7.3.2 Optimality of Donations in the OG Model

The model makes similar predictions about the optimality of the competitive equilibrium as the static model studied earlier regarding the static inefficiency due to the externality. In addition, there is a dynamic efficiency problem as well. To study this issue we will assume agents are identical, $L^h = 1$, and that people only make contributions to the public good when young and only enjoy its benefits when young.

The social planner chooses an infinite sequence $\{c^h_{1t}, c^h_{2t}, g^h_t, K_{t+1}\}$ to maximize social welfare subject to the law of motion for capital. Suppose the social welfare function is given by

$$\Sigma_t(1/(1+\rho))^{t-1}NU(c^h_{1t}, c^h_{2t}, G_t, g^h_t),$$

where $(1/(1+\rho))^{t-1}$ is an intergenerational discount factor. The law of motion for capital is

$$K_{t+1} = F(K_t, N) + (1 - \delta)K_t - N(c_{1t} + c_{2t-1} + g_t).$$

Ihori (2001) showed that a version of the Samuelson rule holds for the public good. In addition, the modified golden rule must hold as well, $F_K(K^g, N) = \rho + \delta$. The competitive equilibrium in this model may be inefficient for two reasons. The Samuelson rule will not hold, as in the static model. Second, it is possible that agents in the competitive economy may accumulate too much physical capital.

More generally, the Samuelson rule must be extended if there is a warm glow motive as well. It is straightforward to show that the following rule holds at the steady state optimum, $NU_G/U_1 + U_g/U_1 = 1$, where the second term on the left captures the warm glow motive. This raises an interesting possibility not mentioned in the literature. It is possible for the competitive equilibrium to satisfy the rule for providing the public good if there is only a warm glow motive for contributing to the public good, $U_g/U_1 = q$, as in the static model. However, it does not necessarily follow that the competitive steady state equilibrium is optimal in this special case since the modified golden rule may not hold under competition.

Two policy instruments are required to remove the inefficiencies. The government can use its debt policy to hold the economy on the modified golden rule path and then implement a Pigouvian tax to induce individuals to contribute the socially efficient amount to the public good. However, if the government cannot use its debt policy in this manner, its choice of the optimal second-best subsidy will have to adjust to take the position of the economy relative to the modified golden rule path into account.

7.4 Conclusion

In this chapter we have studied several extensions of the models studied in the last chapter. First, we studied the charity firm side of the donations market. Charities may pursue policies themselves that are expressly intended to increase donations. In addition, we also studied several additional reasons for donating to charities including status effects.

Second, we presented results from several dynamic games of donating including a sequential game where one player is a Stackelberg leader and the other players are followers and compared it to the outcome where donations are made simultaneously. The Nash equilibrium level of donations is greater than the Stackelberg level. We also presented several interesting results involving mechanism design. It is possible, to design a mechanism that provides individuals with an incentive to make the optimal contribution to the public good. In particular, Falkinger's mechanism is simple in design and potentially can be implemented.

Finally, we presented an overlapping generations model where agents make donations to a public good. Donors respond to an increase in their current income, or an increase in everyone else's current donation to the public good in the same way as in the static model. Donors will also alter their donation today in response to a perceived change in everyone else's contribution to the public good in the future. We also noted that the interest rate may affect the timing of donations in addition to altering the total amount donated. An increase in the interest rate, for example, provides an incentive for donors to save more and this may cause them to shift their donations from the present into the future. We also described the normative properties of the competitive equilibrium with donations. The competitive equilibrium will generally be suboptimal because the Samuelson rule for the public good will not hold and the economy need not be on the modified golden rule path. Two policy instruments will be required to achieve optimality as a result.

---

[1]   This is similar to the so-called Rotten Kid Theorem due to Becker (1974) where the head of a household reallocates income across family members so as to achieve an optimal outcome despite the existence of a rotten kid who behaves in a completely selfish manner.

[2]   Guttman cites the example of intergovernmental grants where a state's highway expenditure is matched by the Federal government. This is, however, not a good example of the private sector solving the free rider problem through matching grants. In addition, he cites private agents solving a free rider problem whenever they decide to split the cost of a shared good, e.g., coffee pot. Unfortunately, while this is certainly the case in many instances, it is unob-

servable to the researcher interested in studying this general phenomenon. In most cases of interest, e.g., public television, large charities like Oxfam, and donations to universities, private matching contributions are a rare exception.

[3] Varian (1994a) also considered a mechanism where each agent reveals a single number in the price setting stage that determines the agent's price of contributing to the public good and then in the second stage agents make a contribution taking price as given. Let q^h be the number revealed by agent h. The agent's price of contributing to the public good is defined under the mechanism as $p^h = \Sigma_{j \neq h} g^j/(N-1)$. In the second stage agent h chooses (x^h, g^h) to maximize utility subject to $w^h - x^h = p^h g^h + \Sigma_{j \neq h} p^j g^j + Q(p)$,

where $Q(p)$ is a penalty term and is given by $(\Sigma_j p^j - 1)^2$. By the definition of G we can write the budget constraint as $w^h - x^h - p^h G = Q(p)$. Varian proves that the Nash equilibrium is unique and coincides with the Lindahl allocation, and the penalty term is zero in equilibrium.

[4] Each series had ten trials, each subject was endowed with w tokens, w = 20 for some series and w = 50 for others, and each subject was told the average contribution on the previous play and their own payoffs. The payoff function was $u^h = w - g^h + \alpha \Gamma + \beta(g^h - G^{-h}/(N-1))$. For the control group $\beta = 0$, and for the mechanism group $\beta > 0$. Group size, the payoff function, and the subsidy parameter were varied across the different series, and in one series the payoffs varied within the groups.

8 Neutrality Results

The possibility that the private sector may respond to government policy in such a way as to frustrate the intention of the policy is well known. Many governments provide goods and programs such as hospitals, public radio, food stamps, and housing subsidies that compete with goods provided through private means like private health clinics, commercial radio, soup kitchens, and homeless shelters. It would not be too surprising to discover that some of the impact of the government's policy is offset by changes in the private sector.

A government's policy is said to be neutral if the response of the private sector perfectly offsets the change in government policy on a one-for-one basis so that the equilibrium allocation is unaffected by the policy. Warr (1983, 1984) and Bergstrom, Blume, and Varian (1986) first provided conditions under which certain government policies are neutral in the context of a privately provided public good.[1] This provided a benchmark for further study by Roberts (1984, 1987), Bergstrom and Varian (1985), Bernheim (1986), Andreoni (1988a), Boadway, Pestieau, and Wildasin (1989), Ihori (1992), Glazer and Konrad (1993), Andreoni and Bergstrom (1996), Ihori (1996), and Helsley and Strange (1998), Andreoni and Payne (2003), among others.[2] It has been shown that under certain conditions the equilibrium is unaffected by a redistribution of income among contributors to a public good and government contributions to the same good financed by a general tax imposed on contributors.

This is a truly remarkable result because traditionally economists have argued that lump sum transfers and taxes be used to adjust the distribution of income. Indeed, this is the basis of the Second Fundamental Theorem of Welfare Economics. However, the neutrality results imply that this cannot be achieved in the subscriptions model of a public good.

In the next section we will derive the two neutrality propositions. In section 8.2 we will study the conditions under which neutrality will fail. These include policies that alter the set of contributing agents, taxing non-contributors, differences in the opportunity cost of contributing to the public good, impure altruism, distorting taxes and transfers, unsophisticated agents who do not see through the government's budget constraint, agents who make contributions to a local public good while behaving atomistically at the federal level, and costly fundraising. In section 8.3 we extend the neutrality propositions to the case of donated labor. A redistribution of income will generally have real effects in this case. However, if all contributors affected by the government's policy donate both cash and labor to the public good, a redistribution of income across such contributors can be neutralized by changes in their cash contributions alone. Section 8.4 concludes the chapter.

8.1 Neutrality Propositions

The most favorable conditions that support neutrality occur in the subscriptions model. It will be recalled that agents care about a private good and a public good and that the public good is the sum of private contributions to it. Each contributor makes a donation based on the belief that he has no impact on the other contributors and takes the actions of the other contributors as given, including the government. The contributor maximizes utility subject to his budget constraint and beliefs about the other contributors. In equilibrium those beliefs are consistent with the observed actions taken by the contributors.

8.1.1 Redistribution

In the Bergstrom, et. al. version of the subscriptions model the contributor's behavior is described by the following donation or contribution function,

$$G = \Gamma^h(w^h - T^h + cG^{-h}, c),$$

where $w^h - T^h + cG^{-h}$ is defined as full income. By differentiating this function and simplifying the following result can be derived. (See the Appendix.)

$$[1 + \Sigma_h(\psi^h/c - 1)]cdG = - \Sigma_h dT^h \qquad (8.1)$$

where $\psi^h = 1/\Gamma^h_f$ is a full income effect. If $\psi^h \geq 1 \geq c$, the square bracketed expression is strictly positive. This is tantamount to assuming the income elasticity of donations is less than or equal to one in magnitude, which seems reasonable. Since $\Sigma_h dT^h = 0$ under a pure redistribution of income, $dG = 0$ in (8.1) and the public good is unaffected by the tax policy as long as the set of contributors is unchanged.[3]

The intuition for this result is that agents who receive a transfer contribute more to the public good while agents who pay a tax reduce their contribution. Contributors also respond to perceived changes in everyone else's contribution as well. Since all agents face the same marginal cost of making a donation, it doesn't matter who makes a contribution at the margin and thus the increased contributions of those receiving a transfer are offset by the decreased contributions of those paying a tax.

Bergstrom and Varian (1985) derived conditions under which the equilibrium would be invariant to the income distribution. Suppose x^i is the individual's choice variable, $X = \Sigma x^i$, the Nash equilibrium can be stated as the solution to a system of equations of the form $x^i = f^i(w^i, X)$ for $i = 1, ...,$ N, and for $(x^1, ..., x^N)$, where each f^i is continuous, and $N > 2$. Then a necessary and sufficient condition for the equilibrium to be independent of income is that each f_i have the form, $x^i = a^i(X) + w^i b(X)$. In the context of the solution to the public goods problem, the supply function is given by $G = F^h(w^h + G^{-h})$. Invert this to obtain $w^h + G^{-h} = \pi^h(G)$, add g^h to both sides, and rearrange to obtain or $g^h = w^h + G - \pi^h(G)$, which is of the required form.

8.1.2 Supplemental Government Provision

Next, suppose the government is convinced that the level of the public good is too low because of the free rider problem and decides to tax each private agent in order to make its own contribution to the public good. Let g^G be the government's contribution and note that the level of the public good is given by $G = \Sigma_h g^h + g^G$. The government's budget constraint is $\Sigma_h T^h = cg^G$, where $T^h > 0$ is a tax imposed on contributor h.

The solution to h's decision problem is the contribution function,

$$G = \Gamma^h(w^h - T^h + c(\Sigma_{j \neq h} g^j + g^g), c).$$

In the Appendix we derive the following result,

$$[1 + \Sigma_h(\psi^h/c - 1)]cdG = cdg^G - \Sigma_h dT^h. \tag{8.2}$$

Differentiate the government's budget constraint,

$$cdg^G = \Sigma_h dT^h. \tag{8.3}$$

The last two equations imply $dG = 0$ and neutrality prevails once again as long as the group of contributors is not affected by the policy.[4]

8.2 The Failure of Neutrality

8.2.1 Non-Neutrality: Non-Participants

One reason for the neutrality result to break down is if the government's policy involves non-contributors. If non-contributors are taxed and the funds are transferred to contributors, then the total amount of the public good available will increase and vice versa if contributors are taxed in order to transfer to non-contributors. To see this note that the term $-\Sigma_h dT^h$ in equation (8.1) will be positive if contributors as a group receive a small transfer. Under our assumptions, $dG > 0$. The reverse is true if contributors are taxed instead. In general, if some contributors are taxed and some receive transfers, the right-hand side of (8.1) will differ from zero and neutrality will fail.

The same conclusion will follow from (8.2) and (8.3) when the government taxes contributors and non-contributors to finance its own contribution to the public good. Suppose there are H contributors and H' non-contributors and both pay taxes. Differentiate the government's budget constraint (8.3) when both groups are taxed, $cdg^G = \Sigma_h dT^h + \Sigma_{h'} dT^{h'}$, where the first sum is over contributors and the second sum is over non-contributors, and use this result in (8.2),

$$[\Sigma_h(\psi^h - c) + c]dG = \Sigma_{h'} dT^{h'}, \tag{8.4}$$

where the square bracket expression is positive, and the sum on the left-hand side is over contributors while the sum on the right-hand side is over non- contributors. Since $\Sigma_{h'} dT^{h'} > 0$, then $dG > 0$ in (8.4) and neutrality will fail. Of course, it also follows that a redistribution among non-contributors will have no effect on the equilibrium. This follows since $\Sigma_{h'} dT^{h'} = 0$ in (8.4) under such a policy.

Another possibility emerges if the government's policy induces some agents to move to a corner solution and not contribute after the policy is imposed, or if the policy induces some agents to begin contributing. If contributor h's tax payment is greater than her contribution, for example, then she will be forced out of the private market for the public good and both neutrality propositions will fail as a result.

8.2.2 Differences in Marginal Cost

Contributors may face a different cost of donating. For example, Ihori (1996) considered cost differentials in a model where different countries contribute to an international public good. If contributors face a different marginal cost of contributing, neutrality will fail.

To see this in the context of our model, suppose the marginal cost of providing the public good differs across agents. The donation function for agent h is

$$G = \Gamma^h(w^h - T^h + c^h(\Sigma_{j \neq h}g^j + g^g), c^h).$$

We can derive an equation similar to (8.2) by differentiating the donation function,

$$[1 + \Sigma_h(\psi^h/c^h - 1)]dG = dg^G - \Sigma_h dT^h/c^h$$

The government's budget constraint becomes $c^G g^G = \Sigma_h T^h$. Differentiate and use the result in the preceding equation to obtain,

$$[1 + \Sigma_h(\psi^h/c^h - 1)]dG = \Sigma_h(1/c^G - 1/c^h)dT^h. \tag{8.5}$$

In general, the right hand side will not be equal to zero. Neither a tax policy for redistribution across agents, nor a general increase in taxes designed to finance greater government spending on the public good, will be neutral. For example, if the cost is the same across private agents, but is different from the government's cost, then the right hand side becomes $(c - c^G)\Sigma_h dT^h/cc^G$. If the government has a cost advantage, an increase in the government's provision of the good financed by a general tax increase will increase the level of the public good. Of course, the opposite is true if the private sector has a cost advantage. In addition, a purely redistributive tax amongst private contributors will not affect the equilibrium in this case since the private agents all face the same cost.

However, neutrality will also fail if the marginal cost of contributing differs across private agents with the same intuition. Suppose the level of the government's provision is fixed and that a transfer is made from contributor two to contributor one. The right hand side of (8.5) becomes $(c^2 - c^1)dT/c^1c^2$, where $dT > 0$ is the tax increase. If contributor one is more (less) efficient at providing the public good, the level of the public good will increase (decrease).

8.2.3 Imperfect Altruism: Contributions as Imperfect Substitutes

Donations may be perceived as being imperfect substitutes and neutrality will fail as a result. Suppose that contributors differ in their productivity of producing the public good so that output of the public good is given by $G = \Sigma_k \phi^k g^k$, where the weights ϕ^k differ across agents. Utility is given by

$u^h(x^h, G)$ and the individual's budget constraint is $w^h - T^h - g^h - x^h = 0$, where $c = 1$ for simplicity. The constraint can be written as

$$w^h - T^h + G^{-h}/\phi^h - G/\phi^h - x^h = 0,$$

by using the definition of the public good where $G^{-h} = \Sigma_{j \neq h} \phi^j g^j$, and where full income is defined as $f^h = w^h - T^h + G^{-h}/\phi^h$. The donation function that solves the contributor's decision problem is

$$G = \Gamma^h(w^h - T^h + G^{-h}/\phi^h, \phi^h).$$

The following result can be derived in the same manner as in the last section,

$$[1 + \Sigma_h(\phi^h \psi^h - 1)]dG = \Sigma_h(\phi^G - \phi^h)dT^h \tag{8.6}$$

In general the right-hand side of (8.6) will not equal zero and neutrality will fail. For example, consider redistribution from contributor two to contributor one, $dT^1 = -dT$, $dT^2 = dT > 0$. From (8.6), the right hand side becomes $(\phi^1 - \phi^2)dT$. If contributor one is perceived as being more productive in producing the public good than contributor two and a transfer from contributor two to contributor one is made, the level of the public good will increase and neutrality will fail. Neutrality will occur only if the transfer is between two agents who are perceived as being equally productive in producing the public good.

If the government is more productive at supplying the public good than the private sector, increased provision by the government financed by a general tax increase will lead to an increase in the total amount of the public good produced, and vice versa if the government is less productive. This generalizes results found in the literature.[5]

8.2.4 Imperfect Altruism: The Warm Glow Model

Consider Andreoni's hybrid model, where the donation function is given by

$$G = \Gamma^h(w^h - T^h + G^{-h}, G^{-h}),$$

where the second argument captures the warm glow effect and $c = 1$ for simplicity. Also assume contributions to the public good are perfect substitutes. In the Appendix we derive the following result,

$$\Omega dG = dg^G - \Sigma_h A^h dT^h, \tag{8.7}$$

where $\Omega = [1 + \Sigma_h(\Psi^h - 1)]$, $\Psi^h = 1/(\Gamma^h_1 + \Gamma^h_2)$, $A^h = \Gamma^h_1/(\Gamma^h_1 + \Gamma^h_2)$, and Γ^h_k is the partial derivative with respect to the kth argument, i.e., Γ^h_1 is a full income effect and Γ^h_2 is a warm glow effect. Next, differentiate the government's budget constraint, $dg^G = \Sigma_h dT^h$ and use this in (8.7),

$$\Omega dG = \Sigma_h(1 - A^h)dT^h = \Sigma_h\Gamma^h_2\Psi^h dT^h \qquad (8.8)$$

Andreoni defines A^h as the altruism coefficient. If the agent is a pure altruist, there is no warm glow from giving and $A^h = 1$. In that case, under a pure redistribution where $dg^G = 0$ and $\Sigma dT^h = 0$, neutrality prevails from (8.7). And from (8.8), a general tax increase designed to finance more government spending will also be neutral. On the other hand, if the agent only receives a warm glow from giving, then $A^h = 0$, and neutrality fails. Consider a transfer of one dollar from agent two to agent one, ceteris paribus. Equation (8.7) implies $\Omega dG = (A^1 - A^2)$. If agent one is more altruistic than agent two, the total amount of the public good increases with the transfer, which should make intuitive sense.

In a sense, if agents do obtain a warm glow from donating to the public good, this is similar to having a different productivity in producing the public good. Transfers to more altruistic agents induce the same type of response in the equilibrium as transfers to agents who are more productive at providing the public good, or face a lower cost.

However, these results may be sensitive to the number of donors. Ribar and Wilhelm (2002) showed that there are two opposing forces at work as the number of donors increases in this model. Crowding out is more likely to occur as the number of donors increases, given the altruism motive. However, the donations of others will eventually come to dominate the individual's own contribution and this may weaken the altruism motive if the marginal utility of the public good is decreasing. The second effect will dominate if the marginal utility falls enough with the number of donors, and crowding out will be incomplete as a result. If the representative donor only obtains a warm glow in the limit, then crowding out is limited to the usual income effects, and is incomplete. For example, a tax increase used to finance the government's contribution lowers income and thus reduces the individual's donation through a simple income effect under the warm glow motive, but not typically on a one-for-one basis. Ribar and Wilhelm showed that the second effect dominates for a wide class of utility functions.

8.2.5 Distorting Taxes and Transfers

The neutrality result also appears to hinge on the use of non-distorting policies, e.g., lump sum taxes. Given the foregoing analysis, one might conjecture that if the government were to use distorting policy instruments, then neutrality would fail. If the government were to adjust subsidy rates at the margin, for example, surely this would cause substitution effects and have an impact on the equilibrium. Indeed, the classic prescription for an externality, such as the one studied in this literature, is to impose Pigouvian taxes and subsidies that affect the margin.

For example, Glazer and Konrad (1993) showed that neutrality would fail under certain circumstances when distorting taxes and subsidies were employed. They assumed donations are subsidized and that there is a maximum allowance. Donations below the allowance are fully subsidized. The subsidy ends for donations above the cutoff. They showed that a change in even a lump sum tax may affect the equilibrium in their model because of the discontinuity introduced by the maximum cutoff allowance.

Surprisingly, however, Bernheim (1986) and Andreoni (1988a) have shown that neutrality will still prevail even if distorting taxes and transfers are imposed under certain conditions. To illustrate this possibility, following Andreoni (1988a), suppose all agents donate and that the government imposes a lump sum tax on each agent and subsidizes private contributions to the public good at the margin. The individual agent's budget constraint becomes

$$w^h - T^h - (1 - s^h)g^h - x^h = 0, \tag{8.9}$$

where s^h is a subsidy rate. The government's budget constraint is

$$\Sigma_j T^j = \Sigma_j s^j g^j + g^G. \tag{8.10}$$

Now imagine the agent chooses consumption and her donation to maximize utility, $u^h(x^h, G)$, subject to (8.9) and (8.10), taking the policy parameters $(T^1, ..., T^N, s^1, ..., s^N, g^G)$ as given. We can rewrite (8.10) as

$$T^h - s^h g^h = g^G + \Sigma_{j \neq h}(s^j g^j - T^j)$$

Use this and $G = g^h + \Sigma_{j \neq h} g^j + g^G$ in the individual's budget constraint to obtain $f^h = x^h + G$, where full income is now defined as

$$f^h = w^h + g^G + \Sigma_{j \neq h}(T^j + (1 - s^j)g^j).$$

If the agent chooses G to maximize utility subject to the constraint $f^h = x^h + G$ and the new definition of full income, then the first order condition of the agent's decision problem is the same as before the subsidy, $u^h_G/u^h_x = 1$. In that case, the subsidy rate does not enter the marginal rate of transformation (MRT) and does not distort the agent's choices at the margin.

The solution to the agent's decision problem in this case is simply a function of full income appropriately defined, as in the case where lump sum policies are employed. Neutrality will essentially prevail. Indeed, there is a stronger neutrality result; the equilibrium is invariant to changes in the distorting subsidy rates as well. If agents see through the government's budget constraint and see through the distortions associated with the subsidy rates, then the subsidy rates essentially act like lump sum policies. Changes in subsidy rates will simply call forth offsetting changes in contributions to the public good leaving the equilibrium unaffected.[6]

In the subscriptions model each agent takes the choices made by the other agents as given under the Nash behavioral assumption. It follows that if the agent chooses a positive donation, then she must believe she can affect the total amount donated, i.e., $g^h > 0$ implies that $G > G^{-h}$ since G^{-h} is taken as given. With government contributions, the same argument holds; $g^h > 0$ implies that $G > G^{-h} + g^G$ since G^{-h} and g^G are taken as given. But if she believes that she can affect the total amount contributed to the public good, then it would seem to follow that she should take the government's budget constraint into account when she optimizes. This is especially so if she takes g^G as given. If she can see through the government's budget constraint, the natural question to ask is why can't she also see through the distortions as well? In addition, if she was in equilibrium prior to the change in policy, it must have been best for her, given her circumstances. If that is so, it seems reasonable to argue that she will seek that equilibrium again by changing her economic behavior after the change in policy. This requires her to take the government's budget constraint and the nature of the distortions into account when optimizing.

The main point to be take here is that the subscriptions model makes predictions that are either inaccurate, or nonsensical. The neutrality theorem possibly falls into the latter category. Many researchers most likely believe that private agents alter their behavior in a manner that partially offsets government policy. Few believe the offset is one-for-one, as the subscriptions model predicts. Therefore, there must be something wrong with the subscriptions model.

This extended neutrality result has been disputed by Boadway, Pestieau, and Wildasin (1989). They pointed out that the key assumptions made by Andreoni and Bernheim are that the individual agent takes the government's own budget constraint into account when solving his decision problem and correctly conjectures that all other agents will seek to offset the government's policy through changes in their donations. If instead the agent takes the policy parameters (g^G, T^h, τ^h) and G^{-h} as exogenous and essentially ignores the government's budget constraint, then the first order condition of the agent's decision problem with the subsidy is $u^h_G/u^h_x = (1 - s^h)$. Now the subsidy rate enters the agent's MRT and will distort the agent's choices. They showed that an increase in the subsidy rate will raise the level of the public good under these assumptions.

Andreoni and Bergstrom (1996) make the interesting point that if the government wishes to have an impact on the equilibrium, it can alter the institutional arrangements in the economy in such a way as to bring that goal about. The institutions set up by the government can be adjusted in order to limit the strategies available to agents in the private sector and this can give the government more latitude in its policy choices. For example, suppose the government imposes a subsidy on private contributions at rate s and also imposes a lump sum tax to finance the subsidy. The agent's budget constraint becomes $w^h - x^h - g^h + sg^h - T^h = 0$, where sg^h is the subsidy. If the agent is assessed a share of the total tax burden of the subsidy program, her tax is given by $T^h = \tau^h sG$, where τ^h is her tax share. Combining this with the definition of G, the agent's budget constraint can be written as,

$$w^h + (1-s)G^{-h} - x^h - (1 - s(1-\tau^h))G = 0.$$

Total tax revenue is $\Sigma_j \tau^j sG$ and total government expenditure on the subsidy is given by sG. Thus, the government's budget constraint is $\Sigma_j \tau^j sG = sG$, as long as $g^G = 0$. Since tax shares sum to one, this budget constraint holds automatically and there really is no government budget constraint to consider. In that case, when the agent solves her decision problem, the first order condition is $u^h_G/u^h_x = (1 - s(1-\tau^h))$ and the subsidy and tax share rates distort the donation decision. The government can adjust the subsidy rate in order to increase donations if it so chooses.

Along these lines, Falkinger (1996) provided a simple transfer scheme that can attain the optimum. Suppose agent h receives a transfer according to $\tau^h = \beta(g^h - G^{-h}/(N-1))$. Agents who contribute more than the average contribution of everyone else receive a transfer while those who contribute less pay a tax instead. Notice that $\Sigma \tau^h = \beta G - \beta(N-1)G/(N-1) = 0$, so the government's budget balances. Falkinger showed that the Nash equilibrium in the subscriptions model is unique and the level of the public good is increasing in the subsidy parameter β even when agents see through the government's budget constraint when $0 < \beta < 1 - 1/N$. He also showed how the mechanism can achieve the optimum through choice of β when the population can be separated into different groups.[7]

8.2.6 Sophisticated and Unsophisticated Agents

One can easily imagine a world where there are sophisticated agents who see through the government's budget and make correct conjectures about the behavior of the other players in the game, and unsophisticated agents who do not. If government policy affects both, then neutrality will most likely fail. To see this suppose there are two types of agent and partition the set of agents into H sophisticated agents and H' unsophisticated agents, where $N = H + H'$. Assume all agents participate and that the government imposes a tax on each agent and pays a subsidy based on the agent's contribution.

An unsophisticated agent solves the following decision problem

$$\max u^{h'}(w^{h'} - T^{h'} - (1 - s^{h'})g^{h'}, g^{h'} + G^{-h'} + g^G),$$

where $G^{-h'}$ includes the contributions of both sophisticated and unsophisticated agents. The solution is a donation function of the form,

$$g^{h'} = \gamma^{h'}(w^{h'} - T^{h'}, G^{-h'} + g^G, 1 - s^{h'}), \tag{8.11}$$

where $dg^{h'}/dw^{h'} = \gamma^{h'}_1$ is an income effect, $dg^{h'}/dG^{-h'} = \gamma^{h'}_2 = -(1 - \gamma^{h'}_1)$, and $dg^{h'}/d(1-s^{h'}) = \gamma^{h'}_p$ is a price effect.

A sophisticated agent solves a more difficult problem as indicated above. Rearrange the government's budget constraint to obtain

$$s^h g^h - T^h = \Sigma_{j \neq h}(T^j - s^j g^j) - g^G.$$

Use this in the sophisticated agent's budget constraint to obtain

$$w^h + \Sigma_{j \neq h}(T^j - s^j g^j) - g^G - x^h - g^h = 0.$$

The agent solves the following decision problem,

$$\max u^h(w^h + \Sigma_{j \neq h}(T^j - s^j g^j) - g^G - g^h, G^{-h} + g^G + g^h),$$

taking as given g^G, $\Sigma_{j \neq h}(T^j - s^j g^j)$, and G^{-h}. The solution is a donation function of the form,

$$g^h = \gamma^h(w^h + \Sigma_{j \neq h}(T^j - s^j g^j) - g^G, G^{-h} + g^G), \tag{8.12}$$

where $dg^h/dw^h = \gamma^h_1$, $dg^h/dG^{-h} = \gamma^h_2 = -(1 - \gamma^h_1)$. The difference between the two types of agent is in the price effects generated when there is a change in the subsidy rate.

Assume $dg^G = 0$, $ds^j = ds$ for all j. Differentiate (8.11), differentiate (8.12), and simplify each equation using the procedure of previous sections, sum each equation within the relevant group, and add the two resulting equations, making sure to use the government's budget constraint to simplify. We obtain the following formula for a change in policy (dT^1, ..., dT^N, ds),

$$[1 + \Sigma_i(1/\gamma^i_1 - 1)](dG/ds) = \Sigma_{h'}g^{h'} - \Sigma_{h'}(1/\gamma^{h'}_1 + s)\gamma^{h'}_p.$$

As before, since the public good is a normal good, $\gamma^h_1 < 1$, and the coefficient on the left-hand side is strictly greater than one in magnitude. The sum $\Sigma_{h'}g^{h'}$ is the total contributed to the public good by the unsophisticated agents and is positive. If the substitution effects dominate, $\gamma^{h'}_p < 0$ and the right-hand side will be strictly positive. Therefore, $dG/ds > 0$ and neutrality fails. Of course, as the number of unsophisticated agents increases, the greater the effect the subsidy rate has on the equilibrium level of the public good. To our knowledge this result is new to the literature.

8.2.7 Local Market Power Versus National Policies

It is somewhat difficult to believe that private individuals think they can influence policy at the national level through their own actions, and, more specifically, take the national government's budget constraint into account when solving their own decision problem. However, they may feel they can influence matters at a local level. In that case, policies imposed at the national level may very well have distorting effects that are not offset by the response of the private sector.

Consider a situation where there are an infinite number of unconnected localities and n agents in each locality. We will index localities by α, which is uniformly distributed on the unit interval. There is no mobility among localities, no trade among localities, and no spillover effects across localities, for simplicity. The technology for producing the public good is the same across localities. Let $G(\alpha) = \Sigma_I g^i(\alpha)$ be the privately produced public good in location α, where $g^i(\alpha)$ is agent i's contribution. Utility is

$$u^h(x^h(\alpha), G(\alpha)) = \ln(x^h(\alpha)) + \beta\ln(G(\alpha)),$$

and agent h in α is endowed with income $w^h(\alpha)$. Suppose the national government imposes a tax of $T^h(\alpha)$ on contributor h at location α and pays a subsidy of $s^h(\alpha)g^h(\alpha)$ to h at α. We will assume for simplicity that $s^h(\alpha) = s$ and $T^h(\alpha) = T$ for all h and all α, where $w^h(\alpha) > T$ for all h and all α. Agent h's budget constraint is

$$w^h(\alpha) - T = x^h(\alpha) + (1 - s)g^h(\alpha).$$

Agent h at location α solves the same decision problem as in the classic subscriptions model where the individual agent ignores the national government's budget constraint and hence believes that the national subsidy policy is distorting at the margin. The solution is

$$g^h(\alpha) = [\beta(w^h(\alpha) - T)/(1-s) - G^{-h}(\alpha))]/(1+\beta).$$

Summing over h in α we obtain,

$$G(\alpha) = [\beta/(n+\beta)(1-s)](w(\alpha) - T),$$

where $w(\alpha) = \Sigma_i w^i(\alpha)$ is local gdp at α. Finally, summing over all locations, the aggregate amount of the public good available is given by

$$G = \int_0^1 G(\alpha)d\alpha = \int_0^1 [\beta/(n+\beta)(1-s)](w(\alpha)-T)d\alpha,$$

and the national government's budget constraint is

$$\int_0^1 [sG(\alpha) - T(\alpha)]d\alpha = sG - T,$$

where T is aggregate tax revenues.

The policy experiment is to increase the subsidy rate at the margin at every location and finance the additional expenditure with an increase in the tax at every location. By differentiating the last two equations and simplifying we obtain

$$dG/ds = [nG/(n+\beta)(1-s)] > 0.$$

An increase in the subsidy rate nation-wide tends to increase the level of the public good since private agents are unable to influence policy at the national level.

Policies at the local level can still be neutralized. To see this notice that if the subsidy is local, $\Sigma_h s^h(\alpha)g^h(\alpha) = \Sigma_h T^h(\alpha)$ is the α-government's budget constraint. It can also be written as

$$s^h(\alpha)g^h(\alpha) - T^h(\alpha) = \Sigma_{j\neq h}[T^j(\alpha) - s^j(\alpha)g^j(\alpha)].$$

Using this in agent h's budget constraint at α,

$$w^h(\alpha) + \Sigma_{j\neq h}[T^j(\alpha) - s^j(\alpha)g^j(\alpha) + g^j(\alpha)] = G(\alpha) + x^h(\alpha).$$

The first order condition for the consumer with the log utility function can be solved toobtain,

$$G(\alpha) = [\beta/(1+\beta)]\{w^h(\alpha) + \Sigma_{j\neq h}[T^j(\alpha) - s^j(\alpha)g^j(\alpha) + g^j(\alpha)]\}.$$

Summing over h and using the local government's budget constraint we obtain $G(\alpha) = [\beta/(\beta+n)]w(\alpha)$. Since the local policy parameters do not enter this function, local policy will not have an effect on the equilibrium.

Thus, federal policy can overcome the externality problem in this context. Indeed, this may be a strong implication of the subscriptions model that has not been noticed. The model does not predict that all policy will fail to alter the equilibrium.

8.2.8 Fundraising

Andreoni and Payne (2003) present a model of costly fundraising where charities use donations to produce a particular "commodity" that contributors derive utility from and fundraising by the charity is required in order to attract potential contributors. They assume charities know the distribution of contributors but not the type of a specific contributor, and that it is costly to contact a sample of contributors to solicit a donation. An increase in government grants to a charity reduces the need for fundraising by the charity and this increases the cost of raising donations at the margin, which in turn lowers the amount of donations.

Neutrality fails for two reasons. First, since charities receiving grants spend less on fundraising, the marginal cost of raising donations is higher and this causes a reduction in donations. Second, some non-donating individuals pay taxes that finance the government grant. The net effect is an increase in total output of the charity. A simple revealed preference argument can be made that implies the charity will never reduce fundraising upon receiving a grant so much so that the total output of the charity is less than it was before the grant.

8.3 Neutrality and Donated Labor

8.3.1 Donated Labor

We can model donated labor in much the same way as donated cash in the subscriptions model to provide the greatest opportunity for the neutrality result to hold. Agents are endowed with one unit of labor and can volunteer h units of it. Agents differ in their labor productivity as measured by their wage. The agent derives utility from the private good and from the sum of donated labor according to $u^i(x^i, H)$ where $H = \Sigma h^i$ is the total level of donated labor. The agent's budget constraint can be written as $w^i(1 - h^i) - x^i - T^i = 0$, or

$$w^i(1+H^{-i}) - w^iH - x^i - T^i = 0,$$

where $w^i(1+H^{-i}) - T^i$ is the agent's full, after-tax, income. The solution to her decision problem is the supply of donated labor,

$$H = H^i(w^i(1+H^{-i}) - T^i, w^i).$$

We can easily derive conditions under which the neutrality propositions hold in this model. In the Appendix we derive the following result,

$$[1+ \Sigma(1/w^i H^i_I - 1)]dH = - \Sigma dT^i/w^i.$$

Under a pure redistribution of income, $\Sigma dT^i = 0$. However, it does not follow that $\Sigma dT^i/w^i = 0$. Therefore, it would appear that neutrality fails in the case of donated labor. This is so because agents face a different opportunity cost of contributing to the public good. If agents are equally productive, $w^i = w$, and we have

$$[1+ \Sigma(1/w^i H^i_I - 1)]dH = - (1/w)\Sigma dT^i = 0,$$

under a pure redistribution of income.

Suppose there are two agents, $w^1 > w^2$ and $dT^1 = - dT^2$. Then

$$[1+ \Sigma(1/w^i H^i_I - 1)]dH/dT^1 = (w^1 - w^2)/w^1 w^2 > 0.$$

Transferring from the agent with the high opportunity cost of donating labor (#1) to the low cost agent (#2), leads to an increase in the total amount of the public good available.

8.3.2 Donated Labor and Cash Contributions

However, if agents can make cash or monetary contributions in addition to donating their labor, neutrality may still occur. Suppose $C = F(G, H)$ is the total level of the public good, G is the total amount of cash contributions, and H is the total amount of donated labor, where the two types of donation may be imperfect substitutes for one another. The representative agent's budget constraint can be written as

$$w^i(1+H^{-i}) + G^{-i} - w^i H - G - x^i - T^i = 0.$$

The agent chooses (x^i, G, H) to maximize utility subject to this budget constraint. The first order conditions are $F_G u^i_C/u^i_x = 1$ and $F_H u^i_C/u^i_x = w^i$, and the solution can be written as a pair of functions,

$$G = G^i(w^i(1+H^{-i}) + G^{-i} - T^i, w^i)$$

and

$$H = H^i(w^i(1+H^{-i}) + G^{-i} - T^i, w^i).$$

Now consider a pure redistribution of income across contributors and suppose $dT^i = - dg^i$. It is straightforward to confirm that $dx^i = dh^i = dH = dG = 0$. This is proven in the Appendix.

Of course, if some contributors only contribute one type of donation and the redistribution is across only the contributors making cash contributions, neutrality will hold; cash contributors will be able to offset any small redistribution among them. However, if the redistribution is across the entire set of contributors, where some only donate labor, then neutrality will fail. This generalizes and extends the neutrality proposition in a significant way.

It also follows from this that if all contributors are donating both types of donation and the government taxes all contributors in order to make its own contribution to the public good, contributors will be able to offset this by altering their cash donations under the same conditions as the original neutrality propositions. However, if some contributors only donate labor and they are also taxed, then neutrality will generally fail.

8.4 Conclusion

In this chapter we studied the famous neutrality propositions whereby private agents are able to offset certain government policies on a one-for-one basis. The two policies studied at length are a pure redistribution of income across agents and government provision of the public good financed by a tax imposed on all agents. These results generated great controversy and much useful research. In particular, we presented and discussed the conditions under which the propositions hold.

We also provided two new reasons for neutrality to fail. First if there are unsophisticated agents who do not see through the government's budget constraint, then certain policies that affect the unsophisticated agents may affect the equilibrium, even though there may be sophisticated agents who do see through the government's constraint and behave accordingly. And, second, if contributors believe they can affect local conditions but cannot affect federal policies, then federal policies will have an impact on the equilibrium.

We also discussed the important case of donated labor. If a public good is produced using donated labor alone, then neutrality will generally fail as long as the opportunity cost of donating labor differs across agents. However, if contributors also make cash contributions, then cash contributions can be adjusted to offset the government's policy and neutrality may still hold.

Our conclusion is that neutrality is a very fragile result theoretically. It will break down under a variety of realistic circumstances. This strongly suggests that the neutrality result will not generally hold in a real economy. Although, policymakers need to recognize that private agents may take actions that offset the impact of the government's intended policy.

Appendix A: Neutrality Results

Redistribution

Differentiate $G = \Gamma^h(w^h - T^h + cG^{-h}, c)$, to obtain

$$dG = \Gamma^h_f(cdG^{-h} - dT^h),$$

where Γ^h_f is the derivative with respect to full income. Divide both sides by Γ^h_f, let $\psi^h = 1/\Gamma^h_f$, use $dG^{-h} = dG - dg^h$, and rearrange to obtain,

$$\psi^h dG = (cdG - cdg^h - dT^h).$$

Sum and collect terms to derive (8.1),

$$[1 + \Sigma_h(\psi^h/c - 1)]cdG = -\Sigma_h dT^h.$$

Supplemental Government Provision

The solution to h's decision problem is $G = \Gamma^h[w^h - T^h + c(\Sigma_{j \neq h}g^j + g^G)]$. Differentiate,

$$dG = \Gamma^h_f[c(\Sigma_{j \neq h}dg^j + dg^G) - T^h].$$

Divide by Γ^h_f, sum, and rearrange to obtain (8.2).

Appendix B: Non-Neutrality Results

Imperfect Altruism: Contributions as Imperfect Substitutes

Differentiate the donation function $G = \Gamma^h(w^h - T^h + (\Sigma_{j \neq h}g^j + g^G)/\phi^h, \phi^h)$, multiply through by ϕ^h/Γ^h_f, add $\phi^h\psi^h dg^h$, sum, and add $\phi^G dg^G$ to both sides to get

$$[1 + \Sigma_h(\phi^h\psi^h - 1)]dG = \phi^G dg^G - \Sigma_h\phi^h dT^h.$$

Differentiate the government's budget constraint $dg^G = \Sigma_h dT^h$ and use this in the preceding equation to obtain (8.6).

Imperfect Altruism: The Warm Glow Model

Differentiate $G = \Gamma^h(w^h - T^h + \Sigma_{j \neq h}g^j + g^G, \Sigma_{j \neq h}g^j + g^G)$,

$$dG = \Gamma^h{}_1(dG^{-h} - dT^h) + \Gamma^h{}_2 dG^{-h} = (\Gamma^h{}_1 + \Gamma^h{}_2)dG^{-h} - \Gamma^h{}_1 dT^h$$

Multiply through by $\Psi^h = 1/(\Gamma^h{}_1 + \Gamma^h{}_2)$, add dg^h to both sides, sum, and add dg^G to both sides to get (8.7). Differentiate the government's budget constraint, $dg^G = \Sigma_h dT^h$ and use this in the last equation to get equation (8.8).

Distorting Taxes and Transfers

Totally differentiate the agent's donation function,

$$dG = \gamma^h{}_1(dg^G + \Sigma_{j \neq h}(dT^j + (1- s^j)dg^j + g^j ds^j)).$$

Add and subtract $(dT^h + (1- s^h)dg^h + g^h ds^h)$, sum over all h, differentiate the government's budget constraint, and combine the resulting two equations to obtain

$$[1 + \Sigma(1/\gamma^j{}_1 - 1)]dG = 0.$$

Sophisticated and Unsophisticated Agents

Assume $dg^G = 0$, $ds^j = ds$ for all j. Differentiate (8.11), differentiate (8.12), and simplify each equation using the general procedure, sum each equation within the group, and add the two resulting equations, making sure to use the government's budget constraint to simplify,

$$[\sum_{j=1}^{N}(1/\gamma_1^j - 1) + 1]dG/ds = \sum_{h'=1}^{H'} g^{h'} - \sum_{h'=1}^{H'}(1 + s\gamma_1^{h'})(\gamma_p^{h'}/\gamma_1^{h'})$$

Neutrality and Donated Labor

To derive the neutrality propositions, differentiate the supply of donated labor to obtain

$$dH = H^i{}_1(w^i dH^{-i} - dT^i) = H^i{}_1(w^i dH - w^i dh^i - dT^i),$$

where $H^i{}_I$ is an income effect. Rearrange, sum, and simplify,

$$[1+ \Sigma(1/w^i H^i{}_1 - 1)]dH = - \Sigma dT^i/w^i.$$

Donated Labor and Cash Contributions

To confirm the conjecture, note that the representative agent's budget constraint is consistent with this conjecture since $dx^i = -w^i dh^i - dg^i - dT^i = 0$. Next, notice that the marginal rates of transformation of the agent's first order conditions are not affected under this conjecture. Finally, differentiate the function governing the agent's choice of G,

$$dG = G^i_1(w^i dH^{-i} + dG^{-i} - dT^i) = G^i_1(w^i dH - w^i dh^i + dG - dg^i - dT^i).$$

Rearranging,

$$(1/G^i_1)dG = w^i dH - w^i dh^i - dg^i - dT^i.$$

Under our conjecture, this becomes $(1/G^i_1)dG = w^i dH - w^i dh^i$, which holds when $dh^i = dH = dG = 0$, which confirms our conjecture.

---

[1] For a geometrical description of a bargaining game involving a public good which emphasizes the indeterminacy of the equilibrium, see Shibata (1971).

[2] This neutrality result is more general; private agents may alter their behavior in order to return to the initial pre-policy equilibrium thus offsetting some or all of the intended effects of a variety of policies. Becker (1974) noted that investment in private post secondary education has fallen as government support for post secondary education has increased and Peltzman (1973) provided some evidence in support of this conjecture. As another example, parents might offset the intended effect of a subsidized school lunch program by feeding their children less at home. Barro (1974) put forth the idea that private individuals could alter their intergenerational transfers within the family so as to offset changes in government debt and social security. See the debate between Barro (1976) and Feldstein (1976) on whether government debt is net wealth or not, Carmichael's (1982) correction of the basic argument, the papers by Bernheim (1986), Bernheim and Bagwell (1988) and Bernheim, Shleifer, and Summers (1986), and Bernheim's (1989) survey. Andreoni's (1989) paper is also of some interest in this regard. See also the paper by Helsley and Strange (1998) on private government, who show that a public sector government may reduce its provision of a public good, e.g., police protection, in response to the provision of the good by a private government, e.g., private security. Finally, Jensen (2004) presents evidence from South Africa that a one rand increase in public pensions to the elderly leads to a 0.25 - 0.30 decrease in private support for the elderly from children living away from home.

[3] Alternatively, following Warr, the first order condition of the contributor's decision problem is given by,
$u^h_G(x^h, G^{-h} + g^h)/u^h_x(x^h, G^{-h} + g^h) = c,$
where c is the marginal cost of the donation. Solve to obtain $x^h = K^h(c, G)$ using the implicit function theorem. Next, substitute this into the agent's budget

constraint, $w^h - T^h = K^h(c, G) + cg^h$, where T^h is a tax if positive and a transfer if negative, and sum across agents,

$\Sigma_h(w^h - T^h) = \Sigma_h K^h(c, G) + cG$.

For a discrete change in the tax, $\Sigma T^h = 0$ and the taxes drop out of the equilibrium condition. For a small change in tax policy we have,

$-\Sigma_h dT^h = \Sigma_h[dK^h(c, G)/dG]dG + cdG$.

Since $\Sigma_h dT^h = 0$ under redistribution, it follows that $dG = 0$.

[4] Again following Warr, we can solve the first order condition of the contributor's problem, substitute into the agent's budget constraint, and sum across agents to obtain

$\Sigma_h(w^h - T^h) + cg^G = \Sigma_h K^h(c, G) + c\Sigma_h g^h + cg^G$.

Using the government's budget constraint in this last equation and the definition of G, and rearranging we have,

$\Sigma_h w^h = \Sigma_h K^h(c, G) + cG$.

Once again the government's policy has no effect on the equilibrium since the variables that it controls have dropped out of the equilibrium condition. For a small change in policy, $dG = 0$.

[5] See Ihori (1992) for a special case of three countries and an international public good.

[6] To see this, totally differentiate the agent's donation function,

$dG = \Gamma^h_f(dg^G + \Sigma_{j \neq h}(dT^j + (1 - s^j)dg^j + g^j ds^j))$.

Divide by Γ^h_f, add and subtract $(dT^h + (1 - s^h)dg^h + g^h ds^h)$, sum over all h, differentiate the government's budget constraint, and combine the resulting two equations to obtain $[1 + \Sigma_h(\psi^h - 1)]dG = 0$. Neutrality prevails even though subsidy rates are allowed to change.

[7] See also Kirchsteiger and Puppe (1997). They show that in the class of linear tax-subsidy policies where each agent's tax depends on the distribution of the contributions of everyone else to the public good, for every interior solution that is efficient there are multiple boundary equilibria, where someone does not contribute, that are inefficient. In addition, an interior solution that is efficient may not be stable.

9 Empirical Evidence on Charitable Contributions

Charitable contributions are a prime example of a privately provided public good. In this chapter we will survey the empirical evidence on charity. This is the single largest area studied to date because of the availability of high quality data. Donations appear to be positively correlated with income and negatively correlated with the tax price of donating to charity, defined as one minus the taxpayer's marginal tax rate, and hence positively correlated with the taxpayer's marginal tax rate. There is also strong evidence that donating increases with age, education, being married, and family size.

The real controversy in this literature is the responsiveness of donations to tax policy. Early studies indicated that charitable contributions were unresponsive. However, Martin Feldstein and his coauthors, Clotfelter, Taylor, and Boskin, challenged this view. In a series of papers, they estimated price elasticities of charity in excess of one in magnitude. However, this view was itself challenged by more recent work. Auten, Cilke, and Randolph (1992) showed that the static model, typically used by researchers in the 1970s, predicted the outcome of tax reforms in 1982, 1984, and 1986 in the U.S. very poorly. And several authors estimated dynamic models using panel data, e.g., Broman (1989) and Ricketts and Westfall (1993), and found the tax price elasticity to be significantly less than one in magnitude.

A number of important public policies hinge on the responsiveness of charitable contributions. If charitable contributions are highly price inelastic, for example, then allowing taxpayers to deduct charitable donations may be an inefficient way of increasing the total supply of charity. On the other hand, if donations are highly responsive, then a subsidy may be warranted. And changes in tax policy may have unintended side effects on donations. The decline in tax rates in the U.S. in the 1980s reduced the incentive to donate and donations fell as a result. In addition, cross price effects may be important. If cash donations and volunteer labor are substitutes (complements), a subsidy for one activity may reduce (increase) the supply of the other activity. Understanding the nature of these responses is critical to designing tax policy.

In the next section we present some additional theory aimed at doing specific empirical work. We also briefly discuss some of the econometric difficulties as well and the data that is available. In section 9.2 we present the work done on charitable contributions using static models. Dynamic models and results from panel data studies are presented in section 9.3. And section 9.4 concludes the chapter.

9.1 Empirical Research on Charity

9.1.1 Econometric Problems

There are several problems confronting empirical researchers in this area, e.g., omitted variables, multicollinearity, measurement error, and simultaneity bias. Multicollinearity may be especially problematic in this area because some of the variables are not directly observable but must be constructed using some common elements. In particular, the tax price depends partly on the taxpayer's level of income since income determines the taxpayer's tax bracket. A high income level implies a high tax rate and a low tax price and vice versa for a low income level. This suggests that the coefficients for the income and tax price variables are biased in opposite directions. Some studies may find a low income elasticity and a high tax price elasticity, while other studies may find the reverse. A cursory glance at Table 9.1 seems to bear this out.

Most likely the greatest problem confronting the empirical researcher is the tax price variable. The tax price depends on the individual's marginal tax rate and this in turn depends on the individual's income, charitable contributions when the taxpayer itemizes, and various other economic parameters capturing the tax bracket structure under a progressive income tax, e.g., special treatment of capital gains, other deductions like home mortgage interest, and so on.[1] It follows that it is an endogenous variable.

One possible solution to this simultaneity problem due to Feldstein (1975a, b), that has become very popular, is to use the 'first dollar' tax price as a proxy, or an instrument for the true price. The 'first dollar' tax price is one minus the marginal tax rate confronting the taxpayer when her donations are zero, $1 - \partial T(w^h, A^h, 0; c^h, \tau^h)/\partial w^h$. However, there are a number of problems with this solution. First, while the 'first dollar' tax price may be uncorrelated with charitable contributions, it still does not reflect the complexity of the tax bracket structure of the income tax in many countries including the U.S., as pointed out by Reece and Zieschang (1985). Second, the estimated coefficient will be biased downward since the 'first dollar' tax price is larger than the 'last dollar' tax price with a progressive tax rate schedule, and it is the 'last dollar' tax price that the taxpayer actually based her decisions on, as discussed by McClelland and Kokoski (1994). Third, there are a number of endogenous choices the taxpayer may make that will influence the 'first dollar' tax price. For example, the 'first dollar' tax price still depends on income and the marginal tax rate, as well as other write-offs, and those variables depend on economic choices, e.g., purchase of a house, that respond to taxation. In addition, some of these decisions may be correlated with charitable contributions. So use of the 'first dollar' tax price does not solve the problem it was intended to solve.

Some of the same problems arise with the income variable, which is also most likely an endogenous variable. A variety of researchers have used disposable income based on the 'first dollar' concept calculated as gross income minus the tax the taxpayer would have paid had there not been any charitable contributions, $y^{h'} = [1 - T_w(w^h + A^h, 0)](w^h + A^h)$ rather than $y^h = [1 - T_w(w^h + A^h, g^h)](w^h + A^h)$. However, Reece (1979) argued that use of the 'first dollar' income variable may lead to a violation of the individual's budget constraint since $y^{h'} < y^h$ when $g^h > 0$ and is large enough to reduce the individual's tax rate. He argued that a more appropriate variable is gross income. Although, this may also cause a violation of the individual's budget constraint since gross income will be larger than the actual level of income net of tax. In addition, even gross income is endogenous since it will generally depend on decisions that are affected by taxation like labor supply and saving.

There is also an omitted variables problem. In a life cycle context, future variables will affect decisions made now, as we argued in earlier chapters. It follows that these variables should be included in the analysis. Some researchers recognized this early on. For example, Feldstein and Clotfelter (1976) and Reece (1979) included a measure of permanent income rather than current income. One might also want to include a measure of wealth as well, yet most data sets do not include such information. To see the importance of this suppose permanent income (w*) is the appropriate proxy to be used in the equation and current income is used instead, w = w* + u, where u is a random variable normally distributed with mean zero and constant variance. It can be shown that the estimated coefficient under OLS will be biased toward zero when current income is used.[2] For example, when Feldstein and Clotfelter (1976) used permanent income in their study, the estimated income elasticity increased. This provides some evidence of a downward bias if current income is used. However, permanent income is not observable and must be constructed.

Another problem arises with the spillover variable. Typically, the individual's contribution, g^h, is small relative to the total, G, for many charities, even local ones. Thus, there would not be much variation in the spillover variable G^{-h} across donors and this might make it difficult to obtain a precise estimate of the coefficient a_3.

Finally, we should also mention that volunteer labor and charitable bequests may be linked to cash donations made earlier in the life cycle. One would really like to estimate a system for donated cash, donated labor, and charitable bequests (made from the estate), in which case the price of cash contributions, the price of charitable bequests, and the opportunity cost of donated labor, the net wage, should be included in each equation. Unfortunately, this data is not available. However, one should keep this in mind when interpreting results. For example, the opportunity cost of donated labor is typically omitted in studies of cash contributions. Other variables may be picking up some of the cross price effect between these two types of donations.

9.1.2 Data Sources

There are two main types of data available on charitable contributions, tax data and survey data. Each has its own strengths and weaknesses. A cross section of tax data typically contains detailed and precise information about the individual's current income and tax bracket allowing for a straightforward calculation of the income and price variables. However, there is usually little information about personal characteristics, or wealth. For example, in the U.S. tax system, the taxpayer must provide information about marital status, the number of dependents, and whether the taxpayer and spouse are over 65 or not. However, there is no specific information on age, education, or other demographic variables of interest. And there is only information on donations if the taxpayer itemizes. This is a significant drawback since many taxpayers give to charity but do not itemize.

A number of researchers have used survey data instead. Typically, such data includes high quality information on the taxpayer's personal characteristics such as the individual's specific age and education. Both age and education may have a strong influence on giving to charity. However, 'age' may proxy for wealth, which is usually omitted. And, the information on income, wealth, and charitable contributions are not objective but are subject to measurement error due to reporting mistakes, poor record keeping, faulty memory, or simple dishonesty. Fortunately, many of these studies

agree with results obtained using other data sources, which lends some cre-
dence to their veracity.

Finally, there are several tax panel data sets available. For example,
there is a ten year panel data set selected from the U.S. Internal Revenue
Service's Special Panel of Tax Returns. This data tracks the same 12,000
individuals for a ten-year period, 1979 - 1988. It also covers two interesting changes in the tax law that took place in 1981 and 1986 when tax rates
were dramatically reduced, which effectively raised the tax price of donating. Several researchers have used this data, notably Randolph (1995).
However, it is short on information on personal characteristics.

9.2 Static Models

9.2.1 Modelling Contributions in a Static Models

Let w^h be the taxpayer's labor earnings, A^h be her exogenous income, g^h be
her donation, τ^h be a vector of tax parameters, and let $T^h(w^h, A^h, g^h, \tau^h)$ be
the tax function for taxpayer h. Her budget constraint is given by

$$w^h + A^h - g^h - x^h - T^h(w^h, A^h, g^h, c^h, \tau^h) = 0,$$

which is non-linear because of the tax function. For example, if charitable
donations are deductible, the tax price of donating is $p^h = 1 - \partial T^h / \partial g^h$,
which changes with the tax bracket under a progressive tax. The tax price
will depend on the choices, e.g., g^h, made by the taxpayer and is endogenous. The agent's budget constraint when monetary contributions to a charity are deductible is $y^h = x^h + p^h g^h$, where $y^h = (A^h + w^h)(1 - \tau^h)$ is after tax
income.

Under the empirical version of the subscriptions model the donor's util-
ity function is given by $u^h(x^h, G; c^h, \varepsilon^h)$, where c^h is a vector of s personal
characteristics like gender, age, and education, and ε^h is a random variable,
which is unobservable. The solution to her decision problem under the
subscriptions model is a charity function,

$$g^h = \gamma^h(y^h, p^h, G^{-h}; c^h, \varepsilon^h). \tag{9.1}$$

A linear version of this equation is given by

$$g^h = a_0 + a_1 y^h + a_2 p^h + a_3 G^{-h} + \Sigma_i \beta_i c^{hi} + \varepsilon^h, \tag{9.2}$$

where $(a_0, a_1, a_2, a_3, \beta_1, ..., \beta_s)$ are the parameters to be estimated.[3] This
model predicts that $a_1 > 0$ if both goods are normal, $a_2 < 0$ if the substitution effect dominates, and crowding out should occur so that $a_3 = -1$. Fi-

nally, if we include government spending on a good that is a substitute for the good provided privately, this can be modeled as the n-th term in the partial sum G^{-h}. We can add a separate variable to (9.2) with coefficient a_4 for the government variable and we have another prediction, $a_3 = a_4$.

Utility in the empirical version of the warm glow model only depends on general consumption of the private good and the donor's own contribution, $u^h(x^h, g^h, c^h, \varepsilon^h)$. As a result, the supply of donations function only depends on the agent's own disposable income, price, and personal characteristics,

$$g^h = \delta^h(y^h, p^h; c^h, \varepsilon). \tag{9.3}$$

The properties of this function are similar to those of (9.1), except that there is no term in the partial sum of contributions. We can also linearize this equation,

$$g^h = b_0 + b_1 y^h + b^h + \Sigma_i \beta_i c^{hi} + \varepsilon^h. \tag{9.4}$$

Normality implies that $b_1 > 0$. And if the substitution effect dominates, $b_2 < 0$.

Finally, we can consider Andreoni's hybrid model where the utility function is given by $u^h(x^h, G, g^h; c^h, \varepsilon^h)$. A linear version of the solution to the decision problem is

$$g^h = c_0 + c_1 y^h + c_2 p^h + c_3 G^{-h} + \Sigma_i \beta_i c^{hi} + \varepsilon^h. \tag{9.5}$$

Equation (9.5) may appear to resemble (9.2). However, $-1 < c_3$ because of the warm glow motive. Indeed, this can be taken as a test of the models. If $-1 = c_3$ is rejected in favor of $-1 < c_3$, then this supports the warm glow hybrid model. Indeed, under the warm glow hybrid model it is even possible for "crowding in" to take place where $0 < c_3$. And if G^{-h} does have an influence on the individual's donation, this is evidence against the pure version of the warm glow model in (9.4).

Empirical researchers interested in charitable donations have focused most of their attention on estimating price and income elasticities and not testing the different models against one another. Typically, a measure of individual charitable contributions is regressed on proxies for income, the tax price, which is usually taken to be one for non-itemizing taxpayers and one minus the taxpayer's marginal tax rate for taxpayers who itemize, and a variety of demographic variables.[4] Estimating price and income elasticites in this manner can be justified by reference to the pure version of the static warm glow model.

9.2.2 Empirical Results

Taussig (1967) first estimated the price and income elasticities using a cross section of data and found that donations were very price inelastic; the price elasticity was not statistically different from zero. His estimated income elasticity was also greater than one in magnitude indicating that charitable donations were a luxury good. Schwartz (1970) studied aggregate time series data and estimated price and income elasticities that were both less than one in magnitude. This suggested that donations were price inelastic.

Feldstein and his coauthors challenged this view in a series of papers.[5] Their estimate of the tax price elasticity was always greater than one in magnitude and the estimated income elasticity was always less than one in magnitude. Clotfelter (1985) summarized 16 studies done prior to 1985.[6] In every study where the price elasticity was greater than one in magnitude, the income elasticity was less than one, and in several of the studies, when the income elasticity was greater than one in magnitude, the price elasticity was less than one, although there were also some exceptions to this.

A typical estimated equation in this work appears in Feldstein (1975a). He used a pooled cross section time series data set aggregated by income class for seventeen income classes for the period 1948 - 1968. His basic estimate is the following,

$$\ln G_{it} = - 1.92 + 0.822 \ln Y_{it} - 1.238 \ln P_{it},$$

where the standard errors are 0.032 and 0.101, respectively, G_{it} is the average charitable contribution in income class i at time t, Y_{it} is average income minus taxes that would have been paid in the absence of the donations in income class i at time t, and P_{it} is the first dollar tax price in income class i at time t. Both elasticities were highly significant.

These results were confirmed by a variety of studies using different data sources and time periods. Feldstein and Clotfelter (1976) used survey data (1963) and an estimate of permanent income, and this increased the income elasticity (0.99) and reduced the price elasticity (-1.07). Feldstein and Taylor (1976) confirmed the result for a cross section tax file (1970), Abrams and Schmitz (1978, 1984) for a pooled time series cross section aggregated by income class (1942 - 1972) and a cross section of seven income classes aggregated by state (1979), where government transfer variables and measures of recipient poverty were included, Reece (1979), who used the Consumer Expenditure Survey (1972) and included government transfers and a measure of recipient income, and Schiff (1985), who used cross section data taken from the National Survey of Philanthropy (1973) and included several variables designed to capture spillover effects. Later support came from Slemrod (1989), who used a cross section tax file (1982) and corrected for tax evasion, Choe and Jeong (1993), who studied a cross section tax file (1985) and corrected for censoring and endogeneity of the tax price, and Andreoni and Scholtz (1998), for a cross section of the Consumer Expenditure Survey (1985), who adjusted the model to include the donor's reference group as a spillover effect.[7]

There were several caveats to this result, however, actually presented by Feldstein (1975a). The price elasticity for the wealthiest group in his original study was significantly lower than one in magnitude (-0.29, s.e. 0.106) and the income elasticity was significantly greater than one (1.37, s.e. 0.063). This suggested there might be some heterogeneity across taxpayers. Second, Feldstein (1975b) discovered that different types of donation exhibit different responsiveness.[8] He estimated a donation function for five separate donation categories: religious organizations, educational institutions, hospitals, health and welfare organizations, and all others. The price elasticity was greater than one in magnitude in the last four categories, but less than one for religious organizations.[9] In addition to this, the estimated income elasticity was greater than one for educational institutions and hospitals, but less than one for the other categories.

This was challenged by Reece and Zieschang (1985), which is the only study we are aware of that attempted to take into account the complicated bracket structure of the U.S. income tax. Some of the problems associated with the tax price and income variables stem from the nature of the bracket structure. If the bracket structure is taken into account, these problems should be mitigated. Consider a simple setting where there is a progressive income tax and there are two brackets, $b_1 - b_0$ and $b_2 - b_1$, where $b_2 > b_1 > b_0$. Let τ be the tax rate for bracket k, assume $\tau_2 > \tau_1$, and consider a taxpayer in the top bracket. His tax liability is

$$T^h = \tau_1(b_1 - b_0) + \tau_2(w^h - b_1),$$

where $b_1 < w^h < b_2$. If charitable contributions can be written off against taxable income, his liability is

$$T^h = \tau_1(b_1 - b_0) + \tau_2(w^h - g^h - b_1),$$

assuming $w^h - g^h > b_1$. The taxpayer's budget constraint is

$$w^h - \tau_1(b_1 - b_0) + \tau_2(w^h - g^h - b_1) - g^h - x^h = 0,$$

or, after rearranging,

$$(1-\tau_2)w^h - \tau_1(b_1 - b_0) + \tau_2 b_1 - (1-\tau_2)g^h - x^h = 0.$$

Table 9.1. Results from Static Models

Study	Data	Dependent variable	Price elasticity	Income elasticity
Feldstein (1975a)	SOI, pooled TS CS, 1948 - '68	total contributions, all 17 classes	-1.24	0.82
		total contributions, highest income class	-0.29	1.34
Feldstein (1975b)	SOI, CS, 1962	gifts to religious organizations	-0.49	0.63
		gifts to educational institutions	-2.23	1.22
		gifts to hospitals	-2.44	1.08
		gifts to health & welfare organizations	-1.19	0.85
		gifts to all others (e.g., libraries)	-2.63	0.65
Feldstein & Clotfelter (1976)	Federal Reserve Survey, CS, 1963	total contributions	-1.07	0.99
Feldstein & Taylor (1976)	Tax Model, CS, 1962	total contributions	-1.09	0.76
	Tax Model, CS, 1970	total contributions	-1.42	0.768
Boskin & Feldstein (1977)	NSP, CS, 1973	total contributions	-2.54	0.69
Dye (1978)	NSP, CS, 1973	total contributions	-2.25	0.53
Abrams & Schmitz (1978)	SOI, pooled TS CS, 1948-'72	total contributions	-1	0.85

Table 9.1. (cont.)

Reece (1979)	CEX, 1972 - '73	gifts to charity (e.g. Red Cross) plus donations deducted from pay	-0.976	1.42
		gifts to charity	*	1.7
		gifts to religious organizations	-1.6	0.397
		gifts to educational organizations	*	1.64
Clotfelter & Steuerle (1981)	Tax Model, CS, 1975	total contributions	-1.27	0.78
Abrams & Schmitz (1983)	SOI, CS, 1977	total contributions	-1.48	0.53
Schiff (1985)	NSP, CS, 1974	total contributions	-2.79	0.76
		contributions to social welfare groups	-4.97	0.43
Reece & Zieschang (1985)	CEX, 1972 - '73	gifts to charity (e.g. Red Cross)	-0.113	1.425
Feenberg (1987)	Tax Model, CS, 1982	total contributions	-1.63	0.74
Slemrod (1989)	IRS Taxpayer Compliance Measurement Program, CS, 1982	reported charitable contributions	-2.04	0.35
		auditor adjusted contributions	-1.7	0.26
Robinson (1990)	Tax Model, CS, 1985	total contributions	itemizers -0.67 non-itemizers -0.67	0.68 0.68

Table 9.1. (cont.)

Choe & Jeong (1993)	Tax Model, CS, 1985	total contributions	OLS estimates: -1.35 / SET estimates: -2.53	0.76 / 0.96
Ribar & Wilhelm (1995)	International aid data and state data, 1988-1991	contributions to international aid agencies	-1.00 to -2.0	1.5 to 2.6
O'Neil, Steinberg, & Thompson (1996)	Tax Model, CS, 1985	total contributions / cash donations / property donations	-0.47 / -0.78 / -2.21	0.6 / 0.5 / 0.32
Auten & Joulfaian (1996)	SOI, linked income and estate tax data, CS, 1981-'82	lifetime charitable giving	-1.108	0.708
Andreoni & Scholtz (1998)	CEX, CS, 1985	total contributions	-0.349	0.283
Duquette (1999)	Tax Model, CS, 1986	total contributions	itemizers -1.241 / non-itemizers -0.637	0.87 / 0.721
Greene & McClelland (2001)	HRS, CS, 1991	total contributions	-1.57 to '-1.73	0.32 to 0.35

All coefficients listed in the table were statistically significant, * - not statistically significant, *NP* - not presented. *SOI* - Statistics of Income, IRS, *NSP* - National Study of Philanthropy, *CEX* - Consumer Expenditure Survey, *CS* - Cross section, *TS* - Time series, *HRS* - Health and Retirement Study

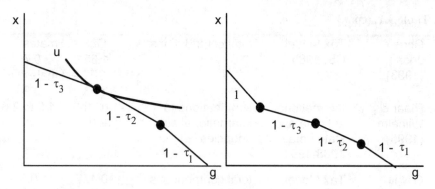

Fig. 9.1. Tax Bracket Structure

We can define the taxpayer's "virtual income" as

$$I^h = (1-\tau_2)w^h - \tau_1(b_1 - b_0) + \tau_2 b_1,$$

where the term $- \tau_1(b_1 - b_0) + \tau_2 b_1 = (\tau_2 - \tau_1)b_1 + \tau_1 b_0 > 0$ is a rate structure premium. The brackets give rise to a non-linear, concave budget constraint for a taxpayer who itemizes. This is depicted in Figure 9.1 in the left-hand diagram, where there are three brackets and $\tau_3 > \tau_2 > \tau_1$, and where we have listed the tax price next to each relevant segment of the constraint. The taxpayer may not be at a point of tangency but at a 'kink' point instead, as depicted in the left panel.

If the taxpayer has a choice of taking a standard deduction, or taking a deduction on the basis of itemizing his allowable expenditures, e.g., home mortgage interest, unusual medical expenses, and charitable donations, this creates an additional linear segment in the budget constraint with a slope of - 1 where the tax price is $p = 1$ for a taxpayer who does not itemize. This is depicted in the diagram on the right in Figure 9.1. This creates the possibility of multiple tangency points, which should also be taken into account in the estimation method.

Reece and Zieschang took the full bracket structure into account in their estimation procedure. They calculated a tax structure elasticity, which is similar to the tax price elasticity, of -0.113 and an income elasticity of 1.425. They also used the 'first price' and 'last price' methods for comparison purposes. The price elasticity under both methods was about - 0.15 and the income elasticity under both methods was about 1.3. The main drawback to their procedure is that it is computationally very expensive and for large data sets prohibitively so.

In studies employing tax file data, taxpayers who do not itemize their deductions are not included in the sample used for estimation. However, a change in the U.S. tax law in the 1980s allowed non-itemizers to deduct some of their charitable donations without itemizing. In 1981 The Economic Recovery Tax Act phased in a deduction for non-itemizers that lasted for five years (1982-86) with dollar limits during the first three years of the policy. Robinson (1990) used Individual Tax Model data for 1985 that included non-itemizers as well as taxpayers who itemize their deductions. He found price elasticities for non-itemizers that were similar to those for itemizers when Maximum Likelihood estimation was used. Furthermore, he found that the income elasticity decreased with income while the price elasticity increased in magnitude with income, being greater than one in magnitude only for the wealthiest taxpayers.

On the other hand, Duquette (1999) found that itemizers were more responsive to price and income than non-itemizers. He used the Individual Tax Model data for 1985 and 1986 and a larger sample that included both itemizers and non-itemizers. The tax price elasticity was much higher in magnitude for itemizers (-1.2) than for non-itemizers (-0.67). He suggested this could be due to the fact that non-itemizers tend to give more to religious organizations than itemizers. In addition, home ownership tends to be greater among itemizers than non-itemizers and homeowners may have greater ties to the community and be more responsive to charity as a result.

O'Neil, Steinberg, and Thompson (1996) argued that results from equations estimated with aggregate data may mask important differences at the disaggregated level. They used a cross section tax file with a broader definition of income and a proxy for wealth and estimated a price elasticity of -0.47 and an income elasticity of 0.6 when 'total contributions' was used as the dependent variable. However, when the dependent variable was disaggregated into cash contributions and property donations, they estimated price elasticities of -0.78 and -2.21, respectively, and income elasticities of 0.5 and 0.32, respectively, all measured very precisely. Furthermore, they also uncovered evidence of significant heterogeneity across income classes. The price elasticity across income classes was U-shaped and the income elasticity was an inverted U-shape when total contributions were used as the dependent variable.

A general theory of lifetime donations would naturally include the tax price of within lifetime charitable gifts, as discussed above, income, wealth, and the tax price of making a charitable bequest as part of one's estate. With their data set, Greene and McClelland (2001) were able to estimate each respondent's life span and used an estimate of each respondent's asset growth to calculate an estimate for each respondent's expected estate and how much they might leave to charity as a bequest. This allowed them to include proxies for all four economic variables in their charity equation.

The estimated own price elasticity was between -1.57 and -1.734, the income elasticity was between 0.317 and 0.352, the wealth elasticity was between 0.115 and 0.163, and the cross price elasticity was between 0.303 and 0.685, depending on the assumption involving asset growth. This suggests that charitable contributions and charitable bequests are substitutes and raises the interesting possibility that tax policy affects the timing of donations in a significant way.

9.3 Dynamic Models

9.3.1 Modeling Contributions in a Dynamic Model

The main drawback to the static models of the early literature is their inability to forecast the response of charitable donations to significant changes in tax policy such as the Economic Recovery Tax Act of 1981, the Deficit Reduction Act of 1984, and the Tax Reform Act of 1986. Auten, Cilke, and Randolph (1992) studied cross-section samples of individual tax returns for 1979 - 1990 taken from the IRS's Statistics of Income, and concluded that "... average contributions also increased in spite of tax law changes that made it generally less tax-favorable for taxpayers to give to charity." (page 288.) And, ".... high income taxpayers do not appear to have decreased their contributions as much as predicted by cross-section regression estimates." (page 288.) Finally, "The typical cross-section regression model does not fully predict some of the observed systematic taxpayer behavior. Most notably, the regression does not account for the short-term timing effects observed in 1981 and 1986." (page 289.)[10]

Researchers turned to dynamic models to analyze the data. However, matters become somewhat more complicated when we admit dynamics into the model. Consider a simple life-cycle setting with a consumer whose lifetime utility function is

$$\Sigma_t \beta^t u^h(x^h_t, G_t, \varepsilon^h_t),$$

where x^h_t is consumption of the private good at time t, G_t is the level of the public good at time t, ε^h_t is a variable that captures shifts in preferences, and β is the discount factor, $0 < \beta < 1$. The agent's wealth constraint under an earnings tax is

$$\Sigma_t R^t[(1-\tau^h_t)w^h_t + p^h_t G^{-h}_t - x^h_t - p^h_t G_t] + (1+r)a^h_{-1} = 0,$$

where $R = 1/(1+r)$, r is the interest rate, g^h_t is h's contribution at time t, G^{-h}_t is the sum of everyone else's contribution at t, p^h_t is h's tax price, τ^h_t is the tax rate confronting the taxpayer at t, and $(1+r)a^h_{-1}$ is the taxpayer's initial wealth. Let λ be the multiplier for the wealth constraint. The agent chooses a sequence of consumption and donation to the public good to maximize lifetime utility subject to the wealth constraint. When the period utility function is given by $u = \ln(x^h_t) + \alpha \ln(G_t)$, the first order conditions of the agent's decision problem are $\beta^t/G_t = \lambda R^t p^h_t$ and $\beta^t/x^h_t = \lambda R^t$.

There are a number of ways of proceeding. For example, by manipulating the first order conditions, we obtain the so-called Euler equation for G_t,

$$p^h_{t+1}G_{t+1} = \beta(1+r)p^h_t G_t.$$

Let $E_k = p^h_k G_k$ be the expenditure on the public good, and solve the preceding difference equation to obtain $E_{t+j} = E_t(\beta(1+r))^j$. It follows immediately that the expenditure on charity will grow at the rate $\beta(1+r)$, given the initial level of contributions at time t. Therefore, donations will grow over time when $\beta(1+r) > 1$ and decline when $\beta(1+r) < 1$, even though the tax price is fixed. Substituting the solution to the Euler equation into the wealth constraint and solving yields

$$(E_t + x^h_t)/(1-\beta) = \Sigma_{j=0}R^j((1-\tau^h_{t+j})w^h_{t+j} + p^h_{t+j}G^{-h}_{t+j}) + (1+r_t)a^h_{t-1}, \qquad (9.6)$$

for $j = 1,2....$ Notice that we can combine the first order conditions for x^h_t and E_t to obtain $\alpha x^h_t = E_t$ for all t. Using this in equation (9.6) we have,

$$E_t = A\{\Sigma_{j=0}R^j[(1-\tau^h_{t+j})w^h_{t+j} + p^h_{t+j}G^{-h}_{t+j}] + (1+r_t)a^h_{t-1}\},$$

where $A = \alpha(1-\beta)/(1+\alpha) > 0$. We can rearrange this last equation to get,

$$g^h_t = A[\Sigma_{j=0}R^j((1-\tau^h_t)w^h_{t+j} + p^h_{t+j}G^{-h}_{t+j}) + (1+r_t)a^h_{t-1}]/p^h_t - G^{-h}_t. \qquad (9.7)$$

This equation instructs us that future income, the future donations of everyone else, and future tax prices affect current donations, in addition to the current tax price and current wealth. A regression of the contribution on current price and current income alone will be incorrectly specified according to (9.7). In that case, other variables that are typically included in the regression equation, like age and education, may be proxying for some of these future variables. For example, old people have acquired more wealth than young people. If the current donation is increasing in future income, then including 'age' in the regression equation may partly pick up the effect of future income. We should not be surprised to find that the estimated coefficient for 'age' is positive.

Alternatively, notice that (9.7) can be written in the following form if we subtract the equation dated t-1 from the equation dated at time t,

$$\Delta E^h_t = A[\Delta(1-\tau^h_t)w_t + \Sigma_{j=0}R^j(\Delta(1-\tau^h_{t+j})w^h_{t+j} + \Delta E^{-h}_{t+j}) + (1+r_t)\Delta a^h_{t-1}] \qquad (9.8)$$

$$+ (A-1)\Delta E^{-h}_t.$$

This version of the equation might be useful if the researcher believes the data is not stationary in levels but is stationary in first differences.[11] It also removes person-specific fixed effects if they are constant over time. This is convenient if such effects are unobservable.[12]

There are two types of comparative statics response to take into account in a dynamic model such as this. The agent may respond to an unexpected shift in a variable at a moment in time. For example, if the agent at time t suddenly comes to believe that her wage at time t+j will increase, then she will adjust her contributions today at time t according to $dg^h_t/dw^h_{t+j} = R^j > 0$, from (9.7). The current response will be smaller the further in the future the change in the wage is expected to occur. Second, the agent will generally respond to an expected 'evolutionary' change in a variable. More specifically, the agent's trajectory of contributions to the public good, $(g^h_t, g^h_{t+1}, g^h_{t+2}, ..., g^h_s,....)$, will respond to the trajectory of labor earnings, $(w^h_t, w^h_{t+1}, w^h_{t+2}, ..., w^h_s,....)$. A 'hump shaped' earnings trajectory may lead to a 'hump shaped' contributions trajectory, for example. Therefore, even if we notice an increase in an individual's giving over time, as we might in a panel data set, this is not necessarily evidence that the individual's earnings profile has shifted. Instead, it may be evidence that the individual's earnings trajectory has positive slope and that the individual has taken this into account in choosing her optimal donations trajectory.

The model also predicts there is a critical difference between permanent and temporary shifts in the exogenous variables of interest. For example, the effect of a permanent increase in earnings on the current contribution is $\Sigma R^t = (1+r)/r > 1$ from (9.7). However, the effect of a temporary increase in earnings in period s on the current contribution is $R^s < 1$. Similar remarks hold for temporary versus permanent changes in the tax price as well. Permanent changes may become confused econometrically with temporary changes if current income and the tax price are the only economic variables included in the equation.

The empirical importance of future variables entering the dynamic donations equation is that donors might alter their charitable donations to 'smooth' their own consumption over the life cycle. In fact, charitable contributions may be a particularly easy form of expenditure to adjust. An increase in the current tax price will induce the individual to give less in the current period. However, a change in the tax law, which alters future tax prices, will also affect current contributions. For example, a tax rate cut in the near future, which raises the price of future contributions, may induce the agent to donate more now. Static models cannot make this prediction; they have nothing to say about the timing of contributions.

We can also use the equation appearing just before (9.7) and the first order condition $\alpha x^h_t = E_t$ to obtain a consumption function for this model,

$$x^h_t = B[\Sigma_j R^j(w^h_{t+j} + p^h_{t+j} G^{-h}_{t+j}) + (1+r_t)a^h_{t-1}], \tag{9.9}$$

where $B = A/\alpha = (1-\beta)/(1+\alpha) > 0$. The innovation here is that the agent's consumption of the private good depends on the current and future partial sums of everyone else's contributions to the public good and the current and future tax price confronting the individual. This particular functional form predicts that an increase in the current partial sum G^{-h}_t, or the partial sum in the future, G^{-h}_s for $s > t$, will induce an increase in private consumption today since the individual experiences an increase in her full income. And an increase in either the current, or a future, tax price will induce an increase in private consumption now.

One way of proceeding that is somewhat data intensive is to estimate equations governing the evolution of the variables on the right hand side of equation (9.7),

$$(1-\tau^h_t)w^h_{t+1} = \omega(1-\tau^h_t)w^h_t + u^h_{wt+1},$$

$$E^{-h}_{t+1} = \varepsilon E^{-h}_t + u^h_{Et+1},$$

where u_w and u_E are serially uncorrelated random error terms that are also uncorrelated with one another and (ω, ε) are the parameters to be estimated. The researcher could then estimate these equations along with (9.7) as a system and exploit the cross equation restrictions to identify the structural parameters. The problem with this methodology is that closed form solutions can be difficult to obtain in all but the simplest cases.

Another way of proceeding is to posit temporary and persistent components to the price and income variables and do so in such a way as to allow identification of the various parameters. One can then posit a linear version of the decision rule and use the data to calculate the persistent price and income elasticities that hold in the long run and the temporary elasticities, which only hold in the short run. This is the method employed by Auten, Sieg, and Clotfelter (2002) and we will go into more detail on this method later in the next section.

The dynamic subscriptions model just described can be rejected when confronted by data for several reasons. First, utility may not be interlinked and thus donors may not care about the total contributed to the public good. Second, the functional form chosen may be wrong. Third, the proxies chosen to represent the theoretical variables may be incorrect. And, fourth, the method of forecasting future parameters may be inaccurate.

We can obtain a dynamic version of the warm glow model if the period utility function's arguments are private consumption and the agent's own contribution instead of the total sum according to $u^h(x^h_t, g^h_t) = \ln(x^h_t) + \alpha\ln(g^h_t)$. After solving the Euler equations we obtain the following supply of contributions instead of (9.7),

$$g^h_t = A[\Sigma_{j=0}R^j(1-\tau^h_{t+j})w^h_{t+j} + (1+r_t)a^h_{t-1}]/p^h_t. \tag{9.10}$$

Only the variables directly confronting the individual enter the supply of contributions in this model. As in the static models, (9.10) is a special case of (9.7). One test of whether the broader model is more appropriate is whether the donation is sensitive to the donations of other private agents and the government's spending on similar goods. Simply observing that the agent responds to future tax policy is not enough to distinguish the two models.

The main new econometric problem associated with time series and panel data that a researcher must confront is the stationarity of the data. Two time series, say, x and y, may both drift upward over time and a regression of y on x may reveal a positive elasticity with a small standard error and a large R-squared statistic. However, the two variables may be unrelated to one another and the regression result may actually be due to the fact that the two variables are simply drifting upward in the same manner rather than being fundamentally related. This is the famous spurious regression problem. One can undertake a variety of diagnostic procedures designed to test for this possibility, e.g., unit root tests, and there are a variety of estimation techniques for dealing with this problem should it arise, e.g., estimation in first differences, dynamic OLS.

9.3.2 Empirical Results

There were a number of significant changes in the income tax in the U.S. during the 1980s including the Economic Recovery Tax Act of 1981, the Deficit Reduction Act of 1984, and the Tax Reform Act of 1986. All of these changes lowered tax rates and raised the price of donating to charity for itemizers. They also reduced the incentive to itemize as well. It is of some interest to see how the static model did in forecasting the effects of those changes on charitable donations.

To that end, Auten, Cilke, and Randolph (1992) used a cross section tax file for 1979 and estimated a price elasticity of -1.11 and an income elasticity of 0.67, which is in accordance with the literature. They then forecast what contributions would have been in the 1980s had there not been any changes in the tax law. For example, the actual average contribution in the sample increased from \$1776 in 1979 to \$1940 in 1989. Holding tax policy, and hence the tax price, constant, they used the model to forecast that donations would have increased from \$1776 to \$1888 by 1989. This is the amount of the increase that the other variables, income and the demographic variables, can explain. Finally, they used the model to forecast what contributions would have been if tax policy were allowed to change and the tax price elasticity was -1.11. According to their forecast, contributions would have been 8.8% lower than the baseline of \$1888, or \$1733. This conclusion was also true when Auten, Cilke, and Randolph looked at the different income classes separately; the model over-predicts the decline in donations. These wildly inaccurate predictions are quite startling.[13]

Dissatisfaction with the static model, the availability of panel data, and new techniques to use in working with such data, led researchers to study the supply of charity in a dynamic context. Table 9.2 contains estimates from some of this work. For example, Broman (1989) used panel data to

Table 9.2. Results From Studies Using Panel Data

Study	Data	Dependent variable	Price	Income
Clotfelter (1980)	Treasury's Panel Study 1970, '72, '73	total contributions	levels: -0.929	0.61
		first difference in total contributions	first differences: -0.333	0.403
Broman (1989)	EY-UM, 1979-1982	total contributions	levels: -1.03	0.82
		first difference in total contributions	first differences: -0.22	0.24
Barrett (1991)	EY-UM, 1979-'86	total contributions	static model: -0.82 dynamic model: -1.086	0.34 0.234
Ricketts & Westfall (1993)	EY-UM, 1979-'86	total contributions	*	0.96

Table 9.2. (cont.)

McClelland & Kokoski (1994)	CEX, 1982-'84	total contributions	-1.159	0.669
		service oriented giving	-0.99	0.36
		religious giving	-0.51	0.485
Randolph (1995)	Special Panel of Tax Returns, IRS, 1979-'88	share of total donations in income	Current variables -1.21 0.82 Permanent variables -0.51 1.14 Transitory variables -2.27 0.58	
Barrett, McGuirk & Steinberg (1997)	EY-UM, 1979-'86	total contributions	-0.471	0.495
Tiehen (2001)	IS Survey, 1987-'95	total contributions	CS estimate ('95 data): -1.8 0.55 Pooled CS TS estimate: -1.14 0.3 Cohort panel estimate: -1.15 0.24 Major motivation: -2.21 0.03* Minor motivation: -0.79 0.2	
Auten, Sieg, & Clotfelter (2002)	IRS, 1979-1993, panel	total contributions	Persistent: -1.26 0.087 Transitory: -0.4 0.29	

All coefficients listed in the table were statistically significant, * - not statistically significant, *NP* - not presented. *EY-UM* - Ernst & Young, Univ. of Mich Panel data, *IS Survey* - Independent Sector Survey, *CEX* - Consumer Expenditure Survey

compare estimation in levels with estimation in first differences. The elasticities are much smaller in magnitude when estimated in first differences.

Second, she included a future price variable and its coefficient was positive strongly suggesting that charitable contributions are a gross substitute over time. Thus, an observed response today may be due to an expected change in the future tax price.

However, some of these studies did not distinguish between permanent and transitory changes in the economic variables. Several early analysts included a measure of permanent income in their studies, e.g., Feldstein and Clotfelter (1976) and Reece (1979). However, Randolph (1995) pointed out that there were indirect effects that work through the tax price that needed to be taken into account as well. For example, a taxpayer with a large permanent income will face a permanently lower tax price, while a taxpayer with a large temporary income but a low permanent income will face a tax price that is low now but high later on. This distinction needs to be incorporated into the estimation procedure.

Randolph used data from the IRS's Special Panel of Tax Returns, a tax file that followed the same group of taxpayers over a ten year period from 1979 to 1988, to estimate the permanent and transitory income and tax price elasticities. First, he estimated a version of the static model, which excludes the permanent income and tax price variables. The estimated tax price and income elasticities were - 1.21 and 0.82, respectively. Next, he included the permanent variables and the results were quite a bit different. The permanent income elasticity was 1.14, while the transitory income elasticity was only 0.58. The permanent and transitory tax price elasticities were - 0.51 and - 1.55, respectively. And he easily rejected the hypothesis that the permanent effects were the same as the transitory effects. Thus, the estimated elasticities in previous studies that ignored the difference between temporary and permanent changes may be estimating an average of the long run and short run elasticities. If one were to base tax policy on such averages, one might seriously misestimate the effects of a change in tax policy.

In a recent study, Tiehen (2001) used a panel of survey data for 1987 to 1995 from the Independent Sector Surveys on Giving and Volunteering that included information on the intensity of the influence of the tax write-off provision on the respondent, e.g., taxpayers were asked how much they were influenced by the deductibility provision. She used the data to estimate equations based on cross sections by year, a pooled cross section time series, a synthetic cohort, and based on the intensity of the influence of the tax write-off as stated by the individual on the questionaire. Most of the tax price elasticities were around one in magnitude and all of the income elasticities were significantly less than one. For example, in the estimates based on cross section by year, which are similar in spirit to the static models, the tax price elasticities are all greater than one in magnitude and the income elasticities are all less than one. However, the elasticities estimated from the pooled dated and the synthetic cohort were much smaller in magnitude than those estimated from the cross sections by year.

Tiehen's most interesting result was that the income elasticity is not statistically significantly different from zero for respondents who stated that tax considerations provide a major motivation for donating, while the tax price elasticity is - 2.21 and is highly significant. Alternatively, for taxpayers who stated that tax considerations are not a motivation, the income elasticity is 0.36 and is highly statistically significant, while the tax price elasticity is essentially zero. Thus, taxpayers who say they are motivated by tax considerations appear to be highly responsive to tax policy. Unfortunately, she cannot take the permanent versus transitory effects of the economic variables into account since the data set is not rich enough.[14]

Perhaps the most technically sophisticated panel data study to date is Auten, Sieg, and Clotfelter (2002). They posited a warm glow version of the dynamic model studied in the last section and assumed that income and price have permanent and transitory components, $w_t = w^p_t - w^t_t$ and $p_t = p^p_t - p^t_t$, where a 'p' superscript refers to the persistent or permanent component, a 't' superscript refers to the transitory component, and where we have left out the 'h' superscript denoting the individual agent for brevity. They used a linear approximation to the dynamic decision rule, in first difference form,

$$\Delta g_t = b_1 \Delta p^p_t + b_2 \Delta p^t_t + b_3 \Delta w^p_t + b_4 w^t_t. \tag{9.11}$$

They also assumed the following processes hold, $w^p_t = w^t_t + \varepsilon_{wt}$, $w^t_t = \varepsilon_t$, $p^p_t = p^t_t + \varepsilon_{pt} + a_1\varepsilon_{wt}$, $p^t_t = \phi_t + a_2\varepsilon_t$, where ε_{wt}, ε_t, ε_{pt}, and ϕ_t are i.i.d. shocks with mean zero and constant variance, and are uncorrelated with one another. It is straightforward to show that the contemporaneous covariance in the first difference in income is[15]

$$\sigma_{\Delta w_t \Delta w_t} = \sigma^2_w + 2\sigma^2_\varepsilon, \tag{9.12}$$

and the first order autocovariance for the first difference in earned income is

$$\sigma_{\Delta w_t \Delta w_{t-1}} = -\sigma^2_\varepsilon. \tag{9.13}$$

Estimates of the left hand side of (9.12) and (9.13) allow one to estimate σ^2_w and σ^2_ε recursively. Continuing in the same manner, one can obtain estimates of the rest of the structural parameters including $b = (b_1, b_2, b_3, b_4)$.

The b parameters are the elasticities with respect to the different changes in income and price when the data is in natural logs.

Auten, et. al. found that the persistent or permanent elasticities were greater in magnitude than the temporary or transitory elasticities and that the persistent price elasticity was greater than one in magnitude. This strongly suggests that tax policy can have an important influence on charitable donations as long as the policy is perceived as permanent. Of course, it might be difficult convincing taxpayers that the new policy is permanent since tax policy is almost constantly being debated and frequently changed. One drawback to their study, however, is that the theory also implies that a measure of wealth should be included in the estimated equation. Unfortunately, there was not enough information in the data to allow wealth to be calculated.

9.4 Conclusion

What can one conclude from this enormous literature? The early work relying on static models depicted in Table 9.1 indicates that most of the price elasticities are at least as great as one in magnitude, while the income elasticities are less than one, although there are a few exceptions. The more recent work estimating dynamic models depicted in Table 9.2 reveals that most of the price elasticities cluster around one in magnitude, while the income elasticities are typically less than one, with a few exceptions. There is also considerable heterogeneity across taxpayers and across different types of donation. Taxpayer responsiveness may differ by income level. Donations to different types of charities may exhibit different responsiveness to policy. And there is also a difference in the responsiveness to permanent versus transitory changes in income and price. We should also mention that age, education, the number of dependents, and being married typically exhibit a positive correlation with charitable contributions. Although, the reader should keep in mind that some of these demographic variables could be proxying for omitted variables like wealth and future income.

The main problem in this area is that some of the variables need to be constructed, e.g., tax price, future tax price, and it is not immediately obvious how to do this in some cases. And in most cases there is only limited information on the demographic variables of interest. However, the fact that most of the studies come to similar conclusions despite using different data and different statistical models is of some importance. We should also mention that the statistical models of donating surveyed in this chapter are based on the warm glow hypothesis mainly because of the limitations of the data. This should not be construed as acceptance of that particular model over the subscriptions model. In the next chapter we will survey several good faith efforts to test the interdependent utility hypothesis that is at the core of the subscriptions model.

---

[1]   The problem is compounded when the donor donates an asset instead of cash in the U.S. Suppose q' is the sale price, q is the original purchase price, τ is the taxpayer's marginal income tax rate, and ϕ is her marginal capital gains tax rate. If the individual keeps the asset and consumes the proceeds her consumption increases by q' - ϕ(q' - q). If she donates it instead, she saves τq' in income tax. At the margin she must be indifferent between these two activities and thus q' - ϕ(q' - q) = τq', or p = 1 - ϕ(1 - q/q') - τ is the tax price. This variable is also not directly observed.

[2]   See Greene (1997).

[3]   This linear equation can also be justified by reference to the indirect utility function and use of duality theory, where indirect utility is given by

$$V^h = [w^h + (a_0 + a_2/a_1 + a_2 p^h + a_3 G^{-h} + \Sigma_i \beta_i c^{hi} + \varepsilon^h)/a_1] \exp(- a_1 p^h).$$

It, thus, stems from optimizing behavior.

[4]   The price of donating may be understated if the taxpayer overstates her charitable contributions in an attempt to illegally evade some of her true tax liability. If this occurs, the price variable will be measured with error and a price elasticity that is large in magnitude may be due to tax evasion rather than to the responsiveness of charitable donations to the price per se. Slemrod (1989) included several variables designed to capture various aspects of tax evasion, such as the probability of being detected evading taxation, in his study of the supply of charitable contributions. He found that when such additional variables are included in his charity regression equation, the price elasticity typically increased in magnitude. It follows that the large magnitude of the price elasticity in regression equations that do not include tax evasion is not due to ignoring tax evasion.

[5]   Feldstein (1975a) used aggregate time series tax data stratified by income for 17 income classes. Feldstein (1975b) studied a cross section of tax data stratified by income containing information on disaggregated charitable donations (religious organizations, hospitals, health and welfare organizations, and educational institutions). Feldstein and Clotfelter (1976) studied a cross section of survey data. Feldstein and Taylor (1976) used a series of cross section of aggregated data. And Boskin and Feldstein (1977) used a cross section of survey data.

[6]   See Clotfelter's Table 2.12 on page 57.

[7]   See Clotfelter (1985) for a summary of the literature of the 1970s and early 1980s and Steinberg (1990) for a survey of studies done in the late 1980s.

[8]   See his specification I in Table 3 on page 217.

[9]   Several analysts have pointed out that donors may make donations to religious organizations because they feel they are buying a service that is very important to them regardless of the "price."

[10] Indeed, Clotfelter (1987) predicted that contributions in 1988 would fall by 15 - 16% after the Tax Reform Act of 1987 lowered tax rates. However, wealthy donors *increased* their contributions by 150% in 1986 to take advantage of the tax write-off before it was reduced in 1987 and then lowered their contributions dramatically after that. See O'Neil, Steinberg, and Thompson (1996). Also see Clotfelter (1992) for a heroic yet disappointing attempt to defend the static model's predictions involving some of the tax changes in the US during the 1980s. His discussion contains so many caveats that it is hard to take his defense seriously. For example, the model dramatically misestimates the response for most income brackets from 1980 - 1984 to ERTA. For seven of eighteen income brackets the model predicted a drop in contributions, or no change, while actual giving increased (See Figure 7.1). As another example, the model significantly misestimates the behavior of nonitemizers for 1985 - 1987. It predicted virtually no change in contributions, yet giving increased significantly across almost all brackets (Figure 7.3).

[11] See Hamilton (1994) on time series analysis.

[12] Consider a regression equation of the form $y^i_t = x^i_t \beta + \gamma^i + \varepsilon^i_t$, where γ^i is a constant person-specific effect that is fixed over time. Taking first differences with panel data eliminates the fixed effect.

[13] Many of the early studies involving static models were used to simulate significant changes in tax policy based on the coefficients estimated in the study. See Feldstein (1975a, b) and Clotfelter (1985) chapter 3 for examples of this sort of simulation exercise. Clotfelter (page 212) forecast the 1986 Tax Reform Act would reduce charitable donations by 15% or more and Lindsay (1986) forecast it would lower donations by $11 billion. Actual donations increased in 1987 and 1988.

[14] Tiehen also included a variable on whether the taxpayer was asked to volunteer, or not. This variable was always highly significant and had a positive correlation with charitable giving.

[15] To see this note that $\Delta w_t = \Delta w^P_t + \Delta w^t_t = \varepsilon_{wt} + \varepsilon_t - \varepsilon_{t-1}$ and $E(\Delta w_t) = 0$. Thus, $\sigma_{\Delta w_t, \Delta w_t} = E(\Delta w_t)^2 = E(\varepsilon_{wt} + \varepsilon_t - \varepsilon_{t-1})^2 = E(\varepsilon_{wt}\varepsilon_{wt} + 2\varepsilon_{wt}(\varepsilon_t - \varepsilon_{t-1}) + \varepsilon_t\varepsilon_t - 2\varepsilon_t\varepsilon_{t-1} + \varepsilon_{t-1}\varepsilon_{t-1})$, from which the result follows.

10 Further Evidence on Privately Provided Public Goods

There are many activities where private agents attempt to supply a public good. In this chapter we will examine the empirical literature on volunteer labor, charitable bequests, and public radio. This last area is of particular importance since private and public dollar donations to the same good should be close substitutes.

Many individuals donate their time to charitable causes. According to the Independent Sector's report Giving and Volunteering in the United States 2001, about 90 million adults volunteered over 15 billion hours at a value of approximately $239 billion in 2000. In addition, 42% of the adult population donated money and time, while only 10% did not donate time or money. Traditionally, women have tended to volunteer more than men (46% versus 42% in 2000), although in some data sets, e.g., Brown and Lankford's (1992) Florida survey, married men tended to volunteer with about the same frequency as married women. And the largest single category was volunteering for religious organizations.

A number of researchers, including Menchik and Weisbrod (1987), Schiff (1990), Brown and Lankford (1992), Andreoni, Gale, and Scholtz (1996), and Duncan (1999), have found evidence that the number of hours an individual is willing to donate decreases with the individual's market wage, increases with other sources of income, and decreases with the tax price of cash contributions. This last possibility indicates that donating time is a complement to donating money and has some interesting policy implications. For example, a decrease in the marginal tax rate, as occurred in the United States in 1981 and 1986, causes the tax price of cash donations to increase. The results just mentioned suggest this would reduce both cash contributions and volunteering.

Some individuals also leave some of their estate to charity. Boskin (1977), Barthold and Plotnick (1984), Clotfelter (1985), and more recently, Joulfaian (1991, 2000), and Auten and Joulfaian (1996), among others, studied this issue. There is some evidence that such donations respond negatively to the tax price of making a charitable bequest and that the tax price elasticity is greater than one in magnitude. In addition, there is some

minor evidence that charitable bequests are substitutes for charitable donations made earlier in the individual's life cycle. For example, a reduction in
the tax price of charitable bequests, as would be the case if the estate tax
were eliminated, would tend to reduce charitable contributions earlier in
the life cycle.

One of the main policy issues in this literature is the question of whether
government donations crowd out private donations. The subscriptions
model predicts unequivocally that there is a one-for-one crowding out. On
the other hand, the warm glow model predicts there is no response. Finally,
hybrid models that incorporate a warm glow motive can be used to derive
a variety of predictions that range from crowding out to crowding in. The
evidence from Kingma (1989) and Kingma and McClelland (1995) suggests there is only partial crowding out using data on dollar donations to
public radio. This is supported by the results of Berry and Waldfogel
(1999), who found evidence that public broadcasting stations tended to
partially crowd out private stations in the classical and jazz music markets.
More recently, Ribar and Wilhelm (2002) also found no support for
crowding out using panel data on donations to 125 international relief and
development organizations.

We study the theoretical models and the empirical work on volunteer
labor in section 10.1. In section 10.2 we present the empirical work on
charitable bequests. The crowding out hypothesis is studied in section
10.3. And section 10.4 concludes the chapter.

10.1 Volunteer Labor

10.1.1 Modeling Volunteer Labor

Consider a version of the warm glow model where the representative agent
is endowed with one unit of labor and can either donate some of it, or work
in the labor market. She cares about consumption of a composite good x,
the amount of labor donated v, and the amount of cash donated g, according to a well-behaved utility function of the form, $u^i(x^i, v^i, g^i)$. Her budget
constraint is given by

$$(1-\tau^i)A^i + w^i(1-\tau^i)(1-v^i) - (1-s^i)g^i - x^i = 0, \qquad (10.1)$$

where $1-v^i$ is her labor supply, w^i is the wage rate, τ^i is the tax on labor
earnings, A^i is exogenous income, and s^i is a subsidy for cash contributions. The donor chooses consumption, donated labor, and cash contributions to maximize utility subject to (10.1). At an interior solution the first

order conditions hold with equality and can be solved to obtain the donations functions,

$$g^i = g^i(w^i(1-\tau^i), p^i, (1-\tau^i)A^i), \tag{10.2a}$$

$$v^i = v^i(w^i(1-\tau^i), p^i, (1-\tau^i)A^i), \tag{10.2b}$$

where $p^i = 1-s^i$ is the tax price of donating cash.

This is the system one would like to estimate for this model. The wage rate is the opportunity cost of donating labor; the higher the wage rate, the less likely it will be that the agent will donate her time, and similarly for the tax price of cash donations. The theory predicts that in general both prices should enter both estimated equations. However, in studies of cash contributions the opportunity cost of donated labor is typically left out.

The comparative statics are easily derived for an interior solution. For example, if we assume the cross partial derivatives u^i_{gx} and u^i_{vx} are non-negative and the cross partial u^i_{gv} is non-positive, then it is straightforward to show that the cash donation is increasing in exogenous income. The response of donated labor is ambiguous even under these extra assumptions. Since labor supply is equal to $1 - v^i$, however, then donated labor is increasing in the wage if labor supply is an inferior good.[1] It is straightforward to show that the compensated donated labor is strictly decreasing in the net wage rate. The compensated supply of cash contributions is increasing in the net wage under the additional assumptions on the cross partial derivatives. In that case, an increase in the wage unambiguously causes an increase in observed cash donations since the income and substitution effects work in the same direction, while the response in observed donated labor is ambiguous. An increase in the subsidy rate for cash contributions will cause the compensated supply of cash donations to increase unambiguously. Thus, observed cash contributions would increase since the income effect is also positive. The compensated supply of donated labor decreases with the subsidy rate. If donated labor is a normal good, then the response in observed donated labor to the subsidy of cash donations is ambiguous.

The choice between the two types of donation is governed by $u^i_v/u^i_g = w^i(1-\tau^i)/(1-s^i)$. Long (1977) pointed out that if the subsidy rate is equal to the tax rate, as would be the case under deductibility of cash donations, then the choice between the two types of donation will not be distorted by government policy. An increase in the subsidy rate in that case would tend to favor cash contributions over donated labor. If only itemizers receive a subsidy for cash contributions and $s^i = \tau^i$, then the decision between the two types of donation will be undistorted only for itemizers. For non-itemizers, we have instead, $u^i_v/u^i_g = w^i(1-\tau^i)$ and the tax distorts their decision.

Next, consider a version of the subscriptions model. If the individual cares about the total amount of labor donated and the total amount of cash donations according to a utility function of the form $u^i(x^i, V, G)$, where $V = \Sigma v^i$ and $G = \Sigma g^i$, then the donation functions for an interior solution will include two spillover effects, V^{-i} and G^{-i},

$$g^i = g^{*i}(w^i(1-\tau^i), p^i, (1-\tau^i)A^i, V^{-i}, G^{-i}), \qquad (10.3a)$$

$$v^i = v^{*i}(w^i(1-\tau^i), p^i, (1-\tau^i)A^i, V^{-i}, G^{-i}). \qquad (10.3b)$$

The responses are easily derived. The new element is that the sum of labor donated by the other agents enters as an income effect. It is a straightforward matter to show that the responses are given by the derivatives,

$$dv^h/dV^{-h} = - [1 - w(dv^h/dA^h)] = - [1 - (wv^h/A^h)\varepsilon_{vA}],$$

$$dv^h/dG^{-h} = - [1 - p(dv^h/dA^h)] = - [1 - (pg^h/A^h)\varepsilon_{vA}],$$

where ε_{vA} is the income elasticity, and similarly for the response of cash donations. These responses will be negative if the ratio of the value of the donations to total assets and the income elasticity are both small in magnitude.

One test of the two models is to include the spillover variables V^{-i} and G^{-i} and test their coefficients. The problem with this is that the individual donations do not alter the total donations by much. This means that there might not be enough variation in the variables V^{-i} and G^{-i} to estimate their coefficients with precision.

10.1.2 Evidence

There have only been a few studies that attempted to estimate the supply function of volunteer labor due to the paucity of data. The early literature used simple regression analysis similar in spirit to the early literature on charitable cash contributions and concluded that volunteer labor and cash contributions were complements.[2] See Table 10.1 for a summary of results. Menchik and Weisbrod (1987) used the data from the National Study of Philanthropy to estimate the supply of volunteer labor. Their regression included an estimate of the market wage, the tax price of cash contributions, full income net of taxes, local government expenditures, and a variety of demographic variables including age, gender, and the presence of young

Table 10.1. Volunteer Labor

Study	Data	Dependent variable	wage	income	tax price
Menchik & Weisbrod (1987)	NSP, 1974, CS	hours donated	-0.41	0.652	-1.2
Schiff (1990)	NSP, 1974, CS	hours donated (aggregate)	*	*	*
		hours donated (lower educ)	-2.64	*	-7
		hours donated (combined appeal)	-1.57	1.46	*
Brown & Lankford (1992)	FCAS, 1983, CS.	hours donated (women)	NA	*	-2.1
		monetary donations (women)	NA	0.4	-1.6
		hours donated (men)	NA	*	-1.1
		monetary donations (men)	NA	0.35	-1.8
Andreoni & Scholtz (1998)	ISS, 1990, CS.	hours donated	-0.823	0.174	-0.1
		monetary donations	-0.138	0.283	-0.3
Duncan (1999)	NSP, 1974, CS	value of total donations	**	*	-1.6
		hours donated	**	*	-1.7
		monetary donations	**	*	-2.2

All coefficients listed are statistically significant, * - not significantlly different from zero, ** - not relevant, *NA* - not available. *NSP* - National Survey of Philanthropy, *CEX* - Consumer Expenditure Survey, *FCAS* - Florida Consumer Attitude Survey, *ISS* - Independent Sector Survey.

children in the family. They found that volunteer labor was negatively related to the own wage, positively related to full income, negatively related to the tax price of cash contributions, and surprisingly, positively related to local government expenditures. The wage elasticity, full income elasticity, and tax price of cash contributions elasticity were -0.41, 0.652, and -1.247, respectively. It is notable that the tax price elasticity was negative, which indicates that volunteering and donating cash are complementary activities.

In addition to this they estimated a positive correlation between volunteering and age, being married, being female, living in a large or medium sized city or a suburb, and respondents whose parents completed high school, and is negatively related to having parents who donated regularly, and where the parents of the respondents attended religious ceremonies regularly. Finally, they also uncovered considerable evidence of heterogeneous behavior when volunteering was disaggregated among four categories: higher education, lower education, social welfare, and natural resources. However, they restricted their attention to one-earner households, which might tend to limit the applicability of their results.

Schiff (1990) extended these results using the same data by including additional explanatory variables in the equation, e.g., state government spending, local government spending, and disaggregated spending variables like cash transfers. Aggregate hours donated were completely insensitive to the economic variables. However, donated time to lower education responded negatively to the net wage and the tax price, while hours donated to combined appeal, or united fund charities, e.g., United Way, responded negatively to the net wage and positively to income.

Brown and Lankford (1992) studied a survey done in Florida in 1984 that contained a great deal of information. Unfortunately, there was no information on wages and not enough demographic information to allow the authors to calculate a wage rate as Menchik and Weisbrod had done. Brown and Lankford argued that labor may be constrained at the margin and the wage would not be a useful measure of the value of time. Instead, they argued the total available amount of time after adjusting for hours worked is a better measure of the opportunity cost of time. They found that most of the coefficients for the variables included in their study were not measured very precisely and were thus not statistically different from zero. Cash contributions were negatively related to the own tax price and being a single parent, and positively related to income, education, family size, and age. It also appeared that the two types of contribution were complements since the cross price elasticity of volunteer labor with respect to the tax price of cash contributions was negative for both men and women. Finally, volunteering by gender was not affected by income. Of course, if labor is not constrained, then this study suffers from a serious omitted variables problem, which could explain the imprecise estimates.

Andreoni, Gale, and Scholtz (1996) used a unique data set, which contained information on each individual's contributions of time and money and various economic and demographic variables, to estimate supply functions for both donated time and money. They assumed donors care about the value of donated labor and the value of cash contributions according to a well-behaved utility function, $u^i(x^i, L^i, g^i, w^{*i}v^i)$, where L is leisure, w^*v is the value of donated labor, and w^* is the hourly value of the individual's donated labor, which may differ from the market wage. It is also assumed that volunteer labor is less productive than market labor, $w^* < w$. They showed that cash donations will precede donated labor when the market wage is strictly greater than the hourly value of volunteer labor, and cash contributions will always exceed the value of volunteer labor.

Andreoni, et. al., estimated the structural parameters of a quadratic utility function under the maximization hypothesis and found income and price elasticities for cash contributions and donated labor well below one in magnitude, which are much smaller in magnitude than typically found in the literature. In addition, they also found that donated labor and donated cash were uncompensated complements but compensated substitutes. Finally, they simulated several important policy proposals. For example, extending the deduction for cash contributions to non-itemizers would increase cash donations by 3% and also increase volunteer labor by 0.6%. This second effect, while small in magnitude, is still an important unintended benefit of the policy.

In order to derive and estimate separate supply functions for donated money and volunteer labor the two activities must be viewed as imperfect substitutes. One might question this, however. After all, if a donor reduces his volunteer effort to a particular charity by one hour, works in the labor market, earns w, and donates w to the same charity, why can't the charity use w to hire an extra hour of labor of the same quality thus replacing the earlier loss in labor? If volunteer labor and donated cash are perfect substitutes, and the individual obtains utility from the sum of the value of both donations, then separate supply functions for donated time and money cannot be derived, only the total value of donations $g^i + w^iv^i$ can, as pointed out by Duncan (1999).

To see this, suppose $C = G + V = \Sigma g^h + \Sigma w^{*h}v^h$ is the public good, where $G = \Sigma g^h$ is total cash donations, $V = \Sigma w^{*h}v^h$ is the total value of volunteer labor, and w^{*i} is i's marginal productivity when donating labor. Utility is given by $u(x, C)$, and satisfies the usual assumptions. The budget constraint is

$$w^h(1-\tau^h)(L^h - v^h) + A^h - (1-\tau^h)g^h - x^h = 0,$$

where τ^h is the income tax rate, L^h is the endowment of labor, $L^h - v^h$ is labor supply to the labor market, A^h is asset income, and $(1-\tau^h)$ is the tax price of cash donations. This constraint can be written as

$$w^h(1-\tau^h)L^h + A^h + p^hC^{-h} = (w^{*h} - w^h)(1-\tau^h)v^h + (1-\tau^h)C + x^h,$$

where $w^h(1-\tau^h)L^h + A^h + p^hC^{-h}$ is 'social income,' I^h. The right hand side is equal to $(1-\tau^h)C + x^h$ if $w^{*h} = w^h$. The first order conditions for donor h are given by

$$u^h_C - (1-\tau^h)u^h_x \leq 0,$$

$$w^{*h}u^h_C - w^h(1-\tau^h)u^h_x \leq 0.$$

In the special case where w^{*h} is equal to w^h, the last two conditions are the same and we cannot solve for distinct supply functions, but only the total, $c^h = g^h + w^hv^h$. Of course, if $w^{*h} < w^h$, the agent will not donate labor since his cash donation buys more charity at the margin.

Following Duncan (1999), suppose $w^{*h} = w^h$ for all h. When we solve the first order conditions we obtain $C = F^h(I^h, p^h)$. It follows that the individual's net contribution is

$$c^h = F^h(I^h, p^h) - C^{-h}, \tag{10.4}$$

where C^{-h} is the value of everyone else's total value of donations, $\Sigma_{i\neq h}(g^i + w^iv^i)$. If there is a labor - leisure choice as well, then we have instead $c^h = F^h(I^h, w^h(1-\tau^h), p^h) - C^{-h}$.

Equation (10.4) forms the basis of Duncan's estimates using the National Survey of Philanthropy (NSP). We can linearize (10.4) to obtain,

$$c^h = X^hB + \alpha_1I^h + \alpha_2C^{-h} + \alpha_3p^h + \varepsilon^h,$$

where X^h is a vector of personal characteristics and G^{-h} contains the government's expenditure as the n+1 agent.

Duncan estimated a linear version of (10.4) and found that total contributions are positively related to full income and negatively related to the tax price, $1 - \tau^h$, the partial sum C^{-h}, and local government spending, although the standard errors for full income and the partial sum C^{-h} were so large that the null hypothesis that their coefficients were zero could not be rejected. In addition, the theory predicts that C^{-h} and government spending will have the same impact on total contributions and this was supported by the data, although, this was true because the standard errors were so large.

Several comments are in order. When the two types of donations are perfect substitutes, the model is formally equivalent to the subscriptions model. From our earlier analysis it follows that $dg^i/dG^{-i} = -(1-dg^i/dw^i)$, or $\alpha_2 = \alpha_1 - 1$. Since $\alpha_1 = \alpha_2 = 0$ from Duncan's estimates, this implication is easily rejected, although Duncan does not mention this. Second, a simple test of the model would be to include the wage as a separate regressor and test its coefficient. Unfortunately, such a test was not performed. Third, if w^i differs from w^{*i}, then if $w^i > w^{*i}$, the individual will never donate time, only money, and a large fraction of individuals do not volunteer time but do give money. This suggests that the market time and donated time are not perfect substitutes.[3] Fourth, it would not be terribly surprising to discover that an individual is not as productive when volunteering after having worked a full day. Finally, the NSP data does not report the distribution of an individual's donations of time and money across all charities. It follows that if an individual makes a cash donation and donates time to a particular charity, it must be assumed that the two types of donation are perfect substitutes for one another, and, more to the point, that each charity's output is a perfect substitute for every other charity's output. This is hard to believe.

10.2 Charitable Bequests

10.2.1 Modeling Charitable Bequests

Contributions to a charity from one's estate upon death can also be considered a public good, where the charity's income is the sum of such donations. Watson (1984) studied a dynamic warm glow model of charitable bequests. We will consider an alternative based on the subscriptions model that is more general.

There are N agents who contribute to charity during their lifetime and also make a bequest at the end of their lifetime from their estate. They can also make a bequest to their own offspring. The representative agent has a T period horizon and her utility function is of the form

$$\sum_{t=1}^{T} \beta^{t-1} u^h(x_t^h, G_t) + \beta^{T+1} \tilde{u}^h(x_{T+1}^{ch}, x_{T+1}^{CB}),$$

where, in addition to the variables already defined, x^{ch} is consumption by the decision maker's child, and x^{CB} is consumption of the charity receiving the charitable bequest. The agent's budget constraint is

$$w_t^h(1-\tau_t^h) + (1+r(1-\tau_t^h))a_t^h - a_{t+1}^h - x_t^h - p_t^h g_t^h = 0, \text{ for } t = 1, 2, ...T-1,$$

where a_t is an asset that pays a one period return of r, and for time the last period at T,

$$w^h_T(1-\tau^h_T) + (1+r(1-\tau^h_T))a^h_T - a^h_{T+1} - (1/(1-\theta))b_T - cb_T - x^h_T - p^h_T g^h_T = 0,$$

where θ is the estate tax rate, cb is a charitable bequest that is exempt from the estate tax, income, $w^h_t + ra^h_t$, is taxed at rate τ^h_t, and where we have assumed that the charitable contribution made during the donor's lifetime g^h_t is deductible from income in determining the base for the income tax, i.e., $p = 1 - \tau$ is the tax price of within lifetime charity. We also have

$$x^{ch}_{T+1} = w^{ch} + b_T,$$

and

$$x^{CB}_{T+1} = w^{CB} + \Sigma_i cb^i_T,$$

where wch is the offspring's income, w^{CB} is the charity's income, b_T is a bequest to the offspring, and $\Sigma_i cb^i_T$ is the sum of charitable bequests to the charity.

Clearly, since utility is increasing in each of its arguments, the individual will not accumulate any assets in the last period. Let $a^h_{T+1} = 0$ and consider the agent's decision problem at time T,

$$\max \; u^h(y^h_t - p_T g_T - cb^h_T - b^h_T/(1-\theta), G_t) + \beta^{T+1}\tilde{u}^h(w^{ch} + b_T, w^{CB} + \Sigma_i cb^h_T),$$

where $y^h_T = w^h_T(1-\tau^h_T) + (1+r(1-\tau^h_T))a^h_T$ is disposable income plus wealth at the beginning of time T, a^h_T. It is straightforward to derive the first order conditions and solve them to obtain functions of the form,

$$z^h_T(y^h_T, p^h_T, G^{-h}_T, 1/(1-\theta_T), w^{ch}, w^{CB} + CB^{-h}_T), \text{ for } z = g, b, cb, \qquad (10.5)$$

where CB^{-h}_T is the sum of everyone else's contribution to the charity in the last period. Notice that wealth at the beginning of the last period of the horizon, $(1+r)a^h_T$, enters each function through the term in income, y^h_T. However, the size of the estate, $b_T/(1-\theta) + cb_T$, does not enter since that is an endogenous choice at time T. This model generalizes Watson's model to include the terms wch and $w^{CB} + CB^{-h}_T$.

There are a number of interesting features associated with the solution (10.5). First, it is unambiguous that the response to a change in w^{CB} is identically the same as the response to CB^{-h}_T. Second, the donation function $g^h( )$ depends on the same variables as the cb^h and b^h functions. Thus, the within lifetime charitable donation g^h depends on the estate tax rate, the economic circumstances of the donor's offspring, and the economic circumstances of the charity receiving the charitable bequest. If true, it suggests that the charity supply functions studied in the last chapter are possibly misspecified since these variables are not included in those studies. This may be especially true for older donors and may be another reason why age and donations tend to be positively correlated. Third, variables which affect the within lifetime charitable donation will also affect the bequest and the charitable bequest and should be included in those regression equations as well.

If the utility function is additively separable, then it can be shown that the charitable contribution $g^h{}_T$ is decreasing in $G^{-h}{}_T$, but increasing in w^{ch}, w^{CB}, and $CB^{-h}{}_T$. The charitable bequest is decreasing in w^{CB} and increasing in $G^{-h}{}_T$. Finally, the bequest is decreasing in wch and increasing in $G^{-h}{}_T$. The rest of the responses are ambiguous. In particular, the estate tax rate causes conflicting income and substitution effects. If the substitution effect dominates, however, then we would expect the bequest to the heirs (b) to fall and the charitable bequest (cb) to rise with the tax rate.

10.2.2 Empirical Results

This area is severely limited by the amount and quality of the data available. Most researchers have relied on estate tax data, with one exception. The main problem is that data on many of the relevant variables is missing. There is usually information on the estate size, which proxies for wealth, and on the estate tax liability, which allows calculation of the tax price for charitable bequests. It is natural then to estimate a linear version of the supply of charitable bequests function, cb = CB(e, q), where e is the estate size and q is the tax price of charitable bequests. Of course, it also follows that this equation is mis-specified and this needs to be taken into account in the estimation procedure. The results are collected in Table 10.2.

Boskin (1977) used a warm glow type model of the last period of the agent's lifetime to model charitable bequests as a function of wealth and various prices. The limitations imposed by the data forced him to use estate size as a proxy for wealth and only include the tax price of charitable bequests, although the price was allowed to vary by level and the data was disaggregated by type of recipient (religion, education - scientific, social welfare, and other). He estimated a tax price elasticity of -1.2 and a wealth elasticity of 0.52 using a data set from the late 1950s. In addition to this, the price elasticity increased from -0.94 for the low price group to -1.8 for the high price group. When the data was disaggregated, the price elasticity ranged between -0.7 and -2.0 and also increased in magnitude with the price. Boskin's general conclusion was that the estate tax was efficient since the tax price elasticity was so large in magnitude. This was reinforced when he studied data collected in 1969 and obtained similar results.

Barthold and Plotnick (1984) challenged this result. They used probate records instead of tax data and found that while income had an effect on charitable bequests, price did not. This challenge did not stand up to other studies, although all of the more recent studies used tax data. Joulfaian (1991), for example, estimated a wealth elasticity of charitable bequests of 0.23 and a price elasticity of -3.0. When the data is disaggregated across different types of bequests, the price elasticity estimates ranged from -0.19 for bequests to the arts and humanities to -1.57 for educational and medical research bequests. Oddly enough, religious bequests were very price sensitive with an elasticity of -1.22.

Table 10.2. Charitable Bequests

Study	Data	Estate Tax Price	Wealth
Boskin (1977)	Treasury Special Study, 1957, 1959, CS	-1.2	0.52
		-0.94 to -1.8a -0.7 to -2.0b	0.54 0.2 to 0.7c
	Federal estate tax file, 1969, CS	-0.2 to -2.53a	0.4
Barthold & Plotnick (1984)	Connecticutt probate data, 1930's, 1940s, CS	*	0.4
Clotfelter (1985)	SOI estate tax data, 1976, CS	-1.67	0.42
		-1.77 to -2.46a	0.39
Joulfaian (1991)	SOI tax file, 1986-88, CS	-0.19 to - 3.0	0.0 to 0.23
Auten & Joulfaian (1996)	SOI, linked income and estate tax data, 1982-83, CS	-11.3	3.945
Joulfaian (2000)	SOI, linked income and estate tax	-0.74 to - 2.57	1.03 to 1.54

All coefficients listed in the table were statistically significant, * - not statistically significant. *HRS* - Health and Retirement Study, *SOI* - Statistics of Income, IRS. *a* - varies by price level, *b* - varies by price and by type of donee, *c* - varies by type of donee

Auten and Joulfaian (1996) studied income tax records that matched data on children and parents. They found that charitable bequests were extremely sensitive to the net worth of the parents and the bequest tax price. The net worth elasticity was 3.945 and the price elasticity was -11.263, which are both incredibly large. The child's own income had no effect on charitable bequests.

Joulfaian (2000) in a recent study also found charitable bequests to be highly sensitive to price, with a price elasticity ranging from -0.738 to -2.57. The wealth elasticity ranged from 1.026 to 1.54. He estimated his regressions with the share of charitable bequests out of income as the dependent variable and found this specification to be superior to the traditional method of regressing the log or the level of charitable contributions on various explanatory variables.

Greene and McClelland (2001) estimated a charitable contributions equation and included the cross price of charitable bequests, in addition to income, wealth, and the tax price of within lifetime charitable contributions. The estimated elasticity for the cross price effect ranged from 0.303 to 0.685, depending on the assumed amount of asset growth in their model. The fact that this elasticity is positive strongly suggests that charitable contributions made during one's lifetime and charitable bequests are substitutes. Thus, a change in tax policy that alters the price of a bequest to charity, for example, will cause donors to alter the timing of their donations.

All in all, it would seem fair to say that charitable bequests are price elastic; most estimates of the own price elasticity are above one in magnitude. In addition, most wealth elasticities are significantly below one in magnitude but positive so that charitable bequests appear to be a normal good. It is also fair to say that the empirical models typically leave out important variables that the theory instructs us should be in the model, with the study by Greene and McClelland being the exception. Since there is not enough information to include these variables, the resulting models suffer from an omitted variables bias. If charitable bequests and lifetime charitable contributions are related, the bequest tax price may be picking up some of the influence of the omitted price variable.

10.3   Testing for Externalities and the Crowding Out Hypothesis

The subscriptions model predicts that private donations will be crowded out on a one-for-one basis by government expenditures. On the other hand, the warm glow model predicts there is no effect. The difference between the two models is whether there is an externality present among the donors, or not. If the externality is weak or non-existent, then only partial crowding out will occur. Of course, under other motives for donating it is possible that crowding in may occur.

One way of testing the externality hypothesis is to include a measure of the private spillover effect and a measure of the government's contribution in the supply equation for the public good and test their coefficients. For example, if we regress the donor's charitable contribution on the donor's tax price, income, the sum of everyone else's contribution, G^{-i}, and the government's contribution, g^g, the coefficient on G^{-i} will allow us to test whether there is a spillover effect across private agents, the coefficient on g^g will allow us to test the impact of government, and a test of the equality of the two coefficients will allow us to test whether there is perfect crowding out, or not. The problem lies in finding appropriate empirical proxies for these effects.

For example, suppose the agent's indirect utility function is given by

$$V^i = (w^i + (\alpha_0 + \alpha_2/\alpha_1 + \alpha_2 P^i + \alpha_3 S^i + \alpha_4 g^g + \gamma Z^i + u^i)/\alpha_1)\exp(-\alpha_1 P^i),$$

where S is a spillover effect, Z is a vector of characteristics and u is a random variable. It is straightforward to show that the supply of the public good is given by

$$g^i = \alpha_0 + \alpha_1 w^i + \alpha_2 P^i + \alpha_3 S^i + \alpha_4 g^g + \gamma Z^i + u^i. \tag{10.6}$$

An estimate of the coefficient α_3 can inform us about the strength of the private spillover effect. If agents obtain utility from the total amount privately contributed, then $S^i = G^{-i}$ as in the pure version of the subscriptions model, where G^{-i} is the partial sum of private contributions. In addition, α_4 informs us of the impact of government activity. And, finally, a test of the hypothesis $\alpha_3 = \alpha_4$ tells us something about the relative spillover effects. In order to test these hypotheses we require data on g^i, w^i, P^i, S^i, g^g, and Z^i with enough variation across agents to allow us to estimate the coefficients with precision.

Roberts (1984) heuristically argued that private efforts to provide certain public goods such as poverty relief have been crowded out by government programs since the 1930s in the United States and he provided some casual evidence in support of this assertion. If true, this would provide some support for the subscriptions model. There are several problems with this assertion, however. First, a variety of other factors were changing during this era, e.g., prices, income, demographic variables, and other government policies, that may have had an influence on this shift. Second, there were also structural changes occurring in the economy that could have affected private donations. For example, if potential donors believe that the federal government will step in and boost the economy to lower the unemployment rate, as it guaranteed to do with the passage of the Full Employment Act in the late 1940s, they may feel they do not have to donate to private charities to help alleviate poverty. Third, the goods provided by the government may not be perfect substitutes for the goods provided by the private sector.

Unfortunately, data availability makes it difficult to do hypothesis testing. Tax data typically lists the total amount contributed to charity, but not its allocation across charities. This makes it impossible to tell which government programs compete with charities receiving donations from an individual donor. It also makes it impossible to tell if two private donors are donating to the same charity. Survey data sometimes lists the amounts given to different types of charity, e.g., religious versus educational, but does not provide any information on amounts given to specific charities. Another major problem is that government programs may not be perfect substitutes for private donations. Finding less than perfect crowding out can easily be due to making the wrong comparison between goods that are not perfect substitutes. For example, it is not immediately obvious that a privately operated soup kitchen for the homeless is the same as a food stamp program run by the government, yet both involve giving food to the needy. Despite these difficulties, a number of researchers have made valiant attempts to uncover the externality effect and test the crowding out hypothesis with a limited amount of success.[4]

Schwartz (1970) first included a variable, non-donor income, to capture a possible spillover effect in his charity equation. The estimated coefficient was significant and negative in sign; the higher non-donor's income, the smaller the donation to charity. This suggests that donors take into account the economic circumstances of the recipient. Hochman and Rodgers (1973) included a measure of income dispersion in their equation for thirty-two SMSA's, although they omitted the price variable. The greater the amount of income inequality, the more likely it is that people will donate to charities that help the poor. Their estimate of the coefficient for the inequality variable was positive and significant suggesting that greater income inequality leads to greater donations. Both of these early results support a model where donors are linked to recipients through their utility function, although they do not support the one-for-one crowding out result.

Feldstein and Clotfelter (1976) recognized that there may be a spillover effect in their study on charitable contributions and included a variable designed to capture such an effect. They argued that donors may mimic the behavior of those who are at least as well off as they are and used income class to measure this. They calculated a weighted average of income in a donor's income class and higher income classes according to the following function,

$$S^i = \Sigma_j W^{ij} \ln(Eg^j)/\Sigma_j W^{ij},$$

with $W^{ij} = (Ew^i/Ew^j)^\lambda$, where W^{ij} is a weight, λ is an integer ranging from 0 to 15, Ez is the mean of the variable z, and where the sum is for $j \geq i$. The sum of squares increased with λ when they estimated the charity equation until $\lambda = 10$ where it stabilized. The estimate of the coefficient for S^i was 0.22, but was not significantly different from zero; the spillover effect was unimportant for their tax data.

However, there are several problems with their method. For such a large value of λ, W^{ij} is very small in magnitude. They used seven income classes ranging from \$0 to \$100,000. Consider the weight applied to the richest class's income (\$100,000) relative to the next to the poorest class (\$5,000), $W^{ij} = (5,000/100,000)^{10} = 9.76 \times 10^{-14}$, which is approximately zero. Even for the second highest income class (\$50,000) compared to the highest class, $W^{ij} = (50,000/100,000)^{10} = 0.00097$, which is again almost zero. Thus, $S^i \approx \ln(Eg^i)$. It may be the case that there is not enough variation in charitable donations across income classes to allow precise estimation of the coefficient for the spillover variable under this method. In addition, they were not really testing the main spillover effect of the subscriptions model where $S^i = G^{-i}$. They also did not include a measure of government expenditures that might compete with private donations. Their estimated coefficients may suffer from omitted variable bias as a result.[5] Finally, an individual may mimic the behavior of an individual of a higher income class but not the entire class. In that case, the method of calculating the spillover variable is biased against the interlinked utility hypothesis.

Andreoni and Scholtz (1998) extended Feldstein and Clotfelter's idea of how agents might be linked and estimated a charity equation of the form,

$$C = X\beta + \phi WC + u,$$

where C is the log of charitable contributions, X is a vector of variables like income, tax price, and personal characteristics, and W is a weighting matrix that combines donors into 'reference groups.' The weights in W are chosen to link an individual to his reference group. The parameter ϕ indicates the influence of the individual's reference group on his charitable contribution. A value of $\phi = 1$ would indicate strong support for utility interdependence. They considered various ways of choosing reference groups. For example, one could combine individuals on the basis of their age and education. When combining donors in this manner, they found mild evidence of crowding in. When agents in the reference group increased their donations by 10%, the individual donor increased his donation by about 2%. This is evidence against the subscriptions model. However, they did not include a variable to capture government spillovers and it is not clear how one should go about combining agents into a reference group.

From Table 10.3 one can easily see that there is not a single study that supports perfect crowding out. There are several studies that do not find any crowding out whatsoever, e.g., Reece (1979) and Posnett and Sandler (1989), some that find partial crowding out, e.g., Abrams and Schmitz (1978, 1984), and several have even found a minor amount of 'crowding in,' e.g., Schiff and Weisbrod (1991), Khanna, Posnett, and Sandler (1995), and Andreoni and Scholtz (1998). Unfortunately, many of the studies done on this issue can be easily criticized. In some studies the government's spillover effect is omitted, while in others the private donor spillover effect is left out. The assumption that the different private charities are perfect substitutes is questionable, especially when the data is aggregated across all charities. And the assumption that the government's expenditures are a perfect substitute for private efforts is problematic. One can come close in testing the hypothesis using appropriate data as Schiff (1985) does, for example, by comparing private donations to social welfare charities with local government spending on welfare. His estimate of crowding out was -$0.66, which was significantly less than one in magnitude but at the high end of the estimates as well. However, evidence against perfect crowding out may actually be evidence against the perfect substitutes part of the hypothesis, or some other part of the hypothesis, rather than evidence against the subscriptions model per se.

In order to adequately test for crowding out the contributions must be perfect substitutes, including the government. The best example of this is the paper by Kingma (1989), who studied donations to public radio. In the public radio market in the United States, individual stations do not compete with one another, make no effort to block or scramble their signal, and receive private and public donations. Thus, public radio is a pure public good and the dollar donations are perfect substitutes. Kingma estimated a linear equation using a cross section of survey data and included a measure of the tax price, income, government donations, the donations of other agents, and several demographic variables, e.g., education and age. The coefficients for the tax price and the contributions of other private donors were not measured precisely and thus not significantly different from zero. The income coefficient was positive and the coefficient for government donations was negative and significant. However, Kingma only found a

Table 10.3. Externalities and the Crowding Out Hypothesis

Study	Data	Dependent variable	Spillover variable	Spillover effect+
Feldstein & Clotfelter (1976)	FRS, 1963-'64, CS.	m.c	weighted sum of other's donations	*
Abrams & Schmitz (1978)	SOI, pooled TS CS, 1948-'72	m.c	government transfers	-$0.28
Reece (1979)	CEX, 1972 - '73, CS	m.c	public assistance	*
		m.c	recipient income	*
Abrams & Schmitz (1983)	SOI, CS, 1977	m.c	state poverty rate	0.23
		m.c	state welfare transfers	-$0.30
Schiff (1985)	NSP, 1974, CS.	m.c	state gov spending	$0.34
		m.c	local gov spending	-$0.66
		s.w.d	state gov cash transfers	-$0.058
		s.w.d	state welfare spending	$0.046
		s.w.d	monetary gifts by others	-18.19a
Menchik & Weisbrod (1987)	NSP, 1974, CS.	h.d	state + local gov spend	0.117
Posnett & Sandler (1989)	CAF - UK, 1987, CS	d.r.b.c	cent govt grants	*
		d.r.b.c	loc govt grants	*

Table 10.3. (cont.)

Kingma (1989)	Public Radio, 1983, CS	d.r.s	gifts by others	*
		d.r.s	gov spending	-$0.135
Schiff (1990)	NSP, 1974, CS.	h.d (aggregate)	state gov	*
		h.d (aggregate)	local gov	*
		h.d (social welfare)	gov cash transfers	4.75
		h.d (social welfare)	gov welfare spending	-4.96
Schiff & Weisbrod (1991)	US Tax file, 1973-'76, averaged into CS.	d.r.b.c	gov payments for services rendered by the charity	$0.06
Kingma & McClelland (1995)	Public Radio, 1983, CS	d.r.s	gov spending	-$0.15 to -$0.19
		d.r.s	donations by others	*
Khanna, Posnett, & Sandler (1995)	CAF - UK, 1983 - 1990, panel	d.r.b.c	govt grants	£0.094
Payne (1998)	US Tax file, 1982 - 1990, panel	d.r.b.c	govt grants	-$0.015 (OLS) -$0.53 (TSLS)
Andreoni & Scholtz (1998)	CEX, 1985, CS	donations	other private donations	0.02 to 0.03

Table 10.3. (cont.)

Duncan (1999)	NSP, 1974, CS	value of time and money gifts	gifts by others	*
			local gov welfare spend	-$0.26
Ribar & Wilhelm (2002)	International aid data, 1986-92, panel	donations	government support	$0.0 to $0.23

The spillover effects are listed as elasticities or in units of currency.
All coefficients listed are statistically significant, * - Not significantlly different from zero.*NSP* - Nationa Survey of Philanthropy, *CEX* - Consumer Expenditure Survey, *FCAS* - Florida Consumer Attitude Survey, *ISS* - Independent Sector Survey,
CAF - Charities Aid Foundation, *FRS* - Federal Reserve Survey,
SOI - Statistics of Income, IRS. *m.c* - monetary contributions,
s.w.d - social welfare donations, *d.r.b.c* - donations received by the charity,
d.r.s - donations to radio station, h.d - hours donated
a - This is a Tobit regression result; greater giving by others reduces one's own private social welfare donations.

small amount of crowding out by the government, about $0.125 per dollar of government spending on public radio. Second, he could not reject the hypothesis that the coefficients for the government variable and the donations of others were the same.

These results were reinforced by Kingma and McClelland (1995), who studied the same data, but used a censored regression analysis instead. They also included a measure of how much each person listened to public radio in their equation. They found the same amount of crowding out as in the earlier study, the coefficient for the contributions of others was not different from zero, and listening exerted a positive effect on donations.[6]

Payne (1998) studied a unique panel data set that matched up government grants to specific charities. She studied crime/disaster related charities, employment and youth activities organizations, charities that provide food or shelter, and those that provide human services. She also controlled for a variety of fixed effects to control for heterogeneity across charities, time, and state. Interestingly enough, the OLS results differed dramatically from the TSLS results. Under OLS there is virtually no crowding out. Under TSLS she found crowding out to be significant, about $0.53 per dollar of government grants, but not one-for-one. However, while she does include the poverty and unemployment rates in her model, a measure of the donations of other private individuals is not included, although this problem may be mitigated by her estimation procedure.

Duncan (1999) suggested the possibility that donated money and time might be perfect substitutes for one another so that the sum of the value of donated cash and time enters the utility function as a separate argument rather than the two types of donation entering separately. If they are perfect substitutes, then a donor may change her cash donations, her labor donations, or both, in response to a change in government policy. It follows that it is not necessarily the case that observing less than dollar-for-dollar crowding out in cash donations is evidence against the crowding out hypothesis, if Duncan's assumption about perfect substitutability is correct. It is only the response of total donations $c^i = g^i + w^i v^i$ that matter.

Duncan compared the impact of government spending on total donations with that on money donations and found that crowding out is over 50% greater when total donations are used in the calculation than when money donations are used alone (-$0.26 versus -$0.17). However, the crowding out effect is still significantly less than dollar-for-dollar, about $0.26 per dollar of local government spending. This suggests that there possibly is a warm glow motive operating, although it need not require the agent to receive utility from donated time and donated money separately. Instead the warm glow may take a form that maintains perfect substitutability, $u^i(x^i, C, c^i)$. Although, local government spending may not be a close substitute for private charity and this may bias the results. Duncan also omitted the net wage. If labor supply is endogenous, it should be included.

Ribar and Wilhelm (2002) also found little evidence of any crowding out in their panel data of contributions to 125 international relief and development organizations for 1986 - 1992 from the U.S. They control for unobserved institution-specific factors, year-to-year changes in recipient need, changes in the leadership of the organizations receiving aid, and crowding out across different organizations that provide goods which could be considered substitutes for one another. And since there are few direct benefits to American donors from such goods, they argue their tests are testing for pure altruism versus a warm glow motive. They find little or no evidence of any crowding out and conclude that a "joy-of-giving" or warm glow motive is driving their results.

It seems reasonable to conclude that there is no econometric evidence for perfect crowding out. While there are several studies that do not find any evidence of crowding out at all, and a few that find crowding in, it is most likely the case that some crowding out does occur but is small in magnitude. This would suggest that neither of the polar cases, the subscriptions model and the warm glow model, characterize the data in general. Some hybrid model is more appropriate. However, many of the studies attempting to test these hypotheses implicitly assume donations are perfect substitutes for one another across charities and for government expenditures on similar types of goods. Rejection of the crowding out hypothesis may be due to these other factors.[7]

10.4 Conclusion

In this chapter we surveyed the empirical literature on volunteer labor, donations of time and money, charitable bequests, and the crowding out hypothesis. First, it would appear that volunteer labor responds negatively to the wage rate, positively to income, negatively to the tax price of cash contributions, and positively to several personal characteristics. The fact that there appears to be a negative correlation between the tax price of cash contributions and volunteer labor suggests the two are gross complements. If true, a policy that alters the tax price of cash donations will also have an impact on volunteer labor.

Studies on charitable bequests indicate that the wealth elasticity is less than one in magnitude, with a few exceptions. The estate tax price elasticity is negative and tends to be greater than one in magnitude. This suggests that a change in tax policy will produce a larger change in such bequests. For example, there have been several proposals to eliminate the so-called "death tax" put forth in the U.S. Congress in recent years. If this were to pass, it would lead to a significant increase in the 'tax price,' and we would expect a large reduction in charitable bequests to occur. Since there is some mild evidence that donations to charity are substitutable over time, this might also change the timing of donations as well.

There is virtually no evidence that supports the subscriptions model, or perfect crowding out.[8] Most studies of the "crowding out" hypothesis either find no crowding out, or a small amount. In particular, Kingma (1989) and Kingma and McClelland (1995), focused on a good where contributions are perfect substitutes, e.g. public radio, and found only a limited amount of crowding out, from $0.12 to $0.19 per dollar of government expenditures on public radio. We believe that it is safe to conclude that perfect crowding out does not occur. It follows from this that the government can increase the amount of a public good available by taxing donors and spending the proceeds on the good in question.

[1] The responses are given by $dg/dA = \{[(1-s)U_{xx} - U_{gx}]H_{vv} + [U_{vx} - w(1-\tau)U_{xx}]H_{gv}\}/\Delta$ and $dv/dA = -\{[(1-s)U_{xx} - U_{gx}]H_{vg} + [U_{vx} - w(1-\tau)U_{xx}]H_{gg}\}/\Delta$, where we have dropped the superscript i for convenience and where $\Delta > 0$.

[2] See Clotfelter (1985) chapter 4 for a summary of this early literature.

[3] There is some evidence that volunteer firefighters are not perfect substitutes for paid firefighters. However, the evidence on whether volunteer labor is generally a perfect substitute for hired labor is an open question. See the references in Duncan. It is not immediately obvious to us that recruiting, training, and managing volunteers is the same as for paid workers.

[4] See Steinberg (1991) for a survey of the literature of the 1980s on the crowding out hypothesis. None of the studies in his survey found perfect crowding out, some found no crowding out at all, and a few found a small amount of crowding in. Unfortunately, Steinberg does not state which studies included the contributions of others as a variable along with the government variables.

[5] Feldstein and Clotfelter also tried $S^i = \ln(Eg^i/Ew^i)$ without success.

[6] Smith, Kehoe, and Cremer (1995) argued that giving to charity is a two-step decision. First, the agent makes a decision to give and then decides how much to give. They studied cross section data on donations to a rural hospital during a fund drive and uncovered some evidence that the two decisions are distinct using a Heckman two-step estimation procedure. They found that the decision to give is positively correlated to whether the individual had given to a national charity in the past and age, but was unrelated to income. The conditional decision of how much to give was positively related to income, whether the person was self employed, employed in agriculture, or owned their own business, and visits to the hospital.

[7] Andreoni (1993) provided experimental evidence against the crowding out hypothesis. In a carefully controlled laboratory experiment, he found crowding out to be about $0.71 per $1. This is higher than empirical estimates possibly because extraneous factors, e.g., social pressure, can be filtered out of an experimental environment, but cannot when doing econometric analysis.

[8] It also did not receive support in explaining military alliances. See Murdoch and Sandler (1984), and Sandler and Murdoch (1990).

11 Experimental Evidence on the Free Rider Problem

In this chapter we will discuss some of the key results of the laboratory experiments on public goods. Experiments allow the researcher to set up a carefully controlled environment and study specific behavior. In the classic linear public goods experiment, for example, subjects are given some tokens and can invest in a private good, or a public good. Typically, the experiment is designed so that the individual subject has an inventive to invest all her tokens privately, while the social optimum is to invest all the tokens publicly. The expectation is that the tokens will be invested privately under the free rider hypothesis. In more recent work an interior solution is predicted under the Nash equilibrium concept.

In the early work of Bohm (1972), and later Marwell and Ames (1979, 1980, 1981), and Schneider and Pommerehne (1981), subjects in experiments contributed a surprisingly large amount to the public good when the incentive was to free ride. This led to further work by Kim and Walker (1984), Isaac, McCue, and Plott (1985), and later, Isaac and Walker (1988a, 1988b) and Isaac, Walker, and Thomas (1984), among others, who studied repeated games where it was noticed that contributions begin at a high level in the early trials but then taper off as the experiment progresses. However contributions were still positive in the last period of the experiment when the incentive was to free ride. This led to further work on group size, learning, communication, altruism, framing, and noise in the data, among other aspects of the results.

In the next section we briefly discuss the nature of experimental design. For more detail, the interested reader is urged to consult a good book on the subject, such as Davis and Holt (1993), the paper by Smith (1982), or the survey by Ledyard (1995). We discuss the early results in section 11.2. In section 11.3 we present the response to the early results by Kim and Walker (1984) and Isaac, McCue, and Plott (1985) using repeated experiments. We study the effects of payoffs, group size, communication, and learning in section 11.4, altruism, the warm glow motive, and noise in section 11.5, framing in 11.6, and determining the WTP in 11.7. Section 11.8 concludes the chapter.

11.1 How Are Experiments Designed?

Following Smith (1982), a microeconomic system consists of an environment and an institution. The environment is made up of a set of agents, a set of commodities, and a set of characteristics, e.g., endowment, technology, utility function, for each agent. The institution is a language, composed of messages, e.g., a stated willingness-to-pay (WTP) for a public good, allocation rules that state each agent's final allocation of goods, and adjustment rules, which explain how the sequence of messages evolve. Individuals transmit messages that are translated into an allocation by the institution. The message function relates the environment and the institution confronting the individual to her message. By adjusting the environment or the institution, the experimenter can map out the response in the agent's message. The final outcome is a composite mapping from the environment to the messages to the final goods. The set of agents, the set of commodities, the endowments, the messages transmitted, and the outcome in terms of the resulting allocation, can be observed. We cannot observe preferences, the technology, or the message functions. The performance of the system is usually judged according to the Pareto criterion.

Smith lists several properties that are critically important for an experiment. First, non-satiation must hold. Second, subjects must have a right to a payoff that is increasing in the goods defined by the institution of the experiment. Third, the payoff must dominate any costs associated with the decision making of the subjects. Finally, information should be private. If these conditions are fulfilled, the experiment is well defined and the experimenter has control of the experiment.

Operationally, a game may be played just once, the one-shot game, or it may be repeated, and, if repeated, there may be a fixed number of trials and subjects may be told this, or the end of the game may be random.[1] Typically, small groups are studied in order to keep the cost of the experiment down. In some experiments subjects have been deceived, by being told they were part of a larger group when in fact they weren't, e.g., Marwell and Ames. Monetary payoffs have typically been used, although, some researchers have used "extra credit" points in class as a means of payment. This allows for larger groups to be studied while the cost of the study is kept within reason. Whether extra credit points and monetary payments are equivalent is not known.

The payoffs are induced by the experimenter in order to control the experiment. They may be listed in a table, or may be described in the instructions if they are simple enough. For example, in the classic linear public goods game subjects are endowed with a fixed number of tokens and a token can be invested in a private good and earn $.05, or may be invested in a public good and earn everyone in the group $.02 each. This provides the individual with an incentive to free ride and is simple enough to explain to the subjects.

The information that subjects have can be carefully controlled as well. In a repeated game subjects may be given complete information about the previous period, or they may only be told part of what happened. For example, in the repeated linear public goods game subjects may be told in trial t their own contribution to the public good in the previous trial, g^h_{t-1}, and the group total, G_{t-1}. Alternatively, they might be given more information such as the contributions of each subject in the previous period, $\{g^1_{t-1}, .., g^n_{t-1}\}$. Clearly, this may influence a subject's optimal strategy.

The payoff must then be translated into utility and this can be problematic since it is unobserved. It is possible that the individual's unobservable utility function may include extraneous influences that may jeopardize control of the experiment. This is especially so in public goods games. If subjects care about fairness, feel a warm glow from cooperating, want to give the "right" answer, or have altruistic feelings, this can affect their behavior and make it difficult to disentangle the various influences at work.[2]

There are several other caveats. Most experiments use college students as subjects. This is a very distinct group and may not represent the population. Second, the experiment is artificial. The subjects know that the results of the experiment will have no impact on them once it is over. Payment is made to provide subjects with incentive to take the experiment seriously, however, it is not known whether this is effective. Third, deception may be a problem. In some areas, e.g., psychology, experiments are sometimes designed to trick subjects. If the students come to understand this is true of some experiments, they may infer it is true of all experiments and this may affect their behavior in ways that are unknown. For example, they may try to give answers they think the researcher wants to hear. Finally, subjects may view the payoffs received in an experiment as transitory income rather than as permanent income and this may influence their behavior as well.

The linear public goods experiment has generated considerable research.[3] Suppose there is one private good and one public good, there are n subjects, and let w^h be h's endowment of tokens, and g^h be h's contribution to the public good. The payoff to contributing to the private good is typically constant across subjects, $r^h = r > 0$. If the public good is a pure public good, then $G = \Sigma g^h$ and the payoff is $\rho \Sigma g^i$, for $\rho > 0$. If it is an impure public good, then $G = \Sigma g^i/n$ and the payoff is $\rho \Sigma g^i/n$, i.e., the impure public good is subject to crowding. In the simplest case the parameters r, ρ, and n are chosen so there is a private incentive to contribute to the private good but a social incentive to contribute to the public good. Thus, free riding is a dominant strategy in a one-shot game or in the last known period of a repeated game. For example, suppose $r = .01$, $\rho = .005$, $w^h = 10$, and $n = 4$. If a subject invests all his tokens in the private good he gets a return of $0.10, but only $0.05 if he invests all his tokens in the public good. However, if each subject invests all his tokens in the public good, each subject receives a return of $0.20.

11.2 Early Studies of the Free Rider Hypothesis

Brubaker (1975) distinguished between the strong free rider hypothesis, where subjects free ride completely, and the weak free rider hypothesis, where contributions are positive but suboptimal. In addition to this, Olson (1965) speculated that small groups would find it easier to provide a public good than large groups since it would be more easily known who was free riding in a small group.

The early experimental evidence cast doubt on the extensiveness of the free rider problem. Bohm (1972) designed a survey to elicit the WTP to watch a new television show discussed in chapter five. The subjects in the study were randomly chosen from the population of Stockholm and were placed into groups that were given different incentives. One group was told their cost would be tied to their stated WTP, giving them the incentive to free ride, while another group was told their cost was constant, giving them an incentive to overstate their preference, and so on. Bohm's main result was that the average stated WTP across groups did not differ significantly, leading him to conclude the evidence did not support the free rider hypothesis.

There are several problems with this study, however. The description of the good to be provided was vague and subjects may have been confused about it. Counter-strategic statements were made to the subjects about the nature of free riding that may have contaminated the results. Preferences were not known, nor were they induced by the researchers setting up the experiment. It follows that the researchers could not know what the optimal level of the public good was. Individuals may have been over, or under-providing the good, yet, that cannot be known from the available data. Finally, payments were small in magnitude and might not have been large enough to provide the appropriate incentive.

Smith (1979, 1980) studied several different mechanisms under laboratory conditions. Under his auction mechanism, for example, subjects communicated through computer terminals and were given induced preferences for the public good and a single private good, and groups of n = 3, 6, and 9 were studied. In one experiment an iterative auction-like process was used whereby each subject proposes a contribution to the public good and a level of the public good to PLATO, an interactive computer simulation program. PLATO then calculates the sum of the contributions and the average level of the public good proposed and relays that information back to the subjects. If the sum of the bids is equal to the marginal cost of the public good, agent h's share of the cost is set equal to his bid, for all h. A vote is then taken, yes or no. If all vote yes, the process ends. If some vote no, the cost shares are adjusted, and the program iterates. If the sum of bids is greater than the cost, a rebate rule is used and the program iterates until either agreement is reached, or the terminal time is reached. If the sum of the bids is less than the cost, then cost shares are transmitted back to the subjects who then propose another bid and level of the public good, and the process continues. The mechanism terminates if unanimous agreement occurs, or if the terminal time arrives.

Smith's main results were that all the groups provided significantly positive levels of the public good and the mean quantities were close to the Lindahl level. These results were invariant to group size. Complete free riders and those who bid their entire endowment were represented equally in the population. Thus, many of the subjects in the experiments followed the incentives presented to them. However, the small sample size used in the study might give one pause; subjects might behave more altruistically in small rather than large groups and thus be more willing to contribute to the public good. Second, the Lindahl level of the public good was five or six units. This discreteness might cause an individual to feel compelled to contribute so as to meet the threshold. Finally, it is not clear whether the government's budget balances out of equilibrium.[4]

In a series of experiments, Marwell and Ames (1979, 1980, 1981) presented significant evidence against the strong form of the free rider hypothesis. In a typical experiment, high school students were contacted by telephone and mail. Some of the subjects were told they were part of a group of four students to create the impression of being in a small group, while others were told they were in a large group of eighty. Subjects never interacted with one another. Each subject was given an endowment of tokens that could either be spent on an "individual exchange" and earn a fixed return, or could be spent on a "group exchange" and earn a return based on the group's contribution. The payoffs were listed in a sheet given to each subject. Subjects as individuals were better off investing in the individual exchange but better off as a group investing in the group exchange. The return on the group exchange contained a "provision point," or discontinuity, in the first experiment, where the return increases dramatically at the provision point. Payment was based on the investments actually made by the individual and his or her group. In some trials one individual received an endowment greater than the provision point and all subjects in the group knew this. Everyone was given complete information about the payoffs, endowments, and the size of their group.

Their main finding was that subjects invested anywhere from 40% to 60% of their tokens on the group exchange in a one-shot game. Second, two thirds of the subjects invested more than half their tokens in the group exchange, 22% invested all their tokens in the group exchange, while only 13% were complete free riders. None of the groups invested the optimal amount. In addition, each subject was asked about the importance of fairness in contributing to the group exchange in a follow-up survey. The correlation between those stating they were concerned with fairness and their contributions was 0.42. They also found less free riding in small groups. In a follow up study, Marwell and Ames (1980) found that their main result was not sensitive to the provision point. Finally, the only group that differed was a sample of first year graduate students in economics who only invested 20% of their tokens in the group exchange. Hence, the title of their provocative article, "Economists Free Ride: Does Anyone Else?"

This work can be criticized on a number of grounds. The provision point and the discreteness induced by the payoffs is not part of the theory. It is an artifact of their set-up. This may inadvertently serve as a focal point and thus explain why contributions were so high. For example, if subjects are confronted with a payment schedule where amounts are listed in thousand dollar increments, e.g., 0 - $49, $50 - $99, $100 - $149, and so on, the numbers $50, $100, and so on, may focus an individual's attention as a goal to achieve, as opposed to being confronted with a continuous payment schedule.

Finally, Schneider and Pommerehne (1981) set up an experiment with three stages. Subjects were told that a publisher was going to come out with a new book written by their professor that would help them study for their exams. In the first stage students were asked to write down their WTP for an advance copy of the book and compete in an auction for the book. The bids were collected and the two top bidders were told they had won and were then excluded from the rest of the experiment. In the second stage students were informed that the author wanted more students to receive the book and had suggested that the publisher send copies to each student if the sum of the bids reached a certain threshold. The subjects then wrote down new bids and it was announced that the threshold had not been reached. Finally, in the third stage, students were told that the professor had anticipated that the threshold might not be reached and had contacted a large donor who would make up the difference if the sum of the bids fell short of the threshold and new bids were then collected. Clearly, students had a strong incentive to free ride in the last stage. Schneider and Pommerehne found that the average WTP for the book in the three rounds, respectively, was SFr 27.62, SFr 26.57, and SFr 16.86. They interpreted the first number as the true WTP for the book. If true, then the subjects were willing to contribute about 96% of their true WTP in the second round and about 61% in the third stage when the incentive was to contribute nothing.

However, tastes and budgets were not known, nor were they controlled for so it is unknown what influence they played in the result. Second, is the first bid really the true WTP for the book? How can we know? Third, did the information that was given in the second stage, namely that they had failed to reach the threshold, inform the subjects about their fellow subjects that would taint the results of the third stage? For example, did failure to meet the threshold in the second stage cause some students to bid more in the third stage than they otherwise would have? Why didn't subjects free ride completely in the third stage? Did they truly believe a large donor would make up the difference? If there was some uncertainty about that, they might have felt compelled to contribute more as a result of the uncertainty.

11.3 An Early Response to the Early Results

Kim and Walker (1984) and Isaac, McCue, and Plott (1985) designed repeated linear public good games to see if subjects might learn to free ride over time. The idea is that naive subjects may begin by cooperating in the early trials, but then gradually learn what their true incentives are and begin free riding. By focusing on one-shot experiments, the early results may have captured the naive behavior of the subjects before learning could take place.

Kim and Walker noted that there are a number of problems that must be confronted when designing an experiment. One must first be explicit about the theory to be tested and carefully derive its predictions. This will aid in designing the experiment that generates data appropriate to the theory. In the classic model, utility is a continuous function of a private good and a pure public good, agents maximize utility subject to their endowments, and the private good and the public good vary continuously. The optimal behavior is to free ride completely by not contributing at all. If one designs an experiment where the public good is discrete, or where it is an impure public good, then this does not constitute a test of the theory just mentioned. Therefore, finding evidence of a lack of free rider behavior from the experiment does not necessarily invalidate the theory.

After listing and discussing nine "invalidating factors" from which earlier studies suffered, Kim and Walker designed an experiment that dealt with as many of them as possible.[5] Subjects were told the experiment would last for about four weeks and would be played every day, but were not told when the experiment would end. Each subject was given the same table of payoffs and was told everyone received the same table. They were also told there were 100 people participating, although there were actually only five participating in the experiment. Each subject chose an amount to pledge to the common fund and called a telephone number leaving that amount on a message machine. Each subject's gross earnings were then determined according to the common schedule later that day, net earnings were determined by subtracting the pledge from gross earnings, and the resulting net payoff was delivered anonymously the same day.

A subject could invest up to $7 in the group exchange each day. The common preferences were defined under Schedule 1 as: $v^h(G) = .02G$ for $G \leq \$700$, where G is the sum of the contributions, and $v^h(G) = 13 + 0.005G$ for $G > \$700$. Schedules 2 and 3 increased the payoffs slightly. To simulate large group size each subject was 'cloned' twenty times and a random term was added to the payoff to disguise this replication. The optimal group investment was $700, i.e., $7 per subject. The cost of a unit of the group exchange was $1 while the marginal valuation $dv^h/dG = v^h_G$ under Schedule 1 was only 0.02 per subject. Thus, free riding was optimal. So, preferences were induced, the strong free rider hypothesis should hold, the group was large, there was an opportunity for subjects to learn from the previous outcomes, payments were made every day so the problem of a transitory endowment was minimized, there was no direct contact among the subjects and between the subjects and the experimenters, and the payments could potentially sum to $35 per week, which could be considered a substantial amount for the early 1980s.

Kim and Walker found strong evidence of free riding. Two of the subjects chose to free ride on all eleven trials. The other subjects typically chose small pledges that tended to decline over the trials. Although there were a couple of anomalies, Kim and Walker stressed the prevalence of free riding behavior in the discussion of their results. However, the incentive to free ride was so stark in their experiment that one could usefully ask why all of their subjects didn't free ride from the start of the experiment. Was learning of the free rider phenomenon occurring? Were they simply learning how to solve a decision problem they had never been confronted with before? Or were they trying to learn something about the other subjects in the game?

Isaac, McCue, and Plott (1985) also set up an experiment with repeated trials and obtained some evidence supporting the free rider phenomenon. They ran nine different experiments, eight with economics undergraduate students and one with sociology undergraduates, most with ten subjects. Subjects were guaranteed $5.00, valuations were induced, and a subject's payoff was determined by the return to the public good plus the return to the private good minus the contribution to the public good. Some subjects were given a high payoff and the rest a low payoff and payoff charts were private information. The marginal cost of the public good was $1.30 and the optimal amount was between 23 and 24 units. At $G = 24$, the Lindahl tax for high payoff individuals was $4.22 and for low payoff individuals it was $2.02. Subjects wrote their bids on a piece of paper that was collected by the experimenter. After the calculations were made, the level of the public good was announced at the end of the period and each subject calculated his or her payoff privately. The last period of the experiment was not known.

The level of the public good on the first trial was typically less than half the Lindahl level and in some experiments less than five units. After five trials the level of the public good was close to zero in most of the experiments. In addition, those with a high payoff tended to contribute more than those with a low payoff. There were two interventions by the experimenter. Lindahl prices were announced after several trials had been run and in other cases some communication was allowed after several trials.[6] In each case where the Lindahl prices were announced contributions increased just after the announcement but the level of the public good was still significantly below the Lindahl level in each case, and declined dramatically afterwards. Each time communication was allowed, contributions increased but were still well below the Lindahl level. In each case, less than three units of the public good were provided. In the one experiment where no intervention took place, more than six units were still being provided when the experiment terminated after nine trials.

Isaac, Walker, and Thomas (1984) studied the effects of group size, repetition, the marginal benefit of the group exchange, and experience on the amount contributed to the group exchange. They used the PLATO computer program to minimize subject-experimenter interaction. Subjects were given an endowment of tokens and told they could invest in an individual exchange that yielded a fixed return ($0.01) or a group exchange where everyone in the group would receive the same payoff from any given investment. In addition, subjects were told their own endowment and the total for their group of n = 4 or n = 10, everyone knew there would be ten trials, and everyone was told what their own private return was and what the group contribution was on the previous trial. Because of the nature of the payoffs, complete free riding is a dominant strategy.

They found that contributions were typically positive, but tended to decrease over the number of trials with only one exception. A significant proportion of subjects contributed even on the tenth trial, e.g., 17% to over 50% under certain conditions. Experienced players, individuals who had taken part in an earlier experiment, tended to contribute less but still gave a significant amount, e.g., 30% contributed on the tenth trial. And subjects tended to give more if their marginal valuation of the public good was higher.

While providing some evidence against the early results, new questions were raised. What explains the decay in contributions? Do some players initially make contributions to the public good in an attempt to signal other players, but after observing others free ride gradually begin to free ride themselves? Are some players simply figuring out how to play the game and start by making contributions but then realize that free riding is a better strategy?

11.4 Underlying Influences

11.4.1 Marginal Returns

Isaac and Walker (1988a) were interested in the impact of the marginal return to the public good on contribution behavior. They noted that if $\rho \Sigma g^h/n$ is the payoff to the public good, the marginal return will fall with larger group size. If ρ increases simultaneously so the marginal return is constant when n increases, then a pure numbers effect is isolated. They studied experiments with ten trials and four or ten subjects, the marginal return was held constant at either 0.3, or 0.75, and groups were homogeneous, i.e., everyone in the group had the same return. They found that contributions across the various groups start at a high level on the first trial and decay, but were still positive in the last trial for many of the subjects in the high return groups. Contributions for the low return groups were zero for most of the subjects in the last trial. Second, for groups of four subjects, they found that there was far more free riding in the low return group (.3) than in the high return group (.75) across all ten trials. A similar but much smaller effect was found for groups of ten. Third, subjects in high return groups contributed more tokens to the public good than subjects in low re-turn groups.

Fisher, Isaac, Schatzberg, and Walker (1995) studied heterogeneous groups that consisted of some high return and some low return subjects in repeated experiments similar to earlier work, in addition to homogeneous groups. They found that low return subjects consistently contributed less than high return subjects. The mixed groups contributed at roughly the same intermediate level as homogeneous baseline groups on average. And there was no statistically significant evidence that high and low return sub-jects in mixed groups moved closer to one another suggesting that being in a mixed group does not affect one's own contribution behavior.

11.4.2 Group Size Effects

Isaac and Walker (1988a) found only very weak group effects. For the high MPCR groups in their study there was no discernable effect of group size whatsoever in comparing groups of four and ten subjects. However, in groups with an MPCR of .3 they found more free riding behavior in smaller groups than in larger groups on all ten trials. They also found a crowding effect when the MPCR was allowed to fall as the group size in-creased; there was more free riding in larger groups when the MPCR was lower.

In a follow up study, Isaac, Walker, and Williams (1994) extended the work to larger groups of 40 and 100. The main difference was that they paid subjects (college students) in extra credit points rather than in money. First, they replicated their earlier results with groups of 4 and 10, which lends some confidence in their results with larger groups. In larger groups they found no discernable group size effect when the MPCR was .75. However, they found that there was less free riding in the larger groups than in groups of 4 and 10, the opposite of what was expected. There was also less decay over the trials as well. They also noticed that some subjects made a large contribution in one period followed by a small one followed by another large contribution, and Isaac at. al. speculated that these sub-jects may be trying to signal other subjects in the game. And contributions in the last period were still positive when they should have been zero.

11.4.3 Communication

Can communication improve matters? One might think that if agents can communicate with one another they will be able to achieve an equilibrium closer to the optimum. However, additional information may make the environment richer and thus increase the strategy space creating multiple equilibria.

Isaac and Walker (1988b) set up a linear public goods experiment to test the hypothesis that non-binding communication in an experiment lasting several trials will serve to increase contributions to a public good. There were four members in each group. An experiment consisted of two series of ten trials for each group and the length of the experiment was known. In one group there was no communication in either series of the experiment and this group exhibited the kind of behavior typical in such experiments; well over 50% of the optimal amount of tokens were invested in the group exchange in the first period and this decayed on average to about 10% by the tenth trial. In the second series subjects began by investing about 40% of the optimum in the group exchange and this fell to zero by the tenth trial.

A second group was allowed to communicate after each trial in the first series of the experiment but not in the second. They achieved a greater level of cooperation contributing 100% of the optimum on the first trial on average. This fluctuated for a few rounds but settled on 100% until the end of the series. On the second series they began at 100% and this began to decay after six trials to about 85% on average. The fact that there was no decay in the last period of the first run and only a small amount of decay in the last period of the second run was somewhat surprising since the last play of the game was known with certainty and complete free riding should have been observed. There were individual groups, however, who cooperated for all ten trials in both series and one group that almost contributed 100% of the optimum for all ten trials of both series.

A third group was not allowed to communicate in the first series but could after each trial in the second series. Their behavior mimicked the first group in the first run. However, in the second run their average contribution was about 60% of the optimum and it drifted upward to about 98% of the optimum. Thus, it would appear that communication among the subjects after each round improves efficiency and reduces the free rider problem. However, contributing in the last period is still anomalous.

11.4.4 Learning

In an innovative study, Andreoni (1988b) distinguished between subjects learning how to play the game and coming to understand the free rider problem versus subjects trying to use complicated strategies in playing the game. The 'learning hypothesis' is that some individuals may figure out the free rider incentive quickly, while others may take some time. So we should notice decay in contributions over the trials of the experiment. Under the 'strategies hypothesis' some subjects may be playing complicated strategies in order to signal the other players in the game about their intentions. Or, a player may play the free rider strategy initially to signal that he understands the free rider concept. However, any cooperation eventually gives way to free riding. In the last play of the game free riding clearly dominates since the last period is a simple one-shot game and so we should observe decay in contributions with complete free riding in the last period.

Andreoni split his sample into two groups. In the 'Strangers' group the subjects were randomly reassigned after every trial period, which eliminated their ability to use complicated strategies. The 'Partners' group played with the same group of anonymous subjects over the course of the entire experiment. Partners can attempt to use strategies since they will be matched up with the same group of people. This method serves to isolate learning in the Strangers group since Partners would be learning and possibly playing complicated strategies, while Strangers would only be learning. Contributions should decay in both groups and we should also observe higher contributions among the Partners if they are trying to use strategies that generate information about themselves that would entail contributing to the public good. We should also observe complete free riding in the last period of the game by both groups. The basic experiment was a repeated linear public goods game.[7]

The results were somewhat unexpected. Contributions to the public good were initially high and decayed over time for both groups. About half the tokens in both groups were invested in the public good in the first period, which decayed to 5.8% for Partners and 12.2% for Strangers. Second, contributions to the public good were positive in the last period of the game for 30% of the Partners and, surprisingly, 57.5% of the Strangers. And, paradoxically, Strangers uniformly contributed more than Partners in each period including the last period and the percent of Strangers contributing was greater. This would seem to reject the notion that there is pure learning taking place. If so, one would have to argue that the partners are learning faster, which is somewhat difficult to understand.[8]

Palfrey and Prisbrey's (1996) experimental data provided support for Andreoni's surprising result that Strangers contributed more than Partners. They attributed this to the possibility that the Partners are accumulating more information than the Strangers as the game progresses. In that case, the environment is less confusing for the Partners than for the Strangers. So they argued that it seems reasonable to expect that Strangers may take more time to learn than Partners, which is supported by their data and Andreoni's data.

On the other hand, this was refuted by the data collected by Weimann (1994) and Burlando and Hey (1997). Weimann found no difference between the Strangers and Partners. In only 4 of 30 cases was there a significant difference and in three of those cases Partners contributed more than Strangers. In their experimental data with UK subjects, Burlando and Hey found that Strangers contributed more than Partners, confirming Andreoni's result. However, the opposite was true of their Italian data. They also found evidence that the incidence of free riding behavior was greater for their sample of UK subjects, which may indicate a possible cultural influence at work.

In addition, Weimann (1994) also included two groups where an attempt was made to control the behavior of the other members of the group confronting an individual subject. The experimenter chose the contributions of N - 1 'phantom' subjects in each of the two groups. In one group a subject was made to believe that the other members, the 'phantom' members, were very cooperative. In the other group a subject was made to believe that the 'phantom' members of the group were uncooperative. Otherwise, the game was a repeated linear public goods game.[9] Weimann found that the contributions of the first group increased from about 62% of the endowment to 72.7% on average after the high contributions of the 'phantom' subjects was observed, but then decayed gradually to only 15.3%, despite the large contributions of the 'phantom' subjects. The second group began contributing 77.1% of the tokens and this fell rapidly once the subjects discovered they were in an uncooperative group to only about 18% by the fifth trial and 10.7% at the end.

This evidence is mixed and difficult to interpret. Not only is the strategy space possibly different between the two groups, so is the information set. Strangers have less information than Partners and this may make it harder for them to learn regardless of whether Partners are trying to play complicated strategies, or not. And just because Partners can play complicated strategies doesn't mean that such players recognize this as a possibility and act on it.

11.5 Altruism, Warm Glow, or Noise?

The linear public good experiment is typically set up so that free riding should be observed in a single-shot game, in the last play of a multi-period game, and in each period of a game where subjects are randomly reassigned after each play. However, there is mounting evidence that refutes these predictions. To explain this, some researchers have suggested there is altruism, a warm glow motivation, some other social norm operating like fairness, or there is simple confusion about the game that induces some to contribute by mistake.

All of the early public good experiments were set up with a solution on the boundary of the strategy space; subjects can only make a positive contribution, or free ride, but cannot choose a negative contribution. However, a solution on the boundary censors the sample of data and the observed lack of free riding behavior could be due to this censoring. If the solution of the game is in the interior of the strategy space, and mistakes are random, then subject confusion should average out to zero in large groups and we should notice decay as subjects become more experienced in playing the game. This would help eliminate mistakes from consideration.

Keser (1996) set up a simple repeated linear public goods game with twenty-five trials and a solution in the interior. The payoffs are given by

$$u^h = 41x^h - (x^h)^2 + 15\Sigma g^i.$$

The marginal payoffs to the private good and the public good are $41 - 2x^h$ and 15, respectively, and the Nash equilibrium occurs where $g^h = 7$ and $x^h = 13$ when the agent has twenty tokens. A subject who is purely individualistic can err by contributing more than seven tokens to the public good or less. If such mistakes are equally likely to occur, they should average out to zero with a sample of forty-eight subjects. Keser found that subjects contributed an average of 11.26 tokens to the public good in the first five trials and an average of 8.9 tokens in the last five trials. And the pattern of decay was very similar to earlier experiments. While this evidence does not distinguish among the various possibilities, e.g., altruism, warm glow, fairness, and so on, it does suggest that subjects have more complicated objectives than simply maximizing their own payoff.

11.5.1 Separating Kindness from Confusion

Andreoni (1995b) designed an experiment to separate out the possible "kindness" component, associated with altruism, warm glow, and a sense of fairness, from the "confusion" component associated with mistakes. He split his sample into several groups. The first group, labeled "Regular," played the game in the classic way. A second group, labeled "Rank," played the game in the same manner, however, a subject's actual monetary payment was determined by a ranking of experimental payoffs across the subjects in the group; the monetary payoff is higher the better the subject's ranking, and the subject's ranking is greater the larger her experimental payoff. This transforms the experiment into a "zero sum" game and provides the subject with a strong incentive to free ride in order to maximize their ranking. A third group served as a control, labeled "Regrank." They played the game in the classic manner and received their payoff in the usual way. However, they were also given information on their relative ranking after each round of play. Subjects were randomly reassigned after each play to eliminate any strategizing.

Subjects in the Rank group should only contribute to the public good by mistake since payment based on rank rather than on experimental results tends to eliminate altruism.[10] On the other hand, subjects in the Regrank group have the same information as those in the Rank group but receive a payment in the usual way. Thus, they might be observed making a contribution because of kindness or confusion. It follows that the difference in contributions between the two groups can inform us about the extent of kindness and how it behaves.

It is expected that the level of the public good will be highest in the Regular group and lowest in the Rank group. This was borne out by the results: only 20% of the Regular group were free riders and contributors in that group gave 56% of their endowment to the public good in trial #1, while 35% in the Rank group were free riders and contributors in that group gave about 33% of their endowment to the public good in trial #1. By the tenth trial, 45% of the Regular group were free riders and contributors gave 26.5% of their endowment to the public good, while 92.5% of the Rank group were free riding and contributors in that group only donated 5.4% of their endowment.

If kindness and confusion are the only two components when contributions to the public good are positive under the Regrank condition, and confusion is the only reason to observe positive contributions under the Rank condition, then the difference in contributions between the two groups is a measure of kindness. This difference fell from 13% of the endowment in trial #1 to 3.6% by trial #10. About 25% of the subjects were contributing out of kindness on the first trial. This increased to 45% by trial #5 but eventually fell to 27% on the last trial. This may explain why subjects contribute on the last play of the game. Confusion, as measured by the Rank condition, starts at 65% of the Rank group and falls to 7.5% by trial #10. This can explain the decay observed in many experiments.

However, as noted by Andreoni, paying subjects according to the ranking of their experimental earnings, rather than on the actual experimental earnings, may create more confusion. This might cause one to overestimate confusion and underestimate kindness. Another problem is that the type of "kindness" matters quite a bit, as noted in earlier chapters. If a warm glow motive exists, then the ranking method of payment need not eliminate all cooperation due to "kindness."[11]

Andreoni's results were confirmed by Houser and Kurzban (2002). In their repeated linear public goods experiment subjects were placed in one of two conditions. Under the "human" condition each subject played against three other subjects, while under the "computer" condition each subject played against three computers and they were told that the play of the computers was predetermined. All interaction took place via computer. Groups composed under the "human" condition contribute out of kindness and/or confusion. Groups composed under the "computer" condition should only contribute out of confusion since there is no point to behaving altruistically in such a group. They found that "computer" groups contributed about 29% of their tokens and "human" groups contributed about 53%. So about 45% of the latter's contributions could be attributed to confusion.

11.5.2 Altruism, Warm Glow, or Noise?

Saijo and Nakamura (1995) set up an experiment where the return to the public good (ρ) was greater than the return to the private good (r) and discovered that only about 70% of the tokens were invested publicly. This was somewhat surprising since subjects should have spent all of their tokens on the public good. Saijo and Nakamura speculated that subjects who chose not to contribute all their tokens were acting out of spite, which they defined as a case where an individual chooses not to take an action that makes himself better off because it makes someone else even better off. Alternatively, the subject may not take the action by mistake, in which case the error is that $g^h < w^h$ when $\rho > r^h$.

Palfrey and Prisbrey set up an environment where the private returns are chosen randomly and where $r^h > \rho$ for some subjects and $r^h < \rho$ for some subjects. This generates a richer data set that can be used to estimate individual decision functions using the micro data or aggregate decision functions using the aggregate data. More specifically, subjects were put into four person groups and participated in four series of ten trials. Each period r^h was chosen for each subject randomly from the set of integers $\{1, 2, ..., 20\}$ with a uniform distribution, ρ was chosen from the set $\{3, 6\}$ in the first study and $\{3, 6, 10, 15\}$ in a second study, and was fixed for the first two series, e.g., $\rho = 3$, and then changed to a new value for the second two series, e.g., $\rho = 6$. The private returns were private information while the public return was publicly known.

They used classification analysis and probit estimation to analyze the data. Consider the simple decision rule:

$$\text{Set } g^h = 0 \text{ if } r^h/\rho > 1 + A^h + \varepsilon^h, \text{ or set } g^h = w^h \text{ otherwise,}$$

where $A^h > 0$ is a measure of altruism (or spite if $A^h < 0$) and ε^h is a random variable. In this context, a classification analysis classifies an action as either an error or not. If a subject should have contributed a token to the public good but did not, or if he should not have contributed a token but did, then an error was made. If $w^h = 9$, then up to nine errors can be made on each trial. For example, if the subject should have contributed all his tokens to the public good ($r^h/\rho < 1$) but only contributed seven of nine, he made two 'errors.' The term $1 + A^h = c^h$ is called a 'cutpoint,' and this type of decision rule is known as a cutpoint rule. Given the data, the estimated cutpoint minimizes the errors made and at the estimated cutpoint c^* the error rate ε^* can be calculated. A cutpoint and an error rate can be estimated for the aggregate data or the micro data. A cutpoint greater than one indicates the possibility of altruism in this context. The same technique can be applied to warm glow giving where the decision rule is

$$\text{Set } g^h = 0 \text{ if } r^h - \rho > \gamma^h + \varepsilon^h, \text{ or set } g^h = w^h \text{ otherwise,}$$

where γ^h is a warm glow parameter and the cutpoint is γ^h. A positive estimate of the cutpoint indicates a warm glow motive in this context.

In Palfrey and Prisbrey (1996), where the focus was on altruism, the estimated cutpoint was $c^* = 1$ for the aggregate data under the altruism rule noted above, indicating that subjects were not altruistic or spiteful per se on average. In addition, under the Strangers-Partners methodology they found that $c^* = 1$ for both groups, but that the error rate was higher for the Strangers group. They argued this was because there is more 'noise' in one-time encounters (Strangers) than in ongoing ones (Partners). In addition, the error rate was negatively correlated with being in a 'Partners' group, experience, and the trial period. At the micro level they estimated the distribution of cutpoints and found that a cutpoint of $c^* = 1$ experienced the highest frequency by far, about 30%, the distribution was roughly symmetric, and that error rates were below 20% for about 85% of the subjects and below 10% for over 60% of the subjects. The error rate also decreased with experience. This coincides with a "noise" interpretation of the data. In their probit analysis, they found that subject error decreased with experience, being in a 'Partners' groups, and with the period of play. Palfrey and Prisbrey concluded that "subjects exhibit statistical fluctuations in their decision-making manifested as random noise in the data." (1996, p.425). When they censored their sample, by omitting cases where $r^h < \rho$, they were able to generate contribution data that was consistent with earlier studies. This strongly suggests that observed contributions in many previous studies were due partly to noise.

In their second paper they included a warm glow motive. When studying the warm glow motive they estimated a cutpoint of $c^* = 1$ using the classification analysis but estimated a slightly higher value using the probit regression model, clearly indicating a warm glow motive was present in the aggregate data. However, when the cutpoints of experienced subjects were compared to inexperienced subjects, the warm glow effect dropped by 40% with experience, strongly suggesting that random errors may account for a large amount of the contributions of inexperienced subjects. In their probit model they related the decision variable to a constant, $r^h - \rho$, and ρ to estimate the warm glow effect, the impact of the relative rate of return, and capture the impact of altruism, respectively. They found that the warm glow effect was positive, the altruism coefficient was statistically zero, and the interactive variables reduced the variance of the random error term for both the aggregate data and the micro data. However, putting $r^h - \rho$ and ρ as separate variables in the same regression equation may not delineate precisely the separate effects due to multicollinearity. It is still possible that altruism exists in their data.

Goeree, Holt, and Laury (2002) set up an experiment where an individual could invest privately and earn \$0.05, or could invest publicly. A token invested publicly yielded an "internal" return for the subject and an "external" return for the other subjects. The internal return plays the role of a warm glow for giving, while the external return captures altruism. Internal returns were varied from \$0.02 to \$0.04 and external returns were varied from \$0.02 to \$0.12 by the experimenters. Subjects were presented with a chart giving them ten scenarios where the returns to the public good and group size varied and subjects were asked to decide how much to invest in the public good under each scenario. They were also told they would be randomly matched up with other players in order to receive payment. In their model, utility is given by

$$U^h = \pi^h + A^h(N\text{-}1)\pi^k,$$

where

$$\pi^h = rx^h + \rho(N\text{-}1)g^k + \gamma g^h.$$

The first term captures the utility from the individual's own payoff (π^h), which includes the return from the private good (rx^h), the internal return

(γg^h), and the utility from the external return from everyone else's invest-ment ($\rho(N-1)g^k$), while the second term in the utility function, ($A^h(N-1)\pi^k$), captures the return to altruism. Goeree, et. al., chose (w, N, γ, r, ρ), and (N, ρ, γ) were allowed to vary across the ten different scenarios as part of their experimental design.

In casually studying the data from their experiment, they found that an increase in the internal return had the strongest effect on contributions to the public good. This suggests that the warm glow motive is important. Second, an increase in the external return tended to increase contributions to the public good. Finally, group size also increased contributions. This supports the contention that there is some altruism since contributions were sensitive to group size and the external return. Under a warm glow motive contributions are invariant to group size and the external return.

A standard logit probabilistic choice model was used to induce "noisy decision-making" in order to estimate the model and disentangle the altru-ism parameter from the error involved in making mistakes. In such a model, the probability of observing g^h is

$$\text{Prob}(g^h) = \exp(U^h/\mu)/\Sigma_{j=0,w}\exp(U^h/\mu),$$

where U^h is given above and g^h can take on integer values from 0 to 25. They easily rejected the Nash equilibrium prediction of no error making, i.e., $\mu = 0$. Second, they estimated the altruism parameter A = 0.1; on aver-age a subject in the sample is willing to give up \$0.10 in order for someone else to receive \$1.00. Third, they tested the warm glow hypothesis by es-timating two additional models, where utility is given by $U^h = \pi^h + \omega g^h$, and $U^h = \pi^h + A^h(N-1)\pi^k + \omega g^h$, a warm glow model and a hybrid model that includes altruism and a warm glow, respectively, where ω is the warm glow parameter to be estimated. As it turns out this parameter was insig-nificant in both models suggesting that a warm glow motive did not exist in their data. However, the internal return already captures a warm glow effect through γg^h so adding another term to capture the warm glow effect (ωg^h) might lead to an insignificant coefficient since it is already included.

11.5.3 Revealed Preference and Altruism

Andreoni and Miller (2002) used a dictator game, where two anonymous players share a surplus between themselves, to study the consistency of al-truistic behavior relative to the Axioms of Revealed Preference. The amount available to be shared and the price of sharing were varied. This made it possible for the researchers to confront subjects with different budget sets and allow the sets to overlap so that violations of the Revealed Preference theorem could be checked. There were π to divide between two subjects, $\$\pi = \$\pi^1 + p\$\pi^2$, where p is the price of sharing and where $\$\pi$ and p varied. For example, when p > 1, sharing is more expensive for subject #1.

They found that almost all of their subjects (98.3%) made choices that were consistent with maximizing a well-behaved quasi-concave utility function. In their data only 22.7% of the subjects were perfectly individualistic utility maximizers who did not exhibit any altruism at all. There was some heterogeneity in those who exhibited altruism. They found that about 6.2% of their subjects' behavior was exactly consistent with altruism as perfect substitutes, where subjects gave everything to their anonymous partner when the price of giving was less than one and kept everything when the price of giving was greater than one, and 13.2% were exactly consistent with altruism under equal division of $\$\pi$.

Andreoni and Miller then estimated utility functions that were consistent with the results for the three groups. For the rest of the subjects they used the data to estimate a CES utility function that fit the data the best. They then used the resulting estimates to forecast the outcome of several other studies involving dictator games, linear public goods games, and prisoner's dilemma games. Surprisingly, the model tended to forecast general results fairly well and thus provides a framework for understanding some of the results obtained in other studies. This suggests that in many of the linear public goods experiments a significant portion of the subjects may be exhibiting altruistic behavior.

11.6 Framing

All of the experiments on public goods frame the issue in a positive manner of contributing to a public good and thus causing a positive externality that benefits others. In contrast, in two other areas of the literature, negative externalities and common resource problems, the issue is framed in a negative manner of harm being done and the theory tends to hold up rather well. Plott (1983) set up an experiment of a market with buyers and sellers where a transaction by one subject would reduce the return to other subjects so the social cost was greater than the private cost. This was designed to mimic a negative externality. He found that the market functioned as the theory predicted; individuals ignored the harmful externality in making their trades and the Nash equilibrium was not Pareto efficient.

Walker, Gardner, and Ostrom (1990) set up an experiment involving a common resource. Subjects were confronted with two markets they could invest in, one of which generated a negative externality similar to a limited access common-pool resource. Theory predicts that self-interested individuals would deplete the resource more quickly than is socially optimal since they ignore the externality they cause, and this is exactly what they found. The common element in these two experiments is that the issue is framed in a negative fashion as causing harm, rather than in a positive way of helping someone.

Extending this idea, Andreoni (1995a) suggested that the subject's responses in a public goods experiment may be influenced by the way in which the problem of free riding is framed. A contribution to the public good also means there is less of the private good available, given the total amount of resources. It follows that an alternative way to frame the issue is to state that investing more in the private good will impose an external cost on the other participants since less of the public good will be produced. The responses from the subjects might differ due to the way the issue is framed, even though the opportunity cost of the two actions is the same regardless of the manner in which it is framed.

To test this framing effect, Andreoni split the subjects into two groups. One group received instructions that included a statement that investing in the group exchange produced a positive payoff of half a cent for every member of the group, as is typically done in the literature. The second group received instructions informing them that an investment in the private good reduced everyone else's payoff in the group by half a cent. Since the opportunity cost of the private good is the public good, and vice versa, the incentives are the same under the two scenarios and the response should be the same if framing doesn't matter. Finally, subjects were randomly reassigned after each of ten trials to eliminate strategies being used.

Andreoni found that the results under positive framing tracked those of the literature; on average over 20% of the tokens were invested in the group exchange by the tenth trial and only about 40% were free riding on the tenth trial. However, contributions to the public good under negative framing tracked the results one would expect from free riding; none of the tokens were invested in the group exchange by the tenth trial in one experiment and only 2.1% were invested in a second experiment. And in one experiment 100% of the subjects were free riding by the tenth trial. So it would appear that the outcome of the experiment may be determined by how the issue is framed. Indeed, Andreoni speculated that the whole issue of free riding behavior might never have been raised had the original experiments been framed in a negative fashion![12]

11.7 Eliciting the WTP Function

Brandts and Schram (2001) set up a linear public goods experiment where an entire "contribution function" was elicited from each subject for each trial of ten trials. Subjects were split into four person groups. Each subject could invest an endowment of nine tokens in a public account, where everyone in the group earned the same amount, or in a private account, where the return varied over ten different values. The return to the public account was fixed at 12 cents (Dutch) per token while the return to the private account increased from 3 cents per token to 57 cents per token, i.e., 3, 9, 15, 21, 27, 33, 39, 45, 51, 57. This gives ten different MRTS between the private and public accounts, 3/12, 9/12, 15/12, and so on. In each play of the game, each subject is given the list of ten MRTS and must choose how much to invest in the public account for each MRTS. This information is then transmitted to the monitor of the experiment. An MRTS is then chosen randomly and the sum of contributions to the public account Σg^h is calculated for that MRTS. In one set of trials all members of the group faced the same MRTS, while in another the subjects each faced their own MRTS. After the information is collected, the game is repeated.

Under this experiment it is a dominant strategy for the individual to invest all his tokens in the public good in scenarios #1 and #2 (because 12 > 3 and 12 > 9), and all of his tokens in the private account for scenarios #3 - #10 under the free rider hypothesis. However, if an individual is a pure altruist and cares equally for the payoff of the other members of the group, then when she invests a token in the public account she receives a return of 48 (4 x 12). Since this is larger than the payoff to the private account until scenario #8, she will invest in the public account for situations #1 - #8 and in the private account for situations #9 and #10. Thus, everyone has an incentive to invest in the public account for situations #1 and #2 and in the private account in situations #9 and #10. In the absence of mistakes, those who invest in the public account in situations #3 - #8 are possibly exhibiting some form of cooperative behavior, i.e., altruism, a warm glow, or a sense of fairness. The disaggregated data for each subject can be used to calculate the contribution function for each subject, or the data can be aggregated to study the "average" contribution function.

Brandts and Schram rejected the strong form of the free rider hypothesis. On average for the aggregate function 22% of the endowments were invested in the public account, decreasing from 29% on the first trial to 12% on the tenth trial. The average contribution function was decreasing in the MRTS. Contributions also decayed over the trials. About 40% of the subjects were free riders, while about 32% tended to cooperate. And quite a large number of individuals chose the correct dominant strategy, 85% for scenario #1, 83% for #2, 79% for #9, and 83% for #10. In a post experiment survey, subjects who contributed were more likely to contribute if they discovered they were in a group of contributors, rather than not. This suggests that a subject's behavior depends on the behavior of others and tends to refute the warm glow idea in favor of pure altruism or some other social norm.

11.8 Conclusion

The early work of Bohm and Marwell and Ames provided evidence against the free rider hypothesis. Subjects in these early experiments contributed a surprisingly large amount to the public good even though free riding is the best course of action.[13] Later researchers confirmed this result in multi-period experiments. Many of the subjects in such experiments typically contribute on the first trial of the experiment, contributions decay as the trials proceed, and many subjects still contribute on the last trial. This could be due to either kindness or confusion, and the kindness can take a number of different forms, e.g., altruism, a warm glow feeling, or a sense of social fairness. More recent work has tried to disentangle these various influences with some minor success.

Finally, an important framing effect has been discovered. Almost all public goods experiments have been framed in the positive manner of making a contribution that helps everyone in the group. This may have inadvertently biased the experiments toward subjects making positive contributions. If the issue is framed as investing more in the private good, or not, and thus making everyone else worse off, free riding becomes more prevalent, even though the tradeoff between the private and public good is the same as when the issue is framed positively.

This work is not without problems. Subjects know they are in an experiment and that when it is over it will have no impact on their lives. Whether this affects their responses in the experiment is not known. It might very well be the case, for example, that a subject in an anonymous experiment will exhibit altruism, but may not do so when confronted with decisions in the real world where it counts. In addition, it might be questioned whether investing in a theoretical "public good" in the lab is the same as contributing to a real public good where the individual might actually have to pay more in taxes, as we discovered in our discussion of CV analysis in chapter five.

[1] See Fudenberg and Tirole (1991) for an excellent introduction to game theory.

[2] Smith (1982) mentions an individual caring about winning the auction per se in addition to the utility of the item being auctioned. If true, this can affect the individual's bid, i.e., message.

[3] There are other experiments on public goods that are also of some interest. For example, Bagnoli and McKee (1991) studied a 'threshold' game where the public good is produced if the subjects contribute a certain total amount that meets the threshold. Contributions are refunded if the threshold is not met. They found that subjects in many of their trials were able to meet the threshold and thus provide the public good.

[4] Banks, Plott, and Porter (1988) provided further evidence on the auction mechanism versus the direct contribution mechanism. They found that the Smith process led to a level of contributions closer to the efficient level than the direct contributions process and that unanimity reduced efficiency. Given success, the Smith process delivered a level of the public good close to the efficient level. However, success occurred only 50% of the periods with unanimity and only 67% of the periods without unanimity. Overall the results were somewhat disappointing. Banks, Plott, and Porter concluded that a unanimous voting rule reduced the success rate but produced reasonably good efficiency results when the process was successful.
Chen and Plott (1996) implemented the Groves - Ledyard (1977) mechanism They found that a dramatic increase in the penalty parameter for deviating from the efficient level raises the average level of the public good, the efficient level is chosen more frequently, and the dispersion of the outcome about the efficient level is reduced. In fact, the penalty parameter was the single most important parameter for inducing individuals to choose their best responses. So it would appear that a mechanism can be designed to elicit a close approximation to the efficient level of the public good under laboratory conditions.

[5] The factors are: an impure public good is being studied rather than a pure public good; a discrete public good is being studied rather than a continuous one; the optimum is unknown; there is vagueness in the instructions leading to confusion, uncertainty and disequilibrium; there is insufficient economic motivation; the group is small rather than large; the income paid in the experiment is viewed as transitory income; and there is a lack of anonymity. They noted that all of the previous studies suffered from one or more of these problems.

[6] Subjects were told they could discuss the experiment but not their own payoffs, or their contributions on previous trials.

[7] It consisted of a game of ten trials with five subjects to a group. Each subject was endowed with fifty tokens. There was an individual exchange that paid $0.01 for each token invested, and a group exchange that paid $0.005 for each token invested to each member of the group (or $0.025 to the group). The subjects were told the amount invested in the group exchange at the end of every period.

[8] Andreoni also imposed a restart condition. After the first play of ten trials, subjects were told a second round of ten trials would commence. Strangers would continue to be randomly reassigned. If learning were solely responsible for the decay of contributions, a restart would not affect the play of the game. If there is a difference in the two groups after a restart, there must be something else other than learning going on. Andreoni found that Strangers were hardly affected by the restart whereas Partners went back to the high level of contributions that occurred in the first period of the game.

[9] Use of deception in experiments is highly controversial. Most experimental economists argue against its use because they do not want to taint the subject pool. If subjects come to believe that they are being deceived, this may significantly affect their behavior and severely limit the veracity of the results. See the discussion in Weimann (1994) and the references he cites.

[10] To see this, consider an experiment with five subjects. Let $m_1 > m_2 > m_3 > m_4 > m_5$ be the ranked payments, i.e., the top ranked subject receives m_1, the second ranked subject receives m_2, and so on. Suppose subject #1 is an altruist and subjects #2 - 5 are individualistic and identical. Subject #1's utility function is given by $U^1 = M^1 + \beta 4M$, where M^1 is #1's monetary payment under the rank condition, M is the monetary payment received by each of the other agents, and β is an altruism parameter. Subjects 2 - 5 are individualistic with preferences $U^k = M^k$. If no one contributes to the public good, everyone is ranked the same and receives an average payment, $M^1 = M = \Sigma_{j=1,5} m_j/5$, hence $U^1 = \Sigma_{j=1,5}(m_j/5 + \beta 4m_j/5)$, where the notation $\Sigma_{j=1,5} m_j$ means the sum runs from 1 through 5. If #1 contributes to the public good and no one else does, then #2 - #5 tie for first and receive a monetary payment of $M^k = \Sigma_{j=1,4} m_j/4$ for $k = 1, 2, 3, 4$, and #1 receives a payment of m_5 since he ranks last and attains utility of $U^1 = m_5 + \beta 4\Sigma_{j=1,4}m_j/4$. It is optimal for #1 to contribute to the public good if $m_5 + \beta\Sigma_{j=1,4} m_j > \Sigma_{j=1,5} m_j/5 + \beta 4\Sigma_{j=1,5} m_j/5$. Rearranging this condition we have, $m_5 > \Sigma_{i=1,5}m_i/5$, which is false, so an altruist does better by not contributing to the public good when payment is based on rank.

[11] To see this suppose the altruist's utility is given by $U^1 = M^1 + 4\beta M + \gamma g^1$, where γ is a warm glow parameter. Utility for subjects #2 - 5 is $U^k = M^k$. If all subjects contribute all of their tokens to the private good, $M^1 = M^k = \Sigma_{i=1,5} m_i/5$. This generates $(1+4\beta)\Sigma_{i=1-5}m_i/5$ in utility for the altruist. If the altruist spends all her tokens on the public good and the other subjects do not, the other four subjects tie for first and each receives $\Sigma_{i=1,4} m_i/4$ while the altruist receives m_5, which generates $U^1 = m_5 + 4\beta\Sigma_{i=1-4}m_i/4 + \gamma w$ for the altruist, where w is her endowment of tokens. If $m_5 + 4\beta\Sigma_{i=1-4}m_i/4 + \gamma w > (1+4\beta)\Sigma_{i=1-5}m_i/5$, then contributing to the public good is optimal for the altruist. Rearranging, $[\Sigma_{i=1-5}m_i/5 - m_5] < \gamma w/(1-\beta)$. Obviously, the larger the unobserved warm glow parameter is, the more likely this condition will hold. And it is interesting to note that the larger the altruism parameter β is, in the presence of a warm glow motive, the more likely this condition is to hold. Two observation-

ally equivalent subjects who both contribute to the public good under these circumstances may do so for different motives of "kindness;" one may have a large value for β and a small γ, while the other may have a large γ and a small β.

[12] These results were confirmed by Willinger and Ziegelmayer (1999) in an experiment with an interior solution and for a step-level public good/public bad by Sonnemans, Schram, Offerman (1998). When confronted with a public good decision, "...subjects act more cooperatively, the public good is provided more often, and the subjects earn more money, than when the decision is to prevent a public bad or not." (page 157.) In addition, Eckel and Grossman (2003) found framing effects in the experimental response by subjects to a matching subsidy versus a rebate subsidy when the response should have been the same.

[13] One simple explanation for this may be that the subjects were simply not paid enough. Smith and Walker (1993) argued that there are costs to solving a decision problem, especially one involving concepts not part of everyday experience, e.g., the WTP for a public good. If the payoff is smaller than these costs, the subject doesn't have an incentive to solve the decision problem properly. Smith and Walker presented evidence that increasing the payoff causes the experimental outcome to move closer to the theoretical prediction. They suggest that when an anomalous result is obtained, the researcher should first increase the payoff and run the experiment again.

12 The Effect of Public Inputs on the Economy in Static Models

In "The Wealth of Nations" Adam Smith argued that an economy based on self-interest, specialization, and competition, will be proficient at providing high quality goods and services at the lowest possible price. However, he also recognized that there is a potential role for government to play in providing support for the market. He noted that private agents would have great difficulty providing public infrastructure and that because of this the provision of public infrastructure becomes the responsibility of the government.[1] However, since Smith's book was published, few economists studied the impact of public capital on the economy until only very recently.

Casual observation strongly suggests that public infrastructure such as docks, harbors, dams and locks, bridges, roads, streets, highways, airports, prisons, communication networks, electric and gas facilities, and water and sewer treatment systems, can have a dramatic impact on the economy, and most such goods are provided by government since they may not exhibit exclusion, depletion, or both. For example, "e-commerce," where sales occur via the Internet, requires a transportation infrastructure capable of handling a large volume of deliveries.[2] Congestion and poor infrastructure can hamper this effort. Recently, a number of researchers have found some empirical support for the hypothesis that public capital has a significant impact on the economy, although this remains somewhat controversial.[3]

In this chapter we will present a sequence of static models designed to delineate the effects of public capital on the economy. In the next section we will study the impact of a public input on the individual firm. In section 12.2 we present a model of a small, multi-sector economy that takes prices as given by the rest of the world. In section 12.3 optimal policy design is studied in a small open economy and a form of the Samuelson - Kaizuka rule is derived in the first-best case and generalized to the second-best case when a distorting tax must be used. In section 12.4 we generalize the results of 12.3 to the n x n case. In section 12.5 we present a general equilibrium model of two trading countries where there are spillover effects that work through relative prices. We study the case where rents exist and show

how the rules must be amended when profits cannot be fully taxed in section 12.6. Section 12.7 concludes the chapter.

There are two issues to consider before we continue. The first issue is whether public capital is a pure public good or not. Some kinds of public capital may allow for exclusion, e.g., a bridge, a city swimming pool, a highway with limited access points, while others may not, e.g., a lighthouse, a dam, city streets, sidewalks. And, congestion may affect some types of public capital, e.g., crowded sidewalks and streets, so depletion may be a factor for some types of public capital. The second issue is whether there is constant returns (CRS) to private inputs alone, or to all inputs including public capital. If the private technology exhibits CRS in private inputs, no economic profit will be generated. Meade (1952) referred to this case as "creation of atmosphere." He cited rainfall in a farming community as an example where all firms benefit equally from the externality. Another example is knowledge. On the other hand, if there is CRS in all inputs, then economic profits will be generated. Meade labeled this the "unpaid factor" case.[4] We will remain agnostic on the first issue and assume there is CRS in private inputs on the second issue. The terms "public capital," "public infrastructure," and "public input" will be used interchangeably.

12.1 The Effect of Public Capital on the Firm

Suppose output of a private good is produced according to a neoclassical production function, $Y = F(K, L, G)$, where K is private capital, L is labor, and G represents the services from public infrastructure. It follows that along an isoquant,

$$F_K(dK/dG) + F_L(dL/dG) + F_G = 0,$$

where a subscript denotes a derivative. If all three inputs are productive, including public capital, $F_j > 0$ for $j = K, L, G$. There are several cases to consider. Two can be ruled out if all inputs are productive. It is impossible for both private inputs to increase or remain unchanged in response to an increase in public capital. However, it is possible for one input to rise while the other one falls. Alternatively, if $C(w, r, Y, G)$ is the firm's cost function and the wage and cost of capital, w and r, are given to the firm, then

$$C_Y(dY/dG) + C_G = 0.$$

If cost is decreasing in public capital, $C_G < 0$, then an increase in public capital must raise output since marginal cost is positive, $C_Y > 0$.

We can also ask how a monopolist might be affected by the public input. The monopolist chooses output y to maximize profit $P(y, G)y - C(w, r, y, G)$, where $P(\ )$ is the inverse demand for the monopolist's output and $C(\ )$ is the cost function. At the optimum, $yP_y + P = C_y$. Differentiate the profit maximization condition to obtain,

$$dy/dG = [C_{yG} - (P_G + yP_{yG})]/D,$$

where the denominator $D = (2P_y + yP_{yy} - C_{yy})$ is negative if marginal cost is non-decreasing ($C_{yy} \geq 0$) and marginal revenue is non-increasing ($0 \geq 2P_y + yP_{yy}$) in output. The first term in the numerator, C_{yG}/D, is positive if the public input is productive and lowers cost. The second term captures the shift in demand due to the public capital and reinforces (reverses) the first effect if demand shifts out (in). For example, provision of a highway might cause the cost of transporting coal to a local power company to fall and thus cause its output to rise. However, if the highway causes some consumers to leave the city for a suburb, and this lowers their demand for the power company's output, then output might fall even though it has become more efficient in delivering power.

12.2 A Static Open Economy Model of Public Inputs

Suppose there are two primary resources, labor and private capital, two private goods, Y_1 and Y_2, and public capital. Let $Y_j = F^j(K_j, L_j, G)$ be a well-behaved technology, where G only affects sector one output. All firms in a sector are identical, and there is CRS in private inputs. This case has been referred to in the literature as "factor augmenting." The output of public capital is also determined by a neoclassical technology that converts units of private capital (K^G) and labor (L^G) into public infrastructure (G) according to a well-behaved function, $G = F^G(K^G, L^G)$, which is CRS in (K^G, L^G). We will also assume that competition prevails throughout the economy.

Consider a firm in industry j. Let $C^j(w, r, G, Y_j)$ be its cost function, where w is the wage and r is the opportunity cost of capital.[5] With CRS, we have $C^j = c^j(w, r, G)Y_j$, where c^j is unit cost. The unit input requirements are $dc^j/dz = c^j_z$ for $j = 1, 2$, and $z = w, r$, where a subscript denotes a derivative. These are the amount of an input required to produce one unit of output. We will also assume that the government minimizes cost and $C^G(w, r, G)$ is its cost function. Under CRS, we have $C^G = c^G(w, r)G$. The input demands for the private sector are $c_w^j Y_j = L_j$ and $c_r^j Y_j = K_j$, and similarly for the government's inputs.

We will assume there is free trade in private goods and factors are mobile across sectors within the economy but otherwise immobile. This is sufficient to imply that relative output prices of the traded private goods are given by the world economy. Let good two be numeraire, $P_2 = 1$, and let $P_1 = p$. Also assume sector one is private capital intensive, $k^1 > k^2$, where $k = K/L$ is the private capital to labor ratio, and $k^j = c_r^j / c_w^j$.

We have the following two price equations when firms maximize profit,

$$p = c^1(w, r, G) \text{ and } 1 = c^2(w, r). \tag{12.1}$$

Under a weak univalence assumption, there is a unique solution to these equations such that the factor prices are a function of relative output prices and the stock of public input.[6] It is their dependence on the stock of public capital that extends the literature.

To obtain the effect of public capital on factor prices, differentiate (12.1),

$$dr/dG = -c^1_G/c^1_w(k^1 - k^2) > 0, \tag{12.2a}$$

$$dw/dG = k^2 c^1_G/c^1_w(k^1 - k^2) < 0. \tag{12.2b}$$

It is immediate that the wage falls with the stock of public capital while the interest rate rises as long as public capital lowers cost in industry one. The intuition is that the public input improves the efficiency of sector one firms and this lowers unit cost in that sector. Firms in sector one increase their production and thus bid up the price of the input they use most intensively, private capital.

It follows from this that factor prices need not be equal across countries; the Factor Price Equalization Theorem need not hold in the presence of public inputs. If two countries are identical except in their endowments and there is free trade in private outputs, then output prices must be equal, hence marginal cost must be equal, $c^h(w, r, G) = c^{*h}(w^*, r^*, G^*)$, for the home and foreign countries, respectively. Clearly, factor prices will differ if the public input differs even if the technology is the same across countries. Thus, observing a real interest rate differential across countries need not imply that there is a capital market imperfection, that investors lack information about foreign capital markets, or that investors are irrational. Instead, it could simply reflect a difference in public capital investments.

Since the demand for inputs can be written in the form $L^j = Y^j c_w^j$, we can state the equilibrium conditions for the factor markets as

$$L - Gc_w^G = Y_1 c_w^1 + Y_2 c_w^2, \tag{12.3a}$$

$$K - Gc^G_r = Y_1 c^1_r + Y_2 c^2_r. \tag{12.3b}$$

The government's demands for labor and capital are given by Gc^G_w and Gc^G_r. Thus, $L - Gc^G_w$ is the net private demand for labor and $K - Gc^G_r$ is the net private demand for private capital. Equations (12.3) determine the private good outputs as a function of L, K, and G for a given set of factor prices.

A change in the stock of public capital will generally have three effects on the output of private goods in system (12.3). (See Appendix A.) First, resources must be transferred from the production of private goods to production of the public input; public capital enters the left hand side of (12.3) in a manner similar to the total endowments of the two primary resource inputs, L and K. This effect is similar to the Rybczynski effect in international trade so we will label it the Public Input Rybczynski effect; an increase in G acts like a decrease in L and K to the private sector. It follows that it is impossible for both private goods to increase in response to an increase in the public input because of this effect. The response depends on the ordering of capital labor ratios. If, for example, $k^1 > k^G > k^2$, the output of both private goods will fall with the public input.

Second, an increase in the stock of public capital will improve the efficiency of the production of the first private good and this lowers its unit cost causing firms producing that good to alter their output; G enters c^h_w and c^h_r as a separate argument on the right hand side of (12.3). We can label this the Public Input efficiency effect. There are a number of cases. One that can be ruled out is where both private goods decrease in response. On the other hand, it is possible for both private goods to increase. If both private goods increase, it is because industry one has become more efficient due to the increase in the public input, and has released resources to the other sector allowing it to increase its output as well.

Third, public capital will also affect factor prices through the price equations and this will in turn alter production of the private goods since factor prices enter the terms c^h_w and c^h_r in (12.3). We will call this the Public Input Factor Price effect. If factor demands are downward sloping and the cross price effects are positive, then output in industry one increases while that of industry two decreases with public capital due to the factor price effect. The intuition is that sector one has become more efficient because of the increase in public capital and it increases output and hence the derived demand for the factor it uses intensively, private capital, as a result. This drives up the real interest rate relative to the wage. Industry one expands while industry two contracts.

The net impact of a change in the stock of public capital on the output of private goods in a small economy is ambiguous. One case that can probably be ruled out is where the output of both private goods falls in response to the public input. On the other hand, if the efficiency of private production is improved enough by the public input, then it is possible for the output of both private goods to increase in response.

12.3 Optimal Provision of a Public Input in the Small Open Economy

Aggregate income is given by $wL + rK$ in the small open economy of the last section. This is equal to expenditures on private goods, $pX_1 + X_2$, plus the expenditure on the public input, $c^G G$. We can represent the expenditures of the representative consumer and hence aggregate expenditure on the private goods with the expenditure function, $E(P, G, U) = \min\{P.X \mid U(X, G) \geq u\}$, where $P.X = pX_1 + X_2$, and $E_p = X_1$, and where we have included a consumption benefit associated with public capital in the utility function for the sake of generality. Thus, the resource constraint is given by,[7]

$$wL + rK = E(P, G, U) + Gc^G. \tag{12.4}$$

We can treat factor prices as being a function of p and G from (12.1). Equation (12.4) is then one equation in the level of the representative agent's utility, U, and the government's control variable G. Differentiating (12.4),

$$dU/\lambda dG = m - c^G + L^P(dw/dG) + K^P(dr/dG), \tag{12.5}$$

where $Z^P = \Sigma_i Z_i$, $Z = K, L$, $E_u = 1/\lambda$, λ is the marginal utility of income, and $m = - E_G(P, G, U)$ is the consumer's WTP for a unit of public capital at the margin. Note that profit in the economy is given by $\pi = pF^1 + F^2 - wL^P - rK^P$. With CRS, $\pi = 0$. Hence, by the envelope theorem,

$$pF^1_G + F^2_G = L^P(dw/dG) + K^P(dr/dG).$$

Using this information in (12.5) we have,

$$dU/\lambda dG = m + pF^1_G + F^2_G - c^G.$$

If the government chooses the public input optimally, $dU/\lambda dG = 0$, and we have the Samuelson-Kaizuka rule[8] for choosing a public input in the first-best case,

$$m + pF^1_G + F^2_G = c^G. \tag{12.6}$$

The term m captures the aggregate consumption benefit at the margin, the sum $pF^1_G + F^2_G$ captures the aggregate production benefit at the margin, and c^G is the marginal cost.

Next, consider the case of a distorting tax imposed on the consumption of good one. Tax revenue is τX_1, where τ is the tax rate, and revenue is spent entirely on public capital so the government's budget constraint is $\tau X_1 = Gc^G$, where $X_1 = E_q = dE/dq$ and $q = p+\tau$ is the consumer price of good one. The resource constraint confronting the economy simplifies to $wL + rK = E(p+\tau, 1, G, U)$. Treating τ and U as endogenous and G as the control variable, it is straightforward to show by totally differentiating the resource constraint and the government's budget constraint, and setting $du/\lambda dG = 0$ that a necessary condition for choosing the public input optimally is,

$$(1 - \theta\sigma_{qq})(m + dY/dG) = c^G - \tau E_{qG} + G(dc^G/dG),$$

where $\theta = \tau/p$, $\sigma_{qq} = - (p/E_q)E_{qq} > 0$, and $Y = wL + rK$. We can write the condition governing the optimum as[9]

$$m + \Sigma_i P_i F^i_G = [c^G - \tau E_{qu} + \theta\sigma_{qq}G(dc^G/dG)]/(1 - \theta\sigma_{qq}). \tag{12.7}$$

There are three additional terms in (12.7) relative to the first-best case. The first extra term, τE_{qG}, captures the provision effect of providing the public input on the private demand for the taxed good. If demand increases (decreases), this brings in more (less) tax revenue and serves to reduce (increase) the social marginal cost of the public input. The second additional term, $\theta\sigma_{qq}G(dc^G/dG)$, captures the impact of the public input on factor prices and hence the cost of providing the public input. If the public input increases the efficiency of the private sector and lowers factor prices as a result, then the marginal cost of providing the public input falls and this reduces the social cost of the public input. Of course, it is possible that the increased demand for private inputs used to produce the public input may cause the marginal cost to rise in which case the social cost increases. Finally, there is the multiplicative term $1/(1 - \theta\sigma_{qq})$, which captures the marginal cost of funds (MCF) effect. If the own price elasticity is less than one in magnitude, the MCF is greater than one in magnitude and this serves to magnify the cost of the public input.

This is similar in spirit to Feehan's (1998) result. He considered the case where output in industry i is given by $h^i(G)F^i(K_i, L_i)$ and showed how the Kaizuka rule could be decomposed in the first-best case into $\Sigma VMP_G +$

DHE = c^G, where ΣVMP_G is the sum of the marginal impact of public capital on private production and DHE is the differential Hicks effect, which occurs when the ratio of private capital to labor changes across industries as the economy responds to the public capital. Resources must be drawn out of private production when public capital is produced causing the production possibility frontier (PPF) for private production to shift in. It shifts out again if the public capital is productive. If there is no differential Hicks effect, the shift outward is a radial expansion of the restricted PPF. However, if there is a differential effect, as seems most likely, then the shift outward will not be uniform; some industries will benefit more than others.

Feehan (1998) also considered the effect of distorting taxation and showed that the optimal rule governing the provision of public capital must be adjusted to account for the distortions of the method of financing the public capital similar in spirit to (12.7). However, Feehan and Matsumoto (2000) showed that if factor supplies are endogenous and the government must impose a distorting tax on all sources of factor income, the first-best rule still applies, $\Sigma_i P_i F^i_G = c^G$. Hence, production efficiency remains operative even though distorting taxes are imposed on factor supplies. The reason for this is that production efficiency will be optimal if the government has a rich enough set of tax instruments available. However, if the government does not have enough policy tools, then production efficiency is not optimal, as indicated by (12.7).

12.4 A Generalization

Suppose there are m inputs and n outputs. We will assume public capital confers both consumption and production benefits, e.g., highway, in contrast to Abe (1992), who only considered the case of a consumption benefit. Let L denote the resource vector of inputs, w the vector of factor prices, y the vector of private good outputs, p the vector of output prices, and L^P_i the resource vector used by firm i. The cost functions are $c^i(w, G)$ and $c^G(w)$ for firm i in sector i and the government, respectively. They are homogeneous of degree one so it follows that $c^i = w.c^i_w$ and $w.c^i_{ww} = 0$ for each i including i = G, where x.z denotes an inner product. We can define the national private income function as,[10]

$$N(P, L^P, G) = \max\{p.y \mid y_i \geq F^i(L^P_i, G), i = 1, 2; L^P \geq \Sigma L^P_j\}.$$

where the derivatives yield the vectors $N_p = y$, $w = N_L$, and $N_G = p.F_G = \Sigma p_i F^i_G$ by the envelope theorem.

Equilibrium in the resource markets requires,

$$L^P = L - Gc^G{}_w(w) = L - Gc^G{}_w(N_L(p, L^P, G)),   \tag{12.8}$$

where we have substituted for the factor price vector. Note that the vector $Gc^G{}_w$ is the government's demand for resources so L^P is what is available for private production. Profit maximization implies $p = c(w, G)$. If $n = m$, we can solve the system of price equations, $w(p, G)$, and the factor prices are independent of the resource endowments. Expenditure on private goods in equilibrium must equal the income generated from the production of private goods, $E(p, G, u) = N(p, L^P, G)$, or, after substituting for the resource vector,

$$E(p, G, u) = N(p, L - Gc^G{}_w(w(p, G)), G).   \tag{12.9}$$

This equation determines utility as a function of public capital. This case corresponds to that of lump sum financing. To see this note that $w.L = p.x + Gc^G{}_w$ but that $w.L^G = Gc^G{}_w$ so the government's budget constraint is given by $T = Gc^G{}_w$.

Next, differentiate (12.9) and simplify using the homogeneity of the cost function, $du/\lambda dG = m + p.F_G - c^G$. Thus, an optimal choice for G must satisfy the following necessary condition,

$$(m + p.F_G) = c^G.   \tag{12.10}$$

This is the Samuelson-Kaizuka rule once again.

What happens if the number of factors differs from the number of outputs? Dixit and Norman (1980) showed that an equilibrium with $n > m$ is very fragile; small changes in the output prices will cause industries to collapse. However, $n < m$ can easily occur. In that case, it is shown in Appendix B that we once again obtain (12.10).

Finally, if $n < m$ but $m-n$ factors are perfectly mobile, final good prices and prices of the mobile factors are equal across countries. Let w' be the price vector of the mobile factors, $p*$ be the world output price vector, and $w*'$ be the world factor price vector for mobile factors. Trade and mobility imply $p = p*$ and $w' = w*'$. The system $p* = c(w, w*', G)$ determines w as a function of $p*$, $w*'$, and G. It can be shown that (12.10) still holds.

12.5 A General Equilibrium Model of Public Infrastructure

Next, we will consider two economies that trade with one another. Suppose there is free trade in private good outputs, resources are immobile, and $n = m$. Suppose the home country or region is as designated in the last section. There is also a foreign country or region, where $N^*(p, L^{p^*}, G^*)$, $E^*(p, G^*, u^*)$, and $L^{p*} = L^* - G^*c^{G*}_w$ are the national private income function, the expenditure function, and the resource constraint, respectively, for the foreign country. Profit maximization implies $p = c(w, G)$ at home and $p^* = c^*(w^*, G^*)$ in the foreign country, and free trade in all private outputs implies $p = p^*$ hence $c(w, G) = c^*(w^*, G^*)$. If the technology is the same between the two countries and countries only differ in tastes and endowments, then this becomes $c(w, G) = c(w^*, G^*)$. Factor prices may not equalize between countries, as before. However, in a symmetric equilibrium where $G = G^*$, it follows that the factor price vectors will be equal, $w = w^*$. Under certain conditions, typically assumed to hold in this literature, we can solve these two systems of profit maximizing equations to obtain $w(p, G)$ and $w^*(p, G^*)$. The resource constraints in the two countries are

$$L^P = L - Gc^G_w(w(p, G)) \text{ and } L^{P*} = L^* - G^*c^{G*}_{w*}(w^*(p, G^*)),$$

where we have substituted for the vector of factor prices.

The following system characterizes the general equilibrium,

$$E(p, G, U) = N(p, L - Gc^G_w[w(p, G)], G),$$

$$E^*(p, G^*, u^*) = N^*(p, L^* - G^*c^{G*}_w[w^*(p, G^*)], G^*),$$

$$E_p + E^*_p - N_p - N^*_p = 0,$$

where we have substituted for L^P and L^{P*}. This system is sufficient to determine (p, u, u^*). Following the trade literature, we will assume the equilibrium is unique and stable.

To see how one might manipulate the model assume $n = m = 2$ and let good two be numeraire. Notice that when we differentiate the resource constraint and premultiply by the vector w we obtain

$$w.dL^P = -(w.c^G_w dG + Gw.c^G_{ww}dw) = -c^G,$$

by the homogeneity properties of the cost function, and similarly for the foreign country, $w^*.dL^{P*} = -c^{G*}$. Differentiate the system and use the last two pieces of information to obtain

$$dp/dG = (1/\lambda\lambda^*\Delta)[(m + pF_G - c^G)x_{II} + (E_{pG} - N_{pG}) - (N_{pL}Gc^G_{ww}w_G)]$$

$$du/\lambda dG = m + pF_G - c^G - (im)(dp/dG),$$

$$du^*/\lambda^* dG = -(im^*)(dp/dG),$$

where $\Delta > 0$ is the Jacobian determinant of the system, λ and λ^* are the private marginal utilities of income, im is the imports of the home country, im* is the imports of the foreign country, and where im + im* = 0, i.e., trade must balance.

There are essentially three effects to consider in the price response, an income effect, an output effect, and an effect that works through factor prices. If the net benefit, $m + pF_G - c^G$, is positive and the taxed good is a normal good, the income effect works in the direction of raising the relative output price. Second, recall that E_{pG} is the direct effect of the public input on demand for good one and N_{pG} is the direct response of production of good one to the productivity effect of the public input. If demand increases more (less) than supply, the price will rise (fall). The last term captures an effect working through the factor markets similar to (12.8) and cannot generally be signed. If $m + pF_G - c^G \geq 0$ (<), $x_{11} > 0$, and $E_{pG} - N_{pG} - N_{pL}Gc^G_{ww}w_G \geq 0$ (<), then the relative price of good one will increase (decrease).

Of greater interest is the response of utility in the home country. If the public input is chosen optimally, then

$$m + pF_G = c^G + (im)(dp/dG).$$

This is similar to the Samuelson-Kaizuka rule. The new term involves the price response. If the home country imports good one and its price rises, then welfare is adversely affected and this will raise the social cost of the public input. This is an unintended side effect. Of course, if the country is exporting the good and its price rises, the opposite will be true.

Finally, the foreign country is affected by a spillover effect that works through relative prices. If it is importing (exporting) good one and the price of the imported (exported) good increases it is worse (better) off. The home country essentially ignores this externality when it chooses its policy. This could entail a subtle form of trade subsidization. If better harbors and highways make it easier to ship goods for the home country, this would lower the relative price of exports and make it easier for the home country to compete.

12.6 A Model with Rents

There are a variety of reasons for rents to exist temporarily and the issue of how they affect policy has been studied at length. We will assume there are decreasing returns in some industries so there are economic profits in equilibrium. Consumers own the firms and thus receive the rents. All rents accrue to residents for simplicity. Rents are initially taxed and there is an excise tax on consumption of good one. We will also focus on the case where the public input only affects the technology.

The economy is small relative to the world and $n = m$ for simplicity. The income constraint in the economy is $\pi(1 - \tau) + w.L = q.x$, where w.L and q.x are inner products of total factor income and expenditures, respectively, π is rents, or economic profits, τ is a tax on rents, and $q = (p_1(1+\theta), p_2, ..., p_n)$. By definition the profit equation is given by $\pi = N(p, L^p, G) - w.L^p$. The government imposes a tax on rents, a tax on consumption of commodity one, and spends the proceeds on the public input. The government's budget constraint is given by

$$\theta p_1 x_1 + \tau\pi = Gc^G = w.L^G$$

where θ is the tax rate imposed on good one. The resource equilibrium condition is $L^p = L - Gc^G{}_w$, as before. Finally, all sectors are competitive. Thus, profit maximization implies the by now familiar pricing equations $p = c(w, G)$.

From the price equations it is immediate that the factor price vector w is determined by output prices, which are given to the economy, and the public input. Thus, the factor price response is $dw/dG = (c_w)^{-1}c_G$, where c_w is the matrix of unit inputs across industries and c_G is a vector capturing the impact of the public input on cost across industries.

The following main result is derived in Appendix C. At the optimum where $du/\lambda dG = 0$, the following is a necessary condition of the model,

$$pF_G = \Omega^{-1}[c^G + \theta^*\sigma_{11}(\tau L^p + L^G)(c_w)^{-1}c_G.]. \qquad (12.11)$$

where $\theta^* = \theta/(1+\theta)$, $\Omega = [1 - (1 - \tau)\theta^*\sigma_{11}]$, and $\sigma_{11} = - (q/x_1)E_{11}$. First, consider the special case where the profit tax is the only tax used to finance the public input. Set $\theta = \theta^* = 0$ in (12.11) and obtain $pF_G = c^G$, the Kaizuka rule. Second, suppose the profit tax is not available and the distorting tax is used to finance the public input. Set $\tau = 0$ and obtain a result similar in spirit to (12.7),

$$pF_G = [1-\theta^*\sigma_{11}]^{-1}[c^G + \theta^*\sigma_{11}L^G(c_w)^{-1}c_G].$$

The marginal production cost must be adjusted by the MCF and there is a factor price effect to take into account. Third, if all profits are taxed away, $\tau = 1$, and the following holds as long as the profit tax cannot fully fund the expenditure on the public input,

$$pF_G = [c^G + \theta^*\sigma_{11}L^G(c_w)^{-1}c_G.].$$

Finally, if $\sigma_{11} < 1$ in the more general case where $1 > \tau$, $\theta > 0$, then $\Omega >$ 1. Thus, the second-best Kaizuka rule must be modified due to the use of the distorting tax. The marginal production cost is magnified by the MCF and the response of factor prices must be taken into account as well for two reasons. The government's production cost will generally be affected when factor prices change and the revenue collected under the profit tax will be affected when factor prices change.

Keen and Marchand (1997) assumed that economic profits exist, capital was perfectly mobile, and showed that taxing mobile capital is inefficient if rents can be fully taxed. If rents cannot be taxed fully, then taxing capital is part of a second-best solution. Furthermore, the composition of public spending is also affected. They considered the case where the government spends on a public good (g) that only confers a consumption benefit, and public capital (g^c) that only confers a production benefit, and showed that a coordinated increase in g coupled with a decrease in g^c, holding the level of total spending constant, improves welfare. This strongly suggests that too much is spent on public capital and too little on the public good in the original uncoordinated equilibrium. Intuitively, governments use public capital to attract private capital when the two are complements in production. This raises the tax base and may also increase rents and the wage under certain circumstances.[11]

12.7 Conclusion

We have studied a number of different models of a public input. The models are typically general equilibrium models and deriving predictions can be difficult at best. However, the models almost invariably predict that public capital can affect the allocation of resources, prices and income, and, more importantly, welfare. In particular, it is highly likely that public infrastructure will affect some industries more than others, especially industries that are heavily reliant on a transportation network like manufacturing, agriculture, and online retailing. Some industries may actually be worse off if they do not directly benefit from the public input and factor prices change in a way so as to raise their cost.

We showed that a change in the publicly provided input would cause three effects on the intersectoral allocation of resources. Resources have to be drawn out of the production of private goods. This induces an effect similar to the Rybczynski effect in international trade theory. Second, industries that benefit from the public capital become more efficient inducing another shift of resources across industries. Finally, factor prices will respond and this will further alter the cost structure across industries. The end result will not only be a shifting of the production possibilities frontier but a twisting of the frontier. Some industries will benefit more than others and some industries may even contract.

We also discussed optimal policy design in the presence of a public input. We derived a generalization of the Kaizuka rule that included a consumption benefit. The rule must be modified to take into account the use of distorting taxes. In that case there will be a provision effect if the public input affects the consumption of taxed commodities, and factor prices will change thus altering the cost of producing the public input. In addition, the price of traded commodities may also respond. This remains true even in the presence of profits if profit taxes are insufficient to finance spending on the public input.

Appendix A: Comparative Statics in the Static, General Equilibrium Model

Suppose industry one is the only industry affected by the public input. The pricing equations under profit maximization become $c^1(w, r, G) = p$ and $c^2(w, r) = 1$. Totally differentiate and solve using Cramer's rule to obtain the result in the text, equations (12.2), noting that $c^1_r/c^1_w = Y_1 c^1_r/Y_1 c^1_w = K_1/L_1 = k^1$ since $Y_1 c^1_r$ is the demand for private capital and $Y_1 c^1_w$ is the demand for labor, and similarly for industry two. Notice that if the univalence conditions hold we can solve to obtain $w(p, G)$ and $r(p, G)$.

The equilibrium conditions in the factor markets are given by

$$L_1 + L_2 = Y_1 c^1_w(w, r, G) + Y_2 c^2_w(w, r) = L - Gc^G_w(w, r),$$

$$K_1 + K_2 = Y_1 c^1_r(w, r, G) + Y_2 c^2_r(w, r) = K - Gc^G_r(w, r).$$

Differentiate with respect to the G on the right hand side of the system, holding factor prices constant.

$$\begin{pmatrix} c^1_w & c^2_w \\ c^1_r & c^2_r \end{pmatrix} \begin{pmatrix} dY^1 \\ dY^2 \end{pmatrix} = - \begin{pmatrix} c^G_w \\ c^G_r \end{pmatrix} dG.$$

Solve and simplify to get the Public Input Rybczynski effect.

Second, differentiate with respect to the G that appears as an argument in c^1_j for $j = r, w$ to get the efficiency effect, holding factor prices and the Public Input Rybczynski effect constant.

$$\begin{pmatrix} c_w^1 & c_w^2 \\ c_r^1 & c_r^2 \end{pmatrix} \begin{pmatrix} dY_1 \\ dY_2 \end{pmatrix} = -G \begin{pmatrix} c_{wG}^G \\ c_{rG}^G \end{pmatrix} dG.$$

Solve to get Public Input efficiency effect.

Finally, note that factor prices depend on G and differentiate the system with respect to this G holding the other effects constant to get the factor price effect.

$$\begin{pmatrix} c_w^1 & c_w^2 \\ c_r^1 & c_r^2 \end{pmatrix} \begin{pmatrix} dY_1 \\ dY_2 \end{pmatrix} = -$$

$$\begin{pmatrix} Y_1 c_{ww}^1 + Y_2 c_{ww}^2 + Gc_{ww}^G & Y_1 c_{wr}^1 + Y_2 c_{wr}^2 + Gc_{wr}^G \\ Y_1 c_{rw}^1 + Y_2 c_{rw}^2 + Gc_{rw}^G & Y_1 c_{rr}^1 + Y_2 c_{rr}^2 + Gc_{rr}^G \end{pmatrix} \begin{pmatrix} dw/dG \\ dr/dG \end{pmatrix}.$$

Invert the matrix on the left to obtain

$$\begin{pmatrix} dY_1 \\ dY_2 \end{pmatrix} = -(1/D) \begin{pmatrix} c_r^2 & -c_w^2 \\ -c_r^1 & c_w^1 \end{pmatrix} \begin{pmatrix} dL^P/dw + dL^G/dw \\ dK^P/dw + dK^G/dw \end{pmatrix}$$

$$\begin{pmatrix} dL^P/dr + dL^G/dr \\ dK^P/dr + dK^G/dr \end{pmatrix} \begin{pmatrix} dw/dG \\ dr/dG \end{pmatrix}$$

where $D = c_w^1 c_r^2 - c_w^2 c_r^1$, $dL^P/dw = Y_1 c_{ww}^1 + Y_2 c_{ww}^2$, $dL^G/dw = Gc_{ww}^G$, and so on, and where dw/dG and dr/dG are obtained from differentiating the pricing equations. Solving, we obtain, for example,

$$dY_1/dG = c^1{}_G[k^2(k^2L^D{}_w - L^D{}_r) - (k^2K^D{}_w - K^D{}_r)]/\Delta,$$

$$dY_2/dG = c^1{}_G c^1{}_w[(k^2K^D{}_w - K^D{}_r) + k^1(L^D{}_r - k^2L^D{}_w)]/c^2{}_w\Delta,$$

where $\Delta = (c^1{}_w)^2(k^1 - k^2)^2 > 0$, $L^D{}_w = dL^P/dw + dL^G/dw$, and so on. If factor demands are downward sloping, $L^D{}_w$, $K^D{}_r < 0$. If cross price effects are positive and factor demands are downward sloping, then $dY_1/dG > 0$, and for industry two we have instead, $dY^2/dG < 0$. This follows since dw/dG < 0 and dr/dG > 0, and since industry one has become more efficient, it increases its output and hence the demand for the factor it uses intensively, private capital, relative to industry two.

Appendix B: Derivation of (12.10) when n < m

To derive (12.10) when $n < m$, differentiate $L^P = L - Gc^G_w(w)$ to obtain

$$dL^P/dG = -c^G_w - Gc^G_{ww}(dw/dG).$$

Next differentiate the equilibrium condition,

$$E(p, G, u) = N(p, L - Gc^G_w(w), G),$$

and use dL^P/dG to obtain,

$$du/\lambda dG = m + p.F_G - [N_L c^G_w + N_L Gc^G_{ww}(dw/dG)].$$

Since $N_L c^G_w = c^G$ and $N_L Gc^G_{ww}(dw/dG) = 0$, we have the same result as before, (12.10).

Appendix C: Derivation of (12.11)

First use the profit equation, the resource equilibrium condition, the expenditure function, and the government cost equation in the income constraint to obtain

$$(1 - \tau)N(p, L^P, G) + \tau w.L^P + Gc^G(w) = E(q, u).$$

Differentiate and simplify, assuming the profit tax rate is fixed, to get

$$(1 - \tau)pF_G dG + (\tau L^P + Gc^G_w)dw = p_1 x_1 d\theta + du/\lambda,$$

where we have used $w.dL^P = -w.c^G_w dG - Gw.c^G_{ww} = -c^G dG$ from the resource equilibrium condition and the homogeneity properties of the cost function. Next, use the profit equation and $x_1 = E_1(q, u)$ in the government's budget constraint, and differentiate,

$$(\tau L^P + L^G)dw - (\tau pF_G - c^G)dG - \theta p_1 x_{11} du/\lambda = p_1 x_1(1 - \theta^* \sigma_{11})d\theta,$$

where $\theta^* = \theta/(1+\theta)$ and $\sigma_{11} = -(q/x_1)E_{11} > 0$ is the compensated demand elasticity. Combine the last two equations to obtain,

$$du/\lambda dG = \Phi\{\Omega pF_G - c^G - \theta^* \sigma_{11}(\tau L^P + L^G)(c_w)^{-1}c_G\},$$

where $\Phi = (1 - \theta^* \sigma_{11} - \theta p_1 x_{11})^{-1} > 0$, $\Omega = [1 - (1 - \tau)\theta^* \sigma_{11}]$, and where we have used the response of factor prices to G. At the optimum where $du/\lambda dG = 0$, we obtain (12.11).

---

[1]   "The third and last duty of the sovereign or commonwealth is that of erecting and maintaining those public institutions and those public works, which,

though they may be in the highest degree advantageous to a great society, are, however, of such a nature, that the profit could never repay the expense to any individual or small number of individuals, and which it therefore cannot be expected that any individual or small number of individuals should erect or maintain." (See Smith, 1937, Book V, Chapter 1, Part 3, pp. 681).

[2]   The so-called "just-in-time" method of production pioneered in Japan requires timely deliveries, which, in turn, requires an efficient transportation network. This method works something like the following. On Monday a firm receives an order from a customer to deliver a certain number of units of its product by Wednesday. The firm immediately contacts its suppliers and places orders for the relevant parts to be delivered on Tuesday. The firm receives the parts from its various suppliers and uses them to produce its output on Tuesday. The output is then shipped to its customer on Wednesday. All shipments are received literally "just in time" for production to take place. No physical inventory of either parts, or the final product is necessary. This obviously requires an infrastructure capable of handling a large volume of deliveries if a lot of firms are relying on this method of production. However, if the transportation network is inefficient, the firm might not receive the parts it needs in time to make its delivery by Wednesday. In that case, a warehouse of parts would have to be maintained. In addition, the firm might also need a second warehouse for its finished product. If the transportation network is inefficient, the firm might have to ship the order on Monday as soon as it is received so that its customer can receive the shipment by Wednesday. Thus, the tradeoff is between the private costs of a warehouse versus the public costs of infrastructure.

[3]   We will survey the extensive empirical literature on the public capital hypothesis in chapter 14.

[4]   See the discussion in Feehan (1989). We would prefer to consider models where there is zero profit in equilibrium for the following reason. Whenever there are economic profits, there is a strong incentive for someone to alter their behavior to capture those rents, either through the introduction of a new product or technology, entry into a new market, or some other action. However, this means that the previous situation where there were rents was not a true equilibrium of the system since there was something inherent in the "equilibrium," namely rents, that generated a change in behavior. We prefer to work with a concept of "equilibrium" that is a true rest point of the system where nothing changes. However, we provide a version of the type of analysis one will find in the literature when rents exist in section 12.6 for the interested reader.

[5]   See Mas-Colell, Whinston, and Green (1995) for the properties of the cost function.

[6]   See Dixit and Sandmo (1980) on the univalence assumption. More generally, we could assume there are m inputs and m outputs and the same results would apply.

[7] This is equivalent to lump sum financing. To see this let T be the aggregate tax revenue collected under a lump sum tax. Disposable income is given by $wL + rK - T$ and this is equal to expenditure $E(P, G, U)$. Thus, $wL + rK - T = E(P, G, U)$. Since $T = Gc^G$, we have (12.4).

[8] See Kaizuka (1965) who extended Samuelson's analysis of a pure public good conferring a consumption benefit to the case where the public good is an input in the production process.

[9] We are indebted to Jim Feehan for this development, which is more complete than the formula provided in earlier versions of this result. Since

$$dY/dG = L^P(dw/dG) + K^P(dr/dG) + L^G(dw/dG) + K^G(dr/dG),$$
$$L^P(dw/dG) + K^P(dr/dG) = \Sigma_i P_i F^i_G,$$

and

$$L^G(dw/dG) + K^G(dr/dG) = G(dc^G/dG),$$

we can simplify to obtain the result in the text.

[10] See Dixit and Norman (1980) for the properties of the national income function.

[11] Feehan and Batina (2004) argued that an equilibrium concept where there are positive economic profits is somewhat awkward. If a sector exhibits positive profits this should induce activity designed to capture those profits. They showed that if firms experiencing positive profit hire more capital and labor to capture more of those profits, it is optimal for them to continue hiring more inputs to capture rents until rents are driven to zero. In that case, taxing capital becomes optimal.

13 The Effects of Public Capital in Dynamic Models

Public inputs can have a significant impact on the economy and the static models considered in the last chapter are important for providing intuition into how public inputs can affect resource flows across sectors of the economy. However, public infrastructure investment is also a dynamic phenomenon and will affect the evolution of the economy, its growth rate over time, and its long run steady state. It thus becomes important to consider the investment aspect of public capital in a dynamic framework.

Marglin (1963), Baumol (1968), Diamond (1968), Ramsey (1969), Usher (1969), Sandmo and Dreze (1971), Harberger (1972), and Dreze (1974), among others, argued that public investment draws resources out of the private sector and an optimal public investment strategy should take into account the source of the funds used to finance the public investment on the basis of the opportunity cost principle. The main conclusion of this work is that a weighted average rule governs the optimal public investment whereby public investment is undertaken until the social discount rate is equal to a weighted average of rates confronting consumers and firms, depending on the source of financing.[1]

Diamond (1968) provided a particularly clear derivation and discussion of this sort of weighted average rule. However, he also disagreed with the result and argued instead for production efficiency. The production efficiency result was carefully derived and discussed by Diamond and Mirrlees (1971, 1976). They showed that it is optimal to choose public investments so that the marginal productivity of a public investment is equal to that of a similar private investment. Another way of stating this is to say that public and private investments should face the same shadow prices. They showed that this was even true if distorting commodity taxes were used to finance the public investment.

Arrow (1966), Arrow and Kurz (1970), Kay (1972), and Pestieau (1974) provided further support for this result in the context of several dynamic models. Arrow (1966) argued that society's rate of time preference should be used even when the impact of a public project on investment in the private sector is taken into account. The idea is that $1 invested in a public project right now will throw off a stream of changes in consumption and investment, the changes in investment will eventually affect consumption by altering income, and thus only the ultimate impact on consumption need be taken into account when considering the cost of the project. Eventually, the investment will pay a rate of return and this will also set up a sequence of changes in consumption and investment but in the opposite direction, and the changes in investment will ultimately affect consumption through income. This leads to the conclusion that the appropriate social discount rate is the social rate of time preference, ρ, and not the opportunity cost of funds, r.[2]

This view is clearly at odds with the weighted average formula result. The issue is resolved, however, when considering the amount of control the government has over consumer prices and government debt. If the government has complete control over consumer prices and debt policy, then public investment should be undertaken until the social discount rate is equal to the social rate of time preference and this will also equal the marginal product of private capital. If there is less than perfect control, then the social discount rate will not be equal to the social rate of time preference. Indeed, it will be greater than the rate of time preference implying that less public investment will be optimal than would otherwise have been the case.

The public capital investment decision and the effects of public capital on an economy are inherently dynamic in nature and several analysts have studied the problem in such a context. Schell (1967) showed how the competitive equilibrium could support an optimal allocation if a tax on income was used to finance the accumulation of "social capital." Arrow and Kurz (1970) derived rules governing the optimal public investment policy in a Ramsey type growth model. Weitzman (1970) showed that growth would occur only after enough "social overhead capital" was accumulated at a sufficient level in a model with a Leontieff technology. Pestieau (1974) derived the conditions under which public investment was optimal in an overlappping generations model. And Barro (1990) studied the issue in an endogenous growth model.

We will discuss the classic production efficiency result in the next section. In section 13.2 we present an analysis of the results in a two period OG model that generalizes Sandmo and Dreze (1971), Pestieau (1974), and Yoshida (1986) to the case of incomplete control and show how a weighted average formula applies. In section 13.3 we will study the impact of public capital on growth in an endogenous growth model with and without congestion effects. And section 13.4 concludes the chapter.

13.1 Production Efficiency

13.1.1 The Basic Result on Production Efficiency

Following Diamond and Mirrlees (1971), suppose there are n commodities and let x be a vector of consumer demands, y be a vector of private production, and z be a vector of public production. A positive value for an element of y or z denotes an output while a negative value denotes an input, and a positive value for an element of x denotes demand while a negative value denotes supply. In equilibrium x = y + z. The technology for private production and public production can be written as $y_1 = f(y_2, ..., y_n)$ and $z_1 = g(z_2, ..., z_n)$, respectively, where there is CRS. The utility function of the representative agent is given by u(x) and is well-behaved.

The social planner chooses consumption and production to maximize the utility function of the representative agent subject to the equilibrium condition and the technologies of the private and public sectors. The constraints can be combined,

$$x_1 - f(x_2 - z_2, ..., x_n - z_n) - g(z_2, ..., z_n) = 0. \tag{13.1}$$

The first order necessary conditions of the planner's problem are easily derived and imply the following conditions, $u_i/u_k = f_i/f_k$, for all i and k, and $f_k = g_k$, for all k. Consumption and private production should be chosen so the marginal rate of substitution is equal to the marginal rate of transformation. Second, public and private production plans should be chosen so that inputs are equally productive at the margin; production efficiency should prevail. In an intertemporal context, u_i/u_k is the rate of time preference if u_i is the marginal utility of consumption of a good next period and u_k is the marginal utility of consumption today, and f_i/f_k is interpreted as the social discount rate. At a first-best solution, public investment should be chosen so that the rate of time preference is equal to the social discount rate which is in turn equal to the private discount rate.

How would a government decentralize this result? Suppose the government can levy commodity taxes τ so that consumer prices become $q = p + \tau$, where p is the producer price vector and τ is a vector of commodity tax rates. Let T be a lump sum tax. The consumer's budget constraint is $\Sigma_j q_j x_j + T = 0$. And let v(q, I) represent indirect utility where $I = -T$ is lump sum income. From duality theory, $v_I = \lambda$ is the private marginal utility of income and demands are given by $x_k = -v_k/\lambda$. Firms engaged in private production maximize profit, $f(y_2, ..., y_n) + p_2 y_2 + ... + p_n y_n$. The first order condition is $f_k + p_k = 0$ for k = 2, 3, ..., n. Solving, we obtain y(p).

The constraints for the government's decision problem can be written as

$$x_1(q, I) - f(y_2(p), ..., y_n(p)) - g(z_2, ..., z_n) = 0, \qquad (13.2a)$$

$$x_i(q, I) - y_i(p) - z_i = 0, \text{ for } i = 2, 3, ..., n. \qquad (13.2b)$$

The government chooses consumer prices and the lump sum tax to maximize indirect utility subject to the constraints (13.2). Production efficiency remains optimal in this setting since z_k only enters the constraints, hence $g_k = f_k$. To see this notice that (13.2b) determines producer prices as a function of control variables (q, T, z). Set up the Lagrangean,

$$L = v + \alpha_1[x_1(q, I) - f(y_2(p), ..., y_n(p)) - g(z_2, ..., z_n)]$$
$$- \Sigma_i\alpha_i[x_i(q, I) - y_i(p) - z_i],$$

where sums run from $i = 2, .., n$, and $\alpha_1, ..., \alpha_n$ are the multipliers. Differentiate with respect to p_k to get $\Sigma_i\alpha_iy_{ik} - \alpha_1\Sigma_if_iy_{ik} = 0$, where y_{ik} is the derivative of y_i with respect to p_k. Since the supply derivatives are generally non-zero, it follows that $\alpha_i/\alpha_1 = f_i$. Next, differentiate with respect to z_k to obtain, $\alpha_k - \alpha_1g_k = 0$. Production efficiency follows immediately from the last two equations, $g_k = f_k$.

We should note that when the government controls all consumer prices aside from the numeriare through commodity taxation, the Ramsey rule for optimal taxation emerges as another policy prescription. If non-distorting lump sum taxation is available, the Ramsey rule implies that distorting tax rates should be set to zero. If lump sum taxes are not available, then the Ramsey rule governs the optimal choice of taxes. However, under complete control, production efficiency remains valid, as was just proven.

13.1.2 Imperfect Control

We can use the same Lagrangean from the last section to study what happens when the government has imperfect control, except that some of the consumer prices are no longer under the control of the government. To illustrate the nature of the problem, for example, there may be a social injunction against taxing food, clothing, or medicine. This means that the producer price of food, clothing, or medicine, that appears in the indirect utility function will respond to the government's policy.

Suppose none of the consumer prices are under the control of the government. In that case the equilibrium conditions determine the vector of producer prices as a function of tax rates, the lump sum tax, and public production, $p(\tau, T, z)$. We derive the following weighted average formula in Appendix A,

$$\Sigma_i(s_{ik} - y_{ik})[g_i + (q_is_{ik} - p_iy_{ik})/(s_{ik} - y_{ik})] = 0, \qquad (13.3)$$

evaluated at the optimum, where we have used $p_i = - f_i$. Equation (13.3) is a general statement of the weighted average formula. Consider the special case where the cross price effects drop out,

$$- g_i = [s_{ii}/(s_{ii} - y_{ii})]q_i - [y_{ii}/(s_{ii} - y_{ii})]p_i.$$

This states that the social marginal product of the kth input, or the social discount rate, should be equal to a weighted average of compensated demand and supply price responses. If supply is perfectly inelastic, then $- g_i = q_i$, and the social discount rate is the price confronting consumers. Since $q_i = u_i/u_1$, this is also equal to the marginal rate of substitution of good i for the numeraire good. In an intertemporal context this is the rate of time preference. On the other hand, if demand is perfectly inelastic instead, then $- g_i = p_i$, the producer price, hence $g_i = f_i$ and production efficiency prevails. However, in general, if the government has incomplete control, then neither the time preference rate, nor the market rate will be appropriate as the social discount rate.

13.1.3 Heterogeneity

Suppose agents differ in their tastes and endowments. Let $x^h(q, T^h, T)$ be the demand vector that solves agent h's decision problem and let $v^h(q, T^h, T)$ be her indirect utility function, where T^h is a person specific lump sum tax, T is a non-person specific lump sum tax, and $q = p + \tau$ is the consumer price vector as before. The government's objective function is a weighted utilitarian sum of utilities, $\Sigma\phi^hv^h$, and its constraints are given by

$$\Sigma_hx^h_1(q, T^h, T) = f(y_2(p), ..., y_n(p)) - g(z_2, ..., z_n),$$

$$\Sigma_hx^h_i(q, T^h, T) = y_i(p) + z_i \text{ for } i = 2, ..., n.$$

The government chooses its policy to maximize its objective function subject to the constraints. We derive the following result in Appendix B,

$$- g_i = [\Sigma_hs^h_{ii}/(\Sigma_hs^h_{ii} - y_{ii})]q_i - [y_{ii}/(\Sigma_hs^h_{ii} - y_{ii})]p_i,$$

when the cross price affects drop out. This formula relies on the availability of person-specific lump sum taxes.

Suppose instead that only the non-person specific taxes are available. Then combining equations in the same manner, we obtain instead,

$$- g_i = [\Sigma_hs^h_{ii}/(\Sigma_hs^h_{ii} - y_{ii})]q_i - [y_{ii}/(\Sigma_hs^h_{ii} - y_{ii})]p_i$$

$$+ cov(\mu^h, x^h_i)/E(\mu^h)(y_{ii} - \Sigma_h s^h_{ii}),$$

where $E(\mu^h) = \Sigma_h \mu^h/N$ is the average of the μ^hs. The last term on the right captures the equity effect associated with the government's investment in the ith input. It takes the sign of the term in the covariance. For example, if the ith input is provided by consumers with a large social marginal utility of income, this term is negative and implies that it is optimal to induce greater social investment that lowers the marginal product of the government's investment, ceteris paribus. On the other hand, if the ith input is provided by consumers with a low social marginal utility of income, this term is positive and the opposite conclusion is true.

13.2   Public Investment in the Overlapping Generations Model

Diamond (1968) and Sandmo and Dreze (1971) both studied a simple two period model of public investment and derived a weighted average rule. In particular, Sandmo and Dreze derived the result that the government's first-best rule for determining public investment is where the social discount rate is equal to the rate facing consumers, which is equal to the rate of time preference. This is consistent with production efficiency. When pure profits are partially taxed in the second-best, the government's social discount rate should be a weighted average of the rate facing the consumer and the tax distorted rate confronting firms, where the weights are the behavioral responses in consumption and the firm's demand for capital investment. However, in their two period model there are no taxes in the first period so all public investment is financed by debt. Thus, debt policy cannot be chosen independently of public investment.

Yoshida (1986) generalized this to the overlapping generations framework where identical individuals live for two periods, as in Sandmo and Dreze, but the economy lasts forever. He showed that the social discount rate is equal to the population growth rate, which is in turn equal to the rate of time preference and that production efficiency is optimal at a first-best allocation. This can be decentralized if there are no distortions and transfers can be made to both generations. Furthermore, it is still optimal to equate the social discount rate to the population growth rate when transfers can be made to both generations even if taxes cause distortions in the decentralized policy. To derive the optimal policy he assumed agents are identical and used the utility function of the representative agent in a steady state as the social welfare function. However, he also assumed that debt policy was used solely to finance public investment and that profits are positive in equilibrium.[3] Since the population growth rate is close to zero in many industrial economies, his policy prescription is essentially to drive the marginal product of public investment to zero.

Pestieau (1974) used Diamond's neoclassical overlapping generations model where the government chooses income tax rates and public investment and showed that it is optimal to equate the rate of return on public capital to the social rate of time preference. This is in turn equal to a weighted average of the rates facing consumers and firms. He used a weighted sum of utilities as the social welfare function and assumed there was CRS in all inputs but that profits were taxed away completely by the government. Of course, the results are sensitive to this last assumption.

We will consider the problem within the context of Diamond's neoclassical overlapping generations with endogenous labor supply, as in Pestieau, but where there is CRS in private inputs and hence no profits in equilibrium. Second, we will assume that debt policy can be chosen independently of public investment by assuming there are additional sources of revenue available through the tax system. This is critical and seems reasonable to us. Finally, we will use a social welfare function following Arrow and Kurz (1970) and Atkinson and Stiglitz (1980).

13.2.1 Socially Optimal Public Investment in the Neoclassical OG Model

Time is discrete and the economy lasts forever. At time t, $N_t = 1$ identical agents are born and each lives for two periods. Each agent is endowed with one unit of labor when young. There is one consumption good produced according to a neoclassical technology that is CRS in private inputs, $Y_t = F(K_t, H_t, G_t)$, where K is private capital, H is labor, and G is public capital. Private capital depreciates at rate δ_K and public capital depreciates at rate δ_G. Private capital and public capital evolve according to

$$K_{t+1} = (1 - \delta_K)K_t + I_{Kt},$$

and

$$G_{t+1} = (1 - \delta_G)G_t + I_{Gt},$$

respectively, where I_j is investment in j. The cost of transforming a unit of the public capital investment into a unit of public capital is $C(I_G)$. The representative consumer's well-behaved utility function is given by

$$u^1(c_{1t}, G_t, 1 - h_t) + \beta u^2(c_{2t}, G_{t+1}),$$

where $\beta = 1/(1+\rho)$ is the discount factor, ρ is the discount rate, h is labor supply, and $L = 1 - h$ is leisure. It follows that $H = hN = h$ since $N = 1$. There are N_0 agents in the initial old generation at time $t = 1$, each of whom owns K_1/N_0 units of private capital that is used to produce the consumption good in the first period. K_1/N_0 and $G_0 > 0$ are taken as given. And the initial old agents only care about their own consumption.

The objective function for the social planner is

$$\Sigma \beta^{t-1}[u^1(c_{1t}, G_t, 1 - h_t) + u^2(c_{2t-1}, G_t)],$$

where the discount factor is the same as the one used by private agents. The constraints confronting the planner are given by

$$(1 - \delta_K)K_t + F(K_t, h_t, G_t) - K_{t+1} - c_{1t} - c_{2t-1} - C(I_{Gt}) = 0,$$

and the law of motion for public capital. The first order conditions are easily derived and can be combined to imply the following conditions, $u^1_{Lt}/u^1_{c1t} = F_H$, $u^1_{c1t}/u^2_{c2t} = \beta(1+F_K-\delta_K)$, $u^1_{c1t} = u^2_{c2t-1}$. In a steady state the last two conditions imply, $F_K - \delta_K = \rho$; the modified golden rule path is optimal. And, finally, we also have,

$$u^1_G/u^1_{c1} + u^2_G/u^2_{c2} + F_G = C_1(F_K - \delta_K + \delta_G) = C_1(\rho + \delta_G). \qquad (13.5)$$

The result where $F_G = F_K = \rho$ is the special case where there is only a production benefit of public infrastructure, no depreciation, and where the cost of public investment is unity. Suppose that cost is equal to one. Then $F_G < F_K$ if the sum of the marginal consumption benefits is positive, and depreciation of private capital is at least as great as that of public capital. In what follows we will assume zero depreciation for both capital stocks and that public investment has a constant marginal cost equal to one.

As is well known, the competitive equilibrium may not be optimal in the overlapping generations model. Under competition, consumers choose consumption so that $U_1/U_2 = \beta(1 + r)$ and firms choose private capital where $r = F_K$. In general, however, there is no reason to expect that F_K will be equal to ρ. In particular, Diamond (1965) showed that $F_K < \rho$ is possible and hence too much private capital might be accumulated under competition.

13.2.2 Decentralized Government Policy

Suppose the government can impose a wage tax, a tax on interest income, and can choose its debt policy optimally so it has complete control over consumer prices. The wage tax distorts the labor supply decision while the tax on interest income distorts the intertemporal consumption decision.

The representative agent's wealth constraint is

$$w_{nt}h_t = c_{1t} + R_{nt+1}c_{2t},$$

where $w_{nt} = w_t(1-\tau_{wt})$ is the wage net of the wage tax τ_w, and $R_n = 1/(1+r_{t+1}(1-\tau_{rt+1}))$ is the net price of second period consumption. The solution to the agent's decision problem is $x(w_{nt}, R_{nt+1})$ for $x = (c_{1t}, c_{2t}, h_t)$ and indirect utility is $V(w_{nt}, R_{nt+1})$, where $V_T = -\lambda$, λ is the private marginal utility of income, $V_w = \lambda_t h_t$, and $V_r = -R^2\lambda_t c_2$. Of course, if public infrastructure produces a consumption benefit as well as a production benefit, then G will enter $x(\ )$ and $V(\ )$ as well. In that case, there will be a behavioral response by consumers when there is a change in public investment. We will simplify by assuming there are no consumption benefits. Finally, firms are identical and choose private inputs to maximize profit, taking the stock of public capital as given. This implies that $r_t = F_K$ and $w_t = F_H$. And profit is zero as a result of assuming CRS in private inputs.

In the classic analysis of optimal policy design in the overlapping generations model it is imagined that the government chooses an infinite sequence of tax policies to impose, generation by generation, $\{(\tau_{wt}, \tau_{rt+1})\}$, and a sequence of one period debt that pays the going market rate of interest, $\{B_t\}$, to maximize a utilitarian sum of utilities, $\Sigma\beta^{\tau-1}V(w_{nt}, T_t, R_{nt+1})$, subject to the resource constraints, the economic behavior of the private sector, and its own budget constraint, where β is the social discount factor.[4] In terms of tax policy, this is equivalent to choosing a sequence of prices, $\{(w_{nt}, R_{nt+1})\}$. It is assumed the capital of the initial old generation cannot be taxed, which rules out exploiting the so-called capital levy.[5]

The main results in the optimal tax literature relying on this model are that the formulae governing the optimal tax rates are very sensitive to the behavioral parameters, e.g., $(w_{nt}/c_2)(\partial c_2/\partial w_{nt})$, and whether the government can choose its debt policy optimally or not. One can easily find a reasonable set of parameters that imply that the optimal tax rate on interest income is negative and another reasonable set where it is positive. In addition to this, some surprising results have been obtained. For example, it is the labor supply elasticities that are critically important in determining whether it is optimal to tax interest income or not in this model, not the interest elasticity of saving, as was originally thought to be the case. The position of the economy relative to the modified golden rule also plays a critical role in the analysis. If the government can choose its debt policy optimally, then it can maintain the economy on the modified golden rule path. If not, then there is an additional effect to consider when evaluating the optimal tax rates, namely, choosing the tax rates to move the economy closer to the modified golden rule path, in addition to minimizing the static deadweight loss.

It is convenient to rewrite the resource constraint using the following substitutions in the resource constraint, $c_{1t} = w_{nt}h_t - s_t = w_{nt}h_t - (K_{t+1} + B_{t+1})$ and $c_{1t} = w_{nt}h_t - R_{nt+1}c_{2t}$, to obtain the following two constraints,

$$F(K_t, h_t, G_t) + K_t + G_t - w_{nt}L_t + B_{t+1} - c_{2t-1} - \phi G_{t+1} = 0,$$

$$F(K_t, h_t, G_t) + K_t + G_t - w_{nt}L_t - K_{t+1} + R_{nt+1}c_{2t} - c_{2t-1} - \phi G_{t+1} = 0.$$

The government chooses the sequence $\{w_{nt}, R_{nt+1}, B_{t+1}, G_{t+1}\}$ when it has full control to maximize social welfare subject to the last two constraints, taking the behavioral functions for labor supply and consumption into account for each generation, and taking the initial capital stocks as given. Let γ_t and α_t be the Lagrange multipliers for the two constraints, respectively.

First, consider the optimal choice of debt. The first order condition for B_{t+1} is $\gamma_t = 0$, when debt is chosen optimally, evaluated at the optimum, where γ_t is a Lagrange multiplier. Next, the choices for G_{t+1} and K_{t+1} must satisfy

$$- (\alpha_t + \gamma_t) + \beta(1+F_G)(\alpha_{t+1} + \gamma_{t+1}) = 0, \qquad (13.6a)$$

$$- \alpha_t + \beta(1+F_K)(\alpha_{t+1} + \gamma_{t+1}) = 0, \qquad (13.6b)$$

respectively. It is immediate from (13.6a) that the social discount rate is equal to the rate of time preference in a steady state, $F_G = \rho$. This is true regardless of whether debt policy can be chosen optimally, or not, as long as the government controls all consumer prices.

It is also immediate that if debt policy can be chosen optimally, (13.6) implies production efficiency, $F_G = F_K$. Therefore, when all prices can be controlled by the government and debt policy is available, $F_G = F_K = \rho$. It also follows that if debt policy cannot be chosen optimally, as is more likely the case, then (13.6) implies $(1+F_G)/(1+F_K) = 1 + \gamma_t/\alpha_t$. In general, F_G will differ from F_K if debt policy cannot be chosen optimally. For example, $\gamma/\alpha > 0$ at the second-best optimum entails choices that imply $F_G > F_K$.

Suppose the government cannot tax interest income so that it no longer controls all consumer prices. In that case the interest rate can be determined by

$$r_t = F_K(K_t, L(w_{nt}, 1+r_{t+1}), G_t).$$

Appending this additional constraint to the government's decision problem we obtain the same condition for the optimal choice of government debt, $\gamma = 0$. In addition, we also have the following conditions for private and public capital, respectively,

$$- \alpha_t + \beta(\alpha_{t+1} + \gamma_{t+1})(1+F_K) - \psi_{t+1}\beta F_{KK} = 0,$$

$$- (\alpha_t + \gamma_t) + \beta(\alpha_{t+1} + \gamma_{t+1})(1+F_G) - \psi_{t+1}\beta F_{KG} = 0,$$

evaluated at the optimum, where ψ is the multiplier for the new constraint. It follows that the social discount rate is no longer equal to the social rate of time preference. In a steady state the last two conditions imply

$$1 - \beta(1+F_G) = - \psi\beta F_{KG}/(\alpha + \gamma).$$

Since $r = F_K$ when firms maximize profit, the additional constraint is binding. Thus, the shadow price of the additional constraint is not zero. It follows that if $F_{KG} > 0$, then $F_G > \rho$ and less will be invested in public capital than when the government has full control, ceteris paribus. This should make intuitive sense.

Also notice that in a steady state we can rearrange the two conditions for G and K to obtain the following result,

$$F_G = [(F_{KK} - F_{KG})/F_{KK}]\rho + [F_{KG}/F_{KK}]r. \tag{13.7}$$

This is a weighted average formula where the weights sum to one but may be of different sign. For example, in the Cobb-Douglas case, $Y = AK^\alpha(LG)^{1-\alpha}$, and it follows that

$$F_G = (1 + K/G)\rho - (K/G)r = \rho + (K/G)(\rho - r).$$

This weighted average formula does not depend on the response of consumption, labor supply, or saving, to taxation, which is quite different from the Sandmo and Dreze formula.

13.3 Public Investment in a Model of Long Run Growth

13.3.1 Public Capital as a Source of Economic Growth

It is possible that public capital investment may be the engine for economic growth in the long run. To see this, we will study a version of the Ramsey model that includes productive public capital, following Barro (1990), but extended to allow for consumption benefits. The growth rate will be endogenous. Time is discrete and the economy lasts forever, $t = 0,$

1, 2, ... There is one consumption good available that is produced using private capital, labor, and public capital according to a Cobb-Douglas technology which exhibits constant returns in private inputs. Hence production in intensive form is $y_t = Ak_t^\alpha G_t^\theta$, where y is private output per worker, k is private capital per worker, and G is the stock of public capital. The economy is initially endowed with k_0 units of private capital per worker and G_0 units of public capital. For simplicity there is complete depreciation in both capital stocks each period.

Identical firms producing the private good maximize profit per worker, y - rk - w, where r is the real interest rate and w is the real wage. Profit maximization implies that the real interest rate is given by $r_t = \alpha y_t/k_t$. There is a representative consumer who experiences an infinite planning horizon. The consumer is endowed with one unit of labor each period that is completely supplied to the labor market in exchange for a wage. We will extend this branch of the literature by allowing for a consumption benefit of public capital. The agent's period utility is $U(c_t) = \ln(c_t) + \zeta\ln(G_t)$, where c is consumption, and his preferences over the horizon are represented by $\Sigma\beta^t[\ln(c_t) + \zeta\ln(G_t)]$. The consumer's period budget constraint is $(w_t + r_t k_t)(1 - \tau_t) - k_{t+1} - c_t = 0$, where τ is the income tax rate. We will also impose a solvency constraint on the consumer, following the literature in this area. As an aside, w + rk = y.

It is imagined that the consumer chooses a consumption path $\{c_t\}$ to maximize lifetime utility subject to her period budget constraint, taking public policy, the initial conditions, and aggregate variables as beyond her control. The first order conditions are

$$\beta^t(1/c_t - \lambda_t) = 0,$$

and

$$-\beta^t\lambda_t + \beta^{t+1}r_{t+1}(1 - \tau_{t+1})\lambda_{t+1} = 0,$$

where λ is the Lagrange multiplier for the budget constraint. By combining these first order conditions, it is straightforward to show that the Euler equation of the consumer's optimization problem is given by

$$c_{t+1}/c_t = \beta r_{t+1}(1 - \tau_{t+1}). \tag{13.8}$$

If $\beta r(1-\tau) > 1$, then consumption grows over time. We seek a path that satisfies the Euler equation and the transversality condition, $\lim_{t\to\infty} \beta^t k_{t+1}/c_t = 0$. One such path is the so-called balanced growth path, where output per worker, private capital per worker, consumption per worker, and public capital per worker all grow at the same rate.[6]

From the technology, we have the following implication,

$$y_{t+1}/y_t = (k_{t+1}/k_t)^{\alpha}(G_{t+1}/G_t)^{\theta}.$$

If $1+\omega_x$ is defined as the gross growth rate of x, then this last equation implies the following result, $1+\omega_y = (1+\omega_k)^{\alpha}(1+\omega_G)^{\theta}$. Thus, $\theta = 1 - \alpha$ is a necessary condition for the existence of a balanced growth path where $\omega_y = \omega_k = \omega_G$. It is necessary that public capital enter the technology in a labor enhancing way according to $y = Ak^{\alpha}G^{1-\alpha}$ for a balanced growth path to exist, where $\theta = 1-\alpha$. In that case there is constant returns to scale in private capital per worker and the stock of public capital taken together. To see this note that aggregate output is $Y = AK^{\alpha}L^{1-\alpha}G^{\theta}$ where $\theta = 1 - \alpha$. This is intuitively plausible; if public capital is labor enhancing and grows at a constant rate, then this will allow firms to overcome diminishing returns in private capital due to labor being fixed.

To close the model we need a resource constraint and the government's budget constraint. The resource constraint is given by the following equation,

$$Ak_t^{\alpha}G_t^{1-\alpha} - k_{t+1} - c_t - \phi G_{t+1} = 0.$$

The government's budget constraint is $\tau_t y_t = \phi G_{t+1}$, where ϕ is the constant marginal cost of producing a unit of public capital. It is straightforward to show that only two equations of the consumer's budget constraint, the resource constraint, and the government's budget constraint are independent.

Following the literature, we will conjecture that a solution to the consumer's optimization problem is linear in form, $c_t = ay_t$, $k_{t+1} = by_t$, and use the method of undetermined coefficients to solve for the constants a and b. Using the conjecture and the government's budget constraint in the resource constraint yields $1 - \tau = a + b$. Using the conjecture in the Euler equation $y_{t+1}/y_t = \alpha\beta(1 - \tau_{t+1})(y_{t+1}/by_t)$ which implies that $b = \alpha\beta(1 - \tau)$. From the previous equation this implies that $a = (1 - \alpha\beta)(1 - \tau)$. Thus,

$$c_t = (1 - \tau)(1 - \alpha\beta)y_t, \tag{13.9a}$$

and

$$k_{t+1} = \alpha\beta(1 - \tau)y_t, \tag{13.9b}$$

constitute a solution to the optimization problem for a balanced growth path.

We can now write the utility function of the representative agent at the beginning of the planning horizon as

$$U = \sum_{t=0}^{\infty} \beta^t [\ln((1 - \tau_t)(1 - \alpha\beta)Ak_t^\alpha G_t^\theta) + \zeta\ln(G_t)], \qquad (13.10)$$

when we restrict attention to growth paths where $\tau > 0$. The government's decision problem is to choose an infinite policy sequence in the first period that it is absolutely committed to, $\{\tau_t, G_t\}$, to maximize U, given by (13.11), subject to the resource constraint, the government's budget, and (13.9). It is straightforward to show that the first order conditions can be written in the following way,

$$\tau = \lambda_2 G/(ydL*/dy), \qquad (13.11a)$$

$$\lambda_2 G = \beta\theta(ydL*/dy) + \beta\zeta, \qquad (13.11b)$$

$$\lambda_1 k = \beta(\alpha - \rho\theta)(ydL*/dy), \qquad (13.11c)$$

where λ_1 and λ_2 are the Lagrange multipliers for the two constraints, L* is the Lagrangean, and $dL*/dy = (1 + \lambda_1 k + \lambda_2 G)/y$ is the impact of an extra unit of output on the Lagrangean and hence on social welfare.

Equations (13.11) can be combined in various ways. For example, if $\zeta = 0$ so there are no consumption benefits associated with public capital, then (13.11a) and (13.11b) imply that $\tau = \beta\theta$, as in Glomm and Ravikumar (1994). More generally, if $\zeta > 0$ instead, we obtain,

$$\tau = \beta\theta + \beta\zeta/(ydL*/dy). \qquad (13.12)$$

The second term on the right in (13.12) captures the impact of the consumption benefit of public capital on the tax rate at the margin and is positive since a gift of a unit of output has positive social value in the absence of satiation. It is also increasing in the benefit parameter ζ. Thus, the optimal tax rate will be higher when there is a consumption benefit than would otherwise be the case. It can also be shown that the ratio of public capital to private capital is constant and is given by

$$G/k = \tau/\alpha\beta(1 - \tau). \qquad (13.13)$$

The growth rate can be calculated in the following way. Substitute the production function and (13.13) into (13.11b) to obtain $k_{t+1}/k_t = 1+\omega = (\alpha\beta(1-\tau))^{1-\theta}A\tau^\theta k^{(\alpha+\theta-1)}$. If there is constant returns to scale in k and G, i.e., public capital is labor enhancing, this becomes

$$1+\omega = (\alpha\beta(1-\tau))^{1-\theta}A\tau^\theta. \qquad (13.14)$$

The growth rate depends on the tax rate in two ways. First, the income tax distorts the accumulation of private capital and this serves to reduce the growth rate. Second, an increase in the tax rate generates more tax revenue and hence allows for an increase in productive public capital investment. Differentiate equation (13.14) to obtain

$$d\gamma/d\tau = (\theta - \tau)(1+\omega)/\tau(1-\tau) = \beta[\rho\theta - \zeta(ydL*/dy)](1+\gamma)/\tau(1-\tau),$$

after using (13.12). Clearly, this derivative takes the sign of $(\theta - \tau)$. If the productivity parameter is larger than the tax rate in this model, then the growth rate increases with the tax rate. On the other hand, if the productivity parameter is less than the tax rate, then the growth rate decreases with the tax rate. Intuitively, if $\theta > \tau$, an extra unit of public capital essentially pays for itself in increased productivity.

Consider the special case where there is no consumption benefit of public capital. Then $\zeta = 0$ and it follows that $\tau = \beta\theta$ and

$$d\gamma/d\tau = \theta\rho\beta(1+\gamma)/\tau(1-\tau) > 0.$$

In this case the net impact of the optimal tax and public capital investment policy is to increase the growth rate. On the other hand, if there is a consumption benefit associated with public capital, there is an additional effect that needs to be taken into account. The growth rate is increasing in the tax rate only if $\rho\theta > \zeta/(ydL*/dy)$. The consumption benefit causes the government to produce more of the public capital than would otherwise have been the case and this causes the tax rate to be higher than it otherwise would have been. This in turn serves to lower the growth rate. So the real tradeoff in providing public capital investment may not be between the distorting effects of the taxes required to finance the additional investment and the productivity of the marginal public capital investment. Instead, the real tradeoff may be between the growth rate and the additional taxes needed to finance the consumption benefits associated with public capital. To our knowledge this point has not been made before.

13.3.2 Congestion

A number of analysts have extended this model by including congestion. Most examples of public infrastructure involve congestion to some degree and so including it in the model is of interest. We will follow the analysis of Glomm and Ravikumar (1994).

The model is similar to that of the last section. However, let K^G be the stock of public capital and let G be the services derived from the stock according to $G = K^G/K^\eta L^\mu$, where $K = Nk$, $L = N$, k is capital per person, and $0 < \eta, \mu < 1$. Given the public capital stock, the services flowing from public capital are decreasing in private capital and labor. This captures the idea that the more private inputs are used, the greater the amount of congestion created. As it turns out, $\eta+\mu$ will play an important role in causing scale effects. If $\eta = \mu = 0$, we have the case of a pure public good.

The representative consumer and firm solve the same decision problems as before and the same conditions will hold since each takes aggregates like congestion as given and beyond their control. By following the same procedure as before it can be shown that the linear decision rules of the consumer are also of the same form. In addition, $y = A(k)^{\alpha-\eta\theta}(K^G)^\theta/N^{\theta(\mu+\eta)}$ is the production function after substituting for G. The individual firm takes G, and hence its determinants, as given. Thus, $1 = \alpha - \eta\theta + 0$ so $\theta = (1 - \alpha)/(1 - \eta)$ is necessary for the existence of a balanced growth path.

Glomm and Ravikumar consider the optimal policy in the same manner as discussed in the last section. The decision rules for the consumer are once again linear and the government chooses an infinite sequence of tax rates and investment in public capital at the beginning of its planning horizon to maximize utility subject to its budget, the equilibrium condition involving the law of motion for private capital, the optimal behavior of the private sector, and the initial conditions. (See Appendix C.) They showed that at the second best optimum, $\tau = \beta\theta$, a special case of our earlier result, and that the ratio of public to private capital is once again constant on the optimal growth path. Interestingly enough, the optimal tax rate does not generally depend on the congestion parameters, nor does it depend on the initial conditions. However, if the economy evolves on a balanced growth path, then $\theta = (1-\alpha)/(1-\eta)$ and the tax rate depends on a congestion parameter, η.

It is straightforward to show that the tax rate is increasing in η. Intuitively, a small increase in η increases the impact of congestion on private capital. To overcome this a higher tax rate is required to finance slightly more investment in public capital. We can calculate the growth rate in exactly the same manner as in the last section to obtain

$$1+\omega = (\alpha\beta(1-\tau))^{1-\theta}A\tau^\theta k^{\alpha+\theta(1-\eta)-1}N^{\theta(1-\mu-\eta)}.$$

If there is constant returns, this becomes

$$1+\omega = (\alpha\beta(1-\tau))^{1-\theta}A\tau^\theta N^{\theta(1-\mu-\eta)}.$$

Once again, this captures the two effects mentioned in the last section; the income tax rate causes a distortion at the margin reducing the growth rate but also finances more public capital which raises the growth rate.

One can see the scale effects from this last equation. If there is constant returns in congestion, then $1 = \eta + \mu$, and the scale effect involving N doesn't exist. If there is increasing returns to congestion, then scale matters and larger economies will grow less rapidly than smaller economies. And, if there is decreasing returns to scale in congestion, then scale matters and larger economies will grow faster than smaller economies.

13.4 Conclusion

The Diamond - Mirrlees (1971) production efficiency result is one of the classic results of the optimal policy design literature. Coincidentally, in another branch of the literature other analysts such as Sandmo and Dreze (1971) derived a weighted average formula. These two views can be reconciled by recognizing that the efficiency result requires the government to have perfect control of consumer prices and its debt policy. If the government does not have complete control over consumer prices, then a weighted average formula will be appropriate and this will depend very sensitively on the policy instruments available to the government. We studied this issue in the context of a static model and an overlapping generations model.

We also showed that the long run growth rate is increasing in the ratio of public capital to private capital in an endogenous growth model where public capital entered the technology in a labor enhancing way. Thus, public capital may be an "engine" of economic growth. This creates a tradeoff between productivity enhancing public investments and the taxes required to finance it. However, the demand for public capital will be greater if there is a consumption benefit associated with it. In that case, the tradeoff is between the higher level of public capital investment due to the consumption benefit and the additional taxes needed to pay for it. Finally, we showed how congestion may affect growth and the demand for public capital. Under certain circumstances congestion creates a negative externality that causes a scale effect and reduces the ability of public capital to be an "engine" of growth.

Appendix A: Derivation of the Weighted Average Formula (13.3)

Differentiate the Lagrangean with respect to p_k,

$$\lambda x_k + \alpha_1 x_{1k} - \Sigma_i \alpha_i x_{ik} + \Sigma_i (\alpha_i - \alpha_1 f_i) y_{ik} = 0.$$

The first three terms are new relative to the case where the government completely controls prices and capture the effect of the kth price on utility and demand. Differentiate the private agent's budget constraint, $x_k + x_{ik} + \Sigma_- q_i x_{ik} = 0$, where the sum is from $i = 2, ..., n$. Using this, the Slutsky equation, and Diamond's definition of the social marginal utility of income we can write the last equation as,

$$(\mu/\alpha_1 - 1)x_k - \Sigma_i(\alpha_i/\alpha_1 + q_i)s_{ik} + \Sigma_i[\alpha_i/\alpha_1 - f_i]y_{ik} = 0.$$

Differentiate the Lagrangean with respect to the lump sum tax and note that it implies that $\mu/\alpha_1 = 1$. Use this information in the last equation,

$$\Sigma_i[(\alpha_i/\alpha_1 - f_i)y_{ik} - (\alpha_i/\alpha_1 + q_i)s_{ik}] = 0.$$

Finally, differentiate the Lagrangean with respect to z_i, to get $\alpha_i - \alpha_1 g_i = 0$. Use this in the last equation to obtain the weighted average formula (13.3).

Appendix B: The Weighted Average Formula with Heterogeneity

The first order conditions with respect to T^h, T, z_k, and p_k are given by

$$\phi^h \lambda^h + \alpha_1 x^h_{1T} - \Sigma_i \alpha_i x^h_{iT} = 0, \tag{B1}$$

$$\Sigma_h \phi^h \lambda^h + \alpha_1 \Sigma_h x^h_{1T} - \Sigma_h \Sigma_i \alpha_i x^h_{iT} = 0, \tag{B2}$$

$$\alpha_k - \alpha_1 g_k = 0, \tag{B3}$$

$$\Sigma_h \phi^h \lambda^h x^h_k + \alpha_1 \Sigma_h x^h_{1k} - \Sigma_h \Sigma_i \alpha_i x^h_{ik} + \Sigma_i(\alpha_i - \alpha_1 f_i)y_{ik} = 0, \tag{B4}$$

where we have assumed the public production agency has no control over prices, and where x^h_{ik} is the derivative of h's demand for good one with respect to the kth price, and so on. Substitute (B1) and (B3) into (B4), use the Slutsky equation and Diamond's definition of the social marginal utility of income, and it is straightforward to derive the weighted average formula, following the steps of Appendix A.

Appendix C: Endogenous Growth and Congestion - The Planner's Problem

The government chooses an infinite sequence of tax rates and investment in public capital at the beginning of its planning horizon to maximize utility $\Sigma\beta^t \ln(c_t)$ subject to the constraints,

$$c_t = (1 - \tau)(1 - \alpha\beta)y_t,$$

$$k_{t+1} = \alpha\beta(1 - \tau)y_t,$$

$$G = K^G/K^\eta L^\mu,$$

$$K = Nk,$$

$$L = N,$$

$$y = A(k)^{\alpha - \eta\theta}(K^G)^\theta/N^{\theta(\mu + \eta)},$$

$$Ak_t^\alpha G_t^{1-\alpha} - k_{t+1} - c_t - \phi G_{t+1} = 0,$$

$$\tau_t y_t = \phi G_{t+1},$$

k_0, and K^G_0 given.

---

[1] This weighted average rule has been discussed by a number of other authors including Sandmo and Dreze (1971), Dreze (1974), Bradford (1975), Pestieau (1975), Baumol (1977), Marchand and Pestieau (1984), Yoshida (1986), Auerbach (1987), and Burgess (1988), among others.

[2] Kay (1972) proved that if (a) a project has only pecuniary benefits, (b) the saving rate s and the opportunity cost of funds r are both constant, (c) sr < ρ, and (d) there is no reinvestment of the pecuniary benefits of the project, then ρ is the appropriate discount rate and a project should be accepted if it has a positive present value when ρ is used as the discount rate. Kay also discussed when the theorem generalizes. For example, if (d) is relaxed and some of the pecuniary benefits are reinvested in future public projects, then the initial rule still holds if those projects also generate a positive present value when ρ is the social discount rate.

[3] It is well known that debt policy is equivalent to making transfers to both generations. Thus, Yoshida implicitly assumed there were two types of debt policy available by assuming transfers can be made to both generations, in addition to using debt policy to finance public investment.

[4]   See Atkinson and Sandmo (1980) and King (1980) for early analyses of optimal taxation in the OG model. For a summary see chapter 3 in Batina and Ihori (2000).

[5]   See chapter 6 in Batina and Ihori (2000) for a summary of the time consistency problem and references to the literature.

[6]   In a similar model that also includes congestion effects, Glomm and Ravikumar (1994) showed that the linear decision rules for c and k satisfy the consumer's decision problem uniquely as long as the sequence $\{G\}$ does not grow too quickly, i.e., if $G_t < \delta^t G_0$ for some $\delta \geq 1$.

14 Empirical Work on the Public Capital Hypothesis

Aschauer's (1989) landmark paper started a large empirical literature testing the impact of public capital on the economy, the so-called "public capital" hypothesis. We will present a summary of some of the various tests of the hypothesis.[1] A variety of different approaches have been taken using different data sets and alternative statistical techniques. The main point is to verify that the marginal product of public capital is statistically positive since this is at the heart of the models studied in the last two chapters. This requires estimating either a production function, or a cost function. The early results were very encouraging, however, later work was not quite as favorable.

In the next section we present Aschauer's and Munnell's results. In section 14.2 we present several critical arguments against the early work since this sets the stage for most of the later work. In particular, we discuss Tatom's (1991a, 1991b, 1993) critical work. Studies using disaggregated data, city and state level data and industry specific data, are studied in section 14.3. Some studies present results favorable to the hypothesis, e.g., Morrison and Schwartz (1996), while others report the opposite, e.g., Holtz-Eakin (1994). Several additional studies using U.S. time series are discussed in section 14.4. We report on the results of studies for other countries in section 14.5, as well as results using a cross section of OECD countries. Certain conditions are required for the stock of capital to be chosen optimally and one can econometrically test whether those conditions hold, or not. We discuss this in section 14.6. Finally, section 14.7 concludes the chapter.

There are a number of complicating factors to testing the main hypothesis. First, there are different types of public capital and not all will have the same impact. The second issue is finding empirical proxies. Not all proxies lead to the same results. For example, the theory is silent on whether "labor" means labor hours, employment, the stock of human capital, or some other variable. Third, the data may not be disaggregated enough. For example, one would like to know whether a new airport will have a bigger impact on the local economy than a new highway but the data may not allow one to make this distinction. Finally, there is the issue of the amount of variation in the data. Some analysts will multiply the public and private capital stocks by the capacity utilization rate. This increases the variability in the data and may improve the parameter estimates. Whether or not this is appropriate is still an open question.

There are also some common econometric problems in the empirical work. First, and foremost, is the simultaneity problem. Many of the variables used to proxy for capital, labor, and public capital, or price variables under the cost approach, are endogenous and there may be a simultaneity bias as a result. A second problem that arises with time series or panel data is the stationarity of the data. Two time series that tend to drift together may yield a positive correlation that is entirely spurious. Techniques are now readily available for dealing with this issue, e.g., unit root testing, but are sometimes not used.[2] Other issues such as measurement problems and multicollinearity also arise. We will point out the various issues along the way as we survey the literature.

14.1 Early Results

Ratner (1983) first included a public capital variable in an aggregate production function and estimated a log-linear version of the function using aggregate, annual, U.S. time series data for 1949 – 1973. His estimate of the output elasticity with respect to public capital, 5.8%, was small in magnitude, but significantly different from zero. It increased substantially to 27.7% when revised data was used by Tatom (1991b) for the same time period. However, when Tatom corrected for serial correlation, the elasticity was not statistically different from zero. See Table 14.1.

Hulten and Schwab (1984) studied the relationship between productivity of manufacturing and the sun and snow belt regions of the U.S. using aggregate data for 1951-1978. Growth in multifactor productivity was the same in both regions. Differences in the growth rates of private inputs completely explained differences in the growth rate of output between regions. And the productivity slowdown was felt in the same way by the two regions despite differences in public infrastructure.

However, it was Aschauer's (1989) paper that sparked the current interest in the literature. He used annual, aggregate, time series data covering the period from 1949 to 1985 for the U.S. and estimated a Cobb-Douglas production function. Suppose there is constant returns to scale in all three inputs and suppose the technology is given by

$$Y = AK^{1-\alpha_2-\alpha_3} L^{\alpha_2} G^{\alpha_3} e^{\alpha_4 \ln(CU)+\alpha_5 T+u} ,$$

where CU is capacity utilization, T is a time trend, and u is an i.i.d. random error term that is uncorrelated with any of the other variables. Take logs and simplify,

$$\ln(Y/K) = \ln(A) + \alpha_2\ln(L/K) + \alpha_3\ln(G/K) + \alpha_4\ln(CU) + \alpha_5 T + u. \quad (14.1)$$

An estimate of α_1 can easily be obtained from $\alpha_1 = 1 - \alpha_2 - \alpha_3$. Aschauer estimated this equation using various techniques.[3] The estimate of the public capital elasticity was 0.39, almost seven times larger than Ratner's estimate. Second, the output elasticity of labor was 0.35, and the output elasticity of private capital can be calculated according to $1 - 0.35 - 0.39 = 0.26$. So it would appear that public capital is more productive than either private capital or labor alone. This result was quite astonishing when first published.

Aschauer also discovered that other forms of government spending did not increase private output, including general government consumption, non-military spending, military spending, and compensation for government employees. Second, almost the entire effect of public capital was due to structures, not equipment. Third, core infrastructure: highways, mass transit, airports, electrical and gas facilities, water, and sewers, had an output elasticity of 0.24 and was highly significant. Although this estimate is about 37% smaller in magnitude than the estimate for total public capital, it was four times larger than Ratner's. And a cross-country comparison of G7 countries revealed a positive correlation between growth in labor productivity and the ratio of public investment to GDP. Aschauer also presented results for the trucking industry that indicated that highway capital had a positive effect on output in the industry.

Furthermore, Aschauer offered the reduction in spending on public capital as an explanation for the infamous productivity slowdown in the U.S. Researchers began to notice a decline in the growth rate of GDP and the rate of growth in labor productivity in the early 1970's in several countries including the U.S. Several explanations were offered and there were supporters and critics for each one.[4] However, Aschauer offered a novel explanation; the slowdown in growth could be explained as a response to the marked decline in spending on public infrastructure. When his model is simulated the decline in public infrastructure spending in the late 1960's and early 1970's can explain about 57% of the slowdown in the growth rate. The policy implication is fairly obvious; growth would improve if more were spent on infrastructure.

Table 14.1. Early Results

Author	Data	Approach	Main result
Ratner (1973)	aggregate 1949 - 73	production function	$E_G = 0.058$
Aschauer (1989)	aggregate 1949-1985	production function	$E_G = 0.39$ (total public capital) $E_G = 0.24$ (core infrastructure) $E_G = 0.00$ (govt consumption) $E_G = 0.00$ (military capital)
Munnell (1990a)	aggregate 1949-1987	production function	$E_G = 0.31$ (total public capital) $E_G = 0.37$ (core infrastructure)
Tatom (1991b)	aggregate 1948-1989	production function	$E_G = 0.132$ (with energy price) $E_G = 0.00$ (first differences)
Lynde and Richmond (1992)	aggregate 1959-1989	translog cost function	Public capital is productive.
Lynde and Richmond (1993)	aggregate 1959-1989	profit function	Public capital is productive.

E_G = output elasticity of public capital.

Munnell (1990a) also found some supporting evidence using similar data.[5] For the period 1949 – 1987, she estimated an aggregate output elasticity for public capital of 0.31, without any constraint on the estimation, 0.37 when constant returns is imposed for private inputs, and 0.33 when constant returns to private inputs and public capital (K, L, G) is imposed. However, the labor coefficient in her equations is implausibly low and sometimes even negative. (See Table 14, equation (1), pp. 18, for example.)

Aschauer (1990) used a panel of data on the fifty states in the U.S. for 1965-1983 and time averaged the data to estimate a production function that captures the long run effect of public capital on output. He estimated the output elasticity of core infrastructure spending to be about 0.055. Since this is well above the share of core infrastructure spending to output ratio, 0.025, he further argued that this strongly suggests that too little had been spent on core infrastructure. However, an elasticity of 0.055 is much smaller than his earlier study. Indeed, as we will see, this is a typical pattern; the elasticity tends to be much smaller when disaggregated data is used.

Of course, one general criticism of applying these results to the productivity slowdown is that the other possible reasons that have been put forth for the slowdown have not been included in the estimation strategy. Therefore, a test of the different explanations, and how well the public capital hypothesis does relative to other explanations, has not been undertaken. It is certainly possible that the public capital hypothesis may dominate the other explanations. Of course, the opposite is also possible.

14.2 Criticism of the Early Work

Other researchers were highly critical of these results. In particular, Tatom (1991a) argued that most of the decline in spending on infrastructure in the US during the early 1970's was due to a decline in spending on highways, streets, and educational buildings by state and local governments. He pointed out that the number of school age children and the amount of miles driven per person were both decreasing during this period. Cutting spending on highways, streets, and educational buildings was a rational response to the decline in demand.

Furthermore, Tatom (1991b, 1993) argued that there were statistical problems with the earlier studies. First, the early work did not take into account the energy crisis. If energy is not taken into account in the estimation, reduced growth in productivity that would have been attributed to energy related problems, especially during the 1970's, would naturally be attributed to other sources including the drop in public investment spending. Second, significant breaks in the time trend were omitted. Trends are included in these studies to account for technological change. Tatom argued there was a break in the trend around 1967. Ignoring this would again bias the public capital elasticity upwards. Third, the data may not be stationary.[6] When two data series, such as output and public capital, are both drifting upwards over time, a regression of one series on the other can lead to a statistically significant positive coefficient even if there is no real relationship between the two variables. This is the spurious regression problem. Tatom (1991b) presented evidence from the Augmented Dickey – Fuller unit root test that the data is not stationary in levels.[7] This strongly suggests that the early results may possibly be spurious. When these various problems are taken into account, Tatom found no evidence that public capital had a large effect on output or growth.[8]

Aaron (1990) and Eisner (1991), among others, argued that causality could go in the opposite direction. Estimating a production function implicitly assumes that public capital "causes" output or growth in output. However, the direction of causality could be the other way. As a society becomes wealthier it may spend more on public infrastructure so an increase in output, which leads to greater wealth, may in fact cause greater spending on public capital. Also, during a recession when output is low, the government may undertake a public infrastructure project to boost output and employment. In that case, low output is causing an increase in infrastructure spending and hence the causality is "reversed." This sort of "simultaneity problem" can bias the estimation of the coefficients.

Both Munnell and Aschauer have revised their earlier view. Munnell (1992) stated that, "the numbers emerging from the aggregate time-series studies are not credible." Similarly, Aschauer (1993) revised his estimates downward as well. He suggested that about 10% of the productivity slowdown can be explained by the decline in public infrastructure spending. However, Lynde and Richmond (1992, 1993) provided further evidence strongly supporting the hypothesis. In their second paper they estimated a profit function for aggregate US data for the period 1948 – 1989 and used an estimation procedure that takes simultaneity and stationarity into account. Their estimates suggested that about 40% of the productivity slowdown could be explained by reduced spending on public capital. While lower than Aschauer's original estimate, this is still quite large.

14.3 Studies Using Disaggregated U.S. Data

14.3.1 Regional and State Studies

Regional economists were especially interested in the public capital hypothesis since many infrastructure projects are locally determined in many countries. The results using disaggregated U.S. data are collected in Table 14.2 below. The evidence is mixed, however, one conclusion is that public capital does not have as large an impact when disaggregated data is studied as it does when aggregate data is used.

Eberts (1986) studied data on 38 U.S. metropolitan areas and estimated an elasticity of 0.03 for public capital, which included highways, water, and sewer capital. He also uncovered evidence that private capital and public capital are complements. Deno (1988) estimated an aggregate translog profit function using data from 36 SMSA's for 1970-1978. All three types of public capital (highway, sewer, and water) had a positive impact on output and all were complementary to both private capital and labor. This would suggest that local policy makers may be able to attract more firms and hence private inputs by investing in public infrastructure.

A number of researchers have studied state data. Costa, Ellison, and Martin (1987) estimated a translog production function using a cross section of the 48 contiguous states in the U.S. for 1972 and found that public capital had a significant positive effect on state manufacturing output. The public capital elasticity was 0.19, and labor and public capital were complements, while private and public capital were unrelated. Munnell (1990b) constructed a panel data set consisting of annual observations on gross state product, private capital, non-agricultural employment, and state and local public capital for the 48 contiguous states of the U.S. for 1970 – 1988. She found that public capital had a positive effect on gross state product and its elasticity was 0.15 when there were no constraints imposed, 0.06 when constant returns in private inputs was imposed, and 0.08 when constant returns in all three inputs was imposed. When public capital was disaggregated the estimated elasticities of highways, water, and sewer systems were 0.06, 0.12, and 0.01, respectively, which are quite small in magnitude.

Eisner (1991) pointed out that Munnell's "overall" regressions average across all time periods and all 48 states and thus combine cross section and time series variances and covariances. He argued that it is the cross sections that dominate in her data. He used Munnell's own data to estimate a state production function and discovered that public capital had no effect on private output. Eisner re-estimated the equation and showed that public capital is not productive when taking time averages alone. (See Table 5B pp.50) When cross sections are taken alone, the results are very similar to Munnell's. (See Table 5C, pp. 51.)

To reconcile the various disparate findings in the literature, Holtz-Eakin (1994) used a panel of state data on gross state product, employment, Munnell's private capital series, and his own estimates for state and local public capital for the US for the period 1969-1986 to estimate a state production function controlling for various fixed effects. The main equation of his model is an aggregate state production function,

$$Y_{st} = \alpha_0 + \alpha_1 K_{st} + \alpha_3 L_{st} + \alpha_4 G_{st} + \varepsilon_{st},$$

where ε is an error term. The s subscript indexes states while the t subscript indexes time. Holtz-Eakin considered the following specification of the error term, $\varepsilon_{st} = f_s + \gamma_t + \mu_{st}$ where f is a state-specific effect, γ is a time-specific effect, and μ is an i.i.d. random variable. The state-specific component of the error term picks up any effects that are invariant over time but may vary across states, while the time-specific component picks up effects that are the same across states but may differ over time, where both effects are unobservable by the econometrician. This is important because other studies using state data did not differentiate these various effects and Holtz-Eakin argued this was the reason for the disparate results.

First, one can assume the state-specific effect f_s and the time-specific effect γ_t each period are both fixed. State dummy variables can then be used to capture the state-specific effects. The estimation results are then contingent on the state-specific effects actually present in the data and the focus is on the time variation within each state, not cross sectional variation across the states. Alternatively, the state-specific effect can be eliminated by first differencing the data. Second, one can assume the state-specific fixed effect is random. However, this may introduce a bias in the estimation because the error terms may be common across states. In that case, GLS will be efficient, but inconsistent and biased.[9] Holtz-Eakin estimated various versions of the model controlling for time effects, state effects, and several additional econometric problems. Only in the simplest model did public capital have a positive effect on gross state product. In every other specification the effect was either zero or negative. In some cases it was negative and statistically significant. Holtz-Eakin concluded that the effect of state and local public capital, "is essentially zero." (pp. 20.)

Garcia-Mila and McGuire (1992) estimated a Cobb-Douglas production function using a panel data set for the 48 contiguous states in the U.S. for 1969 – 1983. They found that the highway elasticity was 0.045 and the elasticity with respect to educational expenditures was 0.165. More recently, Garcia-Mila, McGuire, and Porter (1996) came to the opposite conclusion, namely, that public capital does not affect output. They estimated several Cobb-Douglas functions and found that when state effects were taken into account, the elasticities were typically small in magnitude. For example, when fixed state effects are taken into account, the elasticities were 0.127 and 0.064 for highways, and water and sewer capital, respectively. The public capital variables were not statistically significant when the production function was estimated in first difference form.

Morrison and Schwartz (1996) employed a cost function approach using U.S. data for 1970 – 1987 for public capital (highways, water and sewer systems), private capital, production and non-production labor, and energy. Of course, additional data on relative prices is required under this approach and it is especially difficult to find a proxy for the shadow price of public capital. They defined the shadow value of public capital as $Z_G = -\partial C / \partial G$, which is directly related to the marginal productivity of public capital. They estimated a system of equations that included the demands for the variable inputs (labor and energy), a cost function, that allowed for non-constant returns to scale and fixed inputs, and a pricing equation to capture profit maximization. The model was estimated for four regions (North East, North Central, South, and West) and included fixed effects.[10]

In contrast to the results of Holtz-Eakin, Morrison and Schwartz found that public capital did lower cost. The shadow values of public capital Z_G were positive for all four regions and all time periods in the sample. For example, a $1 million dollar investment in public capital on average would generate a cost saving of $160,000 to $180,000, except in the South where the cost saving was $314,000. Second, a dollar invested in private capital had a greater return than a dollar invested in public capital everywhere except in the South. Third, lower investment in the snowbelt, relative to the sunbelt, corresponded to lower shadow values there suggesting that such differential investment was appropriate. Fourth, calculations of the net benefit, $Z_G - C_G$, depended critically on the proxy for the marginal production cost, C_G. Some proxies led to positive values for the net benefit in most years for all of the regions, while others led to some negative values.

More recently, Aschauer (2001) developed a model that linked public capital to output growth and employment. The relationship between public capital and economic growth was non-linear in his model. This allowed him to estimate the growth-maximizing level of public capital relative to private capital. He estimated the model using several estimation procedures and data for the 48 contiguous states in the U.S. over the period from 1970 to 1990. The first main result of the paper was that public capital generally had a positive effect on economic growth in terms of both output and employment. Second, the estimated value of the growth-maximizing public capital stock was between 50 and 70 percent of the private capital stock. Third, public debt and taxes generally exerted a negative effect on economic growth. Fourth, the effect of public capital was higher in the1980s than the 1970s. Finally, the effect of public capital was higher in the Snowbelt than in the Sunbelt.

Annala and Perez (2001) studied the convergence of public capital investment among the states in the U.S. during the period 1977-1996 and provided evidence that such investment has converged both absolutely and when conditioned on a set of variables. Numerous studies have posed the question of whether income across countries and across regions within a country has been converging or not. In particular, Vohra (1998), among others, provided evidence that income is converging among the states in the U.S. Suppose public capital has a positive impact on economic growth.

Then, if public investment is converging across states or regions of a country, this will increase the speed of convergence in income. Alternatively, if public capital investment is diverging, this may slow the convergence process in income. Annala and Perez found significant evidence of convergence in public investment.

This raises an interesting question of whether state or regional data can measure the productivity of public capital reliably. Suppose there is complete convergence of public capital investment across states but there is some variation in per capita state GDP. In that case, the output elasticity of public capital would be zero in a cross section regression equation, even though public capital might be very productive within a state. Indeed, even if a panel of data was used, the cross section variation may dominate thus making it difficult to measure the impact of public capital on the economy over time. This might be one reason why the aggregate time series studies generally find a larger effect of public capital than the studies that rely on cross section or panel data at the state or industry level.

Table 14.2. Results from Studies Using Disaggregated U.S. Data

Author	Data	Method	Main result
Eberts (1986)	38 SMSA'a 1958-1978	Translog prod. Function	$E_G = 0.03$ for $G = HWY + WT + SWR$
Costa, Ellison, Martin (1987)	48 states, cross section - 1972	Translog prod. function	SP – positive effect on manufacturing.
Deno (1988)	36 SMSAs 1970-1978	profit function	HWY, SWR, WT – positive effect on Y.
Hulten and Schwab (1991)	regional 1951-1986	Growth accounting estimation	Public capital has no effect.
Garcia-Mila and McGuire (1992)	48 states 1970-1983	Cobb-Douglas prod. function	$E_{HWY} = 0.045$ $E_E = 0.165$
Garcia-Mila, McGuire, and Porter (1996)	48 states 1970-1983	Cobb-Douglas prod. function	$E_{HWY} = 0.12$ (levels) $E_{HWY} = 0.0$ (first diff.) $E_{WTSWR} = 0.04$ (levels) $E_{WTSWR} = 0.0$ (first diff.)

Table 14.2. (cont.)

Nadiri and Mamuneas (1994)	12 industries 1956-1986	Cost Function	$C_I = [-.21, 0.0]$[a] $C_{RD} = [-.05, -.0008]$[a] social return$_I$ = 0.72 social return$_{RD}$ = 0.872 social return$_K$ = 0.865
Holtz-Eakin (1994)	48 states 1969-1986	Cobb-Douglas production function	E_{SG} = 0.23 (no fixed effect) E_{SG} = -.05 (fixed effect)
Morrison and Schwartz (1996)	48 states 1970-1987	Generalized Leontief Cost function	SG has small, significant negative impact on cost.
Fernald (1999)	29 industries 1953-1989	Growth accounting estimation	HWY capital causes one time increase in growth; little marginal impact.
Chandra and Thompson (2000)	Rural counties 1969-1973	Earnings equation	Earnings shifts toward counties with a new highway.
Paul, Ball, Felthoven, and Nehring (2001)	48 states 1960-1996	Cost function	HWY reduces cost in Agriculture.
Ashauer (2001)	48 states 1970-1990	System estimation	SG has positive effect on growth.
Annala and Perez (2001)	50 states 1977-1996		SG is converging across states.
Pereira and Andraz (2003)	12 U.S. industries 1956 - 1997	VAR model	Public investment has a positive impact on output, private investment, and employment; effects differ by industry

Y = output, SG = State public capital, HWY = highway capital, SWR = sewer capital, WT = water capital, E = education, I = infrastructure capital, RD = R&D capital, K = private capital. E_D = output elasticity with respect to D, C_D = cost elasticity with respect to D. *a* - The cost elasticity was in this range for all 12 industries.

14.3.2 Industry Studies

The data can also be disaggregated by sector of the economy. Industry studies focus on individual industries over time or on a cross section of industries. Typically, these studies tend to find that public capital has a significant impact on output or cost.

Nadiri and Mamuneas (1994) estimated the cost share equations of the representative firm that stem from cost minimization after imposing certain regularity conditions, e.g., concavity in prices. They used data on twelve two digit-manufacturing industries in the U.S. for 1955-1986. Public capital was measured in two ways, total, non-military net public capital stock, (federal, state and local), and R&D public capital. The latter was constructed from data on total R&D expenditures by the government. They found that both public capital variables exerted a negative effect on cost for most of the industries in their sample. The magnitude of the cost elasticities for public infrastructure services ranged from -0.1153 to -0.2113, and the range for public R&D capital services was -0.0027 to -0.557. The marginal benefits were generally higher in durable manufacturing industries. And estimates of the average social return across industries for public infrastructure and public R&D were 0.0718 and 0.0872, respectively, while the estimated social rate of return to private capital was 0.0865. In addition, the return to both public infrastructure and private capital increased throughout the sample period while the return to R&D capital fell.

Fernald (1999) hypothesized that vehicle-intensive industries would benefit most from road and highway building. He employed a data set on 29 industries in the U.S. that constituted most of the private economy, excluding mining and agriculture, for the period 1953-1989 and used an estimation strategy that took congestion and the possibility of simultaneity bias into account. According to this data, value added productivity grew at an annual rate of 1.6% from 1953-1973 but only grew at 0.3% from 1973-1989. Road and highway building grew at a rate of about 4% prior to 1973 but only about 1% after that. The question is what accounts for the drop in the growth of productivity.

Fernald found that the productivity slowdown after 1973 was concentrated in industries that were vehicle-intensive. Second, marginal increases in the growth rate of road building tended to improve productivity in vehicle-intensive industries but also tended to lower productivity in non-vehicle-intensive industries. Third, the massive road and highway building effort in the 1960s in the U.S. was a one-time event giving a boost to productivity growth during that period, but not after. He also argued that incremental road building projects are unlikely to have the same impact on output in the future, but only bring about small marginal gains. Thus, Fernald was able to explain 1.0 of the 1.3 percent drop in the growth in productivity after 1973, or about 77% of the decline, as a result of the reduction in highway capital, which supports Aschauer's original claim.

Paul, Ball, Felthoven, and Nehring (2001) studied the impact of public capital investment in the highway network on the productivity of agriculture in the US. They measured the cost-saving shadow prices for public infrastructure using state level panel data for 1960-1996. Their approach was based on a cost function model that included land, labor, capital, fertilizer, pesticide and "other" material input demands, augmented by pricing equations for crop and animal outputs that reflect profit maximization. Their results indicated that public infrastructure investment had a significantly positive effect on productivity in U.S. agriculture. This was particularly so for animal products for which an efficient transportation network is important. They also found that public infrastructure capital was a substitute for all inputs in agriculture. Finally, public infrastructure generated greater land-use intensity, lower fertilizer and "other materials" intensity, and also altered the shares of animal and crop outputs so there were sectoral reallocation effects as well.

Pereira and Andraz (2003) studied U.S. data on public investment, private output, employment, and private investment for twelve industries covering the entire economy for the period 1956 to 1997. They used the VAR approach in first differences, which allows them to capture the indirect effects as well as direct effects, and control for the stationarity properties of the data. They found that public investment generally has a positive impact on output, private investment, and employment at the aggregate level. For example, they find that $1 million invested in public capital creates 27 jobs. The impact differs by sector, as one would imagine. The biggest effects were in manufacturing (durables), construction, and services, and there are negative effects in agriculture, mining, communications, and FIRE (finance, insurance, and real estate.) Public investment increased jobs the most in construction, services, retail trade, and manufacturing (durables), but reduced employment in service, agriculture, mining, communication, wholesale trade, and public utilities.

14.4 Additional Time Series Evidence

Several researchers focused on correcting for the stationarity and simultaneity problems in the time series data. Finn (1993) estimated a model where transportation services are produced via public infrastructure but are subject to congestion using aggregate U.S. data for 1950 - 1989. She used

Generalized Method of Moments (GMM), an instrumental variables technique, to estimate the equations of her dynamic model. This technique can take care of the causality problem mentioned earlier. She also transformed the data to make it stationary. Her point estimate of the productivity of public capital was 0.16, about half Aschauer's original estimate, but was unfortunately measured very imprecisely. The 95% confidence interval was [0.001, 0.32], which is quite large.

Table 14.3. Recent Time Series Evidence for the U.S.

Finn (1993)	aggregate 1950-1989	GMM estimation	$E_G = 0.16$ (highway capital)
McMillan and Smyth (1994)	aggregate 1952-1990	VAR	Innovations in G had little effect on Y.
Pereira and Flores (1995)	aggregate 1956-1989 (OECD data on US)	VAR	G is endogenous, innovations to G have long lasting effects.
Batina (1998)	aggregate 1948-1993	VAR/ECM	Strong evidence of cointegration for Y, K, L, and G = SLG, less strong evidence when G = HWY, WT; G is endogenous; innovations to G have long lasting effects.
Batina (1999)	aggregate 1948-1993	Production function – DOLS	$E_G = 0.375$ (total public capital) $E_G = 0.14$ (state and local) $E_G = 0.088$ (highway capital)
Pereira (2000)	aggregate 1927 - 1997	VAR – first differences	Significant feedback effects exist among employment, private investment, output, and various types of public investment; rates of return on G range from 3.4% - 16.1%.

McMillan and Smyth (1994) applied a system approach and used data on output, hours worked, private and public capital, energy prices, and inflation for the U.S. for the period 1952 – 1990 to estimate two VAR models, one in levels and one in first differences. They found that public capital had little effect on output in the impulse response functions they calculated. However, they did not carry out any tests for stationarity or cointegration. Estimating a model in levels when the data is not stationary is inappropriate and estimating a model in first differences tends to ignore valuable information on the long run relationship in the data if the data is cointegrated.

Pereira and Flores (1995) used OECD data on the U.S. for 1956 – 1989 and presented evidence that their data was not stationary. They also used a residual based test for cointegration and rejected the null hypothesis that the residuals from their regression equation were stationary implying that the series in their study were not cointegrated. They proceeded to estimate a VAR model in first differences and presented evidence that public capital was an endogenous variable in that it responded to innovations in other inputs and output. Second, they also showed that an innovation to the public capital stock had significant and long lasting effects on the economy. Finally, they also argued that their model, which included lags of all the variables, could pick up important feedback effects that would be missed in estimating a production function or a cost function.

Batina (1998, 1999) did extensive unit root and cointegration testing using aggregate U.S. data on public and private capital for the period 1949 – 1993. He included several proxies for (Y, K, L, G) and undertook a sensitivity analysis.[11] Each series was stationary in first differences using several different tests and there were multiple cointegrating vectors, using the Johannson test for cointegration. When a shorter period of data was used, e.g., 1948-1985, the cointegration results and some of the unit root tests became ambiguous. Therefore, previous researchers using shorter time periods for their tests may have erroneously concluded the variables were stationary or were not cointegrated. In addition, public capital responded to innovations in the other variables implying that public capital is endogenous. And, innovations to the public capital stock also had a significant and long lasting effect on the economy. Batina (1999) used dynamic OLS to estimate an aggregate production function and dummy variables were included to capture the oil price shocks.[12] His estimate of the public capital elasticity was actually quite close to Aschauer's original estimate when the total public capital stock is used as the proxy for public capital. However, this estimate was sensitive to the proxies used for private capital, labor, and public capital and the inclusion of the oil price shock variables. In particular, the elasticity was lower when the disaggregated state and local infrastructure was used for the public capital variable. Indeed, when highway and street capital was used, the coefficient was only 0.087. Finally, when dummy variables capturing the oil price shocks were included the impact of public capital was always significantly lower than when the shocks were omitted.

Using a longer span of similar data, Pereira (2000) also estimated a VAR model to measure the interaction between private output, private investment, employment, and various public capital investments. Public investment generally crowded in private investment and increased employment. In fact, a $1 increase in aggregate public capital investment increased output in the long run by $4.46, a substantial increase. He also calculated rates of return on public investments that ranged from 3.4% on highway and streets to 16% on electric and gas facilities, transit systems, and airfields, in the long run.

14.5 International Evidence

Other researchers have studied the public capital hypothesis in different countries or using international cross section data. For the most part, they also find that public infrastructure has a positive effect on output and growth and a negative impact on cost. The results are collected in Table 14.4.

Mera (1973) was one of the first to include public or "social" capital in a production function. He used data on the 46 prefectures in Japan and aggregated up to the regional level to study three sectors in Japan. The first sector included agriculture, forestry, and fishing, the second included mining, construction, and manufacturing, while the third included everything else, e.g., retail sales, finance. Four different public capital variables were used. G_1, for example, primarily included soil and conservation capital, flood control, and irrigation. One would hypothesize that this type of public capital would primarily affect the first sector but not the other two.[13] Mera found that public capital generally had an impact on the economy that was sector-specific and that not all sectors benefited from each type of public capital. For example, G_1 had a significant positive effect on the first sector. In his preferred equation for the first sector, the elasticities of output with respect to labor, private capital, and public capital were 0.54, 0.2, and 0.26, respectively.

The Japanese government released new data on public investment in the early 1990s. Since then there have been several studies on the productivity of public capital in Japan. The evidence tends to suggest that the total level of public capital has had a positive impact on the economy. However, Iwamoto (1990), Asako et.al. (1994), Mitsui and Ohta (1995), Yoshino and Nakano (1996) and Doi (1998) conclude that the productivity of public capital has declined recently in Japan.

More recently, Annala, Batina, and Feehan (2004) studied a panel of data on employment, output, private capital, and public capital for the major sectors of the Japanese economy. First, they estimated a Cobb-Douglas production function adjusting for various econometric problems, e.g., stationarity, and found the elasticity of public capital was 0.24 in the manufacturing sector, 0.22 in the finance, insurance, and real estate (FIRE) sector, and 0.12 for the economy as a whole. Second, they also estimated a VAR/ECM and a number of interesting results emerged. For example, the elasticity of employment with respect to public capital was 0.11 for FIRE, 0.087 for manufacturing, and 0.072 for construction.

Shah (1992) estimated a restricted translog cost function where labor and material inputs were variable and private capital and public capital (transportation, electricity, and communications) were treated as fixed inputs to the firm. Data from twenty-six three-digit manufacturing industries in Mexico for 1970 – 1987 was used to estimate a system composed of input demand functions and the cost function. Shah found evidence for increasing returns to scale, and that labor, private capital, and intermediate inputs are substitutes, while private capital and labor are weakly complementary to public capital. The long run output elasticity with respect to private capital was 0.242 while the long run output elasticity with respect to public capital was 0.046. The shadow values of private and public capital were 16.3 and 5.9, respectively, while their estimated prices were 8.8 and 5.7. These results suggest there was significant under-investment in both types of capital in Mexico during this period, relative to the level associated with production efficiency.[14]

Berndt and Hansson (1992) studied time series data on Sweden for the period 1960 – 1988. They pursued a strategy of estimating the cost function and labor demand stemming from the cost function approach. They concluded that public capital was productive in Sweden in lowering cost. They also noted that if one only examined the benefits of public capital accruing to firms and thus ignored the possible consumption benefits, one could calculate whether the public capital stock is optimal or not by comparing the production benefits to the price at the margin. Berndt and Hansson found that the ratio of G*/G was greater than one until 1974 but less than one after, where G* is the optimal level of public capital and G the actual level. This suggests that there had been under-investment in public capital in Sweden followed by over-investment, although the "excess" stock had been falling in the 1980's, relative to the level associated with production efficiency.

Bajo-Rubio and Sosvilla-Rivero (1993) estimated a simple aggregate production function model using data from Spain for 1964-1988. They estimated an error correction model to control for stationarity and found public capital to be highly productive in this period. The estimated long run elasticity of output with respect to public capital was 0.39 when capacity utilization was included as a separate variable in the regression equation and 0.18 when output and each capital stock was adjusted for capacity utilization separately.

Seitz (1994) used German data to gauge the impact of public capital on cost and studied two different kinds of public capital data, the total public capital stock and core infrastructure in West Germany. His data consisted of 31 two-digit industries of the manufacturing sector in West Germany for 1970 – 1989. He estimated demand equations for labor and private capital from the generalized Leontief cost equation and used industry dummy variables to capture fixed effects. His main result was that the average shadow price of the total public capital stock was 0.00218. Thus, an increase in total public capital by 1000 DM would lower cost by 2.18 DM. The average shadow price of core infrastructure was 0.00364; an increase in core infrastructure by 1000 DM would lower cost by 3.64 DM. These effects were somewhat lower than other researchers found for other countries.

Sturm and de Haan (1995) presented evidence that public infrastructure was highly productive in the Netherlands. They did extensive unit root testing on Dutch data for 1960-1990 and concluded that their data on output, labor, private and public capital was stationary in first differences. They then estimated the output elasticity for different types of public capital. The elasticity was 1.16, 0.0, and 0.78 for total public capital, buildings, and infrastructure, respectively. They concluded, "That the data suggest a role for public infrastructure capital, but that the estimated coefficients are so large that the normal interpretation of the results seems not to be justified." (pp. 66) Their data series were not integrated of the same order and cointegration tests failed when the data was in levels. This may be due to the short time series used in their study.

Sturm, Jakobs, and Groot (1995) studied a long sample of historical data for the Dutch economy covering the period 1853-1913. Their data included output, investment in machinery for the private sector, and investment in infrastructure by the government, which included core infrastructure like railways, roads, and canals, and other infrastructure like gas,

electricity, and water supply. Their main result was that public infrastructure had a strong impact on the Dutch economy.

Table 14.4. International Empirical Evidence

Author	Data	Method	Main result
Mera (1973)	Japan, 46 prefectures 1954-1963	CD Production function	G has positive, sector - specific impact.
Shah (1992)	26 industries Mexico 1970 – 1987	Translog Cost function	$E_G = 0.045$
Berndt and Hansson (1992)	Sweden 1960 – 1988	Cost function	G reduces private costs significantly.
Seitz (1994)	31 industries West Germany 1970-1989	Generalized Leontief cost function	$P_G = -0.00218DM$[a] $P_{Core} = -0.00364DM$
Sturm and de Haan (1995)	Aggregate data Netherlands 1960-1990	Production function	$E_G = 1.16$, $E_{Core} = 0.78$
Sturm, Jakobs, and Groot (1995)	Netherlands 1853-1913	VAR	Data was trend stationary, G had long lasting effects.
Sturm (2001)	Netherlands 1953-1993	Generalized McFadden Cost function	G has a significant negative impact on cost in the sheltered industry.
Ford and Poret (1991)	11 OECD countries	CD Production function	E_G is either zero or implausibly large.
Pereira and Morin (1996)	11 OECD countries	VAR	No cointegration, G has a strong positive effect.
Pereira (2000)	12 OECD countries	VARECM	G has positive effect for most countries
Annala, Batina, and Feehan (2004)	Japan industry data, 1970 -1998	CD Production function and VARECM	G has significant impact that differs across sectors.

a - An increase in public capital of 1,000,000 DM would reduce cost across industries on average by 2,200 DM.

More recently, Sturm (2001) studied the public capital hypothesis using a cost function approach. Dutch data was used to estimate the cost model for the post-World War II period for two sectors of the Dutch economy, the sheltered sector, comprised of retail, banking, and other private services, and the exposed sector, made up of agriculture, manufacturing, and transport, which is relatively capital intensive and involves more international trade than the sheltered sector. Sturm concluded that production costs of the total private economy were significantly reduced by public capital. A 10% increase in public infrastructure reduced the cost of the private economy by about 3%. Second, only the sheltered sector of the Dutch economy benefited from infrastructure investment. There were two reasons why the exposed sector may not benefit as much, the exposed sector provides some of its own infrastructure and is not as closely related to the public capital variable used in the study as the sheltered sector is.

Several studies have used OECD data to test the hypothesis. Aschauer, it will be recalled, found some support for the hypothesis among the G-7 nations. Ford and Poret (1991), however, disputed this finding. They studied annual data from eleven OECD countries and estimated a production function for each country as well as for a cross section of countries. Estimates of the public capital elasticity were either small in magnitude or implausibly large. For example, time series estimates of the elasticity range from 1.39 (Canada under a broad definition of public capital) to − 0.55 (Norway under a narrow definition). The main problem with the analysis of Ford and Poret is the paucity of data. There are twenty-five observations or less for the majority of countries in their sample, e.g., Japan, France, UK, Australia, Belgium, Finland, Norway, and Sweden. This is simply not enough data to do effective time series analysis. They also do not examine the stationarity of the data, nor do they include any variables to capture systematic differences across countries, or fixed effects.[15]

Pereira (2001) studied OECD data for twelve countries. He estimated the dynamic effects of public investment in infrastructure capital on private output, private investment, and labor using a VAR/ECM. This model incorporated indirect feedback effects among the variables. For example, if output is low because of a recession, many times the government will undertake public investment to boost the economy. If successful, this will boost demand for labor and private investment and possibly output with a lag as well. He calculated the long run accumulated impact of public capital on private output and the other inputs for horizons of five to ten years, which included all of the direct and indirect effects. The results with regard to the impact of public capital on output, for example, allowed the countries to be divided into two groups. Public capital tended to have a large positive impact for Germany, Japan, Sweden, the U.K., and the U.S., with long run elasticities of 0.194, 0.253, 0.227, 0.143, and 0.257, respectively. For the rest of the countries in the sample, Australia, Belgium, Canada, Finland, France, Greece, and Spain, the elsaticities were positive but much smaller in magnitude, 0.017, 0.076, 0.021, 0.067, 0.078, 0.034, and 0.040, respectively. The key difference between the two groups was that public investment tended to have positive, reinforcing, indirect effects in the first group of countries, but negative indirect effects in the second group.

Demetriades and Mamuneas (2000) studied a panel data set of 12 OECD countries using a flexible functional form for the profit equation and allowed for heterogeneity across countries and for time effects. Their methodology also allowed them to distinguish between the short run, the intermediate run, and the long run. They posed a dynamic decision problem of profit maximization for the individual firm where the firm's technology is affected by public capital and where there are adjustment costs to altering the private capital stock. They found that public capital had a strong positive effect on the firm's output and input decisions. They also calculated rates of return to public capital. The rates of return were always higher in the long run than in the short run and the long run rates of return varied between 19% in Australia to 38% in Japan. The G-7 countries tended to have lower public capital stocks relative to GDP than the other five OECD countries in the sample (Australia, Belgium, Norway, Sweden, Finland) and higher rates of return in the long run.

Mention should also be made of Rioja's (1999, 2002) simulation studies. Rioja (1999) studied a general equilibrium Ramsey type growth model with productive public capital and congestion, where consumers and firms optimize, and there are random shocks to the technology and to the income tax policy of the government. Functional forms for the utility function and the technology were chosen, and the parameters were chosen to mimic seven Latin American countries (Argentina, Brazil, Chile, Colombia, Mexico, Peru, and Venezuela). A number of interesting results emerged. For example, a one percent of GDP increase in infrastructure caused output to increase by 2.5% and welfare to increase by 1.4%. He also calculated the welfare maximizing amount of infrastructure and found that these countries were not spending enough on infrastructure; they should increase their spending on infrastructure from the current 6% of GDP to about 10%.

Rioja (2002) included maintenance expenditures in the model. Depreciation of public capital is determined by maintenance expenditures by the government and the amount of private capital which captures usage of the public infrastructure, and depreciation is assumed decreasing in maintenance and increasing in usage by the private sector. One interesting result that emerged is that if maintenance expenditures were increased by 0.5% of GDP and financed by reducing spending on new public investment, more public capital survives in the long run and the stock in the long run is 7% larger. Both output and consumption increase as well.

14.6 Optimality

From the theoretical results presented in the last chapter, the rule governing the optimal provision of public capital depends on whether there are consumption benefits included in the model and on the government's set of policy tools. If there are no consumption benefits and there are enough policy tools available, then the first-best rule is to choose public investment so that the marginal product of public capital net of depreciation per unit of cost is equal to the marginal product of private capital net of depreciation in a steady state. On the other hand, if the government does not have enough policy tools available, the rule must be adjusted to reflect this. For example, if the government cannot use its stock of debt to keep the economy on the golden rule path and there are no consumption benefits, then we saw in the last chapter that $(F_G - \delta_G)/C_G < F_K - \delta_K$ is optimal, for example. The intuition is that when the two types of capital are complementary and the private capital stock is too low relative to the modified golden rule level, the government can compensate by accumulating more public capital.[16]

This leads to the famous weighted average formulas that relate the social rate of return of a public investment to a weighted average of returns confronting consumers and firms depending on the source of funds for the investment. Unfortunately, these formulae tend to be very sensitive to slight changes in the assumptions used to generate the formulae. This makes it very difficult at best to know whether the public capital stock in a particular country is at the optimal level or not. Another issue involves the social return to different public investments. They need not all be equal. One possibility is to compute the return to each social investment and choose the one with the highest return, or alternatively, all those with returns above a certain level. And, one should keep in mind that comparisons to private returns may be misleading.

Rate of return calculations tend to be a mixed bag of results. Some analysts have calculated exceptionally high rates of return suggesting significant underinvestment in public capital, while others have calculated low rates. Evidence of underinvestment was provided by Shah for Mexico, Berndt and Hansson for Sweden, and Rioja for several Latin American countries. However, using disaggregated industry data, Nadiri and Rosen calculated social rates of return to public capital and found them similar to private rates. And Morrison and Schwartz found that the net return to public capital was positive under certain conditions but negative under others.[17]

Otto and Voss (1998) undertook a more systematic approach to the issue by deriving the optimality rules as a system of Euler equations from a dynamic optimization problem and used country specific data from Australia to estimate the Euler equations directly. They noted that aggregate production in Australia has become more private capital intensive over time and suggested that in the simple case of the Cobb-Douglas production function, the output-private capital and output-public capital ratios should be highly correlated. However, in Australia the two ratios are moving in opposite directions. To explain this, they demonstrated that the relative price of public capital to private capital has risen substantially over their sample period and that this may have caused the shift from public capital toward private capital. It is unclear why relative prices have shifted and if they shifted in other countries as well.

Otto and Voss derived the stochastic Euler equations governing the optimal provision of private and public capital in a version of the Ramsey model that included productive public capital and a relative price of public to private capital, but no consumption benefit. They estimated a series of models. For example, the Euler equation governing the choice of public capital when the technology is Cobb - Douglas, the price of public capital (c^G) is allowed to vary over time, and the utility function is isoelastic in form is

$$E[\beta(c_{t+1}/c_t)^{\sigma-1}(\xi Y_{t+1}/K_{Gt+1}+(1-\delta)\ c^G_{t+1})/\ c^G_t] = 1,$$

where E is the expectations operator, ξ is the elasticity of output with respect to the public capital stock, and the period utility function is isoelsatic, c^σ/σ.

Using quarterly data for 1959:3 - 1992:2 for Australia, Otto and Voss found evidence that supported the model; real rates of return for both types of capital were approximately equal to about an annual rate of 9% and both were stationary when a relative price variable was included in the model. In the case of the Cobb-Douglas technology, the private capital elasticity is about 0.2 and the public capital elasticity is about 0.06. They concluded that the government's choice of public capital was optimal. This is predicated on the economy being on the modified golden rule path and that there were no consumption benefits associated with public capital. If such

Table 14.5. Empirical Results on Optimality

Author	Data	Method	Main result
Otto and Voss (1998)	Australia	GMM	G is optimal[a] when relative investment prices are included.
Kitasaka (1999)	Japan	GMM	G is optimal.
Demetriades and Mamuneas (2000)	12 OECD countries	Non-linear SUR	G is underprovided in all 12 countries
Ihori and Kondo (2001)	Japan	GMM	Total H is optimal, disaggregated G is generally not optimal.
Rioja (2002)	7 Latin American countries	Ramsey simulation model	Public capital maintenance is too low

a - G is optimal in the sense that the marginal product of public capital is approximately equal to the marginal product of private capital.

benefits existed, then the question remains an open one for Australia during this period.

Kitasaka (1999) characterized the efficient allocation conditions of both private and public capital similar in spirit to Otto and Voss and examined whether these conditions were rejected by the data in Japan using GMM. He concluded that the stock of Japanese public capital goods was efficiently provided at the aggregate level. However, even though public capital has been sufficiently provided in the aggregate, it does not necessarily mean that optimality is attained at the disaggregated level. This is also true for Otto and Voss's work.

Demetriades and Mamuneas (2000) studied 12 OECD countries and used a dynamic model of profit maximization where there were adjustment costs to private capital. As mentioned in the last section, they also calculated rates of return to public infrastructure. They operationalize the Kaizuka condition for the optimal provision of public capital and calculated the representative firm's marginal willingness-to-pay for a unit of public capital assuming lump sum taxation, $(\partial \pi_{t+1} / \partial G_t)/C_{Gt}$, from the Euler equation for public capital, where C_{Gt} is the price of a unit of public capital. They compared the optimal WTP to the rate of return on public capital and found that the optimal WTP is always well below the actual long run rate of return implying that public capital is undersupplied. The optimal

WTP for public capital ranged from 13% in the U.S. to 17.55% in the U.K., which is well below the actual long run rate of return.

Ihori and Kondo (2001) investigated the efficiency of different types of public capital for the Japanese economy. They also used GMM to estimate the optimality conditions based on the simultaneous Euler equations from the social planner's problem when public capital is productive but does not provide consumption benefits. Their results suggested that the productivity of the various types of public capital has been relatively high but has also diverged over time. They concluded that the allocation of public capital is not currently optimal in Japan. In particular, not enough infrastructure for railways, telephone networks, telegraph, and postal services has been accumulated.

14.7 Conclusion

Aschauer's paper sparked great controversy and a huge literature on estimating the impact of public infrastructure on the economy. A wide variety of approaches and estimation procedures have been used and data from a variety of sources has been studied. The empirical results in the early literature tended to indicate there was a significant effect. The hypothesis also gained support when data from other countries was used, e.g., the Netherlands. However, critics quickly emerged and found little or no impact, e.g., Tatom, Holtz-Eakin, Aaron, and Eisner. Later work, using more sophisticated empirical tools and different data, tended to confirm the result of a positive effect, but much smaller in magnitude. There are several problems that could bias the results, however. These include simultaneity bias, omitted variable bias, fixed effects, causality, measurement problems, and the stationarity properties of the data. When some of these problems are taken into account, the effect of public capital, and especially core infrastructure, tends to be positive, much smaller than the early literature suggested.

There are also other difficulties that we did not touch on. Some benefits of public capital may be very difficult to quantify but are nonetheless important. For example, a better highway network around a city will lower commuting time and thus may have tremendous value to commuters. Placing a value on improvements in health due to improved sanitation may be difficult to do. On the other side of the ledger, there may be other costs as well. A better highway network might induce more people to drive separately rather than use public transport or car pool. This may in turn increase smog and pollution. Better electric power stations generating more electricity may reduce energy costs. However, they may also create more air pollution as well.

This might leave the reader in a quandary. Does public infrastructure have a significant positive impact on the economy, or not? If so, how large is it? And, if it did in the past, can we rely on the previous results to forecast the effect of future spending on infrastructure? We are taken with the argument of Fernald (1999), who studied industry data for the U.S., and found that vehicle-intensive industries tended to benefit more from highway capital than non-vehicle-intensive industries, but there was little effect at the margin. Based on his results, the hypothesis can be refined in the following way. The effects of a massive injection of new public capital into the economy can be quite large and can last for quite a while, but will eventually dissipate. However, marginal changes in the stock of public capital will only have a small impact.

One can also ask the deeper question regarding the effects of different types of capital. In any country's economic history certain types of public capital may have been important in inducing economic growth and development at one moment in time but are supplanted by another form of capital later. In the United States, for example, canals may have sparked economic growth in the early 19th century. However, the railroads came to dominate canals by the 1850s and may have led to an expansion of the economy later in that century. Still later, cars and trucks came to dominate the railroads and coupled with the interstate highway network possibly fueled the economic growth of the late 1960s. In each era one technology supplanted another. Does it follow that more spending on canals, railroads, or highways now would fuel much growth in the U.S. or other advanced countries? Probably not. Governments need to recognize that the social payoff to marginal adjustments to existing infrastructure may be quite small and that the return to new types of infrastructure may be potentially much larger. One obvious example of a new type of infrastructure is the internet and fiber optic cables. Another example is the exploration of space.

---

[1] See Munnell (1992) and Gramlich (1994) for early summaries of the literature. Some authors make a distinction between public capital, which includes items like fire trucks and police cars, and public infrastructure, which does not. Others use the terms synonymously. We will use the terms synonymously and hope not to create any confusion by doing so.

[2] For example, in using DOLS first differences of the leads and lags of the right hand side regressors are added to the right hand side until the residual is a stationary white noise. This eliminates simultaneity bias and stationarity problems.

[3] The data used was the following. Y is a measure of industrial output, L is aggregate labor hours, and K is a measure of the services of the private capital stock maintained by the BLS, all taken from the Monthly Labor Review. G is the stock of public capital and is taken from the Department of Commerce publication Fixed Reproducible Tanglible Wealth. CU is capacity utilization of manufacturing and is taken from the Federal Reserve Bulletin. Except for private capital, these are the data subsequently used by other researchers working with time series US data.

[4] See Munnell (1990a) for a description of the various explanations on the slowdown in growth including the public capital hypothesis. Most likely, all of these explanations have some explanatory power.

[5] Munnell used similar sources for her data. In particular, both Aschauer and Munnell used a measure of private capital services maintained by the BLS and used to calculate multi-factor productivity. Most other researchers working with US data used a measure of private capital that is published coincidentally with the public capital data. It is taken from Fixed Reproducible Tangible Wealth and is calculated by the BEA.

[6] Suppose y is determined by $y_t = \alpha + y_{t-1} + \varepsilon_t$, where ε_t is a "white" noise, i.e., a mean zero random variable with a constant variance that is not autocorrelated. The variable y is said to be a random walk if $\alpha = 0$ and a random walk with drift if $\alpha \neq 0$. The sequence y will tend to meander away from its mean if it is a random walk, or gradually drift upward over time if it is a random walk with drift and $\alpha > 0$. This behavior is the hallmark of many aggregate time series data. See, for example, Nelson and Plott (1982). The data for y will not be stationary in levels. However, if we take first differences, we obtain $\Delta y_t = \alpha + \varepsilon_t$, which is stationary. In that case the variable y is said to be integrated of order one or I(1). If a variable is stationary after differencing d times, it is said to be integrated of order d or I(d). Now suppose y is determined as above and another variable x is given by $x_t = \beta + x_{t-1} + u_t$, where u_t is also a white noise that is uncorrelated with ε_t. If the level of y is regressed on the level of x, the estimated coefficient in the regression of y on x may be different from zero and statistically significant even if the variables are completely unrelated. This is the spurious regression problem. See Hamilton (1994).

[7] Tatom used a Dickey Fuller test to test for unit roots and actually uncovered mixed results. This may be due to the low power of unit root tests in general and the lack of data.

[8] It is possible for two variables that are not stationary in levels to be stationary when taken in linear combination. Suppose y and x are both stationary in first differences. Then the two variables are said to be cointegrated if the error term u_t in the following regression equation is stationary, $y_t = \alpha + \beta x_t + u_t$. One can apply a unit root test to the residual of this equation. If the unit root test rejects the hypothesis of a unit root, then the residual is stationary and the variables y and x are cointegrated. In that case, an estimate of β does capture the appro-

priate correlation between y and x in a long run sense. A statistical procedure known as Dynamic OLS (DOLS), suggested by Stock and Watson (1993), can be used to estimate the parameters of a cointegrated long run relationship. Tatom applied the DOLS procedure and once again found that public capital does not have a statistically significant effect on output.

[9] See Greene (1997) chapter 14 on panel data and fixed effects models.

[10] The sunbelt tended to have more public capital, relative to both output and private capital, than the snowbelt. The biggest change over the sample period was the increase in private investment and hence private capital in the South, relative to output and public capital.

[11] This is the original source for the aggregate data on public and private capital in the US. Labor hours and employment were used as the proxy for labor. The data maintained by the Bureau of Labor Statistics (BLS) on private capital services and the data on private capital from the BEA were used as the proxy for private capital. Aschauer and Munnell are the only researchers to use the BLS data on capital services. Several proxies were used for public capital including total non-military public capital equipment and structures, state and local public capital, and state and local highway and street capital, all taken from the BEA.

[12] DOLS eliminates bias and yields consistent estimates even in the presence of endogenous variables. See Hamilton (1994).

[13] G_2 included coastal improvements, industrial water supply, vocational training facilities, and public gas and electric facilities. G_3 included transportation and communication facilities. G_4 included health, education, and welfare facilities including public housing.

[14] Shah suggested that this under-investment may be due to government regulation, the high debt servicing of previous debt, and uncertainty about politics and hence the policies that may be pursued in the near future.

[15] They also reported on a cross-section regression where the elasticity is 0.24 under the narrow definition of public capital and 0.44 under the broad definition, where the latter has a very high t-statistic. In addition, they examined a longer time series for the US that goes back to 1890 and again found little evidence in favor of the hypothesis.

[16] Abel, Mankiw, Summers, and Zeckhauser (1989) generalized the definition of dynamic efficiency and found evidence that the major economies (US, Great Britain, France, Germany, Italy, Canada, and Japan) are dynamically efficient. In Diamond's model this means that the real interest rate is at least as great as the growth rate.

[17] It would be of some interest to investigate why there appears to be under-investment in some countries and over-investment in others.

15 Local Public Goods, Club Goods, and the Tiebout Hypothesis

Much of the inspiration for the research done on local public goods (LPGs) and club goods, especially the early literature, comes from the Tiebout (1956) hypothesis, which was a response to Samuelson's (1954) gloomy forecast regarding the provision of public goods. Tiebout argued that if consumers are mobile, there is a large array of different communities offering different packages of public goods and services, agents have full information on the packages offered at the different locations, an optimal size community exists at each location, consumers are atomistic, income is independent of location, and mobility is costless, then consumers will sort themselves into homogeneous communities offering the efficient amount of public goods, where Samuelson's rule would hold. An individual would simply choose one location over another on the basis of the public goods offered there and from this information we could ascertain the WTP for a particular local public project. This was quite a surprising notion because it seems to solve the free rider problem without any government intervention and would also solve problems associated with voting mechanisms, e.g., cycles, since unanimity would prevail in each community. However, not much research was done on Tiebout's hypothesis for almost a decade.[1]

Buchanan (1965) later provided a model where individuals form a club specifically designed to share a quasi-public good, charge a membership fee to be in the club, and exclude non-payers. His model can also be used to study the Tiebout hypothesis. Broadly interpreted, a "club" can be an actual club taken literally, e.g., tennis club, or simply a group that shares certain characteristics such as discussing books online, owning a luxury car, having season tickets to the opera, or watching soccer matches. Under certain conditions goods provided by local governments can be interpreted as a club good, e.g., museum, or library. Later work clarified the implications of Buchanan's model, developed various hypotheses about optimal sorting across communities, and extended the model in various directions.[2] Critics quickly emerged, however, and their work shed light on the conditions under which the results of the basic model hold.[3]

One might usefully ask what the difference is between a club good and a LPG. Exclusion appears to be critically important for club goods. This is what allows the good to be provided by the private sector since firms can charge a price for membership in the club, or for visits to the club, and earn a normal return. There are other goods for which this is not true such as city streets, traffic lights, and police and fire protection. We will refer to an impure public good that exhibits exclusion as a club good. Impure public goods that do not exhibit exclusion will be referred to as a LPG. Both types may exhibit congestion and hence rivalry. Indeed, congestion is evident in both Tiebout and Buchanan's models. And there are other goods that can exhibit exclusion but where one would not wish to exclude because they have other important social benefits, e.g., schools, libraries, and museums. These goods can be considered club goods but would have to be provided by government if private firms are not allowed to exclude.[4]

In the next section we present a model of a club good. We also study a generalization of the model that includes the number of visits to the club facility and another model that makes a distinction between the quality of the public good and choice over its quantity. In 15.2 we explore various aspects of the Tiebout hypothesis and the nature of local public goods. Section 15.3 develops criticism of the Tiebout model and the sorting hypothesis, and 15.4 concludes the chapter.

15.1 Club Goods

15.1.1 The Benchmark Club Good Model

It is imagined that the club provides an impure public good that produces a consumption benefit and there are n members in the club who enjoy the good. To fix ideas, one can imagine a swimming pool or tennis club where the size of the facility is the club good. Let the utility function for consumer h be $u^h(x^h, g)$, where x^h is a numeraire private good and g is the club good. It is assumed the club can practice exclusion so non-members who choose not to join can be excluded from the benefits of the club. There are no spillover benefits from one club good to another and membership in a club is purely voluntary.

In addition, there may be a congestion, or crowding effect. This is reflected in the cost of providing the good, $C(g, n)$, where the number of people using the facility, n, affects cost. We will assume that "crowding" is anonymous; only the number of agents using the club matters, not their specific characteristics. The marginal production cost is given by $dC/dg =$

C_g and $dC/dn = C_n$ is the marginal cost of providing one more consumer with the benefit of the good. For a pure public good, $C_n = 0$. If $C_n > 0$, congestion increases the cost of providing the club good, given the level of g. It is also certainly possible that congestion in the number of people using the club good facility can impose a psychological cost on the consumer as well. In that case the utility function is given by $u^h(x^h, g, n)$, where the last argument captures the disutility of crowding.

We can pose the issues of the optimal provision of the club good and its optimal financing. Suppose there are N identical agents, N/n clubs, where N/n is an integer, utility is given by $u(x, g, n)$ and the cost of the club good is $C(g, n)$. Let w be the agent's endowment of the private good. The resource constraint for the members of the representative club is

$$w - x - C(g, n)/n = 0. \qquad (15.1)$$

The planner chooses (x, g, n) to maximize per capita utility subject to the resource constraint (15.1).[5] It is straightforward to show that the following conditions characterize the optimum,

$$n(u_g/u_x) = C_g, \qquad (15.2)$$

$$n(u_n/u_x) = C_n - C/n. \qquad (15.3)$$

The first condition is the Samuelson rule, while the second condition governs the optimal membership of the representative club. If there is no psychological congestion cost, the optimal club membership occurs where the average cost of membership is equal to the marginal cost of membership, which occurs at the minimum point of the average cost curve if the cost curves are U-shaped. If there is a psychological cost for the consumer as well, then the optimal club size occurs where the average cost is greater than the marginal cost according to (15.3). Let (g^*, n^*, x^*) satisfy (15.1) - (15.3). If N/n^* is an integer, there are N/n^* identical clubs at the optimum.[6]

The new element relative to other models considered so far in previous chapters is the membership dimension. The intuition behind (15.3) is that the optimal club size balances the benefit of extra members lowering the cost of providing the club good with the additional congestion costs. Adding one more member reduces the average cost of providing the good but increases congestion. At the optimum the two balance one another.

The question then becomes whether or not the private market can mimic this stylized outcome. Consider the problem of a private firm that will provide the club good and let P be the price of membership. Profit is $Pn - C(g, n)$. In order to attract members the club must choose the characteristics of the club (g, n, P) so that

$$u(w - P, g, n) \geq u^*, \tag{15.4}$$

where u^* is the utility that can be achieved in another club. This is similar to an incentive compatibility constraint. All it really says is that the firm understands the tastes of its potential members and takes them into account when choosing the characteristics of the club.[7] Since u^* is taken as given, (15.4) at equality determines the price P as a function of (g, n) and w. The firm chooses the characteristics of the club to maximize profit subject to (15.4). The first order conditions imply (15.2) and

$$n(u_n/u_x) = C_n - P. \tag{15.5}$$

In addition, if competition drives profit to zero, the membership fee covers the average cost of the club, $P = C/n$, and (15.5) implies (15.3). Consumption of the private good is given by

$$x = w - P = w - C/n,$$

which matches up with the resource constraint.

It follows that the competitive equilibrium allocation and the partition of agents across clubs satisfies the conditions governing the optimum and the Tiebout result follows, as long as N/n^* is an integer and is large enough to generate competitive behavior. Note that the membership fee is larger than the marginal cost of the size of the club if there is disutility due to congestion. Essentially, the fee adjusts for the consumption externality in (15.5).

Alternatively, let $P(g, n)$ be the membership fee charged by a firm providing a club with features (g, n). Suppose N/n^* is large so firms behave competitively. The representative firm provides a club with characteristics (g, n) to maximize profit, $P(g, n)n - C(g, n)$, taking membership price as given. Consumers choose a club to maximize utility $u(x, g, n)$ subject to the budget constraint $w - P(g, n) - x = 0$, taking membership price as given. And competition drives price to average cost in equilibrium. $P(g, n)$ is an example of a pricing function.

At this level of analysis the competitive market solution appears to mimic the socially optimal outcome. If we interpret the model as a model of a local public good, then as long as individuals have perfect information about the range of locations, mobility is costless, income is independent of location, N/n^* is an integer, and there are enough locations to match preferences, the competitive outcome, where individuals choose their location according to the mix of public goods available, is optimal. Tiebout's self-sorting mechanism appears to solve the free rider problem. The case of identical agents serves as a useful benchmark. Later we will discuss the case where there is heterogeneity.

Following Pauly (1967), we can relate this result to the concept of the core. In this context, a state of the economy is a partition of the population into clubs and an allocation of the club good and the private good in each club. A state is in the core if no group of individuals can form a club and reach a higher level of utility by trading among themselves using only their own endowments. Pauly argued that if $n^* < N$ and N/n^* is an integer, the core will exist. Furthermore, if the core exists, a competitive equilibrium, as described above, is in the core. However, if N/n^* is not an integer, the core will generally be empty. In addition, if N/n^* is small, competition among clubs may not prevail.[8]

Wooders (1980), Scotchmer (1985a, 1985b, 1986), and Scotchmer and Wooders (1987) examined various aspects of the basic model including the existence, stability, and optimality of the equilibrium. In particular, Scotchmer (1985a) modeled a two-stage game where firms decide to enter the 'club good' market in the first stage and then play a Nash game in choosing (g, P), where P is the membership fee. Firms can attract new members through their pricing and club good strategies. With a finite number of firms, each firm will come to believe it has some market power. The resulting equilibrium will not be Pareto optimal since too much entry will occur; essentially, when a firm enters the market it does not take into account the negative impact it has on the profit of the other clubs. Firms still earn positive profit since each has market power even though there are too many firms. Scotchmer also showed that in the limit as the economy is replicated, the club price approaches the congestion cost.

Several remarks are in order. First, the club good is not a pure public good in the Samuelson sense; exclusion is required in order to charge a price, there are no spillover effects from the club good, and with congestion the marginal cost of providing the good for one more person is strictly positive. The self-sorting mechanism, therefore, does not necessarily solve the free rider problem in the presence of a pure public good. If a single locality provided a true pure public good from which all benefited, location would be irrelevant and most of the benefits would accrue to non-residents who could not be charged for them. Indeed, a club good is more closely related to a private good and that is why one expects market provision to be relatively efficient. However, in defense of the basic model, one could also argue that club goods are more realistic than pure public goods, and that studying such a good is of value because of this.

Second, many local public goods do not exhibit exclusion, or exclusion is very costly, and this affects the method of financing the good. Examples include city streets and sidewalks, public parks with many access points, streetlights, traffic lights, police and fire protection, and the local courts. If exclusion cannot be practiced, pricing and membership fees cannot be used to finance the good. A different method of financing must be used and it is entirely possible that agents may choose location partly on the basis of the method of financing the good. For example, given the mix of public goods across locations, a landowner may choose to live in a community that imposes a sales tax rather than another community that relies exclusively on a property tax. In addition, if exclusion is not possible, some other mechanism like voting must be used to determine the appropriate policy.

Third, as pointed out by Scotchmer (1994), if use of the club is a choice and a price per visit is charged, one can reduce one's total expenditure by reducing the use of the facility. However, one's enjoyment of the club also diminishes. With a local public good, one can also reduce one's "expenditure" on the local public good by buying less property (under a property tax), or working less (under a local labor income tax), but still enjoy the same benefit from the local public goods. This, of course, depends on the exclusion mechanism available.

15.1.2 Endogenous Classification

Berglas and Pines (1981) argued that the classification of the club good may depends on the optimal sharing group and is endogenous. Different cases for the optimal sharing group can be distinguished in the following manner, given the level of g. Suppose (x^*, g^*) solves the planner's problem. Then utility can be written as a function of n,

$$u(n) = u(w - c(g^*, n)/n, g^*, n).$$

Differentiate and simplify to obtain,

$$(n/u_x)(du/dn) = C/n - [n(u_n/u_x) - C_n]. \qquad (15.6)$$

If an interior optimum exists such that $0 < n^* < N$, it will satisfy (15.3) and $du/dn = 0$. However, if $du/dn < 0$ for all $n > 0$, then $n^* = 1$ and the good can be classified as a private good. And, if $du/dn > 0$ for all $n \leq N$, then $n^* = N$ and the good may be classified as a local public good with exclusion, according to Berglas and Pines.

The first term on the right hand side of (15.6) is the average cost of membership and the second term in brackets is the impact membership size has on congestion. Suppose $n = 1$. If the average cost of membership is U-shaped and the effect of average cost is greater than the effect of congestion at $n = 1$, it pays to increase membership. An increase in membership will lower average cost but increase congestion. However, at a low level of membership, the former dominates the latter with U-shaped cost curves. If this is true for the entire population, the good is a local public good with exclusion. If the effect of congestion is greater than the effect of average cost for all n > 1, the good is consumed privately instead. For example, they pointed out that a swimming pool will be a private good in some settings, a club good in others, while in still other settings it will be a local public good under the Berglas and Pines classification method.

It should be noted that this classification is done solely on the basis of congestion and assumes the good exhibits exclusion. It may not be appropriate in cases where exclusion is not possible, e.g., city streets and sidewalks. A city street may have an optimal intermediate sharing group size, 0 < n* < N, and be classified as a club good under this method. However, it might be more appropriate to classify it as a LPG since exclusion could not be used to limit the number of users.

15.1.3 Intensity of Use

Berglas (1976a), Berglas and Pines (1981, 1984), Sandler and Tschirhart (1984), Scotchmer and Wooders (1987), and more recently, Sinn (1997), among others, studied a model where the intensity of use of the facility is also a dimension of choice. Following Berglas and Pines, let the utility function be given by $u(x, g, v, V)$, where v is the number of visits the individual makes to the club and $V = nv$ is the total number of visits, which might provide disutility to the agent because of congestion. The number of people using the club might also affect utility. The first order conditions change slightly but the basic argument remains the same. Cost is given by $C(g, V)$ and the resource constraint is

$$w - x - C(g, V)/n = 0.$$

The social planner chooses (x, g, n, v) to maximize utility subject to the resource constraint. Samuelson's rule once again governs the optimal choice of the facility, g. In addition, we also have the conditions for the club membership size and optimal number of visits, respectively,

$$n(u_V/u_x) = C_V - C/V, \tag{15.7}$$

$$(u_v + nu_V)/u_x = C_V, \tag{15.8}$$

where $u_v > - nu_V$. The first equation mimics (15.3), where C_V is the marginal cost of one more visit and C/V is the average cost. The second equation is new and simply states that the marginal rate of substitution between visits and consumption is equal to the marginal rate of transformation. Visits provide direct utility but also create disutility for others due to crowding effects.

Berglas (1976a) showed that a membership fee is not optimal in this setting when the intensity of use was endogenous and that it is actually optimal to charge a price per visit instead. To see this suppose the club firm charges a membership fee equal to average cost, $P = C(g, nv)/nv$. The individual consumer chooses the number of visits to maximize $u(w - P, g, v, V)$, where $V = vn$, taking V, P, and g as given. The first order condition is $u_v = 0$, which does not match up with the social planner's problem. Suppose instead there is a price per visit of q. Then the consumer solves max $u(w - qv, g, v, V)$. The first order condition is $u_v/u_x = q$. If the price is chosen according to

$$q = C_V - n(u_V/u_x), \tag{15.9}$$

then[9]

$$u_v/u_x = C_V - n(u_V/u_x),$$

which is (15.8). In addition, the profit of the club in this case is

$$qnv - C(g, nv) = [C_V - n(u_V/u_x)]nv - C(g, nv).$$

If competition drives this to zero, we have (15.7) and the competitive equilibrium can support the optimum.[10]

15.1.4 Quality Versus Quantity

Another interpretation of the model of the last section is that of a two-dimensional club good where the two dimensions are the quantity of the good and its quality. Many public goods exhibit a quality dimension and a quantity dimension where the individual consumer chooses the quantity of the good to consume and the quantity dimension is a pure private good. For example, the quality of drinking water can be considered a public good, while the quantity of water consumed is a private good.

Following Berglas (1984), suppose agents are identical and the utility of the representative agent is given by $u(x, z, g)$, where g is the quality of the public good and z is a quantity associated with it. The resource constraint is

$$nw = nx + C(g, nz).$$

The model is mathematically similar to that of the last section except there is no psychological cost of congestion in total usage of the private good dimension. The planner chooses (x, g, z, n) to maximize utility subject to the resource constraint. The first order conditions imply the following conditions,

$$u_z/u_x = C_Z,$$

$$n(u_g/u_x) = C_g,$$

$$C_Z = C/Z,$$

in the absence of psychological effects of crowding, where $Z = nz$. The first condition governs the optimal provision of the quantity variable relative to the numeraire. The second condition is the Samuelson rule. And the third condition governs the choice of the optimal sharing group. The quantity of the public good is supplied at the minimum point of the average cost curve and revenue from its sale covers total cost. Once again N/n^* locations or clubs will form, each producing (g^*, z^*) of the public good when agents are identical.

Berglas showed that the optimal allocation can be decentralized by charging a price per unit of the quantity of the public good. Mobility is costless, private agents take price and aggregate variables as beyond their control, and everyone has information about the package of services available at every location. In equilibrium no consumer wishes to move to another location and no developer can enter and form a new development profitably. And the public good is fully financed through the price charged for the private good dimension.

15.1.5 Optimal Sorting with Heterogeneous Agents

A number of analysts provided proofs that a system of segregated clubs is optimal under certain conditions, e.g., McGuire (1974b), Berglas (1976a, b), Berglas and Pines (1981), and more recently, Ellickson, Grodal, Scotchmer, and Zame (1999). This provides a benchmark case that allows us to examine what may happen if an assumption is relaxed. As it turns out there are a variety of circumstances where mixed communities may dominate homogeneous communities.

Consider the Berglas quantity-quality model with two types of agent. Utility is given by $u^h(x^h, z^h, g^h)$ and cost is $C(g^h, n^h z^h)$, where the cost function is the same across locations but the utility function may differ between the two types. We want to compare homogeneous locations with a mixed location. Under the Tiebout hypothesis, utility in mixed locations should be lower than in homogeneous locations.

The social optimum in either type of community occurs where the MRS for the two quantities x and z is equal to the MRT, which is the marginal cost, C_Z, for each type of agent. The Samuelson rule holds for the quality dimension of the public good. And the public good is provided at the minimum point of the average cost curve where the average congestion cost is equal to the marginal congestion cost. Thus, in a mixed community we have,

$$(u^1_z/u^1_x) = (u^2_z/u^2_x) = C_Z,$$

$$\Sigma n^h(u^h_g/u^h_x) = C_g,$$

$$C/(n^1z^1 + n^2z^2) = C_Z,$$

respectively, when there are n^1 type-one agents and n^2 type-two agents. In a homogeneous community, we have instead,

$$(u^h_z/u^h_x) = C_Z,$$

$$\Sigma n^h(u^h_g/u^h_x) = C_g,$$

$$C/n^hz^h = C_Z.$$

With differences in taste, g^1 will differ from g^2. In a decentralized equilibrium developers charge a price for the quantity dimension of the public good. Let P^k be the price in homogeneous location k =1, 2, and let P^m be the price in a mixed location. Thus, $P^k = C_Z(g^k, n^kz^k)$ for k = 1, 2, and $P^m = C_Z(g^m, n^1z^1 + n^2z^2)$. Indirect utility for a segregated community is given by $U(w^h, P^h, g^h)$, and for the mixed location is $U(w^h, P^m, g^m)$. Since (P^m, g^m) was available in the homogeneous location but was not chosen, it must be true that,

$$U(w^h, P^h, g^h) > U(w^h, P^m, g^m) \text{ for } h = 1, 2.$$

Suppose the agent in the mixed community is compensated to achieve the same level of utility as in the homogeneous location. Let τ^h be a transfer such that

$$U(w^h, P^h, g^h) = U(w^h + \tau^h, P^m, g^m) \text{ for } h = 1, 2.$$

However, the budget must balance, $\Sigma_h\tau^h = 0$. It follows that one type of agent must be strictly worse off in the mixed club relative to the homogeneous club. Therefore, mixed communities are not preferred to the homogeneous community.

This may have troubling implications for the Lindahl equilibrium concept, aside from the other problems with that notion of equilibrium, i.e., determining the true WTP for the public good. Imagine a Lindahl equilibrium where there are high demanders and low demanders and agents are immobile. In that case, we would expect the public good to be chosen as the average of the demand of the two types and agents would pay their Lindahl tax shares, where high demanders pay a larger share of the cost than low demanders. Low demanders are forced to consume too much of the public good while high demanders consume too little in such an equilibrium. The Tiebout sorting result suggests, however, that if agents are mobile, both types may be better off by forming homogeneous communities and consuming the optimal amount of the public good.[11, 12]

It would seem to follow that a system of homogeneous clubs is in the core of the economy. However, Scotchmer and Wooders (1987) showed that an equilibrium with mixed clubs is also in the core. For example, a state of the economy in the 'intensity of use club' model is a partition of the population into clubs and an allocation of the private good, visits, and the club good for each club. Scotchmer and Wooders showed that core utilities can be achieved in mixed groups under anonymous crowding if the demand for the facility and congestion coincide across the members of the club. In addition, if core utilities can be achieved in mixed clubs, they can also be achieved in homogeneous clubs, although mixed clubs cannot do strictly better than homogeneous clubs. Furthermore, let p(g, nv) be the price per visit at a club with characteristics (g, nv) under competition, where consumers and firms take prices as given. Scotchmer and Wooders showed there is an equivalence between competitive equilibria and the core; every competitive equilibrium is in the core and every state in the core can be supported by a price system under competition. Since the price allows revenue to cover average cost in a competitive equilibrium, p(g, nv)nv = C(g, nv). It follows that lump sum membership fees are not necessary. And the equilibrium configuration of clubs need not entail homogeneous clubs.

Ellickson, et. al. (1999) studied a model where there are many private goods, there is a continuum of agents, agents are characterized by a variety of characteristics, and agents can join more than one club. A price system under competition includes a price vector for private goods, and a price vector for clubs that has two components, one that finances the club and another that involves possible transfers across members of the club. They showed that if endowments are desirable, i.e., each individual would prefer to consume his endowment and not join any clubs to joining a club and forgoing private consumption, a club equilibrium exists under certain additional technical requirements, every club equilibrium is in the core and is Pareto optimal, and core allocations coincide with club equilibria.

There are a number of other situations where mixed groups may be optimal. Clearly, if the integer condition is not satisfied, mixed clubs may very well be optimal. Second, Berglas (1976b) argued that if different types of labor skills are complementary in the production of the private good, then a mixed club may be optimal.[13] Third, Berglas and Pines (1981) showed that mixed clubs can be optimal when there is more than one club good. For example, suppose there are people who like golf, people who like tennis, and some who like both. An equilibrium in the core may entail a mixed club offering both goods. And mixed clubs are as efficient as homogeneous clubs in Berglas's (1984) quantity-quality model if tastes only differ with regard to the quantity dimension of the public good but not the quality dimension.[14]

Finally, it is not at all clear how important this sorting issue is since, as Scotchmer (2002) put it, ".... typically, no two agents will be alike, and it is not obvious how to stylize their similarities. It is almost tautological that agents with the same tastes who face the same prices will make the same choices. But if they differ in productive skills or other external characteristics, they will not necessarily face the same prices. A competitive economy should get the grouping right under the right kind of pricing scheme, irrespective of what the optimal grouping happens to be." (p 2030.) The issue might be whether the "right kind of pricing scheme" emerges naturally, or whether government has a role to play.

15.2 Local Public Goods and the Tiebout Hypothesis

Tiebout (1956) assumed that consumers are perfectly mobile, have complete information regarding the various policy alternatives available to them in every jurisdiction, income is from dividends and hence independent of location, and consumers are not restricted in their employment. Implicitly, public spending is financed by head taxes. On the other side of the market, he assumed there is a large number of communities, no spillover effects across communities, and an optimal community size exists for every location where the public good is produced at minimum average cost. From this it follows that localities compete for residents on the basis of the mix of local public goods and services and consumers sort themselves into homogeneous communities by "voting with their feet" in choosing a location that is best for them, and an optimum can be achieved.[15] This not only solves the Samuelson problem of determining public spending optimally, it also solves the political problem as well since unanimity will prevail in each community.

Tiebout only provided a heuristic discussion of his result. It was left to later writers to provide the details and critics eventually emerged. One detail is how people express their dissent from policies they don't like. Hirschman (1970), for example, argued that leaving one community for another (exit) because of a disagreement about policy is one way of dissenting. Another equally valuable way of dissenting is to work for change from within the community (voice).[16]

Another detail is the precise definition of a local public good. Some authors have assumed the good is a pure public good locally, i.e., inside the jurisdiction, but a pure private good globally, i.e., outside the jurisdiction. In that case, only local residents benefit from the good and there is no congestion locally. Others have included congestion costs in order to generate an optimal size location where the average cost of providing a public good is minimized. This is what Tiebout assumed. Some actual goods provided by local governments appear to exhibit congestion such as city sidewalks and streets where exclusion is impossible, given the current technology. Other goods such as a bridge or highway with limited access exhibit exclusion. Still other goods such as schools, libraries, and museums may be excludable but may have other benefits that warrant avoiding exclusion.

15.2.1 A Model of an LPG

Consider the following version of a model due to Stiglitz (1977). There are N identical agents and M locations or islands, and each has one unit of homogeneous land. There are n agents at a location and each is endowed with one unit of labor. The utility of the representative agent is given by $u(x, g)$. Output per unit of land is produced from labor and land according to a CRS technology, $y = f(n)$ in intensive form, where $f(n)$ is concave and differentiable. The cost of the public good is $C(g, n)$, where $C_n = 0$ denotes a pure public good and $C_n > 0$ denotes an impure public good with congestion. And the public good does not cause any spillovers across locations.[17]

The social planner chooses (x, g, n) to maximize the representative agent's utility subject to the resource constraint, $f(n) = nx + C(g, n)$. It is straightforward to show that Samuelson's rule holds. In addition, if an interior solution exists for n, say n^*, such that N/n^* is an integer, and $M \geq N/n^*$, we also have the following necessary condition governing the optimal choice of n,

$$f_n - C_n - (f - C)/n = 0,$$

where $df/dn = f_n$. Since f_n is the marginal product of labor and hence the wage, w, and $(f - C)/n = x$, this last equation can be written as

$$w - x = C_n. \tag{15.10}$$

By constant returns, we also have,

$$f = wn + R,$$

where R is total land rents. Combining this last equation with the resource constraint implies

$$n(w - x) + R - C = 0. \tag{15.11}$$

It follows from (15.10) and (15.11) that if there is no congestion externality, $R = C$. This is an example of the Henry George Theorem;[18] land rents are used to finance the public good. However, if congestion occurs, $R < C$ and $w > x$. In that case labor shares in the burden of financing the public good since it causes a congestion externality. This is exacerbated if there is a psychological congestion cost that adversely affects utility. One remedy for this simple externality is to impose a head tax. However, if a head tax is unavailable, a tax on property may be a viable alternative. Indeed, the property tax is used extensively to finance local government spending in some countries like the U.S.

15.2.2 A Model with Housing

The model is easily adjusted to include housing and a property tax. Assume agents are identical and are endowed with w units of the numeraire private good and can spend it on the private numeraire good and housing. Utility is given by $u(x, h, g)$, and the budget constraint is $w = x + (p + \tau)h$, where p is the producer price of a unit of housing and τ is the property tax rate. If there is one unit of land in the local jurisdiction and n agents, each of the identical agents owns $1/n$ units of land and this is used to build a house that costs ph. Total property tax revenue is τhn and the government's budget constraint is $\tau hn = C(g)$, where the local public good is a pure public good for simplicity. If the consumer takes the tax as given, then it will distort his decision making at the margin. If all locations impose a property tax, then it will distort the housing decision in each location and thus capital owners will bear the burden of the tax and this may reduce the amount of capital used in housing.[19]

However, there are land use policies that can convert the property tax into a non-distorting benefit tax. Hamilton (1975, 1976, 1983) argued that this is true of zoning laws. Zoning that fixes the use of property at a given location can convert the decision to own property into a simple choice over location and may make the property tax non-distorting. Suppose the local government imposes a restriction on lot size or the minimum size of a house, say h_{min}. If for consumer i, $h^i = h_{min}$, then his choice is simply which location to reside in and the property tax does not necessarily distort his housing decision.

Zoning may be of even greater importance when agents differ by their income level. Consider two types of agent, rich and poor, and suppose the public good is a normal good. If a head tax is available, agents will sort themselves into homogeneous communities. If the local public good is a normal good, the rich community will enjoy more of the local public good than the poor community. The head tax can be interpreted as the member-ship fee of a "club." Now suppose the head tax is not available and let h^r be the optimal housing choice of the rich and h^p be the housing choice of the poor. If housing is a normal good, $h^r > h^p$. Suppose the representative local government imposes a minimum housing requirement, h_{min} and $h^r = h_{min}$. Once again, the zoning requirement converts the housing decision into a location choice problem and the tax is non-distorting, but does serve to ex-clude the poor.

An equilibrium may not exist without zoning restrictions. If a property tax must be used to finance public spending, the tax base in the rich com-munity will be larger than in the poor community if housing is a normal good. It follows that the tax rate will be lower in the rich community. As pointed out by Henderson (1979), among others, a poor person has an in-centive to move from the poor community into the rich community, buy h^p in the rich community, and enjoy a lower tax rate and a higher level of public spending. As the poor move in, the rich have an incentive to move to a new community. However, the poor will follow them by migrating again, and so on, and an equilibrium will not exist.[20] The rich community can forestall this sort of migration by imposing certain zoning laws on houses and lots. For example, the local government in the rich community, or the developer developing a new community for the rich, can maintain houses and lots above a certain minimum size larger than what the poor can afford, e.g., 3000 square foot houses. Such zoning not only converts the property tax into a non-distorting benefit tax, it also acts as an exclu-sion device.

There are other exclusion devices. For example, the rich community can over-consume the public good thus raising taxes to a level designed to keep the poor out. Let $v^{pp} = v(w^p, t^p, p^p, g^p)$ be indirect utility of a poor person living in a homogeneous poor community, and $v^{pr} = v(w^p, t^r, p^r, g^r)$ be her utility when living in a rich community. The budget of the rich community is $n^r t^r = c(g^r)$ and if one poor person moves in becomes $(1+n^r)t^r$

$= c(g^r)$. Thus, the rich community can choose the level of the public good g^* so that

$$v^{pp} > v(w^p, c(g^*)/(1+n^r), p^r, g^*),$$

and provide an incentive for the poor to stay away.

A third exclusionary device is for the rich community to subsidize public spending in the poor community. This raises the level of taxes in the rich community and raises the level of public spending in the poor community. Both the tax and the transfer tend to keep the poor from leaving their own community.

Finally, the rich community can offer a mix of public goods found to be undesirable by the poor. For example, suppose the rich care about abundant parking, schools, and police protection, and the poor care about public transportation and schools, but not parking, or police protection. Then imposing taxes in the rich community to pay for parking lots, schools, and police protection, and possibly banning buses and other public transportation, may keep the poor out.

More generally, the population can be characterized by a set of characteristics. At an optimum the population is segregated into different homogeneous communities on the basis of the characteristics; mixing is inefficient. The Samuelson condition holds at each location and the optimal size of the group at a location balances the costs of congestion against the benefit of financing local public spending. Decentralizing the optimum when it exists can be problematic. It is imagined that developers set up communities to attract residents of a particular type and provide the optimal amount of public goods and other amenities to that end. Two problems arise, financing local public spending and controlling the size and mix of the population. In terms of finance, there are a number of options available, e.g., income tax, Lindahl tax, property tax, and equal tax shares, among others. Matters are a bit more complicated in terms of controlling the population. Zoning and minimum house or plot sizes can discriminate against agents on the basis of income. And high tax rates and subsequent high local public spending can also be used to keep certain residents out, although, this may be difficult to achieve in practice.

Conley and Wooders (1997, 1998) assumed agents differ by observable characteristics like age and gender, and unobservable characteristics like their endowments, their taste for a public good, or their taste for work versus leisure. The former are referred to as "crowding" types in analogy to the special case where the total number of agents causes observed crowding, and the latter are referred to as "taste" types. Only an agent's "crowding" type enters the utility or production function of others, not his "taste" type. Under anonymous pricing only information about the agent's crowding type is used. With non-anonymous pricing, information on both crowding and taste are used to determine an agent's particular price. For example, with anonymous Tiebout admission pricing agents are charged a price for entry to the club that is based on the crowding type of the individual for each level of the public good at a given location. Agents of different crowding types must be charged a different entry price. Under anonymous Lindahl pricing an agent's Lindahl price for a single level of the public good at a given location is based on his crowding type alone.

Conley and Wooders showed that the core is equivalent to the anonymous Tiebout admission pricing equilibria; the Samuelson rule holds in such a case and the mix of the population using a club is optimal. A property tax can be interpreted as an admission price, for example.[21] Furthermore, they also showed that the core is equivalent to the non-anonymous Lindahl pricing equilibria when both types are used in determining prices. However, the core is larger than the set of anonymous Lindahl equilibria, i.e., there exist allocations in the core that cannot be decentralized through anonymous Lindahl pricing. In a sense this should not be too surprising since anonymous Lindahl prices in this set-up are not truly personalized since they are not based on taste types, e.g., low demand for public goods versus high demand. Indeed, it is the fact that tastes for public goods differ and are unobservable that causes the free rider problem to begin with.

15.2.3 Property Taxation

To be more explicit about the model with housing and the property tax, suppose there are a large number of identical locations, both capital and people are mobile across locations, and agents are identical in tastes and endowments. Each agent is endowed with some of the one consumption good available. An agent living in location i has preferences for the private consumption good, housing, and the LPG, according to $u(x^i, h^i, g^i)$, which is assumed to be well-behaved. The representative consumer's budget constraint at location i is $I - t^i = x^i + q^i h^i$, where q^i is the consumer price of housing, I is income, which is independent of location, and t^i is a head tax. The consumer maximizes utility subject to the budget constraint and the result is a demand for housing, which depends on income, the price of housing, and the level of the LPG, $h^i(I - t^i, q^i, g^i)$, and the indirect utility function, $v^i(I - t^i, q^i, g^i)$. The mobility constraint for the agent is

$$v^i(I - t^i, q^i, g^i) = v^*, \tag{15.12}$$

where v* is given. From the results of Part One we know that $v_g^i = \lambda^i m^i$, where $\lambda^i = v_I^i$ is the private marginal utility of income and m^i is the marginal WTP for the publicly provided good.

Housing is produced using capital and land according to $f^i(k^i)$, where k is capital per unit of land. Profit is $p^i f^i(k^i) - rk^i$, which is land rents, where r is the real interest rate, and is taken as given to the local economy, and p^i is the producer price of housing. The firm maximizes profit so that $r = p^i f_k^i$. Inverting, we obtain the demand for capital, $k^i(r/p^i)$, with $dk^i/d(r/p^i) = 1/f_{kk}^i$ < 0. It follows that the supply of housing is $H^i(r/p^i) = f^i[k^i(r/p^i)]$, where $dH^i/d(r/p^i) = f_k^i/f_{kk}^i$ < 0. The supply is increasing in the price and decreasing in the interest rate. The equilibrium in the local housing market occurs where

$$H^i(r/p^i) = n^i h^i(I - t^i, q^i, g^i). \qquad (15.13)$$

The local government does not have access to perfect zoning, which seems a realistic assumption to make. It imposes a head tax t^i and a property tax on housing and raises $t^i n^i + \tau^i n^i h^i$ in revenue. It spends the proceeds on a publicly provided private good with cost $c^i(n^i g^i)$. Its constraint is

$$t^i n^i + \tau^i n^i h^i = c^i(n^i g^i). \qquad (15.14)$$

Land rents in location i are given by

$$R^i = p^i H^i(r/p^i) - rk^i(r/p^i). \qquad (15.15)$$

The local government's objective function is local land rents and it chooses its policy (t^i, τ^i, g^i) to maximize rents subject to (15.12) and (15.14). Finally, capital market clearing requires

$$k = \Sigma k^i(r/p^i), \qquad (15.16)$$

where k is the economy-wide endowment of capital. The equilibrium is characterized by optimizing behavior on the part of consumers, firms, and local governments, market clearing in the housing market for each location and the capital market, and the migration constraint must hold for each agent, i.e., (15.12) - (15.14) and (15.16) hold.

It is straightforward to show, by deriving the first order conditions of the representative government's decision problem, that if the head tax is available, the property tax should be set to zero. If it is unavailable, it can be shown that the property tax distorts the housing decision and the following modified Samuelson condition governs the optimal choice of the publicly provided good in location i,[22]

$$n^i m^i = [1 + \tau^i h^i_q / h^i]^{-1}(c^i_g + \tau^i h^i_g / g^i). \qquad (15.17)$$

The term $[1 + \tau^i h^i_q / h^i]^{-1}$ is the social marginal cost of funds discussed in Part One and is greater than one in magnitude if the demand for housing is decreasing in the price of housing. And the term $\tau^i h^i_g / g^i$ captures a provision effect. If provision of the LPG increases the demand for housing, this will increase property tax revenue and reduce the social cost of the publicly provided good. Furthermore, for a given level of g the mobility constraint fixes the consumer price of housing. Since $p = q - \tau$ and q is fixed by the mobility constraint, the full incidence of the tax falls on landowners. And $d\pi^i / d\tau^i = -f^i < 0$ is the effect on rents.

Krelove (1993) also derived the same result even if a land tax is also available. And he showed that it is optimal to finance the publicly provided good by the property tax alone, even though a non-distorting land tax may also be available, as long as the population is at its optimal level. The intuition is that the property tax acts like a congestion fee and this is similar in spirit to a head tax in limiting population, while the land tax is not. In addition, he also noted that the second-best equilibrium is not constrained efficient because there is no market mechanism that forces local governments to take into account the indirect effects their policies have on other locations. In a sense there is a system coordination failure that reduces welfare.

With zoning there is a restriction on the use of property. Let h^i_z be the restricted amount of housing at location i, where h^i_z is chosen by the developer, or local government at location i. For example, the restriction may take the form of a minimum amount of housing in terms of the square footage of the structure, or lot size. If the restriction is binding, as it is with perfect zoning, $h^i = h^i_z$. In that case, the agent simply chooses a location on the basis of maximizing $u^i(I - q^i h^i_z, h^i_z, g^i)$, where locations vary by (q^i, g^i, h^i_z). The tax does not distort the housing decision, per se. Of course, if the restriction is not binding, then $h^i > h_z$ and the tax does distort the housing decision.

Several remarks are in order. First, while it is true that the property tax itself may distort the housing decision and cause consumers to consume less housing than would otherwise have been the case, it is also true that other policies may have the opposite effect. For example, in many countries taxpayers can write off mortgage interest on their primary residence against their income tax liability. This serves to increase the demand for housing and may dominate the impact of the property tax, especially for taxpayers in higher tax brackets. Second, the demand for housing may be related to the demand for LPGs, like local schools and police and fire pro-

318   15 Local Public Goods, Club Goods, and the Tiebout Hypothesis

tection. This accounts for the second term in (15.17) that captures the "provision effect." It is certainly possible that this effect can outweigh the effect of the MCF and imply that the second-best level of the LPG is greater than the first-best level. Third, any claims of greater efficiency at the local level must take into account the method of financing local spending. It is not immediately obvious that a shift of responsibility from the national level to the local level is necessarily welfare improving if greater reliance must be placed on a distorting property tax.

15.2.4 Tiebout Without Political Institutions

Epple and Zelenitz (1981) asked whether Tiebout-like mobility could constrain local policymakers from making bad policy choices. Imagine that bureaucrats or politicians wish to run the local government to their own advantage, and not necessarily to the advantage of the local residents. Can the mobility of the residents of the local community preclude the government from choosing policy that is not in the best interest of the residents? Epple and Zelenitz argued that bad policymaking at the local level can still occur even in the presence of consumer mobility. This result hinges on their assumption that jurisdiction boundaries are fixed. This allows local governments to exert monopoly power over landowners by sharing in the land rents.

This raises the question as to whether purely private behavior can achieve the optimum under Tiebout's market analogy without any political institutions. Henderson (1985) argued that developers have an incentive to develop new communities and provide a mix of public services to attract new residents and in so doing would achieve an optimum. Henderson (1985), Henderson and Mitra (1996), and later Henderson and Thisse (2001), cited evidence for the U.S. that the development and formation of new communities was quite significant. For example, from 1910 to 1990 the growth rate of new urban locations was 20% and there have been 123 new, so-called "edge" cities developed since 1970. Many of these new cities appear to be "planned, controlled entities started by land development companies and often administered by 'shadow governments.' Henderson and Mitra found no examples of edge cities not started by a single developer....." (p547.) It is also well known that a significant proportion of the U.S. population migrates each year. Indeed, more than 30% of the young people between the ages of twenty and twenty-nine move each year in the U.S., for example.[23] Given this information, Henderson and Thisse argued that competitive, rent maximizing entrepreneuers would provide an efficient level of public spending on a variety of public goods and services in competing for residents, and that the Tiebout hypothesis did not require politics as a result of this activity.

There are two additional assumptions that appear to be critical to the 'developer efficiency' argument, developing new communities is assumed costless and that communities can be perfectly replicated. In particular, Epple and Zelenitz (1981) and Courant and Rubinfeld (1982) questioned the first assumption. Sandler and Tschirhart (1984) raised the replicability issue against Berglas and Pines (1981, 1984) in their club goods model. However, the literature has not made the case that land and space are necessary to club goods. On the other hand, LPGs appear to require land and space and these are in limited supply. Indeed, Scotchmer (2002) has suggested that this may be one of the defining characteristics that distinguishes the two goods, clubs versus LPGs.

Pines (1991) showed that if locations are not perfectly replicable, the necessary conditions required to prove existence seem overly stringent. He studied a version of Stiglitz's (1977) model mentioned above where it is assumed that each agent owns $1/N$ units of land at each island and the cost of the public good is $c(g) = g$ for simplicity. Income for an agent is $w^i + \Pi$, where Π is a $1/N$ share in total land rents, and his budget constraint is $w^i + \Pi = x^i$. The consumer chooses a location to maximize utility subject to this constraint, which is tantamount to choice over g, when confronted with a wage distribution across islands. A developer at island i chooses (n^i, g^i) to maximize net profit, $\Pi^i = f(n^i) - w^i n^i - g^i$. It is straightforward to show that Samuelson's rule holds. And in equilibrium, markets clear,

$$\Sigma_i n^i = N, \tag{15.18}$$

$$\Sigma_i [f(n^i) - n^i x^i - g^i] = 0. \tag{15.19}$$

At equilibrium consumers and developers optimize and markets clear so that (15.18) and (15.19) hold. Denote the equilibrium as $(x^{i*}, g^{i*}, n^{i*}, \Pi^{i*}, i = 1, .., M; \Pi^*)$ and let the expenditure function for agent i be defined in the following manner,

$$e(1/n^{i*}, u^{i*}) = \min \{x^i + (1/n^{i*})g^i : u^i(x^i, g^i) \geq u^{i*}\},$$

over (x^i, g^i), where $1/n^i$ plays the role of a price in this framework. We can define the surplus of local production over local consumption as

$$s(n^i, u^*) = f(n^i) - n^i e(1/n^i, u^*),$$

and the surplus of the resources available locally over the local use of the resources as

$$\sigma(n^i, u^*, \Pi^*) = f(n^i) - n^i e(1/n^i, u^*) + n^i \Pi^*,$$

where $u^* = u(w(g^{i*}) + \Pi^*, g^{i*})$. Note that $s_n = f_n - e + e_{(1/n)}/n^i = w^i - x^i = -\Pi \leq 0$, where $e_{(1/n)}$ is the partial derivative of the expenditure function with respect to $1/n^i$. The key to the existence question is the behavior of the surplus functions s( ) and σ( ).

Pines assumed land is free if $M > N/\min(n^*)$, where $\min(n^*)$ is the smallest optimal community size. He showed that if there exists at least one optimal community size and land is free, then there exists a unique equilibrium that is efficient. This requires that n* globally maximizes the surplus function σ( ). However, if n* is not a global maximum, if land is scarce, or not perfectly replicable, an equilibrium may not exist.[24] Pines extended these results to a model where there is also housing and congestion. His general conclusion was that an equilibrium with optimizing developers may not exist and that politics may be required to efficiently provide local public services.

15.3 Criticism of the Tiebout Hypothesis

Two problems with the hypothesis that we have already mentioned are that the Tiebout self-sorting mechanism doesn't really solve the free rider problem for a pure public good, and the core might be empty so an equilibrium might not exist because of the integer problem, first pointed out by Pauly (1967). In addition, Stiglitz (1977) showed that the existence of an equilibrium may require transfers between communities. Since it is extremely unlikely that such transfers will be made, existence is problematic.

Examples have also appeared in the literature where there are multiple equilibria and equilibria that are not optimal. For example, an equilibrium may exist that is not Pareto optimal because agents are mismatched; utility can be improved by rearranging residents across communities. Consider the following simple example. Suppose there are two goods, schools and police protection, and two types of agent in the economy, young and old. The young care more about schools while the old care more about police protection. Utility is given by $u^h(S, P)$, where S is schools and P is police. The old agent's indifference curves are depicted as o^1 and o^2 and the young agent's indifference curves are given by y^1 and y^2. The production possibilities for the two locations are given by lines AA' and BB'. Clearly, points A and B' are local equilibria. However, by rearranging agents between the two communities we can attain A' and B where both are better

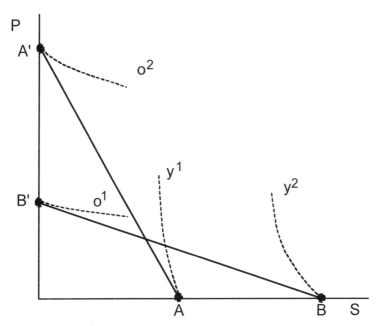

Fig. 15.1. Mismatching

off. Unfortunately, there may be no mechanism where such large-scale migration can be accomplished.

Another issue that has been raised is that if communities stratify by income and the tax base is higher in wealthy communities than in poor communities, the tax rate will be correspondingly lower. As mentioned, the poor then have an incentive to move to wealthier neighborhoods. For example, Wheaton (1975) showed that a head tax would support the optimum of homogeneous communities, but that other taxes, such as an income tax, or a Lindahl tax, cause migration; all agents want to migrate to wealthier communities and an equilibrium will not exist.

Furthermore, Boskin (1973) argued that mobility would lead to a shift in public spending away from welfare programs toward public goods and that this would be inefficient. And Rothenberg (1977) argued that suburbanites who commute to the inner city to work would create greater congestion for inner city residents. This may also be a source of inefficiency since the cost of public goods in the inner city will be greater and the cost in the suburbs will be lower, causing cities to contract and suburbs to expand.

A number of additional issues arise. For example, once the economy is in equilibrium, what happens if new public goods are introduced? How do we ascertain the demand for them? Do all new local projects, like fiber optic cable infrastructure, recycling, and computers for schools, cause a reshuffling of people? It seems almost inevitable that the political system will be involved in this process. This seems to be the case in real world economies.

15.4 Conclusion

In this chapter we have studied various club good models, different models of local public goods, some of which include land as an important factor and housing, the Tiebout hypothesis and criticisms of the hypothesis. The literature in each area has progressed quite remarkably in recent years and is very impressive. In particular, recent work has derived a number of important results on club goods that places it squarely in the tradition of general equilibrium theory and similarly for the work on local public goods. Problems of existence and optimality have received a great deal of attention.

It is probably fair to say that the Tiebout hypothesis about homogeneous sorting is not accurate as a complete description or explanation of the real world. It may not even be appropriate in theoretical models except where the most stringent conditions are satisfied. There is a broad variety of cases where the hypothesis fails; there are existence problems and difficulties associated with the optimality of an equilibrium when it does exist. However, the real value of the hypothesis may be in organizing one's thoughts about modeling economic behavior and studying policy at the local level when resources are mobile.

---

[1]   On the early literature, see Ellickson (1971, 1973, 1977, 1979), Oakland (1972), Flatters, Henderson, and Mieszkowski (1974), Wheaton (1975), Hamilton (1975, 1976), Stiglitz (1977, 1983a, 1983b), Westoff (1977), Henderson (1979, 1985), Brueckner (1979a), Epple and Zelenitz (1981), and Boadway (1982), Wilson (1987a, b), among others. For surveys of the literature on local public goods and the Tiebout hypothesis see Pestieau (1983), Wildasin (1986, 1987), and Rubinfeld (1987). And for some recent work see Conley and Wooders (1997, 1998) and Wellisch (2000).

[2]   See Pauly (1967, 1970a, 1970b), McGuire (1972, 1974a, 1974b), Berglas (1976a, 1976b, 1982, 1984), Berglas and Pines (1981), Scotchmer (1985a, 1985b, 1986), and Scotchmer and Wooders (1987) for some of the early work on club goods, and Sandler and Tschirhart (1980) for a good survey of the

early research. See Ellickson, Grodal, Scotchmer, and Zame (1999) for some more recent work on clubs.

[3] In particular, Buchanan and Goetz (1972), Stiglitz (1977), and Bewley (1981) were especially critical.

[4] It has been suggested in the literature that there are other ways the two goods may differ. For example, it has been pointed out that land and space may be more important to LPGs than to clubs. For some LPGs one must live in the local community to enjoy the public good, e.g., local schools, police and fire protection, and this requires one to either purchase or rent housing. This may act as an indirect exclusion device similar in spirit to being charged for a visit to a tennis or golf club. And some clubs like a golf course may require quite a bit of land. Another way the two goods may differ is that one can lower one's property tax liability by reducing one's expenditure on property, yet still enjoy the same amenities from a LPG. If one lowers one's expenditure on a club good by reducing visits to the club, one will also receive less in benefits. However, this follows from exclusion since the property owner cannot be excluded from enjoying the benefit of local fire protection and traffic lights. See the comments by Scotchmer (2002).

[5] With identical agents the resource constraint of the economy at equality is $Nw = Nx + (N/n)C(g, n)$. With a Benthamite utility function, social welfare is given by $Nu(x, g, n)$. Maximizing this function subject to the economy-wide resource constraint is equivalent to the problem in the text.

[6] Pauly (1967) first noted the integer problem. Stiglitz (1977) presented numerous examples of anomalous outcomes when there are two types of agent and N/n^* is not an integer. In addition, the resource constraint is not convex when population is mobile. Multiple equilibria may exist, suboptimal sorting equilibria may occur, and an equilibrium may not exist. This last possibility can easily occur if $N/2 < n^* < N$. See also Brueckner (1979a) and Bewley (1981). And, it is, of course, true that if N/n^* is finite, the "club industry" will not be competitive; clubs will have market power and this substantially changes the nature of the equilibrium. For example, there may only be a small number of golf courses in a geographic area. Each will obviously come to believe that it has market power in the local market for golf.

[7] Taking utility into account is not as far fetched as it sounds. Successful firms that produce, sell, and market a private good typically take the tastes of its potential customers into account when choosing the characteristics of a product, e.g., lemon scented dishwashing liquid, a DVD with certain special features included like director and actor commentaries, or the power and handling capabilities of a new car.

[8] See the discussion and examples in Stiglitz (1977) when $0 < N/2 < n^*$.

[9] The club's problem is to choose q, n, and g to maximize $[qnv - C(g, nv)]$ subject to the utility constraint needed to attract members, $u(w - qv, g, v, V) \geq u^*$. Differentiate with respect to q, n, and g, and simplify to obtain the appropriate price equation.

[10] See the interesting comment on these results by Sandler and Tshirhart (1984) and the cogent reply by Berglas and Pines (1984). Scotchmer and Wooders (1987) argued that under a price mechanism where p(g, nv) is the price charged by a club per visit when it offers club (g, nv), a lump sum membership fee is not necessary, and the competitive equilibrium is in the core. See also Scotchmer (1985b) who showed that lump sum membership fees are optimal when club firms have some market power. Indeed, she argued that the lump sum fee can actually be thought of as a measure of market power; it is positive in the presence of market power, but zero under competition.

[11] Berglas (1976b) mentions this problem, for example.

[12] This result may hinge on the cost of exclusion. See, for example, Helsley and Strange (1998), who examine coarse exclusion, where a membership fee can be charged, and fine exclusion, where a price per visit can be charged in addition to a membership fee, and the fixed cost of imposing fine exclusion is greater than for coarse exclusion. See also Lee (1991) who studied exclusion when information is asymmetric.

[13] However, if commuting costs are low, people may prefer to live in homogeneous communities and commute to work. And Brueckner (1994) showed that homogeneous clubs may still be optimal when labor types are non-essential in production, when complementarity is weak, or when preferences differ substantially in the population.

[14] Although this might not do justice to Tiebout's hypothesis that agents sort themselves on the basis of their tastes for public goods, which would be the quality dimension in this case.

[15] "The consumer-voter may be viewed as picking that community which best satisfies his preference pattern for public goods......... The greater the number of communities and the greater the variance among them, the closer the consumer will come to fully realizing his preference position." (Tiebout, p 418.) And, "Let the number of communities be infinite and let each announce a different pattern of expenditures on public goods. Given these assumptions...... the consumer-voters will move to that community which *exactly* satisfies their preferences......In this model the demand is exactly the same as it would be if it were determined by normal market forces." (Tiebout, p 421. Emphasis is in the original.)

[16] See Rose-Ackerman (1983) and Inman (1987) for surveys of early research on politics at the local level. For some recent work in this area, see Epple, Romer, and Sieg (2001).

[17] See Conley and Dix (1998) for a recent analysis of the case involving spillovers.

[18] See Henry George (1914).

[19] There is a large literature on the property tax. See Mieszkowski and Zodrow (1989) on taxation in Tiebout models. They contrast the traditional view of the property tax, that it is a benefit tax, with the new view, that it is a tax on capital, specifically housing capital.

[20] This has been dubbed a "Groucho Marx disequilibrium" by Rubinfeld (1994) in his comment on Scotchmer. It stems from a statement once made in jest by Groucho Marx, "I don't care to belong to a club that accepts people like me as members." See brainyquote.com/quotes/authors/g/groucho_marx.html

[21] Of course, as a practical matter, it may be difficult or illegal to charge a differentiated price when this includes the number of children in the family, and other such characteristics, even though that may have an impact on local spending for schools, for example. Second, there may be an equity problem in some circumstances. For example, if low income parents have more children than high income parents, charging the former a higher marginal property tax rate to finance local spending on schools might be viewed as inequitable.

[22] This is similar to equation (8) in Krelove (1993), for example.

[23] See Wildasin and Wilson (1996) note 4, page 180.

[24] It should also be pointed out that under Pines' definition of equilibrium, (5.12) holds and this implies $\Sigma_i s(n^i, u^*) = 0$. Implicitly this assumes that transfers can be made across islands. Without such transfers an equilibrium may not exist. See Stiglitz (1977).

16 Fiscal Competition

Small, open economies, where resources readily flow across the boundary of the economy, can have tremendous difficulty imposing policy. A tax increase used to finance additional spending on schools, roads, and libraries, may cause a shift of resources that frustrates the intension of the policy. For example, an improvement in the local schools may induce migration of families with school age children into the school district thus making it difficult to achieve smaller class size. In a strong sense, a collection of local economies is competing for a mobile tax base and this competition can be a source of inefficiency in contrast to the general thrust of the Tiebout hypothesis.

A number of analysts have studied tax competition among local governments including Starrett (1980), Boadway (1982), Boadway and Flatters (1982), Mintz and Tulkens (1986), Zodrow and Mieszkowski (1986), Wilson (1986, 1991c, 1997), Wildasin (1988, 1989), Hoyt (1991), Bucovetsky (1991), Krelove (1992a, b, 1993), DePater and Myers (1994), and more recently, Brueckner (2000), Hoyt (2001), Lockwood (2001), Keen and Kotsogiannis (2002), Justman, Thisse, and Ypersele (2002), Dahlby and Wilson (2003), Wildasin (2003), Parry (2003), and Kothenburger (2004), among others.[1] The basic idea is that local governments compete with one another for a mobile tax base and this competition has an impact on the optimal tax and spending policies chosen at the local level. For example, it can lead to lower tax rates and hence lower public spending as local governments try to attract private capital with low tax rates. Indeed, it has been suggested that this sort of tax competition may be a way of restraining government spending, at least at the local level.[2]

On the other hand, spending on local infrastructure that is complementary to private capital may cause some private capital to migrate into the community leading to an increase in the local tax base and greater public spending. Indeed, some local governments may even use infrastructure investment, e.g., new stadium, to compete directly for private projects, e.g., new baseball team. In addition, non-residents may pay some of the local taxes implying that some of the local tax burden is exported outside the community. Hotel taxes, taxes on absentee owners of land and other resources, cross border shopping, and taxes imposed on mail orders and internet sales provide examples. Exporting some of the local tax burden may lead to greater local public spending.

The issue then arises as to whether a decentralized Nash game played among a group of local governments in choosing policy has an equilibrium that is optimal, or can support an equilibrium that is optimal. As it turns out, the mobility assumption plays a critical role in answering these questions. When resources and population are perfectly mobile, the Nash equilibrium involving decentralized and uncoordinated local government decision making is Pareto optimal if transfers are made between governments.[3] However, if resources are imperfectly mobile, a role exists for a national government to coordinate policy. Unfortunately, when policy instruments are limited, this can be problematic. Furthermore, population may be immobile in the short run but mobile in the long run. This may have implications for making policy at the local level since there is a tendency to impose policy that exploits immobile resources. Thus, a long run view about policy may differ from a short run view.

In section 16.1 we study the tax competition problem and the impact it has on local government spending for consumption oriented LPGs and public capital, tax exporting, creating a market for rights to the mobile tax base, and tying the Tiebout hypothesis to tax competition. In 16.2 we present several extensions of the analysis including the composition of spending, additional taxes on capital, and the time consistency of tax policy. In section 16.3 we discuss the ramifications of imperfect mobility. Fiscal federalism and the interaction between levels of government is studied in section 16.4 and 16.5 concludes the chapter.

16.1 Tax Competition

A number of researchers have argued that there are spillover effects across the budgets of local governments. For example, Oates (1972) suggested that competition for a mobile tax base, such as business investment, would force local governments to keep taxes and hence spending low, and that this downward bias is inefficient. Zodrow and Mieszkowski (1986) and Wilson (1986) presented the argument in a formal model. In particular, Zodrow and Mieszkowski presented a static model of capital allocation across a number of different locations where public spending is financed by a tax imposed on mobile capital, and labor is immobile. The tax distorts the capital allocation decision. Each local government chooses the local tax rate on capital to maximize local welfare subject to its budget constraint. The critical feature of the analysis is that each local government ignores the impact it has on the other local governments. Under these conditions, the marginal cost of funds is greater than one in magnitude. They showed that the level of a public good conferring a consumption benefit would increase if greater reliance is placed on a non-distorting tax rather than the capital tax, following the analysis of Atkinson and Stern (1974). This suggests that the tax rate on capital and spending on the public good are too low when the mobile factor is taxed due to competition among governments. In the case of public capital that improves productivity, this result is ambiguous. However, if an unusual case can be ruled out, the result will also go through with public capital.[4]

Wildasin (1989) pointed out that the impact of one location's tax system on another community can be thought of as an externality. When one local government raises its tax rate on mobile capital, some of the capital, and hence tax base, will shift to other locations. This increase in the tax base in those other locations is a benefit to them. Unfortunately, the first government does not take this effect into account when choosing its optimal tax rate and this is true of each local government. It follows that each government tends to tax capital at too low a rate and provide less of the LPG than would otherwise have been the case. Wildasin provided an analysis of the spillover effect of a tax on mobile capital, a Pigovian remedy for the externality, and an estimate of the potential magnitude of the subsidy.

Suppose the local government at location h raises its tax rate by dt^h. The outflow of capital to other locations is dk^i/dt^h and the flow of additional tax revenue is $t^i(dk^i/dt^h)$. If S^h is h's subsidy, then $dS^h/dt^h = \Sigma_{i \neq h} t^i(dk^i/dt^h)$ is the marginal effect on the subsidy. Wildasin presented numerical examples which indicated that the size of the subsidy and marginal cost of public funds was substantial. For a reasonable benchmark case, the marginal subsidy rate is about 40% and the social marginal cost of public spending when the externality is taken into account is about 70% of the actual cost as perceived by the local government when it ignores the externality. These results were derived in a partial equilibrium framework that implicitly assumed that the federal government had access to a non-distorting tax to finance the subsidy, as recognized by Wildasin.

Wilson (1986) extended the analysis to trade in private goods and explicit production of the public good. It was shown that taxation of mobile capital will lead to public production of the public good that is too capital intensive relative to the first-best allocation. Krelove (1992a) pointed out that there is also a pecuniary externality since a local government's policy will generally have an impact on trade and resource flows and hence on the prices of traded goods or factors that are mobile, e.g., the interest rate. He proposed a clever market arrangement whereby local communities bid for the tax base in analogy with a private market for a pollution externality. The resulting equilibrium was shown to be optimal. DePater and Myers (1994) extended Wildasin's result to include an adjustment in the corrective subsidy for pecuniary externalities associated with tax competition. However, Sinn (1997) expressed extreme skepticism regarding the possibility that competition among local governments can essentially solve social choice problems. This is because the problems confronting local governments exist because the private sector is incapable of solving them. Expecting competition among governments to solve them is perhaps asking too much. He provided an example involving public capital with congestion where tax competition does not lead to an equilibrium where public capital is lower when private capital is taxed than when it is not taxed.

16.1.1 Taxing Mobile Capital

Consider the following model. There is a large number of jurisdictions or locations, agents are identical, capital is perfectly mobile, while labor is immobile. There are n^i agents residing at location i, and $n^i = 1$ for simplicity. There is one consumption good produced via a well-behaved, neoclassical, CRS technology using capital and labor, according to $y = f(k)$, in intensive form, where k is capital per unit of labor.

Firms producing the numeraire consumption good at location i maximize profit,

$$f^i(k^i) - w^i - (r + t^i)k^i,$$

where w^i is the wage, r is the return to capital, and t^i is a source-based tax on capital used in production at location i. Hence, under profit maximization, $f^i_k = r + t^i$, and $w^i = f^i(k^i) - (r + t^i)k^i$ is the residual paid to labor. We can solve the first equation to obtain the demand for capital, $k^i(r + t^i)$. The wage can be determined from,

$$w^i(r + t^i) = f^i(k^i(r + t^i)) - (r + t^i)k^i(r + t^i).$$

It is straightforward to show that $k_r < 0$ and $w^i_r = - k^i$ by the envelope theorem.

Each consumer is endowed with one unit of labor, which is completely supplied to the local labor market where the individual resides and agent h at location h is endowed with k^{*h} units of capital. Preferences are represented by a utility function $u(x^h, g^h)$. The consumer maximizes utility subject to the constraint

$$w^h + \Sigma r^j k^{hj} - T^h = x^h,$$

where w^h is the wage paid at location h, $r^j k^{hj}$ is the interest income agent h earns from an investment in location j, T^h is a lump sum tax paid by h, and $k^{*h} = \Sigma_j k^{hj}$, where k^{*h} is h's endowment of capital per worker. The first order conditions of the consumer's problem imply $r^a = r^b = r$. The constraint becomes

$$x^h = w^h + rk^{*h} - T^h$$

The consumer's indirect utility function is given by $v^h(w^h + rk^{*h} - T^h, g^h)$. We can easily extend this model to allow for an endogenous saving decision as in Krelove (1992a).[5]

The local government's budget constraint at location i is

$$T^i + \tau^i k^i = c^i g^i / n^i, \tag{16.1}$$

where c^i is the constant unit cost of the LPG, g^i is a public good, and $k^i = \Sigma_j k^{ji}$ is capital invested at location i per unit of labor. The local government chooses (T^h, τ^h, g^h) to maximize indirect utility subject to its constraint, and $k^i(r + \tau^i)$, taking r, and the policies of the other governments, as given. The solution is a function of (r, c^i).

Equilibrium in the capital market requires

$$\Sigma k^{*i} = \Sigma_i k^i. \tag{16.2}$$

An equilibrium is an allocation of capital, a choice of output, and a policy such that consumers, firms, and local governments optimize, and (16.1) and (16.2) hold. And, as mentioned, if we extend the model to allow for a saving decision, then the total capital stock becomes endogenous and will generally respond to policy.

The first order conditions of the representative government's decision problem can be manipulated to obtain the following main result,

$$n^i m^i = [1 + \theta^i \varepsilon_{kr}]^{-1} c^i. \tag{16.3}$$

This is similar in spirit to (15.17). The term $[1 + \theta^i \varepsilon_{kr}]^{-1}$ captures the marginal cost of funds (MCF). Since the demand for capital is negatively related to the cost of capital, then the MCF > 1.

Second, if the person-specific tax is available and can be chosen optimally, then we have the first-best rule instead, $n^i m^i = c^i$. Thus,

$$(n^i m^i)^s / (n^i m^i)^f = [1 + \theta^i \varepsilon_{kr}]^{-1},$$

where the 'f' superscript denotes the first-best level and the 's' superscript denotes the second-best level. It follows that if the aggregate demand for the publicly provided good is strictly decreasing in the level of the good and income effects are small in magnitude, then the second-best level of the publicly provided good is less than the first-best level because of the Pigou effect discussed in Part One.

In addition to this, Hoyt (1991) and Bucovetsky and Wilson (1991) both showed that the tax on capital income goes to zero as the number of locations increases. As the number of locations increases, the ability of mobile capital to escape taxation also increases. In the limit it becomes impossible for local governments to tax capital. And Krelove (1992a, 1993) pointed out that the resulting tax competition equilibrium with a finite number of locations may not be constrained efficient; each local government's policy may have an impact on aggregate prices and may cause a pecuniary externality across locations as a result.

16.1.2 Productive Public Investments

Suppose instead that the publicly provided good improves productivity, $f(k^i, g^i)$ with derivative properties, $f_g > 0$ and $f_{kg} > 0$. Public infrastructure is an example of such a good. Firms maximize profit once again and this implies that $r + \tau^i = f_k(k^i, g^i)$. Solving, $k^i(r + \tau^i, g^i)$. If there is CRS in private inputs, the wage is once again given by

$$w^i(r + \tau^i, g^i) = f[k^i(r + \tau^i, g^i), g^i] - (r + \tau^i)k^i(r + \tau^i, g^i).$$

It has the derivative properties $w^i_r = - k^i < 0$ and $w^i_g = f_g > 0$, by the envelope theorem.

The local government chooses its policy to maximize the indirect utility of the representative resident subject to its budget constraint, the demand for capital, $k^i(r + \tau^i, g^i)$, and taking the interest rate r, and the policies of the other governments, as given. It is straightforward to derive the following formula for public capital,

$$n^i f_g = [1 + \tau^i k^i_r/k^i]^{-1}(c^i - n^i\tau^i k^i_g). \tag{16.4}$$

Once again, the marginal cost of funds is greater than one in magnitude since the demand for capital is decreasing in the cost of capital. And there is also a provision effect. Public capital investment attracts private capital investment if the two types of capital are complements, i.e., $k_g = - f_{kg}/f_{kk} > 0$, and crowds out private investment if the two are substitutes instead.

The comparison between the first-best and second-best levels of the public good becomes ambiguous since the provision effect may work in the opposite direction of the influence of the MCF. In the Appendix we derive the following equation,

$$(g^f - g^s) = - \tau^i [\Gamma f_{kk} MCF - f_{kg}]/\Delta, \qquad (16.5)$$

where and 'f' superscript dentes the first-best and the 's' superscript denotes the second-best, and where $\Gamma = k^i_g + c^i k^i_r / k^i n^i$ and $\Delta = - (f_{kk}f_{gg} - f_{kg}f_{gk}) < 0$. If public capital improves the marginal productivity of private capital and public capital attracts private capital, i.e., $f_{kg} > 0$ and $\Gamma > 0$, then it follows that the second-best level of public capital is greater than the first-best level.[6]

Taylor (1992) argued that local governments can actively use infrastructure investments to compete with one another.[7] Indeed, they may rely on this sort of competition rather than simply reducing taxes in some cases. And in some cases they compete for one big project such as the location of the Saturn assembly plant, or a new football team. One way of modeling this sort of interaction is as a race among a group of agents, e.g., local governments, for a prize. Let $g^i(t)$ be the amount of infrastructure available at location i at time t, and $I^{gi}(t)$ be investment in infrastructure at location i at time t. Hence, the stock changes according to

$$(dg^i/dt) = (I^{gi})^\alpha \text{ for } 0 < \alpha < 1.$$

Let B be the benefit of winning. If r is the discount rate, Be^{-rT} is the present value of winning at time T in the future. To allow for uncertainty, let h be the probability that the local government loses in the next moment, given that it is still in the race and let H(t) be the cumulative probability that it will lose at time t. It follows that $h = H'(t)/[1 - H(t)]$ is the so-called hazard rate; the higher the hazard rate, the greater the probability of losing the race. If $H(0) = 0$, i.e., the probability of immediately losing the race is zero, then we can integrate to get, $H(t) = 1 - e^{-ht}$. The hazard rate will depend positively on the number of local governments competing for the prize.

The local government chooses an investment policy to maximize the expected return,

$$B[1 - H(t)]e^{-rT} - \int_0^T I^{gi}(t)[1 - H(t)]e^{-rt}dt.$$

The solution can be derived using the Calculus of Variations. Taylor showed that the local government will be more likely to compete the greater the reward and the smaller the amount of investment required. In addition, if the reward is large enough, an increase in the probability of losing a big reward will induce the local government to expand its effort and try to complete the project more quickly. On the other hand, if the required amount of investment is large enough, an increase in the probability of losing will cause the local government to give up.

It also follows that resources may be wasted pursuing private investment. If a large number of local governments pursue the same private investment, e.g., a new production facility or sports stadium, but only one community wins, then the infrastructure built by the losers may be underused, and this will be more likely to be the case the more specialized the infrastructure is to a single purpose. This may be viewed as wasteful from a social point of view.

16.1.3 Tax Exporting and Commodity Tax Competition

Mintz and Tulkens (1986) set up a model of regional competition amongst two local governments for a mobile sales tax base. Consumers gain utility from a private good, leisure, and a LPG. The private good can be purchased locally or in another location. Consumers are mobile. However, there is a transportation cost as consumers travel from one location to another. Trade in the private good across locations requires trade in labor. Production occurs under perfect competition and constant cost. Several types of equilibria are possible. There can be autarky where each location is self-sufficient. In that case local prices are lower than anywhere else in the economy and consumers only shop locally. The equilibrium can involve trade across locations, where there is an equality of the net sale price across locations. In that case, shoppers shop in different locations and each location obtains tax revenue as a result. Or it can involve a situation where shoppers do not shop locally. If all shoppers do their shopping for taxed commodities in another location, community i may not collect any revenue at all. Obviously, on the other hand, the more "cross" shopping that occurs for a given location, the more the location can export its tax burden to other communities. If a significant amount of a community's tax burden is exported, then it is possible that this will lower the marginal cost of public spending and the amount of spending will be greater than the first-best level.

Mintz and Tulkens derived the optimal tax-spending policy for a local government that takes the policies of the other local governments as given. It is essentially a Nash reaction function in commodity tax rates since the two governments are linked via the equilibrium conditions confronting the economy. Some possibilities can be easily ruled out. For example, there is a set of possible choices for the local tax rate where the tax rate is so high no one shops at that location. In that case no tax revenue is collected and the public good is not produced. Unfortunately, there are cases where a Nash equilibrium in tax rates may not exist. However, they proved that if the reaction functions in tax rates for the two local governments are non-increasing, there exists at least one Nash equilibrium. They also showed that the Nash equilibrium is not efficient for two reasons, a local government will ignore the impact of its decisions on the tax base of the other governments and it also ignores the impact of its tax exporting on welfare in the other locations.

Another example of tax exporting involves the taxation of income from fixed factors owned by non-residents. If local resources and land, for example, are owned by non-residents, then any tax imposed on those sources of income exports the tax burden. However, high taxes on such income will also reduce the incentive for non-resident ownership, and reduce the demand for such resources and hence the value of those resources. This creates a tradeoff between the tax revenue obtained from such sources and the value of the resources to resident owners. This includes taxes on natural amenities. For example, hotel taxes in Hawaii are probably borne by non-resident owners and tourists, rather than residents.

Myers (1990) and Krelove (1992b) argued that certain taxes act as transfers across communities and serve to provide an incentive for population to migrate so as to distribute itself optimally across communities. It is well known that efficiency requires transfers across communities in general when population is perfectly mobile. Indeed, Myers showed that the individual community has an incentive to make such transfers to other communities so as to cause the population to relocate allowing it to achieve an optimal allocation of goods and people. In a sense, such transfers allow it to "buy" the optimal population size when agents are identical. For example, Krelove studied the taxation of land rents in Stiglitz's model where output of a private good is produced by land and labor, population is mobile, and communities provide a public good financed by land taxes. Krelove showed that a tax imposed on land rents transfers income across communities when individuals own land in other locations. A decentralized equilibrium where local governments choose taxes on rents in a decentralized way is Pareto optimal even though some of the tax burden is exported. Indeed, he also argued that a tax system that is restricted to residents only is not capable of supporting the optimum since it does not transfer across communities.[8]

16.1.4 Bidding for the Tax Base

To solve the problem of tax competition, Krelove (1992a) set up a market in rights to the tax base and applied the logic of inducing an equilibrium extended to include this market from the literature on externalities. Imagine that each local government is endowed with a certain number of "rights" or permits to the capital income tax base and can buy and sell those rights. Further suppose that a local government must have at least as many rights as its capital account surplus, $k^i - s^i$, where s^i is local saving. Let d^i be location i's holding of tax base rights.

The additional restriction imposed on each local government is $d^i \geq k^i - s^i$. If saving is zero and the local government wishes to tax capital, it must obtain the appropriate rights to do so, $d^i = k^i$, for example. If p is the price of such rights and d^{*i} is location i's endowment, $(d^{*i} - d^i)$ is the location's net trade in rights and $p(d^{*i} - d^i)$ is the value of that trade. A location either makes a payment to a central clearing house, or receives a payment based on its own holding of tax base rights, where the sum of payments across locations is zero. If one location wishes to tax capital, it must obtain enough rights to do so at price p. If another location would rather sell its rights rather than tax capital it can do so at price p.

The idea is that the interest rate is sufficient to guide the economic behavior of the private agents in the economy under complete decentralization. However, it is not sufficient to guide the behavior of the local governments. The price of the tax base rights, however, is sufficient to guide this behavior in choosing the appropriate tax on mobile capital. In a sense, the price p coordinates the decentralized behavior of the individual local governments taken as a group.

The main problem with this scheme, however, is the same as for any such artificial market: how are the initial rights to be distributed? This might require tying the rights to some parameter. For example, larger communities might receive more rights than smaller communities. And, more to the point, once it is announced that such a scheme will be used, local governments may have an incentive to alter their behavior so as to receive more rights if the parameter to be used is under their control. This can be somewhat problematic but nicely illustrates the nature of the general problem.

16.1.5 Tiebout and Tax Competition

Brueckner (2000) pointed out that many analyses in the tax competition literature assume that capital is perfectly mobile while population is perfectly immobile, and that this goes against the tradition of the Tiebout hypothesis. In addition, much of the work in the tax competition literature also assumes agents are identical.

Brueckner set up a model in the Tiebout tradition where tastes differ across agents, there are developers who impose a tax on mobile capital and behave atomistically by taking prices and the policies of other developers as beyond their influence, and where the population is also mobile. Developers choose a policy involving the capital tax rate and a level for the LPG that maximizes their profit and consumers choose a location on the basis of the policy package and the wage they can earn at a given location. Developers offer a policy package and the appropriate wage, consumers sort themselves across locations on this basis, and homogeneous communities form.

The key result is that in equilibrium there is a tradeoff between the demand for LPGs and the private capital stock induced by choice of the capital tax rate. Thus, high demand agents sort themselves into a high demand community that chooses a high tax rate on capital and experiences a small private capital stock and low consumption of the private good, and low demand agents sort themselves into a low demand community with a low capital tax rate, a large private capital stock, and high consumption of the private good. Brueckner also showed that low demand agents may be better off under tax competition and high demand agents may be worse off relative to a head tax.

The model is similar to that of previous sections. Output is produced using capital and labor via a neoclassical CRS technology. However, now both inputs are mobile. The developer's profit at location i is $\pi^i = \tau^i k^i - c^i g^i$, where g^i confers a consumption benefit. In equilibrium profit is zero, hence $\tau^i k^i = c^i g^i$, which is the same as the local government's budget constraint used earlier. Under profit maximization in the production of the private good, $r + \tau^i = f_k(k^i)$, as before, and the local wage is given by $w^i = f - (r + \tau^i)k^i$. We can solve the last two equations for the demand for capital and the wage, as before, $k^i(r + \tau^i)$ and $w^i(r + \tau^i)$.

Since the tax rate ultimately depends on the level of the LPG, we an write the wage as $w^i(g^i)$. Clearly,

$$\partial w^i / \partial g^i = (\partial w^i / \partial \tau^i)(\partial \tau^i / \partial g^i) = - k^i(\partial \tau^i / \partial g^i).$$

And,

$$(\partial \tau^i / \partial g^i) = c^i/(k^i + \tau^i k^i_r)$$

from the developer's zero profit equation. It follows that the marginal impact of the public good on the local wage is

$$w^i_g = \partial w^i / \partial g^i = (\partial w^i / \partial \tau^i)(\partial \tau^i / \partial g^i) = - c^i(1 + \tau^i k^i_r/k^i)^{-1}. \tag{16.6}$$

The consumer chooses a location to maximize $u(x^i, g^i)$ subject to $w^i(g^i) + rk^* - x^i = 0$. The necessary conditions imply,

$$m^i = - w^i_g, \qquad (16.7)$$

where m^i is the marginal WTP. Combining the last two equations, (16.6) and (16.7), we obtain another version of (16.3).

We can extend Brueckner's result to the case where the publicly provided good affects productivity. From our earlier results we have, $k^i(r+\tau^i, g^i)$ and $w^i(r+\tau^i, g^i)$, with $k^i_g = - f_{kg}/f_{kk}$ and

$$w^i_g = - (c^i - \tau^i k^i_g)(1 + \tau^i k^i_r/k^i)^{-1} + f_g. \qquad (16.8)$$

And, from the representative consumer's location choice, $m^i = - w^i_g$. Combining this with (16.8),

$$m^i + f_g = (c^i - \tau^i k^i_g)(1 + \tau^i k^i_r/k^i)^{-1}. \qquad (16.9)$$

If there is no consumption benefit associated with the public good, then (16.8) is the same as before and the consumer's choice involves $w^i_g = 0$. This implies (16.9) with $m^i = 0$.

Brueckner also showed that if the individuals can be ranked by their WTP, m^i, the highest demand agents, with the largest WTP, are worse off under tax competition relative to the head tax equilibrium. Intuitively, suppose the initial equilibrium is one where the head tax is being used but that it must be replaced at the margin with a tax on mobile capital. The highest demand agents are actually worse off because capital shifts out of the location they are in thus lowering the wage, and the amount of the public good available also falls. Agents at other locations may be better off or worse off depending on how the wage and public good vary in their specific location.

16.2 Extensions

16.2.1 Composition of Spending

Keen and Marchand (1997) posed the question as to whether the composition of public spending between consumption oriented public goods and goods that improve the productivity of local private producers is optimal when local governments must compete for the tax base. Under certain conditions public investments in local infrastructure may attract private capital and this may have a beneficial effect on the local economy. Consumption oriented public goods may have value because residents gain utility from such goods, but not because they attract private capital. This strongly suggests that there may be a bias toward publicly provided goods that attract private capital and away from consumption oriented public goods, as communities compete with one another.

Keen and Marchand extend the model to allow for both types of public spending and endogenous labor supply. They also include a tax on labor, which is assumed to be immobile, in addition to the tax on mobile capital. It is shown that too much reliance is placed on the labor income tax relative to the taxation of mobile capital. And tax competition also leads to greater spending on public capital and less on public consumption goods than would otherwise have been the case had there not been competition.

In particular, they showed that if revenue and hence the total amount of spending is fixed, welfare actually improves if there is a common decrease in public capital spending across all locations coupled with a common increase in spending on consumption oriented public goods. It follows that in a Nash equilibrium among local governments there is too much spending on public infrastructure and too little on consumption oriented public goods like libraries, parks, and museums. This is of great interest since it strongly suggests that there is a bias in public spending induced by competition among local governments.

16.2.2 Residence-Based Capital Income Taxes

Bucovetsky and Wilson (1991) set up a two period framework of tax competition among local governments with endogenous saving in the first period and endogenous labor supply in the second period. Capital is mobile while labor is not. Each government is allowed to impose taxes on capital and labor. It is also assumed that governments choose their tax policies first and then consumers and firms make their optimal choices taking policy as given. Each local government is absolutely committed to its policies. This avoids the so-called time consistency problem. Only the case of a consumption-oriented public good is considered. And utility is separable in the level of the public good so savings and labor supply do not specifically depend on the public good. This eliminates any provision effects.

They derived a number of interesting results. In particular, utility increases if there is a common increase in either the labor income tax or the tax on capital, which is used to finance a common increase in the public good across locations. Second, they showed that too much reliance is placed on the taxation of labor income relative to capital income under a source-based tax. Third, they also considered a residence-based tax on capital income. If local governments can impose both a source-based and a residence-based tax on capital, the resulting equilibrium is Pareto efficient. This is because local governments can control the incentives to move capital perfectly if both types of capital income tax are available. If a resident must pay a tax on his capital income regardless of where it is invested, and if all capital invested locally is also taxed, it becomes impossible for capital to escape taxation by the local government. Unfortunately, such residence-based taxes are very difficult to impose because of tax evasion. Indeed, most of this branch of the literature simply assumes competition among governments takes place in source-based taxes on capital and ignores residence-based taxes altogether. The point though is that part of the problem associated with mobile capital is that such a residence-based tax is unavailable.

16.2.3 The Time Consistency of Tax Policy

The time consistency problem refers to a situation where a decision maker's optimal rule for future actions is no longer optimal when the future actually arrives because the initial conditions have changed. If the decision maker can solve its decision problem again as the future arrives, it will generally find it better to deviate from the rule that was initially optimal.[9] For example, the government should state that it will not help anyone who moves to a flood plain, but then once people have moved to the flood plain and a flood has occurred, it is optimal to bail them out. As another example, it is optimal for a professor at the beginning of the semester to promise to give a hard final exam to get students to study, but then when finals week arrives give an easy exam. As a third example, it is initially optimal for a kidnap victim to promise not to reveal the identity of the kidnapper if released, but then once released to immediately contact the police.

The famous capital levy is another example of this general problem. In a closed economy the national government should promise to impose a low tax rate on capital in the future to provide an incentive for people to save and invest, as a simple application of the Ramsey rule of optimal tax theory. However, when the future arrives, the government will notice that the capital stock is fixed by saving and investment decisions in the past. If it can optimize again, the government will reapply the Ramsey rule, and impose a very high tax rate on capital since it is now in fixed supply. In each of these examples, the initial conditions at a moment in time include a stock variable that responds to policy, e.g., people living in the flood plain, the knowledge of the students, the captivity of the victim, and the private capital stock. The problem is that the agents involved can figure this inconsistency out and choose suboptimal behavior as a result. People will move to the flood plain, students will not study as hard, the kidnapper will not release the victim, and consumers will not save as much.

In the context of the tax competition problem, imagine the following sequence. First, local governments solve the Ramsey tax-spending problem and announce their optimal rules, e.g., (16.3) or (16.4). Second, private agents then choose their saving and allocation decisions. Finally, the local governments impose their announced policies.[10] In equilibrium everyone is behaving optimally, markets clear, and each government's budget balances. This is the equilibrium the literature has focused on. However, suppose a local government can solve its decision problem again just before it is supposed to impose its policy. The capital invested at that location is now in fixed supply, say k^{+i}. This means that the wage is given by

$$w^{+i} = f(k^{+i}) - (r + \tau^i)k^{+i}.$$

If the representative agent's indirect utility is given by $v^i(w^i(\tau^i) + rk^{*i}, g^i)$ and the government's budget constraint is $\tau^i k^{+i} = c^i g^i$, then differentiating with respect to g^i and τ and combining equations yields Samuelson's first-best rule for the LPG, $m^i = c^i$.

More generally, if output is produced by capital, labor, and land, and the technology is CRS, profit is given by

$$\pi^i = f(k^{+i}, n^i) - (r + \tau^i)k^{+i} - (w^i + \theta^i)n^i,$$

where k is capital per unit of land, n is labor per unit of land, and θ is a tax on labor. If the government moves first and imposes its policy it will choose tax rates and a level of the public good according to the second-best Ramsey and Samuelson rules and it will generally be optimal to tax both capital and labor. However, if the government moves after capital has been allocated, the capital tax becomes lump sum. It is then optimal not to tax labor if labor is in elastic supply. So there will also be a shift in the composition of taxes as well.

The main point is that instead of imposing a small tax rate on capital, as per the Ramsey rule of (16.3), it chooses a much higher tax rate when it re-applies the Ramsey rule after capital has been allocated since the tax is non-distorting. Thus, the first-best Samuelson rule will govern the optimal choice of a LPG conferring consumption benefits, or the Kaizuka rule will characterize the optimal choice of public capital that confers production benefits. This suggests that local governments may impose a high tax rate on capital if policy is inconsistent and that this may lead to a high level of spending rather than a low level, as discussed in the literature.

Unfortunately, consumers and firms understand this, or can eventually figure it out. Several possibilities emerge. For example, consumers may save less as a result if the return to saving is perceived to be low. Firms might reduce the capital intensity of production in favor of other inputs like labor or land. And this might lower the wage, which might in turn cause consumers to save less as well. Land rents may also be adversely affected. So the real issue might not be that tax rates are too low because of tax competition, but that there are strong incentives to impose high tax rates on current capital investments since they are momentarily in fixed supply locally.

If the economy lasts forever and local governments must decide on a capital income tax rate each period, there is a strong incentive to tax existing capital at a higher rate than future capital. To circumvent this, the local government can try to establish a reputation for imposing (16.3) over time and stick to it. However, governments are easily replaced in a democracy and a new government may deviate from the last government's policy. Another possibility is that taxpayers may evade some or all of their capital tax liability. If effective, this can limit the government's ability to exploit the capital levy. However, there is a cost to doing so if caught.

16.3 Imperfect Mobility

A number of analysts have studied models where capital is imperfectly mobile. In the last section we presented one such possibility. Capital is perfectly mobile in the classic timing sequence where the government moves first and imposes its policy before capital has been allocated, but is perfectly immobile if the timing is reversed so that the government moves last.

Lee (1997) studied a simple two period model where agents can locate their capital in the first period without cost but must pay a cost in the second period if they wish to relocate their capital. The rest of the model is very similar to the models studied so far. Consumers have utility for consumption in each period and public spending in each period, $u^i(x^i_1, g^i_1) + \beta^i u^i(x^i_2, g^i_2)$, where β^i is a discount factor. Production is once again neoclassical CRS in both periods. The only difference is that capital is mobile in the first period and imperfectly mobile in the second period, while labor is immobile throughout.

The way to solve the policy game is by backward recursion. The resulting equilibrium will be subgame perfect. We solve each agent's decision problem in the second period which delivers functions that depend on the parameters in the second period. Then we step back and solve the decision problem of each agent in the first period taking into account how first period actions affect the variables in the second period. There are two cases to consider, a large transaction cost of relocating capital in the second period and a low cost. In both cases, each local government chooses its policy taking the policies and aggregate variables as given.

First, consider the case where the cost of relocating is high enough so that capital is effectively immobile in the second period. At the beginning of the second period the local government chooses its tax and spending policy to maximize the representative resident's utility subject to its constraint. Since the capital tax is non-distorting in this case, we obtain a solution similar to the last section. We can solve the equations governing the local government's policy as a function of the state variable, which in this case is the local capital stock at time $t = 2$. Thus, $\tau^i_2(k^i_2)$ is the capital tax rate at time $t = 2$ and $g^i_2(k^i_2)$ is the level of the LPG at $t = 2$. Indirect utility in the second period depends on this parameter. Each local government in the second period chooses its policy believing that it doesn't have to compete for capital at all since the allocation of capital is fixed.

In the first period, the local government again chooses policy to maximize the lifetime utility of the representative resident but now must take into account the dependence of its second period tax rate on the first period capital allocation, in addition to its first period budget constraint, while taking the other local governments' policies as given. We obtain derivatives like

$$\hat{\partial}v^i_1/\hat{\partial}g^i_1 + \beta^i[(\hat{\partial}v^i_2/\hat{\partial}\tau^i_2)(\hat{\partial}\tau^i_2/\hat{\partial}k^i_2) \tag{16.10}$$
$$+ (\hat{\partial}v^i_2/\hat{\partial}g^i_2)(\hat{\partial}g^i_2/\hat{\partial}k^i_2)](\hat{\partial}k^i_2/\hat{\partial}\tau^i_1) + \gamma(k^i_1 + \tau^i_1 k^i_{1r}) = 0,$$

where γ is the multiplier. We also have,

$$\hat{\partial}v^i_1/\hat{\partial}g^i_1 + \beta^i[(\hat{\partial}v^i_2/\hat{\partial}\tau^i_2)(\hat{\partial}\tau^i_2/\hat{\partial}k^i_2) \tag{16.11}$$
$$+ (\hat{\partial}v^i_2/\hat{\partial}g^i_2)(\hat{\partial}g^i_2/\hat{\partial}k^i_2)](\hat{\partial}k^i_2/\hat{\partial}g^i_1) - \gamma c^i = 0.$$

The terms in square brackets are new and capture feedback effects from policy choices today to the state variable and hence policy in the future.

Lee presents a special case where local governments compete more aggressively for the mobile tax base in the first period because this attracts more private capital that it can exploit in the second period when capital is immobile. To achieve this it imposes a smaller tax rate than would otherwise have been the case in the first period. If tax revenue declines in the first period as a result, then spending is lower as well. So less competition later may imply more competition now. Imperfect mobility can lead to a shift in spending over time as well. In the case where the transactions cost of moving capital is low in the second period, local governments will once again compete for mobile capital in the second period and this will put downward pressure on the tax rate in the future. In addition, however, in the first period the government will have to take feedback effects into account when choosing policy since the policy choices in the first period will affect the capital state variable in the second period, as in (16.10) and (16.11).

We can apply the imperfect mobility idea to the case where there are two kinds of capital, mobile capital like equipment, and immobile capital such as buildings and structures. Ex ante, it is clearly optimal to tax the two kinds of capital at different rates unless the supply and demand elasticities are the same for the two types of capital. However, if one type of capital is mobile later in the government's planning horizon, while the other type is immobile, it will be optimal to tax the mobile capital at a lower rate than the immobile capital later in the planning horizon. Working backwards to the first period, the local government may want to attract more of the immobile capital in order to exploit it later on. It can do this by imposing low taxes now on capital that will later be immobile and higher taxes now on capital that will be mobile later on. The impact of this on public pending is unclear.

Wildasin (2003) studied a model where there are capital adjustment costs so that capital cannot adjust instantaneously to policy, but only gradually. It is imagined there is a fixed group of agents who experience an infinite planning horizon. Output is produced using capital and labor and there are costs associated with adjusting the stock of capital. Labor is in fixed supply and immobile. Consumers can own capital in other jurisdictions. The individual consumer gains utility from a consumption good and a LPG each period. The representative local government maximizes the representative consumer's lifetime utility subject to its budget constraint, taking the gradual adjustment of capital into account. The only other tax instrument is a non-distorting tax and it is implicitly assumed there is government debt, which allows the local government to smooth its tax receipts over time.

The model has a number of interesting implications. The stock of capital decreases monotonically to an unanticipated increase in the capital income tax rate. The gradual response is due to the adjustment cost. Second, the optimal capital tax rate in a steady state depends on the fraction of local capital owned by non-residents; the greater this fraction is, the larger the tax rate on local capital. If residents own the entire local capital stock, the optimal tax rate is zero since there is a non-distorting tax available. The intuition is that the local government is able to export some of the capital tax burden to non-residents. The tax rate is also inversely related to the demand elasticity, as is usually the case. In addition, the tax rate is inversely related to the speed of adjustment; the faster the speed of adjustment, the higher the tax rate. The local government would like to exploit non-resident owners. A slow speed of adjustment means the local government has more time to exploit the tax, a faster speed of adjustment means it has less time. If the adjustment is instantaneous, it is impossible to exploit the tax and the optimal capital tax rate is zero. Finally, if the tax rate increase is anticipated, this will affect the optimal tax. The earlier the tax rate increase is anticipated, the lower the subsequent tax rate will be. The intuition is that if taxpayers anticipate a tax increase they will begin to adjust their capital stocks. The further in advance of the tax increase non-resident capital owners begin to do this, the less point there is to exploiting them later when the tax is imposed.

16.4 Fiscal Federalism

Fiscal federalism refers to the relationship between the different levels of government.[11] The main issue involves deciding what role is appropriate for each level of government. Some activities are clearly the responsibility of the national government such as defense of the country, while others are more appropriately handled at the local level like police and fire protection. When there are economies of scale in providing a public good or service, obvious externality effects where some of the benefits of the good spillover to other communities, or possibly inefficiencies due to tax competition, then there is a role for the national government to play. On the other hand, a local government may be more efficient in tailoring policy to meet the needs at the local level than the national government. It may be easier for local government to discover the precise tastes of the local community for a particular service. And when new problems emerge local governments may be more innovative and more willing to experiment than the national government. Unfortunately, there is a great deal of leeway and hard and fast rules are difficult to come by.[12]

16.4.1 Mobility and Pareto Optimality

One important key to results in this area is the mobility of the population. A number of analysts, including Boadway (1982), Boadway and Flatters (1982), Krelove (1992b), Wellisch (2000), Hoel and Shapiro (2003), and Hoel (2004), among others, have shown that if population is perfectly mobile, a Nash equilibrium, where local governments choose tax and spending policies in a decentralized manner, is Pareto optimal and that a Pareto optimal allocation can be supported by such decentralized behavior on the part of local governments. However, this result breaks down if population is imperfectly mobile.

Following Wellisch, assume for simplicity that there are two communities, agents are identical, there are two goods, a private good and a public good, the private good is produced according to a CRS technology using land and labor, and population is perfectly mobile. Consumers care about the private good consumed locally and the public good in both locations according to a well defined utility function, $u(x^i, g^1, g^2)$, so there is a spill-over effect. The technology is given by $F(L^i, N^i)$, where L is land and N is labor. Firms at location i producing the private good maximize profit,

$$\pi^i = F(L^i, N^i) - \rho^i L^i - w^i N^i,$$

where w is the wage and ρ is the rental per unit of land used in production. It follows that $F_L = \rho^i$ and $F_N = w^i$. Each consumer owns an equal share of land, and receives an equal share of land rents, $\Sigma_j(\rho^j - \theta^j)L^j/N$, where N is total population and θ^j is a tax on land rents in location j. The consumer's budget constraint is $I^i = w^i + \Sigma_j(\rho^j - \theta^j)L^j/N = x^i$. The consumer chooses a location to maximize $u(I^i, g^1, g^2)$. This function can also be taken as the indirect utility function.

The ith local government taxes local rents and obtains $\tau^i L^i$ in revenue. This is spent on the local public good. Its budget constraint is $\tau^i L^i = c(g^i)$. It also confronts a mobility constraint, $u^i = u^k$. It chooses the tax rate and level of local government spending to maximize local welfare subject to its budget constraint and the mobility constraint. The resulting policy contains two distortions. If the mobility of the population is ignored, then the local government ignores the spillover effects of its spending on the public good and it only internalizes the part of the tax borne by local residents and not the burden of non-residents. However, if it takes mobility into account, i.e., $u^i = u^k$, then it will internalize both of these effects and the resulting allocation is Pareto optimal.

An optimal mix of population across locations must satisfy $F^i_N - x^i = F^k_N - x^k$. Since $\Sigma(\rho^j - \theta^j)L^j/N$ is the same across agents, it follows that $w^i - x^i = w^k - x^k$. Under profit maximization, $w = F_N$ and the population is allocated efficiently between the two locations under decentralized decision making. Land taxes are exported and this takes the place of the necessary transfer between regions that generates the optimal mix of population.

Hoel (2004) argued that perfect mobility was critically important for this optimality result. The equilibrium is only optimal if the common level of utility, $u^i = u^k$ is maximized. If mobility is costless this can be achieved when local governments impose their policies in a decentralized manner and there are transfers of some form across locations. If, however, mobility is costly, or if some agents are immobile, this will no longer be true. In that case, there may be a role for the national government to play in coordinating policies at the local level.

16.4.2 Vertical Fiscal Competition

Vertical fiscal competition refers to a situation where policies at different levels of government affect one another across levels. There are a number of possibilities. For example, the national government may share the tax base with local governments as it does under an income tax where both levels tax the same sources of income. And local governments may be connected to one another through the national government's budget.

Keen and Kotsogiannis (2002) presented an analysis that nicely illustrates the various tradeoffs. They studied a two period version of the Zodrow - Mieszkowski model, where consumers choose how much to save of their endowment of the numeraire good in the first period, local governments tax mobile capital and rents of immobile factors, and the national government taxes mobile capital. Under decentralization there is horizontal tax competition among the local governments and vertical tax competition between the national and local governments since they share part of the same tax base. They consider a general increase in the local tax rate imposed on capital and derive the conditions under which this improves welfare. The results depend on the interest elasticity of saving relative to the demand for capital, and whether rents are taxed or not. For example, if rents are untaxed, Keen and Kotsogiannis showed that the horizontal externality dominates if saving is interest inelastic, the vertical externality dominates if saving is highly elastic relative to the demand for capital, and both externalities fail to exist if the demand for capital is perfectly interest inelastic. On the other hand, if rents are fully taxed, the horizontal externality dominates regardless of the interest elasticity of saving relative to the interest elasticity of the demand for capital.

Many analysts have argued that spending at the local level is suboptimal because of competition among local governments, typically too low, and that some sort of national government policy that coordinates local policy is required to reduce or eliminate the fiscal externality. However, on the other side of the coin, Brennan and Buchanan (1980) strongly argued that there is much wasteful spending and that tax competition serves to reduce it. Under this view, coordination of tax policy that serves to increase spending simply increases waste and is socially inappropriate as a result.

Edwards and Keen (1996) contrasted these two opposing ideas. They used the Zodrow and Mieszkowski model with a social welfare function that captures these two opposing viewpoints. Local governments are assumed to choose a tax on mobile capital in competition with one another, and use their revenue to provide a public good that confers a consumption benefit for its residents and also use it on wasteful spending designed to capture over-spending at the local level. They showed that a system wide increase in the capital tax rate will strictly improve welfare if

$$MEB/(1 + MEB) > dW/dR,$$

where R is revenue, W is wasteful spending, and where MEB is the marginal excess burden of taxation,

$$MEB = -\tau^i k^i_r/(k^i + \tau^i k^i_r),$$

i.e., the deadweight loss per dollar of tax revenue collected. Tax policy coordination is similar to a transfer from the taxpayers to the government. If dR is transferred by a system wide tax rate increase, taxpayers lose to the extent that this revenue is wasted. The transfer allows a reduction in distorting taxes. The benefit of this is captured by the reduction in deadweight loss. If this outweighs the increased waste, then coordination is beneficial.

Since the marginal cost of funds is given by $MCF = 1/(1+\tau^i k^i_r/k^i)$, we can rewrite the condition as $(MCF - 1)/MCF > dW/dR$. And since $m^i = MCF$, where m^i is the WTP for the public good, the condition can also be written as $(m^i - 1)/m^i > dW/dR$. The left hand side is the ratio of the second-best benefit, $m^i - 1 > 0$, when distorting taxes are used, to the first-best benefit when non-distorting taxes are used, $m^i = 1$. If this ratio is greater than the increased waste when revenue increases, coordination is optimal.

Different analysts have studied a variety of cases on vertical externalities across governments depending on which level of government moves first in the policy game. The implications of the analysis are somewhat ambiguous regarding the impact on public spending. For example, Boadway and Keen (1996) considered the case where the national government moves first taking into account the state's optimal behavior. Hoyt (2001) considered the case where the two levels, national and local, moved simultaneously and thus ignored the impact each had on the other level. And Kothenburger (2004) assumed states moved first and took the national government's policy into account. In what follows we will describe the results of a model where local governments move first anticipating the response of the national government, to give the reader a feel for the revent literature.

Following Kothenburger, there are J communities, population is fixed and immobile, and capital is perfectly mobile. There is one private good produced using capital and fixed factors. Local governments impose a source-based tax on capital taking into account the impact their policy has on the national government's budget but not the other local governments' budgets. Then the national government chooses transfers to the local governments that sum to zero, taking local tax rates as given. Each government is entirely benevolent. The timing of decisions is designed to reflect decision making in the European Union, where the individual countries dominate policymaking.

The policy game is solved backwards to obtain the subgame perfect equilibrium. It is straightforward to show that the transfer made by the national government to a local government is chosen to equalize spending on the LPG across communities. An increase in the ith local tax rate causes the jth tax base to increase as capital relocates. A best response for the national government is to reduce the transfer to community j and to raise the transfer to i in order to equalize local public spending. In addition, i's tax revenue increases with its own tax rate and this causes the national government to lower its transfer. The optimal response balances these various effects. Thus, the transfers are designed to neutralize tax competition as revenue is shared optimally across locations.

Local governments then choose their tax rates knowing how the national government's transfer will respond. Under this policy, the marginal cost of funds is J and hence Samuelson's rule is modified, $m^i = J$. This follows because an increase in tax revenue by one dollar reduces private consumption by one dollar. However, because of the revenue sharing across locations, it only increases spending on the LPG by $1/J$ dollars. Since $J > 1$, $m^i > 1$, and there is a downward bias in public spending. And Kothenburger shows that as J increases the revenue sharing effect dominates so that the tax rate under revenue sharing and hence public spending is lower than under pure tax competition without national transfers. And it is possible that welfare may actually be higher under the latter scenario as well.

16.5 Conclusion

We have studied the impact that mobility of resources can have on local and national government policy. In a strong sense local governments compete for a mobile tax base. Taxation of mobile capital is the classic example. Such taxes shift the base from one jurisdiction to another and provide a beneficial spillover effect. This can cause too little spending on public goods since the local government may not internalize this effect. However, if tax revenue is spent on public infrastructure that is complementary to private capital this may be reversed since this type of expenditure may attract private capital that enhances the local tax base. Indeed, local governments themselves may use public infrastructure to attract private firms to relocate. However, such competition may actually be wasteful if some localities lose the competition for private resources. Tax exporting may also lead to overspending as well.

We also showed that if labor is perfectly mobile, an optimal allocation can be supported by fully decentralized and uncoordinated local government policy if certain tax instruments are available. For example, taxes on land rents can serve to redistribute income across locations so as to support the optimal distribution of population across communities. However, if resources are not perfectly mobile, especially population, then some form of coordination by a national government may be appropriate.

Finally, we also studied the interaction among different levels of government. Vertical externalities may exist across different levels of government where the policy at one level of government affects the tax base of another level. There are cases where the national government can design transfers that will coordinate tax policy at the local level and eliminate harmful fiscal externalities. However, the implications of this literature for the provision of public goods are not clear. In some cases public spending may increase, while in others it may decrease.

Appendix

In the first-best equilibrium, $r = f_k(k^f, g^f)$, and in the second-best equilibrium, $r + \tau = f_k(k^s, g^s)$. Combining, $\tau = f_k(k^s, g^s) - f_k(k^f, g^f) > 0$. Approximating the marginal product of private capital, $f_k(k^s, g^s) \cong f_k(k^f, g^f) + (k^s - k^f)f_{kk} + (g^s - g^f)f_{kg}$. Thus,

$$\tau = (k^s - k^f)f_{kk} + (g^s - g^f)f_{kg} > 0. \tag{A1}$$

Next, note that the Samuelson rule holds in the first-best equilibrium, $n^i f_g(k^f, g^f) = c^i$. Subtract this from (16.4) and simplify to obtain.

$$n^i[f_g(k^s, g^s) - f_g(k^f, g^f)] = -\tau^i[n^i k^i_g + c^i k^i_r/k^i]MCF.$$

where $MCF = 1/(1 + \tau^i k^i_r/k^i)$. We can approximate the marginal product of public capital with,

$$f_g(k^s, g^s) \cong f_g(k^f, g^f) + (k^s - k^f)f_{gk} + (g^s - g^f)f_{gg}.$$

Using this in the last equation,

$$n^i[(k^s - k^f)f_{gk} + (g^s - g^f)f_{gg}] = -\tau^i[n^i k^i_g + c^i k^i_r/k^i]MCF. \tag{A2}$$

We can write (A1) and (A2) as a system,

$$\begin{pmatrix} f_{gk} & f_{gg} \\ f_{gg} & f_{kg} \end{pmatrix}\begin{pmatrix} k^{si} - k^{fi} \\ g^{si} - g^{fi} \end{pmatrix} = \tau^i \begin{pmatrix} -\Gamma MCF \\ 1 \end{pmatrix},$$

where $\Gamma = k^i_g + c^i k^i_r / k^i n^i$. We can solve to obtain,

$$(k^f - k^s) = \tau^i [f_{kg}\Gamma MCF + f_{gg}]/\Delta,$$

$$(g^f - g^s) = - \tau^i [f_{kk}\Gamma MCF - f_{kg}]/\Delta,$$

where $\Delta = - (f_{kk}f_{gg} - f_{kg}f_{gk}) < 0$. The conclusions described in the text follow from this solution.

---

[1]   See Musgrave (1969) and Oates (1972) for early statements of the problem. For useful surveys of the tax competition literature see Wildasin (1986, 1987), Zodrow and Mieszkowski (1986), and, more recently, Wilson (1999), and Wilson and Wildasin (2004).

[2]   Brennan and Buchanan (1980) have made this argument forcefully.

[3]   A tax on the land rents of absentee owners serves to transfer resources across communities and serves the purpose, for example.

[4]   If the third derivatives of the production function F(K, L, G) are zero, for example, where K is capital, L is immobile labor, and G is public capital, then the result that less reliance on the distorting tax will raise the level of public capital provided goes through.

[5]   Suppose there are two periods and utility is given by $u(c^h_1, c^h_2, g^h)$. The wealth constraint is $e^h + RI^h = c^h_1 + Rc^h_2 = 0$, where e^h is the first period endowment, I^h is income, and R is the price of intertemporal consumption. The consumer maximizes utility subject to the constraint and consumption is given by $C^h(e^h + RI^h, R)$. Saving is given by $s^h = e^h - C^h(e^h + RI^h, R)$.

[6]   Sinn (1997) provided an example of public investment where tax competition does not necessarily cause underprovision to occur. He studied the case of a club-type good with congestion that enhances the use of private capital and showed that at the optimum the source-based capital income tax is set equal to the marginal congestion cost. He also argued that the policy would not cover the total amount spent on the good and that the deficit would have to be made up in some other manner. Finally, when all factors are mobile, an equilibrium does not exist.

[7]   See also Justman, Thisse, and Ypersele (2002), who set up a model where local governments choose the quality of the local infrastructure in an attempt to attract certain types of private industry. This allows communities to segment the market into firms that can use the local infrastructure and those that cannot. Some forms of infrastructure support advanced research and engineering design, e.g., SEMATECH in the U.S., and the VLSI program in Japan, while

other forms are more basic and support simpler activities, e.g., standardizing quality control.

[8] This assumes that land rent taxes are sufficient to finance all local spending.

[9] See Kydland and Prescott (1977) for the original statement of the problem. A summary is contained in Batina and Ihori (2000). See Kehoe (1989) for a study relating the problem to the international taxation of capital. He assumed that individuals could choose their capital location after the governments had chosen their tax rates on capital. Capital flight inhibits individual governments from exploiting the capital levy. Coordination of tax policy across governments that eliminates so-called safe havens, however, does allow the individual government to impose high taxes on capital income.

[10] This is the so-called open-loop policy game.

[11] See Oates (1972) and Gordon (1983) for some early work on the subject and Oates (1999) for a recent survey.

[12] There is a great deal of heterogeneity across countries in terms of the responsibilities given to each level of government. Some countries such as France and Japan are highly centralized, while others like the U.S. are very decentralized.

17 Empirical Testing with Local Public Goods

In this chapter we will describe some of the empirical work that has been done on the Tiebout hypothesis, estimating the demand for LPGs, and estimating the relationship between the tax policy of different governments. A number of analysts argued that local policies become capitalized into the price of land or housing and that this is a hallmark of the Tiebout hypothesis. The seminal work is due to Oates (1969, 1973), followed by Pollakowski (1973), Edel and Sclar (1974), Hamilton (1975, 1976), King (1977), Rosen and Fullerton (1977), Brueckner (1979b, 1982, 1983), Starrett (1981), and Yinger (1982), among others.[1] A reasonable model of this process should include the housing decision and the location or mobility decision in the analysis. A second avenue for testing a subsidiary implication of the hypothesis has to do with whether competition among local governments actually leads to reduced public spending or not. This has become known as the Leviathan hypothesis. Brennan and Buchanan (1980) forcefully argued this point. Oates (1985, 1989), Nelson (1987), Marlow (1988), Grossman (1989), and Zax (1989) provided the early results designed to shed light on this issue.[2]

A number of researchers have estimated the demand for a particular LPG. Bergstrom and Goodman (1973), Deacon and Shapiro (1975), and Bergstrom, Rubinfeld, and Shapiro (1982), provided the early work on estimating demand functions for LPGs, and Rubinfeld, Shapiro, and Roberts (1987) provided further guidance on the so-called Tiebout bias problem.[3] Essentially, conditions were provided under which the median voter in each community is decisive in determining the level of a LPG. Epple, Filimon, and Romer (1984) and Epple, Romer, and Sieg (2001) generalized this work. They provided conditions for existence in a model where agents vote and are mobile. Not surprisingly, the conditions are a bit more stringent than in simpler models. In particular, Epple, Romer, and Sieg (2001) recently provided empirical evidence in support of the sophisticated "utility constant" voter model who takes into account the effects of migration on the local economy when voting for policy.

Finally, we also consider empirical models of the relationship among governments. Under horizontal fiscal competition local governments at the same level choose their policies taking the policies of other governments as given. This leads to a policy rule that relates a tax policy parameter, the property tax rate, for example, to the tax policy parameters of the other governments in the form of a reaction function. Under vertical competition different levels of government compete. There is now significant evidence that governments act strategically in a variety of countries. This includes Case, Rosen, and Hines (1993) for state governments in the U.S., Besley and Rosen (1998) for state gasoline and cigarette taxes in the U.S., Heyndels and Vuchelen (1998) for local taxes in Belgium, Brett and Pinske (2000) for property taxes in Canada, Brueckner and Saveedra (2001) for property taxes in the Boston area, Esteller-More and Sole-Olle (2001) for state sales and income taxes in the U.S., Feld and Kirchgassner (2001) for personal income taxes in Switzerland, Buettner (2001) for local business taxes in Germany, and Hayashi and Boadway (2001) for corporate income taxes in Canada.

In the next section we present various tests of the Tiebout hypothesis. In section 17.2 we study estimating the demand for LPGs. Section 17.3 presents the recent literature on government reaction functions and 17.4 concludes the chapter.

17.1 Testing the Tiebout Hypothesis

17.1.1 A Model of Capitalization

Consider the simple model studied in the last chapter. There are n^i agents living in jurisdiction i, each is endowed with an equal share of income so that income is independent of location, as might be the case in a large metropolitan area, and preferences are represented by a well-behaved utility function of the form $u^i(x^i, h^i, g^i)$, where x is the numeraire good, h is housing, and g is a LPG. The consumer maximizes utility subject to her budget constraint. In general, the housing decision will be distorted by the tax and the demand for housing will depend on the policy variables, $h^i(I, p^i(1+\tau^i), g^i)$, where p is the price of a unit of housing, τ is the property tax rate, and I is income which includes an endowment of the consumption good, a payment to labor, and a payment to land owners. If utility is separable in the LPG, then we have instead, $h^i(I, p^i(1+\tau^i))$. Firms hire land and labor to produce housing according to a neoclassical CRS technology. Firms maximize profit and the result is a demand for labor per unit of land and a housing supply function. Equilibrium in the local housing market and the labor market determines the relative prices of housing and labor. If consumers are mobile, then there is also a mobility constraint.

The incidence of the local government's policy will differ depending on whether resources are mobile or not. If the population and the stock of housing is fixed, as might be the case in the short run, and housing is separable from the LPG in the utility function, then any change in the tax rate is completely capitalized into the price of housing, $[(1+\tau^i)/p^i](dp^i/d\tau^i) = -1$. A ten percent increase in the local tax rate induces a ten percent decline in the producer price of housing in the short run. On the other hand, if new communities can form in the long run so that the supply of housing is perfectly elastic, then $dp^i/d\tau^i = 0$ and no capitalization occurs. The distinction between the short run and the long run becomes critically important for the final result.

The mobility constraint takes the form of

$$v^i[I, p^i(1+\tau^i), g^i] = v^*, \tag{17.1}$$

where $v^i(\ )$ is the indirect utility function. We can solve (17.1) to obtain a pricing function that relates the producer price of a house to the public policy variables, $p(g^i, \tau^i; v^*)$. It is straightforward to show by differentiating (17.1) that the price of housing is increasing in the level of the public good and decreasing in the property tax rate, i.e., $p_g > 0$ and $p_\tau < 0$.

Consider two agents, i and i', with the same preferences and endowment. Suppose they live in different locations and that the level of the public good is the same across locations, but that the property tax rate is higher for i than for i'. Since utility must be the same across locations, the pre-tax price of housing must be lower in location i than in location i' to compensate i for paying more in tax at the margin. Thus, capitalization may act as a substitute for migration. However, this does not guarantee that the equilibrium is efficient, as pointed out by a number of writers. It is possible that it is efficient to have only one community containing both i and i', for example. But this analysis does suggest a well-behaved relationship between the public policy variables and the price of housing, at least in the short run depending on the supply response.

However, if tastes differ, matters become much more complicated. In that case, the pricing function need not be well behaved and there may not be a well-defined relationship between the policy variables and the price of housing. It is possible, for example, to have different communities with the same price of housing but different levels of public services and different tax rates in an equilibrium where agents are perfectly mobile when tastes differ. The implication of this is that it is not immediately clear that testing capitalization constitutes a test of the Tiebout hypothesis, although there may be other good public policy reasons for studying the empirical relationship between prices and public policy variables like the property tax rate and various LPGs.

17.1.2 Testing the Capitalization Hypothesis

Many of the tests of the capitalization hypothesis essentially relied on estimates of the following equation,

$$p^i H^i = a + b_1 g^i + b_2 \tau^i + \gamma Z^i + \varepsilon^i, \qquad (17.2)$$

where Z is a vector of community characteristics. Under the maintained hypothesis, $b_1 > 0$ and $b_2 < 0$; a greater level of spending on the LPG should make the community more desirable and thus increase the demand for housing and hence its price, while a higher tax rate should have the opposite effect.

Suppose developers choose the level of the public good and the property tax rate to maximize property values. If the optimum is unique, then small changes in the level of the LPG should not affect property values. In that case,

$$d(p^i H^i)/dg^i = b_1 + b_2(d\tau^i/dg^i) = 0.$$

Oates (1969, 1973) first tested the capitalization hypothesis. He studied data from 53 communities in New Jersey for 1960 and used the median house value in each community as the dependent variable and school expenditures per student as a proxy for the LPG, the property tax rate, and several other variables designed to capture various features of the local housing market. He found that school expenditures exerted a positive effect and the property tax a negative effect, and both were significantly different from zero. About two-thirds of the tax was capitalized into the house value, however, this was approximately offset by the effect of school expenditures. A follow up study by Heinberg and Oates (1970) on the Boston area confirmed this result. The result was also confirmed by a second follow up study by Oates (1973), which included per capita municipal spending in his original equation.

A number of critics emerged, notably, Pollakowski (1973), Edel and Sclar (1974), Meadows (1976), King (1977), Rosen and Fullerton (1977), Sonstelie and Portney (1980), among many others.[4] A variety of adjustments were made to the empirical model; the tax variable was adjusted in different ways, different variables designed to capture public output were included, a broad array of socioeconomic variables were added, and different estimation techniques were eventually employed. Furthermore, other researchers began using cross section data and micro data to test the hypothesis.

The main conclusion of this literature is that a great deal of capitalization occurs and that it is somewhere between 50 and 100 per cent. Studies using cross section data and micro data studies also concluded that there is significant capitalization taking place. It is unclear whether or not this confirms the Tiebout hypothesis and what implications it has for the level or composition of local government spending. Edel and Sclar, for example, argued that Oates only considered the demand side of the model and not the supply side response. In particular, they suggested that if the Tiebout hypothesis is correct, then two communities that are in every way identical except that one spends more on LPGs and imposes a higher tax rate to finance the extra spending than the other may experience a higher price for housing in the short run. However, the two communities should experience the same tax rate, same level of public spending, and the same house price in the long run after the economy has completely adjusted. Therefore, capitalization is not evidence that supports the Tiebout hypothesis, but evidence against it. The mechanism is only working properly if capitalization is falling over time as the economy adjusts toward the equilibrium. However, the actual adjustment process was not modeled.

Two comments are in order. The Tiebout model is static in nature and discussing results in the context of an adjustment process may be inappropriate unless the details are mathematically worked out. The adjustment process has not been fully specified in the literature. Second, capitalization may be important in its own right. For example, a change in policy designed to improve welfare may lower house prices making current homeowners worse off. Therefore, studying the capitalization process has great validity regardless of how it may relate to the Tiebout hypothesis per se.

17.1.3 Testing Leviathan

Under the Leviathan hypothesis government is not a benevolent agent that chooses policy to maximize welfare but an agent that seeks higher taxes in order to increase its spending and hence power. This is socially inefficient. Brennan and Buchanan (1980) suggested that fiscal competition that limits taxation and hence spending can improve efficiency. Greater decentralization may reduce the national government's size but lead to larger local governments as they take on greater responsibility. Is the net effect an increase in total government, or a reduction? This is ultimately an empirical question.

Typically, a measure of the size of government is regressed on a measure of decentralization and various other conditioning variables such as income, growth in income, inflation, borrowing restrictions, independence of
the central bank, and so on. The evidence is mixed, and unfortunately, a
consensus has not emerged. This may be due to the difficulty in measuring
what is meant by decentralization. Different proxies for this variable may
lead to different conclusions. Some units of government are classified as
single-purpose units like a school district, while others are multi-purpose
such as a county or state. Do individuals move from one location to another on the basis of single-purpose units, multi-purpose units, or both?
How does one aggregate across such units and are they all in competition
with one another?

In a recent paper, Jin and Zou (2002) studied a panel data set of 32
OECD countries and estimated linear functions of the form,

$$G_{it} = \alpha_i + \beta_1 D_{it} + \beta_2 Pol_{it} + \beta_3 Con_{it} + \varepsilon_{it},\tag{17.3}$$

where G is a measure of the size of government for country i at time t, e.g.,
the ratio of expenditures to GDP, D is a measure of decentralizaton, e.g.,
local government expenditure to total government expenditure, Pol measures various political variables, e.g., independence of the central bank, and
Con is a control variable, e.g, real per capita GDP, or growth in real GDP.

For their sample of OECD countries, Jin and Zou found that expenditure
and revenue decentralization is positively correlated with the size of local
government but negatively correlated with the size of national government.
They also found that there was a negative correlation between revenue decentralization and the size of total government and some mild evidence of
a positive correlation between expenditure decentralization and the size of
total government. Finally, the percent of local government spending financed by transfers from the national government was positively associated with the size of local government, national government, and total
government.

17.2   Estimating the Demand for LPGs: Politics and the Tiebout Hypothesis

One major criticism of the Tiebout model is that it ignores any political
mechanism that helps residents choose the local policies to be pursued. It
would be nice to have a model that combines Hirschman's (1970) exit and
voice. However, problems of existence and stability arise when trying to
introduce locational choice and voting into a model with a housing market.

This should not be surprising since such problems arise when considering each of these dimensions alone; cycles can exist in voting models and a number of writers, e.g., Stiglitz (1977) and Bewley (1981), have noted that the problems exist in Tiebout's model.

First, consider the classic model due to Bergstrom and Goodman (1973). They assumed that there is a constant cost of the LPG, consumers know their own tax share of the total cost of the LPG, the median voter hypothesis holds so the quantity of the LPG is that which is chosen by the median voter in the community, the median voter is identified as the agent with the median level of income in the community, and the income distributions across locations are proportional to one another. They estimated a model of the form,

$$\ln(g^i) = \alpha + b_1\ln(n^i) + b_2\ln(t^i) + b_3\ln(y^i) + \Sigma_j\phi^{ij}Z^{ij} + \varepsilon^i, \qquad (17.4)$$

where g is expenditures on police, or parks and recreation spending, or total municipal spending except for schools and welfare, n^i is the number of households in community i, t is the tax share of the median voter in the community, y is the income of the median voter in the community, and Z is a list of socioeconomic variables for the community. This captures the possibility that community size may affect the value placed on the LPG. As a proxy for the tax share they used the property tax and assumed that the median voter lived in the median house. The value of such a house was computed from the 1960 Census and the tax was calculated from information complied by state governments.

They used income and socioeconomic data on 826 municipalities in 10 states with population between 10,000 and 150,000 from the 1960 census and government spending data from the 1962 census of governments. They generally found that estimates of the income elasticity were positive and statistically significant, and the estimate for parks and recreation was greater than one in magnitude. Estimates of the tax price elasticity were negative and statistically significant. In addition, they also included a crowding parameter γ. This follows from assuming the level of the public good is given by $g = g*/n^\gamma$, where g* is spending on the level of the public good and g is the service provided. If γ is close to zero, the LPG is almost a pure public good and there are economies of scale in providing the good. On the other hand, if γ is close to one in magnitude, then the good is almost a private good. They found that estimates of γ tended to be at least as great as one in magnitude. Finally, the population elasticity was positive and was greater than one in magnitude for parks and recreation.

The subsequent literature has uncovered several problems that can arise. All potential voters are assumed to vote, political parties are deemed ir-

relevant to determining the outcome of the political process, renters are ignored and yet may exhibit behavior very different from home owners, and
the proxy used for the "price" may be problematic. A more serious problem is known as "Tiebout bias," first described by Goldstein and Pauly
(1981).[5] If agents locate themselves on the basis of local public service
packages, then the income distribution at any given location may change
over time because of this kind of migration. In that case causality not only
runs from income to LPGs, but also from LPGs to income. The same is
also true of the tax price variable because of the manner in which it is constructed. Therefore, the income and tax price variables may be endogenous
and this simultaneity bias can lead to biased estimates.

Epple, Filimon, and Romer (1984) extended the literature by incorporating mobility into the model of voting. They provided conditions that can
be used to prove existence in a model where there is perfect mobility and
where agents vote. Consider the following model. There is a continuum of
agents, a fixed, finite number of locations, and mobility is costless. Consumers have the same preferences but differ in their income. They choose
housing and consumption of a numeraire good to maximize utility, u(x, h,
g), subject to their budget constraint, taking income (I) and the price of
housing (q) as given. Firms use land and the numeraire good as inputs to
produce housing according to a CRS technology and maximize profit. The
local government provides a LPG (g) and imposes a tax on housing consumption, and the cost of the public good is convex in g. In equilibrium
agents optimize, markets clear in each community, and no agent chooses to
move between communities. Policy is chosen through majority rule voting
and the median voter hypothesis holds.

One critical assumption is that the slope of an indifference curve in (g,
q) space increases in income, and it is also concave in g. The population
partitions itself so that locations are stratified by income, there is a consumer on the boundary between two communities who is indifferent between them for any two communities, and an equilibrium satisfies the condition that $q^j > q^k$ and $g^j > g^k$ if and only if $I^j > I^k$, where I^h is the largest
level of income in community h = j, k. This is known as the ascending
bundles property. Epple, et. al. provided sufficient conditions and sketched
a proof of existence under certain additional restrictions on the cost function of the public good and preferences in the case of two communities.[6]
They also provided a numerical example. Interestingly enough, if the equilibrium is unique, it is unstable. It follows that for a stable equilibrium to
occur, multiple equilibria must exist, some of which will be unstable.

Epple, Romer, and Sieg (2001) extended the earlier analysis by assuming that both income and preferences for the LPG can differ and agents

will stratify on both dimensions. In their model communities can be ranked on the basis of their policy packages and more desirable communities experience a higher price of housing in order to reduce the incentive to migrate in, in accordance with the ascending bundles property. The model's implications can be separated into those involving location and those involving voting. A joint distribution of income and taste parameters, a locus of (g, q) pairs, and a locus of pivotal voters are determined in equilibrium. Epple, et. al., parameterize their model and follow a two-step estimation procedure. In the first step the quantiles of the actual income distribution in their data are matched up with the model's predictions and estimates of the mean and standard deviation of the income distribution, the correlation between tastes for the LPG and income, and the income elasticity of housing are obtained, subject to community size restrictions imposed by the data. The rest of the parameters of the model can be estimated in the second step using data on LPGs, local tax rates, and house prices, across communities, once an assumption is made about voting behavior.

Two models of voting behavior were contrasted, a myopic voter model and a "utility-taking" model. In the former model voters ignore all of the effects of migration in making their choices. The effect of a LPG on the consumer price of housing at the margin takes a very simple form, $dq^i/dg^i = c_g(g^i)/H^i$, where H^i is the demand for local housing. This only depends on the LPG and housing demand. On the other hand, voters in the "utility-taking" model take the LPG and house prices in other locations, and hence utility in those other locations, as given. However, they do anticipate some of the changes that local policy might cause for neighboring communities, where by "neighboring" is not meant by location, but in terms of the variables that determine the partition of agents across locations. For example, if income is the only determining factor in the partition, then two communities are adjacent if their incomes are similar. The marginal impact of a LPG on the consumer price of housing becomes much more complicated and closed form solutions do not exist even for simple functional forms.

Epple, et. al. used data from 92 cities and townships in the greater Boston area that ranged in size from the city of Boston (pop. 560,000) to Boxborough (pop. 3,126). Cities and school districts are coterminus in Massachusetts and the property tax is the main source of finance. The data is from the 1980 Census prior to passage of Proposition 2 1/2 when communities were likely to have been competing with one another. Education expenditures were used as the proxy for the LPG. The data resoundingly rejected the myopic voting model in favor of the "utility taking" model. The real value of this work, however, lies in providing an estimation technique for a fairly complicated general equilibrium model of location choice and voting behavior.

Hoyt and Rosenthal (1997) provided some evidence that households do sort themselves on the basis of local amenities, at least at the street level. They contrasted two fixed effects models, one that controlled for location specific effects and another model that controlled for house specific effects. If the Tiebout hypothesis is correct, the marginal benefit of a public good service package is the same across households within a location. If the benefits differ within a location and such differences are related to the features of the house, then the location specific effects model will suffer from an omitted variables bias while the house specific effects model will not. On the other hand, if the benefits differ but are not correlated with the features of the house, then the two models are both consistent. Obtaining similar estimates from the two models is a necessary condition for the Tiebout hypothesis; the hypothesis can be rejected if the estimates differ. The American Housing Survey collected information from a subset of 680 urban housing units of their sample and collected data from each unit's ten closest neighbors in 1985 and again in 1989. Hoyt and Rosenthal used the information from the survey to estimate the two models based on a Tiebout sorting model that included housing and a property tax. They found that they could not reject the hypothesis that the estimates were the same, which provided support for the hypothesis.

These results suggest that there is evidence in support of the Tiebout model, which is quite remarkable given that it is a general equilibrium model. One conclusion from this literature is that local governments need to be aware of resource flows when they impose policy.

17.3 Strategic Government Behavior

17.3.1 Models of Government Interaction

Much of the work described in the last chapter involved models where governments interact with one another. There is a new and fascinating body of empirical work that attempts to test the nature of this interaction. Recently, a number of researchers have estimated government policy reaction functions where a policy variable of one government is regressed on the policy variables of other governments and a variety of other socioeconomic variables. The studies in this area generally find that governments behave strategically vis-a-vis one another.

Imagine there are s governments and that each government chooses a policy vector to maximize its objective function subject to various constraints. The result is an optimal decision rule for choosing its policy. Let π^i be the policy vector for the representative government, $\pi = (\pi^1, ..., \pi^s)$ be the vector for the collection of governments, and let $\pi^{-i} = (\pi^1, \pi^2, ..., \pi^{i-1}, \pi^{i+1}, ... \pi^s)$ be the policy vector of every government but the representative government. Suppose the representative government's objective function is $\Omega^i(\pi^i, \pi^{-i}, y; \phi^i)$, and its constraint is $\Psi^i(\pi^i, \pi^{-i}, y; \psi^i) = 0$, where ϕ^i is a vector of location specific characteristics that affect the objective function, ψ^i is a vector of characteristics that affect the constraint, and y is an aggregate variable. There is also an equilibrium condition that ties the governments together and determines the aggregate variable, $E(y; \pi) = 0$. Notice that the policy choices of the other governments enter the objective function and constraint of the representative government. Of course, without spillover effects these become instead $\Omega^i(\pi^i, y; \phi^i)$ and $\Psi^i(\pi^i, y; \psi^i) = 0$.

There are a number of possibilities governing the interaction of the governments. If all governments are *completely atomistic*, then they take the policy choices of the other governments and all aggregate variables as given. The representative government chooses π^i to maximize its objective function subject to its own constraint.[7] The first order condition is easily derived and the solution is a policy rule of the form $\pi^i = \Pi^i(\pi^{-i}, y; \phi^i, \psi^i)$. An equilibrium is a vector π and a y such that each policy rule holds and the equilibrium condition is satisfied. Horizontal tax competition on the part of local governments is a classic example of this sort of interaction.[8] It also covers the case of spillover models. For example, it includes the case where public spending in one community affects other communities close by. Without spillover effects we obtain $\Pi^i(y; \phi^i, \psi^i)$ instead.

A second possibility is where one of the governments has a special status and acts as a Stackelberg leader.[9] For example, a national government in a federation may act as a leader while the local governments act as followers. This is the case of a vertical fiscal externality. The representative follower solves the same problem as described in the last paragraph. The solution is $\Pi^i(\pi^{-i}, y; \phi^i, \psi^i)$. The leader takes this into account when choosing its optimal policy. Suppose there are three governments and the first government acts as leader. Then

$$\pi^2 = \Pi^2(\pi^1, \pi^3, y; \phi^2, \psi^2),$$

and

$$\pi^3 = \Pi^3(\pi^1, \pi^2, y; \phi^3, \psi^3),$$

are the optimal policy rules for the followers. Solving we obtain

$$\pi^2 = \Gamma^2(\pi^1, y; \phi^2, \phi^3, \psi^2, \psi^3),$$

$$\pi^3 = \Gamma^3(\pi^1, y; \phi^2, \phi^3, \psi^2, \psi^3).$$

These reaction functions relate each follower's decision to the leader. Substituting these into the leader's decision problem, the leader's objective and constraint become

$$\Omega^1(\pi^1, \Gamma^2(\pi^1, y; \phi^2, \phi^3, \psi^2, \psi^3), \Gamma^3(\pi^1, y; \phi^2, \phi^3, \psi^2, \psi^3), y; \phi^1),$$

and

$$\Psi^1(\pi^1, \Gamma^2(\pi^1, y; \phi^2, \phi^3, \psi^2, \psi^3), \Gamma^3(\pi^1, y; \phi^2, \phi^3, \psi^2, \psi^3), y; \psi^1) = 0,$$

respectively. The solution to the leader's problem is $\pi^1 = P(y; \phi^1, \phi^2, \phi^3, \psi^1, \psi^2, \psi^3)$. The leader doesn't have a reaction function per se but simply chooses a point on the reaction functions of the followers that is optimal for it. An equilibrium is a vector π that satisfies the reaction functions of the followers, the leader's optimal decision rule, and also satisfies the equilibrium condition.

Finally, each government may come to understand that it can influence some or all of the aggregate variables through its policy choices. When the governments are *decision atomistic* they take the policy choices of the other governments as given, but take into account their own influence on the aggregate variables. In that case the governments will interact through the equilibrium condition. To see this, assume there are no spillover effects. Government i's decision problem is to maximize $\Omega^i(\pi^i, y; \phi^i)$ subject to $\Psi^i(\pi^i, y; \psi^i) = 0$, and $E(y; \pi^i, \pi^{-i}) = 0$, taking as given π^{-i}. The solution is a policy rule of the form, $\Phi^i(\pi^{-i}; \phi^i, \psi^i)$. The policy vector of the other governments only enters because it influences the aggregate variable.

The main empirical problem is that it may be difficult to distinguish between these various possibilities. For example, a spillover model where π^{-i} enters the objective function implies a policy rule of the form $\Pi^i(\pi^{-i}, y; \phi^i, \psi^i)$. Solve the equilibrium condition, $y(\pi)$, and substitute to get $\Pi^i(\pi^{-i}, y(\pi); \phi^i, \psi^i)$. A model without any spillovers but where the government takes its impact on the aggregate variable into account yields a rule of the form $\Phi^i(\pi^{-i}; \phi^i, \psi^i)$. The implications of these two models are very similar and so empirical researchers may not be able to distinguish between them.

17.3.2 An Example: Horizontal Tax Competition

As a concrete example, consider the tax competition model of the last chapter where output is produced using labor and capital and capital is mobile. When firms maximize profit, we have the condition, $r + \tau^i = f_k(k^i)$. Solve to obtain the demand for capital per worker, $k^i(r + \tau^i)$. The objective function is $\Omega^i = u^i(x^i, g^i; \phi^i)$, the private agent's budget constraint is $x^i = w^i + rk^{*i}$, and the wage is given by $w^i(r + \tau^i) = f - (r + \tau^i)k^i(r + \tau^i)$. The government's budget constraint is $\tau^i k^i = g^i$, and the equilibrium condition in the capital market is $k^* = \Sigma k^i(r + \tau^i)$.

If the government is completely atomistic it chooses the tax rate to maximize

$$u^i(w^i(r + \tau^i) + rk^{*i}, \tau^i k^i(r + \tau^i); \phi^i),$$

taking r as given. The solution is $\tau^i = A^i(r; \phi^i, k^{*i})$. This is a policy function where there is no response to the policy of the other governments. Suppose instead that g^{-i} enters the utility function. The local government's objective function can be written as

$$u^i(w^i(r + \tau^i) + rk^{*i}, \tau^i k^i(r + \tau^i), g^{-i}; \phi^i),$$

where $g^j = \tau^j k^j(r + \tau^j)$. The solution to the government's decision problem in the presence of a spillover effect is $\tau^i = B(\tau^{-i}, r; \phi^i, k^{*i})$. The distinguishing feature of this second model is that the tax rates of the other governments now enter the representative government's policy rule.

Finally, suppose that each government recognizes its influence on the equilibrium but feels it has no effect on the policy of the other governments, and there are no other spillover effects. In that case it chooses its tax rate to maximize the same objective function as in the first model but takes the equilibrium condition into account.[10] The solution is the rule $\tau^i = C(\tau^{-i}; \phi^i, k^{*i}, k^*)$. This rule also differs from the A( ) rule because of the presence of the other governments' tax rates. It also differs in a very subtle way from the B( ) rule that may be difficult to test. To see this, note that r is endogenous to the system and solve the equilibrium condition, $r(\tau, k^*)$. The decision rule is given by $B(\tau^{-i}, r(\tau, k^*); \phi^i, k^{*i})$. This will be difficult to distinguish from C( ).

17.3.3 An Example: Vertical Tax Competition

Next, suppose there are two levels of government, local and national. The national government moves first and chooses its tax and spending policy taking into account the response of the local governments. The representative local government then chooses its policy taking the national government's policy as given. To solve this policy game we first solve the local government's decision problem and then solve the national government's problem.

Using the model of the last section, the representative local government chooses a tax rate on mobile capital and a level of a LPG to maximize $u^i(w^i(r + \tau^i + t) + rk^{*i}, g^i, g; \phi^i)$, subject to its budget constraint, $\tau^i k^i (r + \tau^i + t) = g^i$, taking r and t as given, where t is the capital tax rate imposed by the national government and g is a national public good. The solution is a tax rate function, $\tau^i = \Pi^i(t, g, r; \phi^i, k^{*i})$, for $i = 1, ..., s$.

The national government takes this function $\Pi^i(t, g, r; \phi^i, k^{*i})$ into account when solving its decision problem. Equilibrium in the capital market is given by

$$k^* = \Sigma k^i(r + \tau^i + t).$$

The national government chooses its policy to maximize a Benthamite social welfare function subject to its budget constraint $\Sigma_{i'} tk^{i'}(r + \tau^{i'} + t) = g$, where it imposes the tax on a subset of locations, denoted by i', and the equilibrium condition in the capital market, taking the behavioral response of the local governments into account. The solution is a function for the tax rate,

$$t = P(y; \phi^1, ..., \phi^s, k^*, k^{*1}, ..., k^{*s}).$$

Once this function is known we can substitute it into the reaction functions of the local governments to obtain a complete solution.

17.3.4 Some Empirical Results

We will describe the results of Brueckner and Saveedra (2001) to give the reader a feel for the work being done in this area. Consider a linear tax reaction function of the form

$$\tau^i = \beta \Sigma_{h \neq i} \omega^{ih} \tau^h + Y^i \delta + \varepsilon^i, \tag{17.5}$$

where the ω^{ih} are weights and Y^i is a vector of local characteristics that influence the local demand for LPGs. The weights aggregate across the tax rates of the competing communities and are chosen arbitrarily.[11] For example, the weights could be chosen to reflect the inverse of the distance between communities h and i. We can write (17.5) for all h and stack the equations according to

$$\tau = \beta W\tau + Y\delta + \varepsilon,$$

where W is a matrix with zero elements on the diagonal and τ is a column vector. Solve to get the reduced form,

$$\tau = (I - \beta W)^{-1}(Y\delta + \varepsilon).$$

The main parameter to be estimated is β. A non-zero value indicates that there is strategic interaction among the local governments, while a zero value indicates there is not.

Several comments are in order. First, even if $\beta = 0$, tax competition of a non-strategic sort might still exist. So finding that $\beta = 0$ does not necessarily imply the complete absence of tax competition and it also does not necessarily imply that the level of LPGs is efficient. Second, it is possible in some models of tax competition that the level of spending on the LPG is greater than the first-best level especially when the competition is not symmetric.[12] It is not clear that a non-zero value for β has any implications that support this. Third, the empirical test will not distinguish between a pure spillover model where aggregate variables are taken as given and a tax competition model where aggregate variables are taken into count. Finally, other taxes such as local sales taxes and income taxes and their interdependence have been ignored and this may affect the estimated coefficients.

Brueckner and Saveedra used cross section data from 70 cities in the Boston Metropolitan area for 1980, before the tax limitation proposition, Proposition 2 1/2, was introduced, and for 1990, after the Proposition was imposed, to estimate β. For 1980 they found that $\beta > 0$ and statistically significant. Thus, the local governments in the greater Boston area responded to a property tax rate increase on the part of nearby communities by raising their own property tax rate.[13] In addition, per capita income exerted a negative effect on the property tax rate, per capita state aid had a positive effect, the number of highly educated people had a positive effect, and public sector earnings, a proxy for the cost of LPGs, also had a positive effect. They hypothesized that higher income meant a larger tax base and allowed for a lower tax rate. Highly educated people would probably have a greater demand for education and hence a greater desire to pay a higher tax rate to finance education. And public sector costs also contributed to a higher tax rate for obvious reasons. The one anomaly was the positive effect of state aid. One would think this would exert a negative influence, i.e., greater state aid would allow the local government to cut the tax rate and still finance its desired level of spending. However, it is possible that this is actually proxying for other underlying characteristics not included in the equation.

The results for 1990 were completely different due to the tax limitation law. The proposition limited property tax revenue to 2.5% of the total property value. Any city above the limit was required to lower its tax each year by 15% until the provision was met. Over half the municipalities in Massachusetts were forced to reduce their tax rate. By 1990, 300 of the 351 municipalities were taxing at the limit. This strongly suggests that the property tax could no longer be used strategically and this was exactly what Brueckner and Saveedra found. Essentially, β was not significantly different from zero in the 1990 data.

17.4 Conclusion

In this chapter we have presented some of the empirical work done on the Tiebout hypothesis on optimal sorting, testing the capitalization hypothesis, the Leviathan model and the ability of fiscal competition to restraint government spending, estimation of the demand for LPGs, and strategic government interaction. The best way to begin thinking about the empirical work is in the framework of a simple model where agents are mobile across locations, housing is produced by profit maximizing firms, local governments impose taxes on property and use the proceeds to provide local public goods.

The evidence of the last twenty-five years indicates that property values capitalize a significant portion of local policies. The consensus view appears to be that somewhere between fifty percent and one hundred percent is capitalized, depending on the policy and location. In addition, there is virtually no consensus on whether local competition acts as a restraint on government spending. First, it is possible that local policies may lead to over-spending at the local level. Examples involving public capital exist in the literature where such is the case. Second, there may be a relationship across levels of government that counteracts a tendency toward reduced government spending. Road building and repair projects cut at the local level may be more than replaced by national road projects and subsidies, for example. One must be careful to distinguish between the response on one level with the response when aggregated across all levels. There is little evidence that interaction among governments, both vertical and horizontal, leads to less government spending.

We also described some work on the estimation of LPGs and tests of several voting models. The early work provided a set of assumptions that implied the median voter hypothesis would hold in each community. This allowed researchers to collect data on the median voter across communities and greatly simplified the analysis. However, it was also assumed that the median voter had the median income and bought a house of median value. Estimation proceeded on these maintained hypotheses. And some of the variables had to be constructed like the tax price. Generally, this work found that LPGs are normal goods and experience negative price effects. However, another maintained hypothesis in much of this work is that agents are not mobile. If they are, then LPGs will cause migration and generally alter the income distribution. Thus, a simultaneity bias would result known as "Tiebout bias;" income econometrically "causes" the demand for LPGs and the pattern of LPGs across communities causes migration which in turn econometrically "causes" income. More recent work allows for a test of different voting models while identifying a rather complicated general equilibrium model of mobility and voting. These models include myopic voter models and models where voters are a bit more sophisticated, taking into account the impact migration may have on local housing prices. As it turns out, the myopic voter model has been rejected and there is some recent evidence in favor of the sophisticated voter version of the model.

Finally, we also described some recent work estimating local government reaction functions. The idea here is that one local government chooses its policies taking aggregate variables and the policies of all other governments as given. A policy variable in one community, like the local property tax rate, will be a function of the property tax rate in other communities, and also possibly a function of the national government's policy variables as well. Unfortunately, the local government's response to a change in any of these variables is theoretically ambiguous in all but the simplest cases. For example, in the simplest case where two governments impose a property tax to finance a LPG, tax competition suggests that the tax rate chosen by each will be too low relative to a first-best optimum. A decrease in one location's tax rate causes capital to migrate from other locations thus reducing the tax base at those other locations. Other governments can respond by lowering their tax rate, which causes a reduction in spending. On the other hand, the second government may wish to maintain its level of spending and so will raise its tax rate instead. The net result is an empirical issue and a consensus has not formed yet on this issue.

---

[1]   See Dowding, John, and Biggs (1994) for a survey of the early literature.
[2]   See Tanzi (1996) for a review.
[3]   Rubinfeld (1987) provides a brief summary of some of this work.

[4] See Bloom, Ladd, and Yinger (1983) and Yinger, Bloom, Borsch-Supan, and Ladd (1988) for useful surveys.

[5] See also Reid (1990) and Roberts (1992).

[6] The cost of the public good is linear in g, there are additional restrictions on the slope of the indifference curves in (g, q) space (See note 7 (p 292)), and utility is greater if some of each of the three goods is consumed than when one of the goods is not consumed (See the discussion on p 296.).

[7] It is presumed in this literature that a solution exists and in many cases that it is unique. Unfortunately, the decision problem confronting the government is not generally a concave programming problem and hence typically does not admit of a unique solution. The literature has tended to focus on cases where such a solution most likely exists.

[8] See Wilson (1999) and Wilson and Wildasin (2004) for surveys.

[9] See Boadway and Keen (1996) and Keen and Kotsogiannis (2002) for the case where the national government is the leader and local governments are the followers. See Kothenburger (2004) for a model where the local governments are the leaders relative to the national government but play a Nash game against each other. He argues that the European Union is an example of this sort of policy game.

[10] The first order condition will now contain terms in $\partial r / \partial \tau^i$.

[11] In a more general model $\phi = 1$ and the weights would be treated as coefficients to be estimated.

[12] See Bucovetsky (1991) and Wilson (1991c).

[13] Others have also found evidence of strategic complementarity at the local level. Heyndels and Vuchelen (1998) found a positive relationship for the property tax in Belgium. Hayashi and Boadway (2001) found that some provinces in Canada raise their business tax rate in response to an increase by other provinces, but that they lower their tax rate in response to an increase in the federal business tax rate. Buettner (2001) found a positive relationship for business taxes in Germany.

References

Aaron, Henry, 1990, Discussion of 'Why Is Infrastructure Important?,' in A. Munnell, ed., Is There a Shortfall in Public Capital Investment?, *Conference Series No. 34, Federal Reserve Bank of Boston*, 51 – 63.

Abe, Kenzo, 1992, Tariff Reform in a Small Open Economy with Public Production, *International Economic Review, 33, 209-222.*

Abel, Andrew, N. Gregory Mankiw, Lawrence H. Summers, and Richard Zeckhauser, 1989, Assessing Dynamic Efficiency: Theory and Evidence, *Review of Economic Studies*, 56, 1 - 20.

Abrams, B. and M. Schmitz, 1978, The Crowding Out Effect of Government Transfers on Private Charitable Contributions, *Public Choice*, 33, 29 - 39.

Abrams, B. and M. Schmitz, 1984, The Crowding Out Effect of Government Transfers on Private Charitable Contributions: Cross Sectional Evidence, *National Tax Journal*, 37, 563-568.

Aghion P. and P. Howitt, 1999, Endogenous Growth Theory, Cambridge, MA: MIT Press.

Aldritch, John H., 1997, When is it Rational to Vote?, in Dennis C. Mueller, ed., *Perspectives on Public Choice: A Handbook,* Cambridge, UK: Cambridge University Press, 373-390.

Alesina, Alberto, and Howard Rosenthal, 1995, *Partisan Politics, Divided Government, and the Economy,* Cambridge: Cambridge University Press.

Alesina,A., N. Roubini, with G. Cohen, 1997, *Political Cycles and the Macroeconomy,* Cambridge, MA: MIT Press.

Andreoni, James, 1988a, Privately Provided Public Goods in a Large Economy: The Limits of Altruism, *Journal of Public Economics*, 35, 57 - 73.

Andreoni, James, 1988b, Why free Ride? Strategies and Learning in Public Goods Experiments, *Journal of Public Economics*, 37, 291-304.

Andreoni, James, 1989, Giving with Impure Altruism: Applications to Charity and Ricardian Equivalence, *Journal of Political Economy*, 97, 1447 - 1458.

Andreoni, James, 1990, Impure Altruism and Donations to Public Goods: A Theory of Warm-Glow Giving, *Economic Journal*, 100, 464 - 477.

Andreoni, James, 1993, An Experimental Test of the Public-Goods Crowding-Out Hypothesis, *American Economic Review, 83*, 1317 - 1327.

Andreoni, James, 1995a, Warm-Glow Versus Cold-Prickle: The Effects of Positive and Negative Framing on Cooperation in Experiments, *Quarterly Journal of Economics*, 110, 1-21.

Andreoni, James, 1995b, Cooperation in Public-Goods Experiments: Kindness or Confusion?, *American Economic Review*, 85, 891-904.

Andreoni, James, 1998, Towards a Theory of Charitable Fund-Raising, *Journal of Political Economy*, 106, 1186-1213.

Andreoni, James, and Theodore Bergstrom, 1996, Do Government Subsidies Increase the Private Supply of Public Goods?, *Public Choice*, 88, 295-308.

Andreoni, James, William G. Gale, and John Karl Scholtz, 1996, Charitable Contributions of Time and Money, mimeo, University of Wisconsin-Madison.

Andreoni, James and John Miller, 2002, Giving According to GARP: An Experimental Test of the Consistency of Preferences for Altruism, *Econometrica*, 70, 737—753.

Andreoni, James, and Abigail Payne, 2003, Do Government Grants to Private Charities Crowd Out Giving or Fundraising?, *American Economic Review*, 93, 792—812.

Andreoni, James and John Scholtz, 1995, An Econometric Analysis of Charitable Giving with Interdependent Preferences, *Economic Inquiry*, 36, 410-428.

Annala, Christopher N., and Stephen Perez, 2001, Convergence of Public Capital Investment Among the United States, 1977-1996, *Public Finance and Management*, 1, 214-229.

Annala, Christopher N., Raymond G. Batina, and James P. Feehan, 2004, Public Inputs and the Private Economy: A Study of Japan, mimeo.

Arrow, Kenneth, 1951, *Social Choice and Individual Values*, New York: John Wiley.

Arrow, Kenneth, 1966, Discounting and Public Investment Criteria, in *Water Research,* eds. A. V. Knees and S. C. Smith, Baltimore: Johns Hopkins Press for Resources for the Future, 13-32.

Arrow, Kenneth, 1975, Gifts and Exchanges, in *Altruism, Morality, and Economic Theory*, E. S. Phelps, ed., Russell Sage Foundation.

Arrow Kenneth, 1979, The Property Rights Doctrine and Demand Revelation Under Incomplete Information, in *Economics and Human Welfare: Essays in Honor of Tibor Scitovsky*, edited by Michael Boskin, New York: Academic Press, 23-39.

Arrow, Kenneth, 1981, Optimal and Voluntary Income Distribution, *Economic Welfare and the Economics of Soviet Socialism: Essays in Honor of Abram Bergson*, Steven Rosefield, ed., Cambridge: Cambridge University Press.

Arrow, Kenneth and Mordecai Kurz, 1970, *Public Investment, the Rate of Return, and Public Investment*, Baltimore, MD: Johns Hopkins University Press.

Asako, Kazumi, Atsushi Tsuneki, Shin-ichi Fukuda, Hiroshi Teruyama, Takashi Tsukamoto and Masanori Sugiyama, 1994, Productivity of Government Capital and Welfare Evaluation of Government Investment Policy, *Economic Analysis*, 135, Economic Planning Agency (in Japanese).

Aschauer, D., 1989, "Is Public Expenditure Productive," *Journal of Monetary Economics* 23, pp. 177-200.

Aschauer, D., 1990, Why Is Infrastructure Important?, in *Is There a Shortfall in Public Capital Investment?*, A. Munnell, ed., Conference Series No. 34, Federal Reserve Bank of Boston, 21– 50.

Aschauer, D., 1993, Public Capital and Economic Growth, in The Jerome Levy Economics Institute of Bard College, *Public Infrastructure Investment: A Bridge to Productivity Growth?*, Public Policy Brief, no. 4, 9-30.

Aschauer, D., 2001, Output and Employment Effects of Public Capital, *Public Finance and Management*, 1, 135-160.

Atkinson, Anthony, and Nicholas Stern, 1974, Pigou, Taxation, and Public Goods, *Review of Economic Studies*, 41, no.1, 119-128.

Atkinson, Anthony, and Agnar Sandmo, 1980, Welfare Implications of the Taxation of Savings, *Economic Journal*, 90, 529-549.

Atkinson, Anthony and Joseph Stiglitz, 1980, *Lectures on Public Economics*, New York: McGraw-Hill.

Auerbach, Alan, 1987, Weighted-Average Discount Rates in Public Expenditure Analysis: A Generalization, in *Modern Developments in Public Finance: Essays in Honor of Arnold Harberger,* Michael J. Boskin, ed., Oxford: B. Blackwell.

Auten, Gerald E., James M. Cilke, and William C. Randolph, 1992, The Effects of Tax Reform on Charitable Contributions, *National Tax Journal*, 45, 267 - 290.

Auten, Gerald E. and David Joulfaian, 1996, Charitable Contributions and Intergenerational Transfers, Office of Tax Analysis, U S Department of the Treasury, Working Paper.

Auten, Gerald E., Holger Sieg, and Charles T. Clotfelter, 2002, Charitable Giving, Income, and Taxes: An Analysis of Panel Data, *American Economic Review*, 92, 371 - 382.

Azariadis, Costas, 1993, *Intertemporal Macroeconomics*, Oxford: Oxford University Press.

Bagnoli, Mark, and Michael McKee, 1991, Voluntary Contribution Games: Efficient Private Provision of Public Goods, *Economic Inquiry,* XXIX, 351-366.

Bajo-Rubio, O. and S. Sosvilla-Rivera, 1993, Does Public Capital Affect Private Sector Performance? An Analysis of the Spanish Case, *Economic Modeling* 10, 179-185.

Ballard, Charles L., and Don Fullerton, 1992, Distortionary Taxes and the Provision of Public Goods, *Journal of Economic Perspectives*, 6, 117-131.

Bandara, Ranjith, and Clem Tisdell, 2004, The Net Benefit of Saving the Asian Elephant: A Policy and Contingent Valuation Study, *Ecological Economics*, 48, 93-107.

Banks, Jeffrey, Charles R. Plott, and David P. Porter, 1988, An Experimental Analysis of Unanimity in Public Goods Provision Mechanisms, *Review of Economic Studies*, LV, 301-322.

Barrett, Kevin, 1991, Panel-Data Estimates of Charitable Giving: A Synthesis of Techniques, *National Tax Journal*, 44, 365 - 381.

Barrett, Kevin, Anya M. McGuirk, and Richard Steinberg, 1997, Further Evidence on the Dynamic Impact of Taxes on Charitable Giving., *National Tax journal,* 50, 312-34.

Barro, Robert J., 1974, Are Government Bonds Net Wealth?, *Journal of Political Economy,* 82, 1095-1117.

Barro, Robert J., 1976, Perceived Wealth in Bonds and Social Security and the Ricardian Equivalence Theorem: Reply to Feldstein and Buchanan, *Journal of Political Economy,* 84, 343-350.

Barro, Robert, 1990, "Government Spending in a Simple Model of Endogenous Growth," *Journal of Political Economy* 98, pp. S103-S125.

Barthold, Thomas, and Robert Plotnick, 1984, Estate Taxation and Other Determinants of Charitable Bequests," *National Tax Journal* 37, 225-37.

Batina, Raymond G., 1990a, Public Goods and Dynamic Efficiency: The Modified Samuelson Rule, *Journal of Public Economics,* 41, 389 - 400.

Batina, Raymond G., 1990b, On the Interpretation of the Modified Samuelson Rule for Public Goods in Static Models With Heterogeneity, *Journal of Public Economics,* 42, 125 - 133.

Batina, Raymond G., 1998, On the Long Run Effects of Public Capital and Disaggregated Public Capital, *International Tax and Public Finance,* 5, 263-281.

Batina, Raymond G., 1999, On the Long Run Effect of Public Capital on Aggregate Output: Estimation and Sensitivity Analysis, *Empirical Economics,* 24, 711-717.

Batina, Raymond G., and Toshihiro Ihori, 2000, *Consumption Tax Policy and the Taxation of Capital Income,* Oxford: Oxford University Press.

Baumol, William J., 1968, On the Social Discount rate, *American Economic Review,* 58, 788 - 802.

Baumol, William J., 1977, On the Discount Rate for Public Projects, in Public Expenditure and Policy Analysis, eds. Robert H. Haveman and Julius Margolis, Rand McNally: Chicago.

Becker , Gary S., 1974, A Theory of Social Interactions, *Journal of Political Economy,* 82, 1063-1093.

Bennett, E. and D. Conn, 1977, The Group Incentive Properties of Mechanisms For the Provision of Public Goods, *Public Choice,* 29, 95-102.

Berglas, Eitan, 1976a, On the Theory of Clubs, *American Economics Review,* 66, 116-121.

Berglas, Eitan, 1976b, Distribution of Tastes and Skills and the Provision of Local Public Goods, *Journal of Public Economics,* 6, 409-423.

Berglas, Eitan, 1982, User Charges, Local Public Services, and Taxation of Land Rents, *Public Finance,* 178-188.

Berglas, Eitan, 1984, Qualities and Multiple Public Service in the Tiebout Model, *Journal of Public Economics,* 25, 299-321.

Berglas, Eitan, and David Pines, 1981, Clubs, Local Public Goods and Transportation Models: A Synthesis, *Journal of Public Economics,* 15, 141-162.

Berglas, Eitan, and David Pines, 1984, Resource Constraint,Replicability and Mixed Clubs: A Reply, *Journal of Public Economics,* 23, 391-397.

Bergstrom, T., D. Rubinfeld, and P. Shapiro, 1982, Micro-Based Estimates of Demand Functions for Local School Expenditures, *Econometrica*, 50, 1183-1205.

Bergstrom T.C., and H. Varian, 1985, When are Nash Equilibria Independent of the Distribution of Agent's Characteristics?, *Review of Economic Studies*, 52, 715 - 718.

Bergstrom T.C., L. Blume, H. Varian, 1986, On the Private Provision of Public Goods, *Journal of Public Economics*, 29, 25 - 49.

Bergstrom T.C., L. Blume, H. Varian, 1992, Uniqueness of Nash Equilibrium in Private Provision of Public Goods, *Journal Of Public Economics*, 49, 391-392

Berndt, E. and B. Hansson, 1992, Measuring the Contribution of Public Infrastructure in Sweden," *The Scandinavian Journal of Economics*, 94, 151-168.

Bernheim, B. Douglas, 1986, On the Voluntary and Involuntary Provision of Public Goods, *American Economic Review*, 76, 789-793.

Bernheim, B. Douglas, 1989, Neoclassical Perspective on Budget Deficits, *Journal of Economic Perspectives*, 3, 55-72.

Bernheim, B. Douglas, Andrei Shleifer, and Lawrence H. Summers, 1986, The Strategic Bequest Motive, *Journal of Political Economy*, 93, 1045-1076.

Bernheim, B. Douglas, and Kyle Bagwell, 1988, Is Everything Neutral?, *Journal of Political Economy*, 96, 308-338.

Berry, Steven T.; Waldfogel, Joel, 1999, Public Radio in the U.S.: Does it Correct Market Failure or Cannibalize Commercial Stations?, *Journal of Public Economics*, 71, 189-211.

Besley, T., and H. Rosen, 1998, Vertical Externalities in Tax Setting: Evidence from Gasoline and Cigarettes, *Journal of Public Economics*, 70, 383-398.

Bewley, Truman F., 1981, A Critique of Tiebout's Theory of Local Public Expenditures, *Econometrics*, 49, 713-740.

Bilodeau, Marc, 1992, Voluntary Contributions to United Charities, *Journal of Public Economics*, 48, 119-133.

Bilodeau, Marc, and Al Slivinski, 1996, Toilet Cleaning and Department Chairing: Volunteering a Public Service, *Journal of Public Economics*, 59, 299-308.

Black, Duncan, 1948, On the Rationale of Group Decision Making, *Journal of Political Economy*, 56, 23-34.

Black, Duncan, 1958, *The Theory of Committees and Elections,* Cambridge: Cambridge University Press.

Bloom, H.S., H. Ladd, and J. Yinger, 1983, Are Property Taxes Capitalized into Property Values? in *Local Provision of Public Services: The Tiebout Model After Twenty-Five Years*, G. R. Zodrow, ed., New York: Academic Press.

Boadway, R., 1982, On the Method of Taxation and the Provision of Local Public Goods: Comment, *American Economic Review,* 72, 846-851.

Boadway, R., and F. Flatters, 1982, Efficiency and Equalization Payments in a Federal System of Government: A Synthesis and Extension of Recent Results, *Canadian Journal of Economics*, 15, 613-633.

Boadway, R., and M. Keen, 1996, Efficiency and Optimal Direction of Federal-State Transfers, *International Tax and Public Finance,* 3, 137-155.

Boadway, R., P. Pestieau and D.Wildasin, 1989, Tax-Transfer Policies and the Voluntary Provision of Public Goods, *Journal of Public Economics*, 39, 157-176.

Bockstael, Nancy E., and Catherine L. Kling, 1988, Valuing Environmental Quality: Weak Complementarity With Sets of Goods, *American Journal of Agricultural Economics*, 70, 654 - 662.

Bohm, Peter, 1972, Estimating Demand for Public Goods: An Experiment, *European Economic Review*, 3, 111 - 130.

Bohm, Peter, 1984, Revealing Demand For An Actual Public Good, *Journal of Public Economics*, 24, 135-151.

Bohm, Peter, 1994, CVM Spells Responses to Hypothetical Questions, *Natural Resources Journal*, 34, 37-50.

Boskin, M., 1973, Local Government Tax and Product Competition and the Optimal Provision of Public Goods, *Journal of Political Economy*, 81, 203-210.

Boskin, Michael J., 1977, Estate Taxation and Charitable Bequests, *Journal of Public Economics*, 5, 27-56.

Boskin, Michael J., and Martin S. Feldstein, 1977, Effects of the Charitable Deduction on Contributions by Low and Middle Income Households; Evidence from the National Survey on Philanthropy, *Review of Economics and Statistics*, 59, 351 - 354.

Bowen, Howard, 1943, The Interpretation of Voting in the Allocation of Economic Resources, *Quarterly Journal of Economics*, 58, 27-49.

Bradford, David F., 1970, Benefit Cost Analysis and Demand Curves for Public Goods, *Kyklos,* 23, 775-791.

Bradford, David, 1975, Constraints on Government Investment Opportunities and the Choice of Discount Rate, *American Economic Review*, 65, 887 - 899.

Bradford, David, and Gregory Hildebrandt, 1977, Observable Preferences for Public Goods, *Journal of Public Economics*, 8, 111 - 131.

Brandts, Jordi and Arthur Schram, 2001, Cooperation and Noise in Public Goods Experiments: Applying the Contribution Function Approach, *Journal of Public Economics*, 79, 399-427.

Brennan, G. and J. Buchanan, 1980, *The Power to Tax: Analytical Foundations of a Fiscal Constitution,* Cambridge: Cambridge University Press.

Brett, C., and J. Pinske. 2000. The Determinants of Municipal Tax Rates in British Columbia. *Canadian Journal of Economics,* 33, 695-714.

Broman, Amy, 1989, Statutory Tax Rate Reform and Charitable Contributions: Evidence from a Recent Period of Reform, *Journal of the American Taxation Association,* 10, 7-20.

Brown, Eleanor, and Hamilton Lankford, 1992, Gifts of Money and Gifts of Time, *Journal of Public Economics*, 47, 321 - 341.

Browning, Edgar, 1976, The Marginal Cost of Public Funds, *Journal of Political Economy,* 84, 283-298.

Browning, Edgar, 1987, On the Marginal Welfare Cost of Taxation, *American Economic Review*, 77, 11-23.

Browning, Edgar, and Liqun Liu, 1998, The Optimal Supply of Public Goods and the Distortionary Cost of Taxation: Comment, *National Tax Journal*, 51, 103-116.

Brubaker, E. R., 1975, Free Ride, Free Revelation, or Golden Rule, *Journal of Law and Economics,* 18, 147-161.

Bruce, Neil, 1990, Defense Expenditures by Countries in Allied and Adversarial Relationships, *Defense Economics*, 1, 1749-195.

Brueckner, Jan K., 1979a, Equilibrium in a System of Communities with Local Public Goods: A Diagrammatic Exposition, *Economics Letters*, 2, 387-393.

Brueckner, J., 1979b, Property Values, Local Public Expenditure, and Economic Efficiency, *Journal of Public Economics,* 11, 223-245.

Brueckner, J., 1982, A Test for Allocative Efficiency in the Local Public Sector, *Journal of Public Economics,* 14, 311-332.

Brueckner, J., 1983, Property Value Maximization, *Journal of Urban Economics*, 14, 1-16.

Brueckner, Jan K., 1994, Tastes, Skills, and Local Public Goods, *Journal of Urban Economics*, 35, 201-220.

Brueckner, Jan K., 2000, A Tiebout/Tax Competition Model, *Journal of Public Economics,* 77, 285-306.

Brueckner, J. K., and L. A. Saavedra, 2001, Do Local Governments Engage in Strategic Tax Competition?, *National Tax Journal*, 54, 203-29.

Buchanan, James M., 1965, An Economic Theory of Clubs, *Economica*, 32, 1-14.

Buchanan, James M. and Goetz, Charles J., 1972, Efficiency Limits of Fiscal Mobility: An Assessment of The Tiebout Model, *Journal of Public Economics*, 1, 25-43.

Bucovetsky S., 1991, Asymmetric Tax Competition, *Journal of Urban Economics,* 30, 167-181.

Bucovetsky S. and Wilson, J. D. 1991, Tax Competition With Two Tax Instruments, *Regional Science and Urban Economics,* 21, 333-350.

Buettner, T., 2001, Local Business Taxation and Competition for Capital: The Choice of the Tax Rate, *Regional Science and Urban Economics*, 31, 215-45.

Burgess, David F., 1988, Complementarity and the Discount Rate for Public Investment, *Quarterly Journal of Economics*, 12, 527-514.

Burlando, Roberto, and John Hey, 1997, Do Anglo-Saxons free-ride More? *Journal of Public Economics*, 64, 41-60.

Calfee, John, and Winston, Clifford, 1998, The Value of Automobile Travel Time: Implications for Congestion Policy, *Journal of Public Economics*, 69, 83-102.

Cameron, Trudy and James, Michelle, 1987, Efficient Estimation Methods for "Closed-Ended" Contingent Valuations Surveys, *The Review of Economics and Statistics*, 269-276.

Cameron, Trudy Ann, Gregory L. Poe, Robert G. Ethier, and William D. Schultze, 2002, Alternative Non-market Value Elicitation Methods: Are the Underlying

Preferences the Same?, *Journal of Environmental Economics and Management*, 44, 391-425.

Campbell, Donald E., 1987, *Resource Allocation Mechanisms*, Cambridge: Cambridge University Press.

Carmichael, Jeffrey, 1982, On Barro's Theorem of Debt Neutrality: The Irrelevance of Net Wealth, *American Economic Review*, 72, 202-213.

Carson, Richard T., 2000, Contingent Valuation: A User's Guide, *Environmental Science Technology,* 34, 1413-1418.

Carson, Richard T., Nicholas E. Flores, and Norman F. Meade, 2001, Contingent Valuation: Controversies and Evidence, *Environmental and Resource Economics,* 19, 173-210.

Case, A. C., H. S. Rosen, and J. C. Hines, 1993, Budget Spillovers and Fiscal Policy Interdependence: Evidence From the States, *Journal of Public Economics,* 52, 285-307.

Chamberlin, John, 1974, Provision of Collective Goods as a Function of Group Size, *American Political Science Review*, 68, 707-716.

Chang, Ming Chung, 2000, Rules and Levels in the Provision of Public Goods: The Role of Complementarities Between the Public Good and Taxed Commodities, *International Tax and Public Finance*, 7, 83 - 91.

Chen, Yan, and Charles Plott, 1996, The Groves-Ledyard Mechanism: An Experimental Study of Institutional Design, *Journal of Public Economics*, 59, 335-364.

Choe, Yong S. and Jinook Jeong, 1993, Charitable Contributions by Low and Middle Income Taxpayers: Further Evidence, *National Tax Journal*, 46, 33 - 39.

Ciriacy-Wantrup, S.V., 1947, Capital Returns from Soil Conservation Practices, *Journal of Farm Economics*, 29, 1181-1196.

Clarke, Edward H., 1971, Multipart Pricing of Public Goods, *Public Choice*, 11, 17-33.

Clotfelter, Charles, 1980, Tax Incentives and Charitable Giving, *Journal of Public Economics*, 13, 319 - 340.

Clotfelter, Charles, 1985, *Federal Tax Policy and Charitable Giving*, Chicago: University of Chicago Press.

Clotfelter, Charles T., 1987, Life After Tax Reform, *Change,* July-August, 12-18.

Clotfelter, Charles T., 1992, The Impact of Tax Reform on Charitable Giving: A 1989 Perspective, in *Do Taxes Matter*, Joel Slemrod, ed., Cambridge, MA: MIT Press, 203 - 235.

Clotfelter, Charles T., and C. Eugene Steuerle, 1981, Charitable Contributions, in *How Taxes Affect Economic Behavior,* Henry J. Aaron and Joseph A. Pechman, eds., Washington D.C.: The Brookings Institution, 403-446.

Coase, Ronald, 1974, The Lighthouse in Economics, *The Journal of Law and Economics*, 17, 357 - 376.

Conn, D., 1983, The Scope of Satisfactory Mechanisms for the provision of Public Goods, , *Journal of Public Economics,* 20, 249-263.

Conley, John P. and Manfred Dix, 1999, Optimal and Equilibrium Membership in Clubs in the Presence of Spillovers, *Journal of Urban Economics*, 46, 215-229.

Conley, John P. and Myrna H. Wooders, 1997, Equivalence of the Core and Competitive Equilibrium in a Tiebout Economy with Crowding Types, *Journal of Urban Economics,* 41, 421-440.

Conley, John P. and Myrna H. Wooders, 1998, Anonymous Lindahl Pricing in a Tiebout Economy with Crowding Types, *Canadian Journal of Economics,* 31, 952-974.

Cornes, Richard, and Todd Sandler, 1984a, Easy Riders, Joint Production, and Public Goods, *Economic Journal*, 94, 580 - 598.

Cornes, Richard, and Todd Sandler, 1984b, The Theory of Public Goods: Non-Nash Behavior, *Journal of Public Economics*, 23, 365 - 379.

Cornes, Richard, and Todd Sandler, 1985a, The Simple Analytics of Pure Public Good Provision, *Economica*, 52, 103 - 116.

Cornes, Richard, and Todd Sandler, 1985b, On the Consistency of Conjectures with Public Goods, *Journal of Public Economics*, 25, 117 - 124.

Cornes, Richard, and Todd Sandler, 1994, The Comparative Static Properties of the Impure Public Goods Model, *Journal of Public Economics*, 54, 403 - 421.

Cornes, Richard, and Todd Sandler, 1996, *The Theory of Externalities, Public Goods, and Club Goods,* Cambridge: Cambridge University Press.

Costa, Jose da Silva, Richard Ellison, and Randolph C. Martin, 1987, Public Capital, Regional Output, and Development: Some Empirical Evidence, *Journal of Regional Science*, vol. 27, no.3, 419-437.

Courant, P., and D. Rubinfeld, 1982, On the Measure of Benefits in an Urban Context: Some General Equilibrium Issues, *Journal of Urban Economics*, 13, 346-356.

Crawford,V., 1979, A Procedure for Generating Pareto-Efficient Egalitarian-Equivalent Allocations, *Econometrica,* 47, 49-60.

Cummings, Ronald G., and Glenn Harrison, 1994, Was the Ohio Court Well Informed In its Assessment of the Accuracy of the Contingent Valuation Method?, *Natural Resources Journal*, 34, 1-36.

Cummings, Ronald G., Steven Elliot, Glenn Harrison, and James Murphy, 1997, Are Hypothetical Referenda Incentive Compatible?, *Journal of Political Economy*, 105, 609-621.

Cummings, Ronald G., and Laura O. Taylor, 1999, Unbiased Value Estimates for Environmental Goods: A Cheap Talk Design for the Contingent Valuation Method, *American Economic Review,* 89, 649-665.

Dahlby, Bev, and L. Wilson, 2003, Vertical Fiscal Externalities in a Federation, *Journal of Public Economics,* 87, 917-930.

Danziger, L. and A. Schnytzer, 1991, Implementing the Lindahl Voluntary-Exchange Mechanism, *European Journal of Political Economy*, 7, 55-64.

Davis, Douglas D., and Charles A. Holt, 1993, *Experimental Economics*, Princeton, NJ: Princeton University Press.

Davis, O.A., M.H. DeGroot, and M.J. Hinich, 1972, Social Preference Orderings and Majority Rule, *Review of Economic Studies*, 40, 147-157.

Dawes, R.M., J.M. Orbell, R.T. Simmons, and A.J.C. van de Kragt (1986), Organizing Groups for Collective Action, *American Political Science Review*, 1171-1185.

dAspremont, C., J. Cremer, and L.A. Gerard-Varet, 1990, Incentives andthe Existence of Pareto-Optimal Revelation Mechanisms, *Journal of Economic Theory*, 51, 233-254.

d'Aspremont, Claude, J. Jaskold Gabszewicz, and J.F. Thisse, 1979, On Hotelling's "Stability in Competition," *Econometrica*, 47, 1145-1150.

d'Aspremont, Claude, and Louis-Andre Gerard-Varet, 1979, Incentives and Incomplete Information, *Journal of Public Economics,* 11, 25-45.

d'Aspremont, Claude, and Louis-Andre Gerard-Varet, 1983, On Bayesian Incentive Compatible Mechanisms, in *Aggregation and Revelation of Preferences,* Jean-Jacques Laffont, ed., North Holland: Amsterdam, 269-288.

d'Aspremont, Claude, Herve Moulin, and Louis-Andre Gerard-Varet, 1990, Incentives and the Existence of pareto-Optimal Revelation Mechanisms, *Journal of Economic Theory,* 51, 233-254.

Deacon, R., and P. Shapiro, 1975, Private Preference for Collective Goods Revealed Through Voting on Referenda, *American Economic Review,* 65, 943-955.

de Bartolome, Charles A. M., 1998, Is Pigou Wrong? Can Distortionary Taxation Cause Public Spending to Exceed the Efficient Level?, mimeo.

Demetriades, P., and T. Mamuneas, 2000, Intertemporal Output and Employment Effects of Public Capital: Evidence From 12 OECD Economies, *Economic Journal*, 110, 687-712.

Deno, Kevin, 1988, The Effect of Public Capital on US Manufacturing Activity: 1970 to 1978, *Southern Economic Journal*, vol. 55, no. 4, 400-411.

DePater, James, and Gordon Myers, 1994, Strategic Capital Tax Competition: A Pecuniary Externality and a Corrective Subsidy, *Journal of Urban Economics*, 36, 66-78.

Diamantaras, Dimitrios and Simon Wilkie, 1994, A Generalization of Kaneko's Ratio Equilibrium for Economies with Private and Public Goods, *Journal of Economic Theory*, 62, 499 - 512.

Diamond, Peter, 1965, National Debt in a Neoclassical Growth Model, *American Economic Review*, 55, 1025 - 1150.

Diamond, Peter, 1968, The Opportunity Costs Of Public Investment: Comment, *Quarterly Journal of Economics*, 82, 682-688.

Diamond, Peter, 1975, A Many Person Ramsey Tax Rule, *Journal of Public Economics*, 4, 335-342.

Diamond, Peter, and Jerry A. Hausman, 1994, Contingent Valuation: Is Some Number Better than No Number?, *Journal of Economic Perspectives*, 8, 45-64.

Diamond, Peter, and James Mirrlees, 1971, Optimal Taxation and Public Production, *American Economic Review*, 61, nos.1 and 3, 8-27, 261-278.

Diamond Peter, and James Mirrlees, 1976, Private Constant Returns and Public Shadow Prices, *Review of Economic Studies*, 43, 41 - 47.

Dixit, Avinash and Agnar Sandmo, 1980, *Theory of International Trade,* Cambridge: Cambridge University Press.

Dixit, A.K.; V. Norman, 1980, *The Theory of International Trade*, Cambridge, Cambridge University Press.

Doi, Takero, 1998, Panel Analysis of Public Capital in Japan, *Kokumin Keizai*, 161, 27-52 (in Japanese).

Dowding, K., P. John, and S. Biggs, 1994, Tiebout: A Survey of the Empirical Literature, *Urban Studies,* 31, 767-797.

Downs, Anthony, 1957, *An Economic Theory of Democracy*, New York: Harper and Row.

Drazen, Allen, 2000, *Political Economy in Macroeconomics*, Princeton: Princeton University Press.

Dreze, Jacques H., 1974, Discount Rates and Public Investment: A Post-Scriptum, *Economica*, 41, 52-61.

Dubourg, W. R., M. W. Jones-Lee, and Graham Loomes, 1997, Imprecise Preferences and Survey Design in Contingent Valuation, *Economica*, 64, 681-702.

Duquette, Christopher M., 1999, Is Charitable Giving by Nonitemizers Responsive to Tax Incentives? New Evidence, *National Tax Journal*, 52, 195-206.

Duncan, Brian, 1999, Modeling Charitable Contributions of Time and Money, *Journal of Public Economics*, 72, 213 - 242.

Dye, Richard F., 1978, Personal Charitable Contributions: Tax Effects and Other Motives, in *Proceedings of the Seventieth Annual Conference on Taxation*, 311-321. Columbus: National Tax Association, Tax Institute of America.

Ebert, Udo, 1998, Evaluation of Non-Market Goods: Recovering Unconditional Preferences, *American Journal of Agricultural Economics*, 80, 241-254.

Eberts, 1986, Estimating the Contribution of Urban Public Infrastructure to Regional Growth, Working Paper 8610, Federal Reserve Bank of Cleveland.

Eberts, R. 1986, Public Infrastructure and Regional Economic Development, *Federal Reserve Bank of Cleveland Economic Review*, Quarter 1, 15 – 27.

Eckel, Catherine, and Phillip Grossman, 2003, Rebate Versus Matching: Dos How We Subsidize Charitable Contributions Matter?, *Journal of Public Economics,* 87, 681-701.

Edel, M., and E. Sclar, 1974, Taxes, Spending and Property Values: Supply Adjustment in a Tiebout-Oates Model, *Journal of Political Economy*, 82, 941-954.

Edwards, J., and M. Keen, 1996, Tax Competition and Leviathan, *European Economic Review,* 40, 113-134.

Eisner, Robert, 1991, Infrastructure and Regional Economic Performance, *New England Economic Review Federal Reserve Bank of Boston*, Sept/Oct, 47-58.

Ellickson, B., 1971, Jurisdictional Fragmentation and Residential Choice, *American Economic Review,* 61, 334-339.

Ellickson, B., 1973, A Generalization of the Pure Theory of Public Goods, *American Economic Review,* 63, 417-432.

Ellickson, B., 1977, The Politics and Economics of Decentralization, *Journal of Urban Economics,* 4, 135-149.

Ellickson, B., 1979, Competitive Equilibrium with Local Public Goods, *Journal of Economic Theory,* 21, 46-61.

Ellickson, Bryan, Birght Grodal, Suzanne Scotchmer, and William R. Zame, 1999, Clubs and the Market, *Econometrica,* 67, 1185-1217.

Enelow, J., 1997,Cycling and Majority Rule, in *Perspective on Public Choice: A Handbook,* D. Mueller, ed., Cambridge: Cambridge University Press, 149-162.

Epple, Dennis, and Allan Zelenitz, 1981, The Implications of Competition Among Jurisdictions: Does Tiebout Need Politics?, *Journal of Political Economy,* 89, 1197-1217.

Epple, Dennis, Allan Zelenitz, and Michael Visscher, 1978, A Search for Testable Implications of the Tiebout Hypothesis, *Journal of Political Economy,* 86, 405-425.

Epple, Dennis, Radu Filimon, and Thomas Romer, 1984, Equilibrium Among Local Jurisdictions: Toward an Integrated Treatment of Voting and Residential Choice, *Journal of Public Economics,* 24, 281-308.

Epple, Dennis, Thomas Romer, and Holger Sieg, 2001, Interjurisdictional Sorting and Majority Rule: An Empirical Analysis, *Econometrica,* 69, 1437-1465.

Esteller-More, A., and A. Sole-Olle, 2001, Vertical Income Tax Externalities and Fiscal Interdependence: Evidence for the U.S., *Regional Science and Urban Economics*, 31, 247-272.

Falkinger, J., 1996, Efficient Private Provision of Public Goods by Rewarding Deviations From Average," *Journal of Public Economics*, 62, 413-422.

Falkinger, J., E. Fehr, S. Gchter, R. Winter-Ebmer, 2000, A Simple Mechanism for the Efficient Provision of Public Goods – Experimental Evidence, *American Economic Review*, 90, 247-264.

Feehan, James, 1989, Pareto – Efficiency with Three Varieties of Public Input, *Public Finance*, vol. 44, no. 2, 237-248.

Feehan, James, 1998, Public Investment: Optimal Provision of Hicksian Public Inputs, *Canadian Journal of Economics,* 31, 693-707.

Feehan, James, and Mutsumi Matsumoto, 1999, Public Input Provision with Income Taxation and Variable Factor Supply, mimeo.

Feehan, J., and M. Matsumoto, 2000, Productivity-Enhancing Public Investment and Benefit Taxation: The Case of Factor-Augmenting Public Inputs, *Canadian Journal of Economics* 33, 114-121.

Feehan, James, and Raymond G. Batina, 2004, Public Inputs as Common Property, mimeo.

Feenberg, Daniel, 1987, Are Tax Price Models Really Identified: The Case of Charitable Giving, *National Tax Journal*, 40, 629-633.

Feld, L. P., and G. Kirchgassner, 2001, Income Tax Competition at a State and Local Level in Switzerland, *Journal of Public Economics,* 31, 181-213.

Feldstein, Martin, 1975a, The Income Tax and Charitable Contributions, Part I: Aggregate and Distributional Effects, *National Tax Journal*, 28, 81 - 100.

Feldstein, Martin, 1975b, The Income Tax and Charitable Contributions Part II: The Impact on Religious, Educational and Other Organizations, *National Tax Journal*, 28, 209 - 226.

Feldstein, Martin, 1976, Perceived Wealth in Bonds and Social Security: A Comment, *Journal of Political Economy*, 84, 331-336.

Feldstein, Martin J., 1997, How Big Should Government Be?, *National Tax Journal*, 50, 197-213.

Feldstein, Martin J., 1980, A Contribution to the Theory of Tax Expenditures: The Case of Charitable Giving, in *The Economics of Taxation*, Henry Aaron and Michael Boskin, eds., Washington D. C.: The Brookings Institution, 99 - 122.

Feldstein, Martin, and Charles Clotfelter, 1976, Tax Incentives and Charitable Giving: Evidence from a Panel of Taxpayers, *Journal of Public Economics*, 5, 1 - 26.

Feldstein, Martin, and Amy Taylor, 1976, The Income Tax and Charitable Contributions, *Econometrica*, 44, 1201-1222.

Fernald, John, G., 1999, Road to Prosperity? Assessing the Link Between Public Capital and Productivity, *American Economic Review*, vol. 89, no. 3, 619-638.

Finn, Mary, 1993, Is All Government Capital Productive?, *Federal Reserve Bank of Richmond Economic Quarterly*, vol. 79, Fall, 53-80.

Fiorina, Morris, 1997, Voting Behavior, in Dennis C. Mueller, ed., *Perspectives on Public Choice: A Handbook,* Cambridge: Cambridge University Press, 391-414.

Fisher, Franklin, 1977, On Donor Sovereignty and United Charities, *American Economic Review*, 67, 632 - 638.

Fisher, J., R. M. Isaac, J. W. Schatzberg, and J. M. Walker, 1995, Heterogeneous Demand for Public Goods: Behavior in the Voluntary Contributions Mechanism, *Public Choice,* 85, 249-266.

Flatters, F., J.V. Henderson, and P. Mieszkowski, 1974, Public Goods, Efficiency, Regional Fiscal Equalization, *Journal of Public Economics,* 3, 99-112.

Foley, Duncan, 1967, Resource Allocation and the Public Sector, *Yale Economic Essays*, 7, 43-98.

Foley, Duncan, 1970, Lindahl's Solution and the Core of an Economy, *Econometrica*, 38, 66-72.

Ford, R. and P. Poret, 1991, Infrastructures and Private Sector Productivity, *OECD Economic Studies*, 17, 63-89.

Fraser, Clive, 1992, The Uniqueness of Nash Equilibrium in the Private Provision of Public Goods: An Alternative Proof, *Journal of Public Economics*, 49, 389-90.

Freeman, A. Myrick, 1981, On Measuring Public Goods Demand From Market Data, *Advances in Applied Microeconomics*, 1, 13 - 29.

Freeman, A. Myrick, 1993, *The Measurement of Environmental and Resource Values*, Washington D. C.: Resources of the Future.

Fries, Timothy L., Edward Golding, and Richard Romano, 1991, Private Provision of Public Goods and the Failure of the Neutrality Property in Large Finite Economies, *International Economic Review*, 32, 147 - 157.

Fudenberg, Drew, and Jean Tirole, 1991, *Game Theory*, Cambridge, MA: MIT Press.

Garcia-Mila, Theresa, Therese J. McGuire, 1992, The Contribution of Publicly Provided Inputs to States' Economies, *Regional Science and Urban Economics*, 22, 229-241.

Garcia-Mila, Theresa, Therese J. McGuire, and Robert H. Porter, 1996, The Effect of Public Capital in State-Level Production Functions Reconsidered, *Review of Economics and Statistics*, vol. 78, no. 1, 177-180.

Gary-Bobo, R.J., and T. Jaaidane, 2000, Polling Mechanisms and the Demand Revelation Problem, *Journal of Public Economics*, 76, 203-238.

Gaube, Thomas, 2000, When Do Distortionary Taxes Reduce the Optimal Supply of Public Goods?, *Journal of Public Economics*, 76, 151 - 180.

George, Henry, 1914, *Progress and Poverty*, New York, Doubleday.

Gibbard, A., 1973, Manipulation of Voting Schemes: A General Result, *Econometrica,* 41, 587-602.

Glazer, Amihi, and Kai Konrad, 1993, Private Provision of Public Goods, Limited Tax Deductibility, and Crowding Out, *Finanz Archiv*, 50, 203-216.

Glazer, Amihai, and Kai Konrad, 1996, A Signaling Explanation for Charity, *American Economic Review*, 86,1019-1028.

Glomm, G. and B. Ravikumar, 1994, "Public Investment in Infrastructure in a Simple Growth Model," *Journal of Economic Dynamics and Control* 18, pp. 1173-1187.

Goeree, Jacob K., Charles A. Holt, and Susan K. Laury, 2002, Private Costs and Public Benefits: Unraveling the Effects of Altruism and Noisy Behavior, *Journal of Public Economics*, 83, 255-276.

Goldstein, G., and M. Pauly, 1981, Tiebout Bias on the Demand for Public Goods, *Journal of Public Economics,* 16, 131-144.

Goodspeed, T., 2000, Tax Structure in a Federation, *Journal of Public Economics,* 75, 493-506.

Gordon, R., 1983, An Optimal Taxation Approach to Fiscal Federalism, *Quarterly Journal of Economics,* 98, 567-586.

Gramlich, Edward, M., 1994, Infrastructure Investment: A Review Essay, *Journal of Economic Literature*, vol. 32, 1176-1196.

Green, D., Jacowitz, K., Kahneman, D. and McFadden, D., 1998, Referendum Contingent Valuation, Anchoring, and Willingness to Pay for Public Goods, *Resource and Energy Economics*, 20, 85-116.

Green, Jerry, Elon Kohlberg, and Jean-Jaques Laffont, 1976, Partial Equilibrium Approach to the Free Rider Problem, *Journal of Public Economics*, 6, 375-394.

Green, Jerry, and Jean-Jacques Laffont, 1977, Characterization of Satisfactory Mechanisms for the Revelation of Preferences for Public Goods, *Econometrica,* 45, 427-438.

Green, Jerry, and Jean-Jacques Laffont, 1979, *Incentives in Public Decision-Making,* Amsterdam: North Holland.

Greenberg, J., R. Mackay, and N. Tideman, 1977, Some Limitations of the Groves-Ledyard Optimal Mechanism, *Public Choice,* 29, 129-137.

Greene, Pamela and Robert McClelland, 2001, The Effects of Federal Estate Tax Policy on Charitable Contributions Congressional Budget Office, Washington, DC.

Greene, William H., 1997, *Econometric Analysis,* New Jersey: Prentice Hall.

Gronberg, Timothy and Liqun Liu, 2001, The Second-Best Level of a Public Good: An Approach Based on the Marginal Excess Burden, *Journal of Public Economic Theory,* 3, 431-453.

Grossman, P., 1989, Fiscal Decentralization and Government Size: An Extension, *Public Choice,* 62, 63–69.

Groves, Theodore, 1973, Incentives in Teams, *Econometrica,* 41, 617-631.

Groves, Theodore, and John Ledyard, 1977a, Optimal Allocation of Public Goods: A Solution to the "Free Rider" Problem, *Econometrica,* 45, 783-810.

Groves, Theodore, and John Ledyard, 1977b, Some Limitations of Demand Revealing Processes, *Public Choice,* 29, 107-124.

Groves, Theodore, and John Ledyard, 1980, The Existence of Efficient and Incentive Compatible Equilibrium with Public Goods, *Econometrica,* 48, 1487-1506.

Groves, Theodore, and John Ledyard, 1987, Incentive Compatibility Since 1972, in *Information, Incentives, and Economic Mechanisms,* T. Groves, R. Radner, and S. Reiter, eds., Oxford: Blackwell, 48-111.

Groves, Theodore, and M. Loeb, 1975, Incentives and Public Inputs, *Journal of Public Economics,* 4, 211-226.

Guttman, Joel, 1978, Understanding Collective Action: Matching Behavior, *American Economic Review,* 68, 251-255.

Guttman, Joel, 1987, A Non-Cournot Model of Voluntary Collective Action, *Economica,* 54, 1-19.

Hamilton, B., 1975, Zoning and Property Taxation in a System of Local Governments, *Urban Studies,* 12, 205-211.

Hamilton, B., 1976, Capitalization of Intrajurisdictional Differences in Local Tax Prices, *American Economic Review,* 66, 743-753.

Hamilton, Bruce, 1983, A Review: Is the Property Tax a Benefit Tax?, in *Local Provision of Public Services: The Tiebout Model After Twenty-Five Years,* George Zodrow, ed., New York, Academic Press, 85-108.

Hamilton, James, 1994, *Time Series Analysis.* Princeton, NJ: Princeton University Press.

Hanemann, W. Michael, 1984, Welfare Evaluations in Contingent Valuation Experiments with Discrete Responses, *American Journal of Agricultural Economics,* 66, 332-341.

Hanemann, Michael W., 1994, Valuing the Environment through Contingent Valuation, *Journal of Economic Perspectives,* 8, 19-43.

Harberger, Arnold, C., 1972, The Opportunity Cost of Public Investment Financed by Borrowing, in *Cost-Benefit Analysis*, R. Layard, ed, Penguin, 303-310.

Harbaugh, William, 1998a, What Do Donations Buy? A Model of Philanthropy Based on Prestige and Warm Glow, *Journal of Public Economics*, 67, 269-284.

Harbaugh, William, 1998b, The Prestige Motive for Making Charitable Transfers, *AEA Papers and Proceedings*, 88, 277-282.

Hausman, J.A., 1993, *Contingent Valuation: A Critical Assessment*, Amsterdam: North Holland.

Hayashi, M., and R. Boadway, 2001, An Empirical Analysis of Intergovernmental Tax Interaction: The Case of Business Income Taxes in Canada, *Canadian Journal of Economics,* 34, 481-503.

Head, J. G., 1962, Public Goods and Public Policy, *Public Finance*, 17, 197-219.

Heinberg, J. D., and Oates, W. E., 1970, The Incidence of Differential Property Taxes on Urban Housing Values: A Comment and Some Further Evidence, *NationalTax Journal*, 23, pp . 92-98.

Helsely, Robert W., and William C. Strange, 1998, Private Government, Journal of Public Economics, 69, 281-304.

Henderson, J. Vernon, 1979, Theories of Group, Jurisdiction, and City Size, in *Current Issues in Urban Economics*, P. Mieszkowski and M. Strazheim, eds. Baltimore: The Johns Hopkins Press, 235-269.

Henderson, J. Vernon, 1985, The Tiebout Model: Bring Back the Entrepreneurs, *Journal of Political Economy*, 93, 248-264.

Henderson, J. Vernon, and A. Mitra, 1996, The New Urban Landscape: Developers and Edge Cities, *Regiona Science and Urban Economics,* 26, 613-643.

Henderson, J. Vernon, and J.F. Thisse, 2001, On Strategic Community Development, *Journal of Political Economy,* 109, 546-569.

Herriges, Joseph A., Catherine Kling L. , and Daniel Phaneuf, 2004, What's the Use? Welfare Estimates from Revealed Preference Models When Weak Complementarity Does Not Hold, *Journal of Environmental Economics and Management,* 47, 55-70.

Heyndels, B., and J. Vuchelen, 1998, Tax Mimicking Among Belgian Municipalities, *National Tax Journal,* 51, 89-101.

Hines, James, 2000, What is Benefit Taxation?, *Journal of Public Economics,* 75, 483-492.

Hirschman, Albert, 1970, *Exit, Voice, and Loyalty*, Cambridge: Harvard University Press.

Hochman, Harold M., and James Rodgers, 1969, Optimal Pareto Redistribution, *American Economic Review*, 59, 542 - 557.

Hochman, Harrold M., and James D. Rodgers, 1973, Utility Interdependence and Income Transfers Through Charity, in *Transfers in an Urbanized Economy,* K. E. Boulding et. al., eds., Belmont.

Hoel, Michael, 2004, Interregional Interactions and Population Mobility, *Journal of Economic Behavior and Organization*, 55, 419-433.

Hoel, M. and P. Shapiro, 2003, Population Mobility and Transboundary Environmental Problems, *Journal of Public Economics*, 87, 1013–1024.

Holtz-Eakin, Douglas, 1994, Public-Sector Capital and the Productivity Puzzle, *The Review of Economics and Statistics*, vol. 76, no.1, 12-21.

Holtz-Eakin, Douglas, and Mary Lovely, 1996, Scale Economies, Returns to Variety, and the Productivity of Public Infrastructure, *Regional Science and Urban Economics*, 26, 105-123.

Holtz-Eakin, Douglas, and A. E. Schwartz, 1995, Infrastructure in a Structural Model of Economic Growth, *Regional Science and Urban Economics*, 25, 131-151.

Hori, H, 1975, Revealed Preferences for Public Goods, *American Economic Review*, 65, 978 - 991.

Horowitz, J. and K. McConnell, 2002, A Review of WTA/WTP Studies, *Journal of Environmental Economics and Management,* 44, 426-447.

Houser, Daniel, and Robert Kurzban, 2002, Revisiting Kindness and Confusion in Public Goods Experiments, *American Economic Review*, 92, 1062-1069.

Howe, C. W., B. J. Lee, and Lynne Bennett, 1994, Design and Analysis of Contingent Valuation Surveys Using the Nested Tobit Model, *The Review of Economics and Statistics*, 385-389.

Hoyt, William H., 1991, Competitive Jurisdictions, Congestion, and the Henry George Theorem: When Should Property Be Taxed Instead of Land, *Regional Science And Urban Economics*, 21, 351-370

Hoyt, W., 2001, Tax Policy Coordination, Vertical Externalities, and Optimal Taxation in a System of Hierarchical Governments, *Journal of Urban Economics,* 50, 491-516.

Hoyt, W., and S. Rosenthal, 1997, Household Location and Tiebout: Do Families Sort According to Preferences for Locational Amenities?, *Journal of Urban Economics,* 42, 159-178.

Hurwicz, Leonid, 1972, On Informationally Decentralized Systems, in *Decisions and Organizations: A Volume in Honor of Jacob Marschak*, C. McGuire and R. Radner, eds., North Holland: Amsterdam, 297-336.

Hurwicz, Leonid, 1973, The Design of Mechanisms for Resource Allocation Problems, *American Economic Review,* 63, 1-30.

Hurwicz, Leonid, 1979a, On Allocations Attainable Through Nash Equilibria, in *Aggregation and Revelation of Preferences,* J. J. Laffont, ed., North Holland: Amsterdam, 397-419.

Hurwicz, Leonid, 1979b, Outcome Functions Yielding Walrasian and Lindahl Allocations as Nash Equilibrium Points, *Review of Economic Studies,* 217-225.

Hulten, Charles, and Robert Schwab, 1984, Regional Productivity Growth in US Manufacturing: 1951-1978, *American Economic Review*, vol. 74 no. 1, 152-162.

Hulten, Charles, and Robert Schwab, 1991, Public Capital Formation and the Growth of Regional Manufacturing Industries, *National Tax Journal*, XLIV no. 4, 121-134.

Ihori, Toshihiro, 1992, Impure Public Goods and Transfers in a Three Agent Model, *Journal of Public Economics*, 48, 385 - 401.

Ihori, Toshihiro, 1994, Immiserizing Growth with Interregional Externalities of Public Goods, *Regional Science And Urban Economics*, 24, 485-496.

Ihori, Toshihiro, 1996, International Public Goods and Contribution Productivity Differentials, *Journal of Public Economics*, 61, 139 - 154.

Ihori, Toshihiro, 2001, Public Good Contributions and Capital Accumulation, mimeo.

Ihori, Toshihiro, and Hiroki Kondo, 2001, Public Capital Productivity in Japan, *Public Finance and Management,* 1, 161-182.

Inman, Robert, 1987, Markets, Governments, and the "New" Political Economy, in *Handbook of Public Economics vol 2,* A. Auerbach and M. Feldstein, eds., Amsterdam: North-Holland, 647-777.

Isaac, R. Mark, Kenneth F. McCue, and Charles R. Plott, 1985, Public Goods Provision in an Experimental Environment, *Journal of Public Economics*, 26, 51-74.

Isaac, R., D. Schmidtz, and M. Walker, 1988, The Assurance Problem in a Laboratory Market. *Public Choice*, 62, 217–236.

Isaac, R. Mark and James H. Walker, 1988a, Group Size Effects in Public Goods Provision: The Voluntary Contribution Mechanism, *Quarterly Journal of Economics*, 53, 179 - 200.

Isaac, R. Mark and James H. Walker, 1988b, Communication and Free-riding Behavior: The Voluntary Contribution Mechanism, *Economic Inquiry*, 27, 585 - 608.

Isaac, R. Mark, James M. Walker, and S. Thomas, 1984, Divergent Evidence on Free Riding: An Experimental Environment, *Public Choice*, 43, 113-149.

Isaac, R. Mark, James M. Walker, and Arlington W. Williams, 1994, Group Size and the Voluntary Provision of Public Goods: Experimental Evidence Utilizing Large Groups, *Journal of Public Economics*, 54, 1-36.

Iwamoto, Yasushi, 1990, An Evaluation of Public Investment Policy in Postwar Japan, *Economic Review*, 41(3), 250-261 (in Japanese).

Jackson, Matthew, and Herve Moulin, 1993, Implementing a Public Project and Distributing Its Cost, *Journal of Economic Theory*, 57, 125-140.

Jensen, Robert T., 2004, Do Private Transfers 'Displace' the Benefits of Public Transfers? Evidence From South Africa, *Journal of Public Economics*, 88, 89-112.

Jin, J., and H. Zou, 2002, How Does Fiscal Decentralization Affect the Aggregate, national, and Subnational Government Size?, *Journal of Urban Economics*, 52, 270-293.

Johansen, Leif, 1963, Some Notes on the Lindahl Theory of Determination of Public Expenditures, *International Economic Review*, 4, 346-358.

Johansen, Leif, 1977, The Theory of Public Goods: Misplaced Emphasis?, *Journal of Public Economics*, 7, 147-152.

Joulfaian, David, 1991, Charitable Bequests and Estate Taxes, *National Tax Journal,* 44, 169-180.

Joulfaian, David, 2000, Estate Taxes and Charitable Bequests by the Wealthy, *National Tax Journal*, 53, 743 - 763.

Justman, M., J.F. Thisse, and T. van Ypersele, 2002, Taking the Bite out of Fiscal Competition, *Journal of Urban Economics,* 52, 294-315.

Kaizuka, Keimei, 1965, Public Goods and Decentralization of Production, *Review of Economic Studies*, vol. 47, no. 2, 118 – 120.

Kaneko, M. 1977, The Ratio Equilibrium and a Voting Game in a Public Goods Economy, *Journal of Economic Theory*, 16, 123 - 136.

Kaplow, Louis, 1996, A Note on the Optimal Supply of Public Goods and the Distortionary Cost of Taxation, *National Tax Journal,* 49, 513-533.

Kaplow, Louis, 1998, The Optimal Supply of Public Goods and the Distortionary Cost of Taxation, *National Tax Journal*, 51, 117-125.

Kay, J.A., 1972, Social Discount Rates, *Journal of Public Economics*, 1, 359-378.

Keen, M. and Marchand, M. 1997, Fiscal Competition and the Pattern of Public Spending, *Journal of Public Economics,* 66, 33-53.

Keen, M. and C. Kotsogiannis, 2002, Does Federalism Lead to Excessively High Taxes, *American Economic Review*, 92, 363-370.

Kehoe, P. J. 1989, Policy Cooperation Among Benevolent Governments May Be Undesirable, *Review of Economic Studies,* 56, 289-296.

Keser, Claudia, 1996, Voluntary Contributions to a Public Good When Partial Contribution is a Dominant Strategy, *Economics Letters,* 50, 359-366.

Khanna, Jyoti, John Posnett, Todd Sandler, 1995, Charity Donations in the UK: New Evidence Based on Panel Data, *Journal of Public Economics*, 56, 257-272.

Kim, Oliver and Mark Walker, 1984, The Free Rider Problem: Experimental evidence, *Public Choice*, 43, 3-24.

King, A.T., 1977, Estimating Property Tax Capitalization: A Critical Comment, *Journal of Political Economy*, 85, 425-431.

King, Mervyn A., 1980, Savings and Taxation, in *Public Policy and the Tax System,* ed. G.A. Hughes and G. M. Head, London: Allen and Unwin.

King, Mervyn A., 1986, A Pigovian Rule for the Optimum Provision of Public Goods, *Journal of Public Economics*, 30, 273-291.

Kingma, Bruce, 1989, An Accurate Measurement of the Crowd-out Effect, Income Effect, and Price Effect for Charitable Contributions, *Journal of Political Economy*, 97, 1197-1207.

Kingma, Bruce, and Robert McCleland, 1995, Public Radio Stations are Really Really Not Public Goods: Charitable Contributions and Impure Altruism, *Annals of Public and Cooperative Economics,* 66, 65-76.

Kirchsteiger, Georg, and Clemens Puppe, 1997, On the Possibility of Efficient Private Provision of Public Goods Through Government Subsidies, *Journal of Public Economics,* 66, 489-504.

Kitasaka, Shin-ichi. 1999. Some Tests of the Efficiency of Public Capital Provision: Euler Equation Approach, *JCER Economic Journal.* 39: pp. 76-96 (in Japanese).

Klein, Daniel, 1990, The Voluntary Provision of Public Goods? The Turnpike Companies of Early America, *Economic Inquiry*, 28, 788 - 812.

Kocherlakota, N., and K. Yi, 1996, A Simple Time Series Test of Endogenous vs. Exogenous Growth Models: An Application to the United States, *Review of Economics and Statistics*, vol. 78, no. 1, 126 – 134.

Konrad, Kai, 1994, The Strategic Advantage of Being Poor: Private and Public Provision of Public Goods, *Economica*, 61, 79-92.

Kothenburger, Marko, 2004, Tax Competition in a Fiscal Union with Decentralized Leadership, *Journal of Urban Economics*, 55, 498-53.

Kramer, Gerald, 1973, On a Class of Equilibrium Conditions for Majority Rule, *Econometrica*, 41, 285-297.

Krelove, R., 1992a, Competitive Tax Theory in Open Economies, *Journal of Public Economics*, 48, 361-375.

Krelove, R. 1992b, Tax Exporting, *Canadian Journal of Economics*, 32, 324-453.

Krelove, R., 1993, The Persistence and Inefficiency of Property Tax Finance of Local Public Expenditures, *Journal of Public Economics*, 51, 415-435.

Kydland, Finn and Edward Prescott, 1977, Rules Rather than Discretion: The Inconsistency of optimal Plans, *Journal of Political Economy*, 85, 473-491.

Laffont, Jean-Jacques, and David Martimort, 2000, Mechanism Design with Collusion and Correlation, *Econometrica*, 68, 309-342.

Ledyard, John, 1995, Public Goods: A Survey of Experimental Research, in *Handbook of Experimental Game Theory*, J. Kagel and A. Roth, eds., Princeton: Princeton University Press.

Ledyard, John, and Thomas Palfrey, 1994, Voting and Lottery Drafts as Efficient Public Goods Mechanisms, *Review of Economic Studies*, 61, 327-355.

Ledyard, John, and Thomas Palfrey, 1999, A Characterization of Interim Efficiency with Public Goods, *Econometrica*, 67, 435-448.

Lee, K., 1991, Transaction Costs and Equilibrium Pricing of Congested Public Goods With Imperfect Information, *Journal of Public Economics*, 45, 337-362.

Lee, K. 1997, Tax Competition With Imperfectly Mobile Capital, *Journal Of Urban Economics*, 42, 222-242.

Lindahl, Erik, 1919, Just Taxation - a Positive Solution, in *Classics in the Theory of Public Finance*, R. A. Musgrave and A. T. Peacock, eds., Macmillan, London.

Lindsay, Lawrence, 1986, The Effect of the President's Tax Reform Proposal on Charitable Giving, *National Tax Journal*, 39, 1 - 12.

Lockwood, Ben, 2001, Tax Competition and Tax Co-ordination Under Destination and Origin Principles: A Synthesis, *Journal of Public Economics*, 81, 279-319.

Long, Stephen, 1977, Income Tax Effects on Donor Choice of Money and Time Contributions, *National Tax Journal*, 30, 207-212.

Lynde, Catherine, and J. Richmond, 1992, The Role of Public Capital in Production, *Review of Economics and Statistics*, vol. 74, no. 1, 37-44.

Lynde, Catherine, and J. Richmond, 1993, Public Capital and Total Factor Productivity, *International Economic Reviews*, vol. 34, no.2, 401 – 414.

Mailath, George, and Andrew Postlewaite, 1990, Asymmetric Information bargaining Problems with many Agents, *Review of Economic Studies,* 57, 351-367.

Maler, K. G., 1971, A Method of Estimating Social Benefits From Pollution Control, *Swedish Journal of Economics,* 73, 121-133.

Maler, K. G., 1974, *Environmental Economics: A Theoretical Inquiry*, Johns Hopkins University Press: Baltimore, for Resources for the Future.

Marchand Maurice and Pierre Pestieau, 1984, Discount Rates And Shadow Prices For Public Investment, *Journal of Public Economics*, 24, 153-169.

Marglin, Stephen, 1963, The Social Rate of Discount and The Optimal Rate of Investment, *Quarterly Journal of Economics*, 77, 95-111.

Margolis, Julius, 1955, A Comment on the Pure Theory of Public Expenditure, *Review of Economics and Statistics*, 37, 347-349.

Marlow, M., 1988, Fiscal Decentralization and Government Size, *Public Choice*, 56, 259–269.

Marwell, Gerald and Ruth E. Ames, 1979, Experiments on the Provision of Public Goods. I. Resources, Interest, Group Size and the Free-Rider Problem, *American Journal of Sociology*, 84,1135-1159.

Marwell, Gerald and Ruth E. Ames, 1980, Experiments on the Provision of Public Goods. II. Provision Points, Stakes, Experience, and the Free-Rider Problem, *American Journal of Sociology*, 85, 926-937.

Marwell, Gerald and Ruth E. Ames, 1981, Economists Free Ride, Does Anyone else? Experiments on the provision of public goods, IV, *Journal of Public Economics*, 15, 295-310.

Mas-Colell, Andreu and Joaquim Silvestre, 1989, Cost Share Equilibria: A Lindahl Approach, *Journal of Economic Theory*, 47, 239 - 256.

Mas-Colell, Andreu, Michael D. Whinston, and Jerry R. Green, 1995, *Microeconomic Theory*, Oxford: Oxford University Press.

Mayshar, Joram, 1990, On Measures of Excess Burden and Their Application, *Journal of Public Economics*, 41, 263 - 289.

Mayshar, Joram, 1991, On Measuring the Marginal Cost of Funds Analytically, *American Economic Review*, 81, 1329 - 1335.

McClelland, Robert, 1989, Voluntary Donations and Public Expenditures in a Federalist System: Comment and Correction, *American Economic Review*, 79, 1291 - 1296.

McClelland, Robert, and Mary F. Kokoski, 1994, Econometric Issues in the Analysis of Charitable Giving, *Public Finance Quarterly*, 22, 498 - 517.

McConnell, K., 1990, Models for Referendum Data: The Structure of Discrete Choice Models for Contingent Valuation, *Journal of Environmental Economics and Management,* 18, 19-34.

McFadden, D., 1994, Contingent Valuation and Social Choice, *American Journal of Agricultural Economics,* 76, 689-708.

McGuire, Martin, 1972, Private Good Clubs and Public Good Clubs: Economic Models of Group Formation, *Swedish Journal of Economics*, 84-99.

McGuire, Martin, 1974a, Group Size, Group Homogeneity, and the Aggregate Provision of a Pure Public Good under Cournot Behavior, *Public Choice*, 18, 107-124.

McGuire, Martin, 1974b, Group Segregation and Optimal Jurisdictions, *Journal of Political Economy*, 82, 112-132.

McGuire, Martin C. 1991, Group Composition, Collective Consumption, and Collaborative Production, *American Economic Review*, 81, 1391-1407.

McKelvey, 1979, General Conditions for Global Intransitivities in Formal Voting Models, *Econometrica*, 47, 1085-1111.

McMillan W., and D. Smyth, 1994, A Multivariate Time Series Analysis of the United States Aggregate Production Function, *Empirical Economics*, 19, 659-673.

Meade, James E., 1952, External Economies and Diseconomies in a Competitive Situation, *Economic Journal*, 62, 54 - 67.

Meadows, G.R., 1976, Taxes, Spending and Property Values: A Comment and Further Results, *Journal of Political Economy*, 84, 869-880.

Menchik, P. and B. Weisbrod. 1987, Volunteer Labor Supply, *Journal of Public Economics* 32, 159-183.

Mera, Koichi, 1973, Regional Production Functions and Social Overhead Capital: An Analysis of the Japanese Case, *Regional and Urban Economics*, 3, 157-186.

Mieszkowski, Peter, and George R. Zodrow, 1989, Taxation and the Tiebout Model: The Differential Effects of Head Taxes, Taxes on Land Rents, and Property Taxes, *Journal of Economic Literature,* XXVII, 1098-1146.

Mintz, J. and Tulkens, H. 1986, Commodity Tax Competition Between Members States of a Federation: Equilibrium and Efficiency, *Journal of Public Economics,* 29, 133-172.

Mirrlees, James, 1971, An Exploration in the Theory of Optimal Income Taxation, *Review of Economic Studies*, 38, 175 - 208.

Mirrlees, James, 1986, The Theory of Optimal Taxation, in *The Handbook of Mathematical Economics, Volume III,* Kenneth J. Arrow and Michael D. Intrilogator, eds., Amsterdam: North Holland, 1197-1250.

Mitchell, Robert, and Richard Carson, 1989, *Using Surveys to Value Public Goods: The Contingent Valuation Method,* Washington D.C.: Resources for the Future.

Mitsui, Kiyoshi and Kiyoshi Ohta, 1995, Productivity of Public Capital and Public Finance. *Nihon Hyoron Sha* (in Japanese).

Mitsui, K. and Sato, M. 2001, Ex Ante Free Mobility, Ex Post Immobility, and Time Consistency in a Federal System, *Journal of Public Economics,* 82, 445-460.

Moore, John, and Rafael Repullo, 1988, Subgame Perfect Implementation, *Econometrica,* 56, 1191-1220.

Moulin, Herve, 1979, Dominance Solvable Voting Schemes, *Econometrica,* 47, 1337-1351.

Morrison, Catherine, J. and Amy Ellen Schwartz, 1996, State Infrastructure and Productive Performance, *American Economic Review*, vol. 86, no. 5, 1095-1111.

Mueller, Dennis C., 1989, *Public Choice II,* Cambridge: Cambridge University Press.

Mueller, Dennis C., 1997, *Perspective on Public Choice: A Handbook*, Cambridge: Cambridge University Press.

Muench, Thomas, 1972, The Core and the Lindahl Equilibrium of an Economy with a Public Good: An Example, *Journal of Economic Theory*, 4, 241-255.

Muench, Thomas, and Mark Walker, 1983a, Are Groves-Ledyard Equilibria Attainable?, *Review of Economic Studies*, 50, 393-396.

Muench, Thomas, and Mark Walker, 1983b, Identifying the Free Rider Problem, in *Aggregation and Revelation of Preferences,* edited by Jean-Jacques Laffont, Amsterdam: North Holland, 61-90.

Munnell, A., 1990a, Why Has Productivity Growth Declined? Productivity and Public Investment, *New England Economic Review*, January/February, 3-22.

Munnell, A., 1990b, How Does Public Infrastructure Affect Regional Economic Performance? *New England Economic Review*, September/October, 11-32.

Munnell, A., 1992, Infrastructure Investment and Economic Growth, *Journal of Economic Perspectives*, vol. 6, no. 4, 189-198.

Murdoch, James, and Todd Sandler, 1984, Complementarity, Free Riding, and the Military Expenditures of NATO Allies, *Journal of Public Economics,* 25, 83-101.

Murdoch, James, and Todd Sandler, 1997, The Voluntary Provision of a Pure Public Good: The Case of Reduced CFC Emissions and the Montreal Protocol, *Journal of Public Economics*, 63, 331-349.

Musgrave, Richard, 1939, The Voluntary Exchange Theory of Public Expenditure, *Quarterly Journal of Economics*, 53, 213-217.

Musgrave, Richard, 1959, *The Theory of Public Finance*, New York: McGraw-Hill.

Musgrave, Richard, 1969, Theories of Fiscal Federalism, *Public Finance*, 24, 521-532.

Musgrave, Richard, and Alan Peacock, 1958, *Classics in the Theory of Public Finance*, London: Macmillan.

Myers,G. 1990, Optimality, Free Mobility, and the Regional Authority in a Federation, *Journal of Public Economics*, 43, 107-121.

Nadiri, M. Ishaq and Theofanis P. Mamuneas, 1994, The Effects of Public Infrastructure and R&D Capital on the Cost Structure and Performance of U.S. Manufacturing Industries, *Review of Economics and Statistics*, vol. 76, no. 1, 22-37.

Neill, J. R., 1988, Another Theorem on Using Market Demands to Determine Willingness to Pay for Non-traded Goods, *Journal of Environmental and Resource Economics and Management,* 15, 224 -232.

Nelson, Charles, and Charles Plott, 1982, Trends and Random Walks in Macro-economics Time Series: Some Evidence and Implications, *Journal of Monetary Economics*, 10, 139-162.

Nelson, M., 1986, An Empirical Analysis of State and Local Tax Structure in the Context of the Leviathan Model of Government, *Public Choice*, 49, 283-294.

Nelson, M., 1987, Searching for Leviathan: Comment and Extension, *American Economic Review*, 77, 198–204.

Nett, Lorenz, and Wolfgang Peters, 1993, The Uniqueness of the Subscription Equilibrium with Endogenous Labor Supply, *Economics Letters*, 24, 139-142.

Ng, Yew-Kwang, 2000, The Optimal Size of Public Spending and the Distortionary Cost of Taxation, *National Tax Journal*, 53, 253-272.

Niemi, R., 1969, Majority Decision-Making with Partial Unidimensionality, *American Political Science Review*, 63, 488-497.

Niemi R., and H.F. Weisberg, 1968, A Mathematical Solution for the Probability of the Paradox of Voting, *Behavioral Science*, 13, 317-323.

Nunes, Paolo, and Erik Schokkaert, 2003, Identifying the Warm Glow Effect in Contingent Valuation, *Journal of Environmental Economics and Management*, 45, 231-245.

Oakland, W., 1972, Congestion, Public Goods, and Welfare, *Journal of Public Economics*, 1, 339-357.

Oates, W.E ., 1969, The Effect of Property Taxes and Local Public Spending on Property Values : An Empirical Study of Tax Capitalization and the Tiebout Hypothesis, *Journal of Political Economy*, 77, pp. 957-971.

Oates, W.E., 1972, *Fiscal Federalism*, New York: Harcourt Brace.

Oates, W. E., 1973, The Effects of Property Taxes and Local Public Spending on Property Values: A Reply and Further Results, *Journal of Political Economy*, 81, 1004-1008 .

Oates, W.E., 1985, Searching for Leviathan: An Empirical Study, *American Economic Review*, 75, 748-757.

Oates, W.E., 1989, Searching for Leviathan: A Reply and Some Further Reflections, *American Economic Review*, 79, 578-583.

Oates, W., 1999, An Essay of Fiscal Federalism, *Journal of Economic Literature*, 37, 1120-1149.

Oates, W. E. and Schwab, R. M. 1988, Economic Competition Among Jurisdictions: Efficiency Enhancing or Distortion Inducing? *Journal of Public Economics*, 35, 333-354.

Olson, Mancur, 1965, *The Logic of Collective Action*, Cambridge, MA: Harvard University Press.

O'Neil C. J., R. S. Steinberg, and G. R. Thompson, 1996, Reassessing the Tax-Favored Status of the Charitable Deduction for Gifts of Appreciated Assets, *National Tax Journal*, 49, 215-231.

O'Reilly, Terrance, 1995, Observable Preferences for Public Goods: A Note on the Incentive Compatibility of Inferring Demand for Public Goods from Private Goods Demand, *Journal of Public Economics*, 58, 309-317.

Otto, Glenn D., and Graham M. Voss, 1998, Is Public Capital Provision Efficient?, *Journal of Monetary Economics*, 42, 47 - 66.

Palfrey, Thomas, Rosenthal, Howard, 1984, Participation and the Provision of Discrete Public Goods: A Strategic Analysis, *Journal of Public Economics*, 24, 171-193.

Palfrey, Thomas, and Howard Rosenthal, 1988, Private Incentives in Social Dilemmas, The effects of Incomplete Information and Altruism, *Journal of Public Economics*, 35, 309-332.

Palfrey, Thomas, and Jeffrey Prisbrey, 1996, Altruism, Reputation and Noise in Linear Public Goods Experiments, *Journal of Public Economics*, 61, 409-427.

Palfrey, Thomas, and Jeffrey Prisbrey, 1997, Anomalous Behavior in Public Goods Experiments: How Much and Why?, *American Economic Review*, 87, 829-845.

Parry, Ian W. H., 2003, How Large are the Welfare Costs of Tax Competition, *Journal of Urban Economics,* 54, 39-60.

Parsons, George, Paul Jakus, Ted Tomasi, 1999, A Comparison of Welfare Estimates From Four Models for Linking Seasonal Recreational Trips to Multinomial Logit Models of Site Choice, *Journal of Environmental Economics and Management,* 38, 143-157.

Paul, Catherine J. Morrison, V. Eldon Ball, Ronald G. Felthoven, and Richard Nehring, 2001, Public Infrastructure Impacts on U.S. Agricultural Production: A State-Level Panel Analysis of Costs and Netput Composition, *Public Finance and Management*, 1, 183-213.

Pauly, Mark V., 1967, Clubs, Commonality, and the Core: An Integration of Game Theory and the Theory of Public Goods, *Economica*, 34, 314-324.

Pauly, Mark V., 1970a, Optimality, "Public" Goods, and Local Governments: A General Theoretical Analysis, *Journal of Political Economy*, 78, 572-585.

Pauly, Mark V., 1970b, Cores and Clubs, *Public Choice,* 9, 53-65.

Payne A. Abigail, 1998, Does the Government Crowd-Out Private Donations? New Evidence From a Sample of Non-Profit Firms, *Journal of Public Economics,* 63, 323-45.

Peltzman, Sam, 1973, The Effect of Government Subsidies-in-Kind on Private Expenditures, *Journal of Political Economy*, 81, 1 - 27.

Pereira, Alfredo, 2000, Is All Public Capital Created Equal?, *Review of Economics and Statistics,* 82, 513-518.

Pereira, Alfredo, 2001, Public Investment and Private Sector Performance: International Evidence, *Public Finance and Management*, 1, 261-277.

Pereira, Alfredo, and J.M. Andraz, 2003, On the Impact of Public Investment on the Performance of U.S. Industries, *Public Finance Review*, 31, 66-90.

Pereira, Alfredo, and Rafael Flores de Frutos, 1995, Public Capital Accumulation and Private Sector Performance in the US, mimeo, The College of William and Mary.

Pereira, Alfredo, and Norman Morin, 1996, Public Investment and Private Sector Performance: International Evidence, mimeo, The College of William and Mary.

Persson, Torsten and Guido Tabellini, 1990, *Macroeconomic Policy, Credibility, and Politics,* Chur, Switzerland: Harwood Academic Publishers.

Pestieau, Pierre, 1974, "Optimal Taxation and Discount Rate for Public Investment in a Growth Setting," *Journal of Public Economics*, 3, pp. 217 - 235.

Pestieau, Pierre, 1975, The Role of Taxation in the Determination of the Social Discount Rate, *International Economic Review*, 16, 362-368.

Pestieau, Pierre, 1983, Fiscal Mobility and Local Public Goods: A Survey of the Empirical and Theoretical Studies of the Tiebout Model, in *Location Analysis of Public Facilities*, J.F. Thisse and H.G. Zoller, eds., Amsterdam: North Holland, 11-42.

Pigou, Arthur C., 1928, *A Study in Public Finance*, London: Macmillan.

Pigou, Arthur C., 1947, *A Study in Public Finance*, third edition, London: Macmillan.

Pines, D., 1991, Tiebout Without Politics, *Regional Science and Urban Economics*, 21, 469-489.

Pirttila, Jukka, and Matti Tuomala, 2001, On optimal Non-Linear Taxation and Public Good Provision in an Overlapping Generations Economy, *Journal of Public Economics*, 79, 485 - 501.

Plott, Charles, R., 1967, A Notion of Equilibrium and its Possibility Under Majority Rule, *American Economic Review*, 57, 787-806.

Plott, Charles, R., 1983, Externalities and Corrective Policies in Experimental Markets, *Economic Journal*, 93, 106 - 127.

Pollakowski, H .O., 1973, The Effects of Property Taxes and Local Public Spending on Property Values: A Comment and Further Results, *Journal of Political Economy*, 81, 994-1004.

Posnett, J. and T. Sandler, 1989, Demand for Charity Donations in Private Non-Profit Markets, *Journal of Public Economics*, 40, 187-200.

Prescott, E.C., and M. Visscher, 1977, Sequential Location Among Firms with Foresight, *The Bell Journal of Economics*, 8, 378-393.

Ramsey, D., 1969, On the Social Rate of Discount: Comment, *American Economic Review*, 59, 919-924.

Randall, Alan, Berry C. Ives, and Clyde Eastman, 1974, Bidding Games for Valuation of Aesthetic Environmental Improvements, *Journal of Environmental Economics and Management,* 1, 132-149.

Randolph W C, 1995, Dynamic Income, Progressive Taxes, and the Timing of Charitable Contributions. *Journal of Political Economy,* 103, 709-38.

Ratner, J, 1983, Government Capital and the Production Function for US Private Output, *Economics Letters*, 13, 213-217.

Reece, William S., 1979, Charitable Contributions: New Evidence on Household Behavior, *American Economic Review*, 69, 142 - 151.

Reece, William S., and Kimberly D. Zieschang, 1985, Consistent Estimation of the Impact of Tax Deductibility on the Level of Charitable Contributions, *Econometrica*, 53, 271 - 292.

Reid, G., 1990, The Many Faces of Tiebout Bias in Local Education Demand Parameter Estimates, *Journal of Urban Economics,* 27, 232-254.

Ribar, David C., and Mark O. Wilhelm, 1995, Charitable Contributions to International Relief and Development, *National Tax Journal*, 48, 229-244.

Ribar, David C., and Mark O. Wilhelm, 2002, Altruistic and Joy-of-Giving Motivations in Charitable Behavior, *Journal of Political Economy*, 110, 425-457.

Ricketts, Robert C., and Peter H. Westfall, 1993, New Evidence on the Price Elasticity of Charitable Contributions, *Journal of the American Taxation Association*, 15, 1-25.

Richter, D.K., 1982, Weakly Democratic Regular Tax Equilibria in a Local Public Goods Economy With Perfect Consumer Mobility, *Journal of Economic Theory*, 27, 137-162.

Rioja, Felix K., 1999, Productiveness and Welfare Implications of Public Infrastructure: A dynamic two-sector general equilibrium analysis, *Journal of Development Economics*, 58, 387-404.

Rioja, Felix K., 2002, Filling Potholes: Macroeconomic Effects of Maintenance vs. New Investments in Public Infrastructure, forthcoming in *Journal of Public Economics*.

Rob, Rafael, 1982, Asymptotic Efficiency of the Demand Revealing Mechanism, *Journal of Economic Theory*, 28, 207-220.

Rob, Rafael, 1989, Pollution Claims Settlements Under Private Information, *Journal of Economic Theory*, 47, 307-333.

Roberts, Donald, 1974, The Lindahl Solution for Economies with Public Goods, *Journal of Public Economics*, 3, 23-42.

Roberts, John, 1976, The Incentives for Correct Revelation of Preferences and the Number of Consumers, *Journal of Public Economics*, 6, 359-374.

Roberts, J., 1992, A Comment on the Many Faces of Tiebout Bias, *Journal of Urban Economics*, 29, 45-51.

Roberts, Russell, 1984, A Positive Model of Private Charity and Public Transfers, *Journal of Political Economy*, 92, 136 - 148.

Roberts, Russell, 1987, Financing Public Goods, *Journal of Political Economy*, 93, 420 - 437.

Robinson, John R., 1990, Estimates of the Price Elasticity of Charitable Giving: A Reappraisal Using 1985 Itemizer and Nonitemizer Charitable Deduction Data, *Journal of the American Taxation Association*, 12, 39 - 59.

Romano, Richard, and Huseyin Yildirim, 2001, Why Charities Announce Donations: A Positive Perspective, *Journal of Public Economics*, 81, 423-447.

Rose-Ackerman, Susan, 1982, Charitable Giving and Excessive Fundraising, *Quarterly Journal of Economics*, XCVII, 193-208.

Rose-Ackerman, Susan, 1983, Beyond Tiebout: Modeling the Political Economy of Local Government, in *Local Provision of Public Services: The Tiebout Model After Twenty-Five Years,* G. Zodrow, ed., New York: Academic Press, 55-84.

Rose-Ackerman, Susan, 1987, Ideals versus Dollars: Donors, Charity Managers, and Government Grants, *Journal of Political Economy*, 95, 810-821.

Rose-Ackerman Susan, 1996, Altruism, Nonprofits, and Economic Theory, *Journal of Economic Literature,* 34, 701-28.

Rosen, Harvey, 2004, *Public Finance*, New York: McGraw-Hill.

Rosen, H., and D. Fullerton, 1977, A Note on Local Tax Rates, Public Benefit Levels, and Property Values, *Journal of Political Economy*, 85, 433-440.

Rothenberg, J., 1977, Endogenous City-Suburb Governmental Rivalry Through Household Location, in *The Political Economy of Fiscal Federalism*, W. Oates, ed., Lexington.

Rubinfeld, Daniel L., 1987, The Economics of the Local Public Sector, in *Handbook of Public Economics vol 2*, A. Auerbach and M. Feldstein, eds., Amsterdam: North-Holland, 571-645.

Rubinfeld, Daniel L., 1994, Comments (on Chapter 4), in *Modern Public Finance*, J Quigley and E. Smolensky, eds., Cambridge: Harvard University Press, 120-125.

Rubinfeld, D.L.; P. Shapiro and J. Roberts, 1987, Tiebout Bias and the Demand for Local Public Schooling, *Review of Economics and Statistics*, 69, 426-37.

Rubinstein, Ariel, 1979, Equilibrium in Supergames with an Overtaking Criterion, *Journal of Economic Theory,* 21, 1-9.

Saijo, T, and H. Nakamura, 1995, The Spite Dilemma in Voluntary Contribution Mechanism Experiments, *Journal of Conflict Resolution*, 39, 535-560.

Samples, Karl, and James Hollyer, 1990, Contingent Valuation of Wildlife Resources in the Presence of Substitutes and Complements, in *Economic Valuation of Natural Resources: Issues, Theory and Applications,* Rebecca Johnson and Gary Johnson, eds., Boulder: Westview Press, 177-192.

Samuelson, Paul A., 1954, The Pure Theory of Public Expenditure, *Review of Economics and Statistics*, 36, 389-389.

Samuelson, Paul A., 1955, Diagrammatic Exposition of a Theory of Public Expenditure, *Review of Economics and Statistics*, 37, 350-356.

Samuelson, Paul A., 1958, Aspects of Public Expenditure Theories, *Review of Economics and Statistics*, 40, 332-338.

Samuelson, Paul A., 1969, Pure Theory of Public Expenditures and Taxation, in *Public Economics*, J. Margolis and H. Guitton, eds, London: Macmillan.

Sandler, Todd, and James Murdoch, 1990, Nash-Cournot or Lindahl Behavior? An Empirical Test for the NATO Allies, *Quarterly Journal of Economics*, 105, 875-894.

Sandler, Todd, and John T. Tschirhart, 1980, The Economic Theory of Clubs: An Evaluative Survey, *Journal of Economic Literature,* 18, 1481-1521.

Sandler, Todd, and John T. Tschirhart, 1984, Mixed Clubs: Further Observation, *Journal of Public Economics*, 23, 381-389.

Sandmo, Agnar, 1973, Public Goods and the Technology of Consumption, *Review of Economic Studies,* 40, 517 -528.

Sandmo, Agnar, 1980, Anomaly and Stability in the Theory of Externalities, *Quarterly Journal of Economics*, 94, 799-807.

Sandmo, Agnar, 1998, Redistribution and the Marginal Cost of Funds, *Journal of Public Economics,* 70, 365-382.

Sandmo, Agnar and Jacques H. Dreze, 1971, Discount Rates for Public Investment in Closed and Open Economies, *Economica*, 38, 395-412.

Sargent, Thomas J., 1987, *Macroeconomic Theory,* New York: Academic Press.

Satterthwaite, M. 1975, Strategy-Proofness and Arrow's Conditions: Existence and Correspondence Theorems for Voting Procedures and Social Welfare Functions, *Journal of Economic Theory,* 10, 187-217.

Scafuri, Alan, 1988, On Consistency of Conjectures in the Private Provision of Public Goods, *Journal of Public Economics,* 37, 395 - 398.

Schell, Karl, 1967, A Model of Inventive Activity and Capital Accumulation, in ed. Karl Schell, *Essays on the Theory of Optimal Economic Growth,* Cambridge, MA: MIT Press.

Schiff, Jerald, 1985, Does Government Spending Crowd Out Charitable Contributions?, *National Tax Journal* 38, 535-546.

Schiff, Jerald, 1990, *Charitable Giving and Government Policy,* Greenwood Press, New York.

Schiff, Jerald, and Burton Weisbrod, 1991, Competition Between For-Profit and Non-Profit Organizations in Commercial Markets, *Annals of Public and Cooperative Economics,* 62,619 - 639.

Schneider, Friedrich and Werner W. Pommerehne, 1981, Free Riding and Collective Action: An Experiment in Public Microeconomics, *Quarterly Journal of Economics,* 96, 689-704.

Schofield, N., 1978, Instability of Simple Dynamic Games, *Review of Economic Studies,* 45, 575-594.

Schwartz, R. A., 1970, Personal Philanthropic Contributions, *Journal of Political Economy,* 78, 1264 - 1291.

Scotchmer, Suzanne, 1985a, Profit-Maximizing Clubs, *Journal of Public Economics,* 27, 25-45

Scotchmer, Suzanne, 1985b, Two-Tier Pricing of Shared Facilities in a Free-Entry Equilibrium, *Rand Journal of Economics,* 16, 456-472.

Scotchmer, Suzanne, 1986, Local Public Goods in an Equilibrium: How Pecuniary Externalities Matter, *Regional Science and Urban Economics,* 16, 463-481.

Scotchmer, Suzanne, 1994, Public Goods and the Invisible Hand, *Modern Public Finance,* eds. J Quigley and E. Smolensky, Cambridge: Harvard University Press, 93-119.

Scotchmer, Suzanne, 2002, Local Public Goods and Clubs, in *Handbook of Public Economics,* A. Auerbach and M. Feldstein, eds., Netherlands: Elsevier, 1998-2042.

Scotchmer, Suzanne , and Myrna Holtz Wooders, 1987, Competitive Equilibrium and the Core in Club Economics with Anonymous Crowding, *Journal of Public Economics,* 34, 159-173.

Sefton, Martin, and Richard Steinberg, 1996, Reward Structures in Public Good Experiments, *Journal of Public Economics,* 61, 263-287.

Seitz, H. 1994. Public Capital and Demand for Private Inputs, *Journal of Public Economics* 54, 287-307.

Shah, A. 1992, Dynamics of Public Infrastructure, Industrial Productivity and Profitability, *Review of Economics and Statistics,* Vol. 74, No. 1, 28-36.

Shibata, Hirofumi, 1971, A Bargaining Model of the Pure Theory of Public Expenditure, *Journal of Political Economy*, 79, 1-29.

Sinn, Hans Werner, 1997, The Selection Principle and Market Failure in Systems Competition, *Journal of Public Economics,* 66, 247-274.

Slemrod, Joel, 1989, Are Estimated Tax Elasticites Really Just Tax Evasion Elasticites? The Case of Charitable Contributions, *Review of Economics and Statistics,* 71, 517 - 522.

Slemrod, Joel, 1992, *Do Taxes Matter?,* Cambridge: MIT Press.

Slemrod, Joel, and Shlomo Yitzhaki, 1996, The Social Cost of Taxation and the Marginal Cost of Funds, *International Monetary Fund Staff Papers*, 43, 172-198.

Slemrod, Joel, and Shlomo Yitzhaki, 2001, Integrating Expenditure and Tax Decisions: The Marginal Cost of Funds and the Marginal Benefit of Projects, *National Tax Journal*, 54, 189-202.

Slutsky, S., 1977, A Characterization of Societies with Consistent Majority Decision, *Review of Economic Studies*, 44, 211-225.

Slutsky, S., 1979, Equilibrium with α-Majority Voting, *Econometrica,* 47, 1113-1125.

Smith, Adam, 1937, *The Wealth of Nations*, New York: Modern Library.

Smith, V. Kerry, and Yoshiaki Kaoru, 1990, Signal or Noise? Explaining the Variation in Recreation Benefit Studies, *American Journal of Agricultural Economics,* 72, 419-433.

Smith, V. Kerry, 2000, JEEM and Non-market Valuation: 1974-1998, *Journal of Environmental Economics and Management,* 39, 351-374.

Smith, Vernon L., 1976, Experimental Economics: Induced Value Theory, *American Economic Review*, 66, 274-279.

Smith, Vernon L., 1979, An Experimental Comparison of Three Public Good Decision Mechanisms, *Scandinavian Journal of Economics*, 198-211.

Smith, Vernon L., 1980, Experiments with a Decentralized Mechanism for Public Good Decisions, *American Economic Review*, 70, 584-599.

Smith, Vernon, 1982, Microeconomic Systems as an Experimental Science, *American Economic Review,* 72, 923-955

Smith, Vernon L. and James M. Walker, 1993, Monetary Rewards and Decision Cost in Experimental Economics, *Economic Inquiry*, XXXI, 245-264.

Smith, Vincent, Michael Kehoe, and Mary Cremer, 1995, The Private Provision of Public Goods: Altruism and Voluntary Giving, *Journal of Public Economics*, 58, 107-126.

Snow, Arthur, and Ronald S. Warren, 1996, The Marginal Welfare Cost of Public Funds: Theory and Estimates, *Journal of Public Economics*, 61, 289 - 305.

Sonnemans, Joep, Arthur Schram, and Theo Offerman, 1998, Public Good Provision and Public Bad Prevention: The Effect of Framing, *Journal of Economic Behavior and Organization*, 34, 143-161.

Sonstelie, J., and P. Portney, 1980, Gross Rents and Market Values: Testing the Implications of Tiebout's Hypothesis, *Journal of Urban Economics*, 5, 102-118.

Starrett, D., 1980, On the Method of Taxation and the Provision of Local Public Goods, *American Economic Review*, 70, 380-392.

Starrett, D., 1981, Land Value Capitalization in Local Public Finance, *Journal of Political Economy*, 89, 306-327.

Steinberg, Richard, 1987, Voluntary Donations and Public Expenditures in a Federalist System, *American Economic Review*, 77, 24 - 36.

Steinberg, Richard, 1990, Taxes and Giving: New Findings, *Voluntas*, 1, 61-79.

Steinberg, Richard, 1991, Does Government Spending Crowd Out Donations? Interpreting the Evidence, *Annals of Public and Cooperative Economics*, 62, 591-618.

Stiglitz, Joseph E., 1974, The Demand for Education in Public and Private School System, *Journal of Public Economics*, 53, 36-67.

Stiglitz, Joseph E., 1977, The Theory of Local Public Goods, in *The Economics of Public Services,* M. Feldstein and R. Inman, eds., London: Macmillan.

Stiglitz, Joseph E., 1983a, Public Goods in Open Economies with Heterogeneous Individuals, in *Location Analysis of Public Facilities*, eds. J.F. Thisse and H.G. Zoller, Amsterdam: North Holland, 55-78.

Stiglitz, Joseph E., 1983b, The Theory of Local Public Goods Twenty-Five Years After Tiebout: A Perspective, in *Local Provision of Public Services: The Tiebout Model After twenty-Five Years,* ed. George R. Zodrow, New York: Academic Press, 17-53.

Stiglitz, Joseph, and Partha Dasgupta, 1971, Differential Taxation, Public Goods, and Economic Efficiency, *Review of Economic Studies*, 38, no. 2, 151–174.

Stock, James, and Mark Watson, 1993, A Simple Estimator of Cointegrating Vectors in Higher Order Integrated Systems, *Econometrica*, 61, 783-820.

Strotz, Robert H., 1958, Two Propositions Related to Public Goods, *Review of Economics and Statistics*, 40, 329-331.

Stuart, Charles, 1984, Welfare Costs Per Dollar of Additional Tax Revenue in the United States, *American Economic Review*, 74, 352 - 362.

Sturm, J. and J. de Haan, 1995, Is Public Expenditure Really Productive? New Evidence for the USA and The Netherlands, *Economic Modeling*, 12, 60-72.

Sturm, J., J. Jakobs, and P. Groot, 1995, Productivity Impacts of Infrastructure Investment in the Netherlands: 1853-1913, SOM Research Report.

Sturm, Jan-Egbert, 2001, The Impact of Public Infrastructure Capital on the Private Sector of the Netherlands: An Application of the Symmetric Generalized McFadden Cost Function, *Public Finance and Management*, 1, 230-260.

Sugden, Robert, 1982, On the Economics of Philanthropy, *Economic Journal*, 92, 341 - 350.

Sugden, Robert, 1984, Reciprocity: The Supply of Public Goods Through Voluntary Contributions, *Economic Journal*, 94, 772 - 787.

Sugden, Robert, 1985, Consistent Conjectures and Voluntary Contributions to Public Goods: Why the Conventional Theory Does Not Work, *Journal of Public Economics*, 27, 117 - 124.

Tanzi, V., 1996, Fiscal Federalism and Decentralization: A Review of Some Efficiency and Macroeconomic Aspects, in *Annual World Bank Conference on Development Economics*, 1995, Washington, DC: The World Bank.

Tatom, John, 1991a, Should Government Spending on Capital Goods be Raised?, *Federal Reserve Bank of St. Louis Review*, March/April, 3-15.

Tatom, John, 1991b, Public Capital and Private Sector Performance, *Federal Reserve Bank of St. Louis Review*, May/June, 3-15.

Tatom, John, 1993, Is an Infrastructure Crisis Lowering the Nation's Productivity?, *Federal Reserve Bank of St. Louis Review*, November/December, 3-21.

Taussig, Michael, 1967, Economic Aspects of the Personal income Tax Treatment of Charitable Contributions, *National Tax Journal*, 20, 1 - 19.

Taylor, L. 1992, Infrastructural Competition Among Jurisdictions, *Journal of Public Economics,* 49, 241-259.

Thisse, J.F., and H.G. Zoller, 1983, *Location Analysis of Public Facilities,* Amsterdam: North Holland.

Thompson, Earl A., 1968, The Perfectly Competitive Production of Collective Goods, *Review of Economics and Statistics*, 50, 1-12.

Thompson, Earl, 1974, Taxation and National Defense, *Journal of Political Economy*, 82, 755-782.

Tian, G., 2000, Implementation of Balanced Linear Cost Share Equilibrium Solution in Nash and Strong Nash Equilibria, *Journal of Public Economics*, 76, 239-261.

Tideman, N. and G. Tullock, 1976, A New and Superior Process for Making Social Choices, *Journal of Political Economy,* 84, 1145-1159.

Tiebout, Charles M., 1956, A Pure Theory of Local Expenditures, *Journal of Political Economy*, 64, 416-424.

Tullock, G ., 1977, Demand-Revealing Process, Coalitions and Public Goods, *Public Choice,* 29, 103-105.

Tullock, G., 1981, Why so much Stability?, *Public Choice*, 37, 189-202.

Tullock, G., and C. D. Campbell, 1970, Computer Simulation of a Small Voting System, *Economic Journal,* 80, 97-104.

Tiehen, Laura, 2001, Tax Policy and Charitable Contributions of Money, *National Tax Journal*, 54, 707-723.

Usher, D., 1969, On the Social Rate of Discount: Comment, *American Economic Review*, 59, 925-929

Varian, Hal, 1994a, Sequential Contribution to Public Goods, *Journal of Public Economics*, 53, 165-186.

Varian, Hal, 1994b, A Solution to the Problem of Externalities When Agents are Well-Informed, *American Economic Review,* 84, 1278-1293.

Vickrey, W., 1961, Counterspeculation, Auctions, and Competitive Sealed Tenders, *Journal of Finance,* 16, 1-17.

Vicary, Simon, 1997, Joint Production and the Private Provision of Public Goods, *Journal of Public Goods*, 63, 429 - 445.

Vohra, R., 1998, Convergence (Divergence) and the U.S. States, *Atlantic Economic Journal*, 26, 372-378.

Vossler, Christian A. and Joe Kerkvliet, 2003, A Criterion Validity Test of the Contingent Valuation Method: Comparing Hypothetical and Actual Voting Behavior For a Public Referendum, *Journal of Environmental Economics and Management,* 45, 631-649.

Vossler, Christian A. and Joe Kerkvliet, Stephen Polasky, and Olesya Gainutdinova, 2003, Externally Validating Contingent Valuation: An Open-Space Survey and Referendum in Corvallis, Oregon, *Journal of Economic Behavior and Organization,* 51, 261-277.

Walker, M., 1980, On the Nonexistence of a Dominant Strategy Mechanism for Making Optimal Public Decisions, *Econometrica,* 48, 1521-1540.

Walker, M. 1981, A Simple Incentive Compatible Scheme for Attaining Lindahl Allocations, *Econometrica,* 49, 65-71.

Walker, M. 1984, A Simple Auctioneerless Mechanism with Walrasian Properties, *Journal of Economic Theory,* 32, 111-127.

Walker, James M., Roy Gardner, and Elinor Ostrom, 1990, Rent Dissipation in a Limited-Access Common-Pool Resource: Experimental Evidence, *Journal of Environmental Economics and Management,* 19, 203 - 211.

Warr, Peter, 1983, The Private Provision of a Public Good is Independent of the distribution of income, *Economics Letters*, 13, 207 - 211.

Warr, Peter, 1984, Pareto Optimal Reedsitribution and Private Charity, *Journal of Public Economics*, 19, 131 -138.

Watson, Harry, 1984, A Note on the Effects of Taxation on Charitable Giving Over the Life Cycle and Beyond, *Quarterly Journal of Economics*, 99, 639-647.

Weimann, Joachim, 1994, Individual Behavior in a Free Riding Experiment, *Journal of Public Economics*, 54, 185-200.

Weitzman, M. L., 1970, Optimal Growth with Scale Economies in the Creation of Overhead Capital, *Review of Economic Studies*, 37, 555-570.

Wellisch, Dietmar, 2000, *Theory of Public Finance in a Federal State,* Cambridge: Cambridge University Press.

Westoff, F., 1977, Existence of Equilibrium in Economies With a Local Public Good, *Journal of Economic Theory,* 14, 84-112.

Wheaton, William C., 1975, Consumer Mobility and Community Tax Bases: The Financing of Local Public Goods, *Journal of Public Economics*, 4, 377-384.

Wicksell, Knut, 1896, A New Principle of Just Taxation, reprinted in Musgrave and Peacock, 1967, *Classics and the Theory of Public Finance*, 72-118.

Wildasin, David, 1979, Public Good Provision With Optimal and Non-Optimal Public Good Provision: The Single Consumer Case, *Economics Letters*, 4, 59-64.

Wildasin, David E., 1984, On Public Good Provision with Distortionary Taxation, *Economic Inquiry*, XXII, 227-243.

Wildasin, David E., 1986, *Urban Public Finance*, New York: Harwood.

Wildasin, David E., 1987, Theoretical Analyses of Local Public Economics, in *Handbook of Urban Economics,* Edwin S. Mills, ed., 1131-1178.

Wildasin, David, E., 1988, Nash Equilibria in Models of Fiscal Competition, *Journal of Public Economics,* 35, 229-240.

Wildasin, David, E., 1989, Interjurisdictional Capital Mobility: Fiscal Externality and a Corrective Subsidy, *Journal of Urban Economics,* 25, 193-212.

Wildasin, David E., 2003, Fiscal Competition in Space and Time, *Journal of Public Economics,* 87, 2571-2588.

Wildasin, David E. and Wilson, John D., 1996, Imperfect Mobility and Local Government Behavior in an Overlapping-Generations Model, *Journal of Public Economics,* 60, 177-198.

Williamson, Oliver E., and Thomas J. Sargent, 1967, Social Choice: A Probabilistic Approach, *Economic Journal,* 77, 797-813.

Willig, Robert, 1978, Incremental Consumer's Surplus and Hedonic Price Adjustment, *Journal of Economic Theory,* 17, 227-253.

Willinger, Marc, and Anthony Ziegelmayer, 1999, Framing and Cooperation in Public Good Games: An Experiment With an Interior Solution, *Economics Letters,* 65, 323-328.

Wilson, John D., 1986, A Theory of Interregional Tax Competition, *Journal of Urban Economics,* 19, 296-315.

Wilson, John D., 1987a, Trade, Capital Mobility, and Tax Competition, *Journal of Political Economy,* 95, 835-856.

Wilson, John D., 1987b, Trade in a Tiebout Economy, *American Economic Review,* 431-441.

Wilson, John D., 1991a, Optimal Public Good Provision in the Ramsey Tax Model: A generalization, *Economics Letters,* 35, 57-61.

Wilson, John D., 1991b, Optimal Public Good Provision with Limited Lump-Sum Taxation, *American Economic Review,* 81, 153-166.

Wilson, John D., 1991c, Tax Competition With Interregional Differences in Factor Endowments, *Regional Science and Urban Economics,* 21, 423-451.

Wilson, John D., 1997, Property Taxation, Congestion, and Local Public Goods, *Journal of Public Economics,* 64, 207-217.

Wilson, John D., 1999, Theories of Tax Competition, *National Tax Journal,* 52, 269-304.

Wilson, John D., and David E. Wildasin, 2004, Capital Tax Competition: Bane or Boon, *Journal of Public Economics,* 88, 1065-1091.

Wooders, Myrna, 1980, The Tiebout Hypothesis: Near Optimality in in Local Public Good Economies, *Econometrica,* 48, 1467-1485.

Yinger , J., 1982, Capitalization and the Theory of Local Public Finance, *Journal of Political Economy*, 90, 917-943.

Yinger, J., H. Bloom, A. Borsch-Supan, and H. Ladd, 1988, *Property Taxes and House Values-The Theory and Estimation of Intrajurisdictional Property Tax Capitalization*, London: Academic Press.

Yoshida, Masatoshi, 1986, Public Investment Criterion in an Overlapping Generations Economy, *Economica,* 53, 247 - 263.

Yoshino, Naoyuki and Hideo Nakano, 1996, Interregional Distribution and Productivity Effect of Public Investment, *Financial Review*, 4, 16-26 (in Japanese).

Young, Douglas, 1982, Voluntary Provision of Public Goods, *Public Choice*, 38, 73 - 85.

Zax, J .S., 1989, Is there a Leviathan in Your Neighborhood?, *American Economic Review*, 79, 271-283.

Zodrow, George R., 1983, *Local Provision of Public Services: The Tiebout Model After twenty-Five Years,* New York: Academic Press.

Zodrow, George R., and Peter Mieszkowski, 1986, Pigou, Tiebout, Property Taxation, and the Underprovision of Local Public Goods, *Journal of Urban Economics,* 19, 356-370.

Index

Author Index

Musgrave, 27, 351
Myers, 327, 330, 335

Nadiri, 282
Nakamura, 221
Nakano, 287
Nehring, 283
Neill, 88
Nelson, C, 297
Nelson, M, 353
Nett, 114
Ng, 51
Niemi, 60
Norman, 241, 250
Nunes, 84

Oakland, 322
Oates, 328, 351, 352, 353, 356
Offerman, 231
Ohta, 287
Olson, 208
O'Neil, 167, 179
Orbell, 99
O'Reilly, 93
Ostrom, 226
Otto, 293

Palfrey, 67, 72, 76, 217, 222
Parry, 327
Parsons, 96
Paul, 283
Pauly, 303, 320, 322, 323, 360
Payne, 112, 135, 148, 200
Peacock, 27
Peltzman, 114, 153
Pereira, 283, 285, 286, 290
Perez, 279
Persson, 75
Pestieau, 135, 143, 251, 252, 257,
    269, 322
Peters, 114
Phaneuf, 91
Pigou, 29, 50, 51
Pines, 304, 305, 307, 310, 319, 322,
    324

Pinske, 354
Pirttila, 43
Plotnick, 181, 192
Plott, 60, 73, 75, 205, 211, 213, 225,
    229, 297
Poe, 82
Polasky, 87
Pollakowski, 353, 356
Pommerehne, 205, 210
Poret, 290
Porter, David P, 229,
Porter, Robert H, 278
Portney, 356
Posnett, 197
Postlewaite, 66, 72, 76
Prescott, 61, 75, 352
Prisbrey, 217, 222
Puppe, 154

Ramsey, 251
Randall, 95
Randolph, 155, 159, 168, 172, 175
Ratner, 272
Ravikumar, 264, 265, 270
Reece, 156, 157, 161, 162, 175, 197
Reid, 370
Repullo, 68
Ribar, 111, 141, 182, 201
Richmond, 276
Ricketts, 155
Rioja, 291
Rob, 66, 75, 76
Roberts, D, 28
Roberts, John, 53
Roberts, Judith, 370
Roberts, Russell, 100, 135, 194, 353
Robinson, 167
Rodgers, 195
Romano, 114, 115, 124
Romer, 324, 353, 360
Rose-Ackerman, 115, 116, 117, 324
Rosen, 353, 354, 356
Rosenthal, H, 62, 74, 75,
Rosenthal, S, 362
Roubini, 74, 75